P9-CJY-909

Atlas of
American Military History

SIEGE OF YORKTOWN, APRIL 1862 Shown above is a bird's-eye view of the Union siege of Yorktown in 1862. This color lithograph was created from a map drawn on the spot by Sergeant Charles Worret, a Union soldier in the 20th New York Volunteers.

Atlas of
American
Military History

STUART MURRAY

☑®

Facts On File, Inc.

ATLAS OF AMERICAN MILITARY HISTORY

Copyright © 2005 by Media Projects Inc.

MEDIA PROJECTS INC.
Executive Editor: Carter Smith
Project Editor: Aaron R. Murray
Graphic Designer: Ron Toelke
Production Manager: James Burmester
Editorial Assistant: Timothy Murray

CONSULTING EDITORS:
Steve R. Waddell, Associate Professor, United States Military Academy
Clifford J. Rogers, Associate Professor, United States Military Academy
Ron Toelke, Ron Toelke Associates

Facts On File, Inc.
132 West 31st Street
New York, NY 10001

Library of Congress Cataloging-in-Publication Data
Murray, Stuart, 1948-
    Atlas of American Military History / Stuart Murray.
        p. cm.
    Includes bibliographic references and index.
    ISBN 0-8160-5578-5 (hardcover: alk. paper)
    1. United States—History, Military. 2. United States—History, Military—Maps.
        I. Title: Atlas of American military history. II. Title.

E181.M94 2004
355'.00973'022—dc22

2004008994

Facts On File books are available at special discounts when purchased in bulk quantities
for businesses, associations, institutions or sales promotions. Please call our
Special Sales Department in New York at (212) 967-8800 or (800) 322-8755.

You can find Facts On File on the World Wide Web at http://www.factsonfile.com

Acquisitions Editor: Owen Lancer
Cover design by Cathy Rincon
Text design and layout by Ron Toelke
Maps by Dale Williams

Printed in Hong Kong

Creative pkg 10 9 8 7 6 5 4 3 2 1

This book is printed on acid-free paper.

The unparalleled perseverance of the Armies of the United States,
through almost every possible suffering and discouragement,
for the space of eight long years was little short of a miracle.

—George Washington, Farewell Address to his Army; November 2, 1783

From St. Mihiel to the Vesle,
    With the night wind's mournful wail,
Goes a sound that's understood,
    "Gather here in Argonne Wood."
Thru the night winds wet and dreary,
    Word goes on to Château-Thierry,
Ghostly Phantoms hear the call,
    "Gather those who gave their all."

—From "Phantoms," by L.C. McCollum, 308th Infantry; 1919

In the heroism of the battle, both sides can be commended.

—Preface to "Hill 882," by Ted McCormick, B Co., 1/327th Infantry,
101st Airborne Division; about Vietnam in May 1970

We here highly resolve that these
dead shall not have died in vain. . . .

—Abraham Lincoln, the Gettysburg Address, November 19, 1863

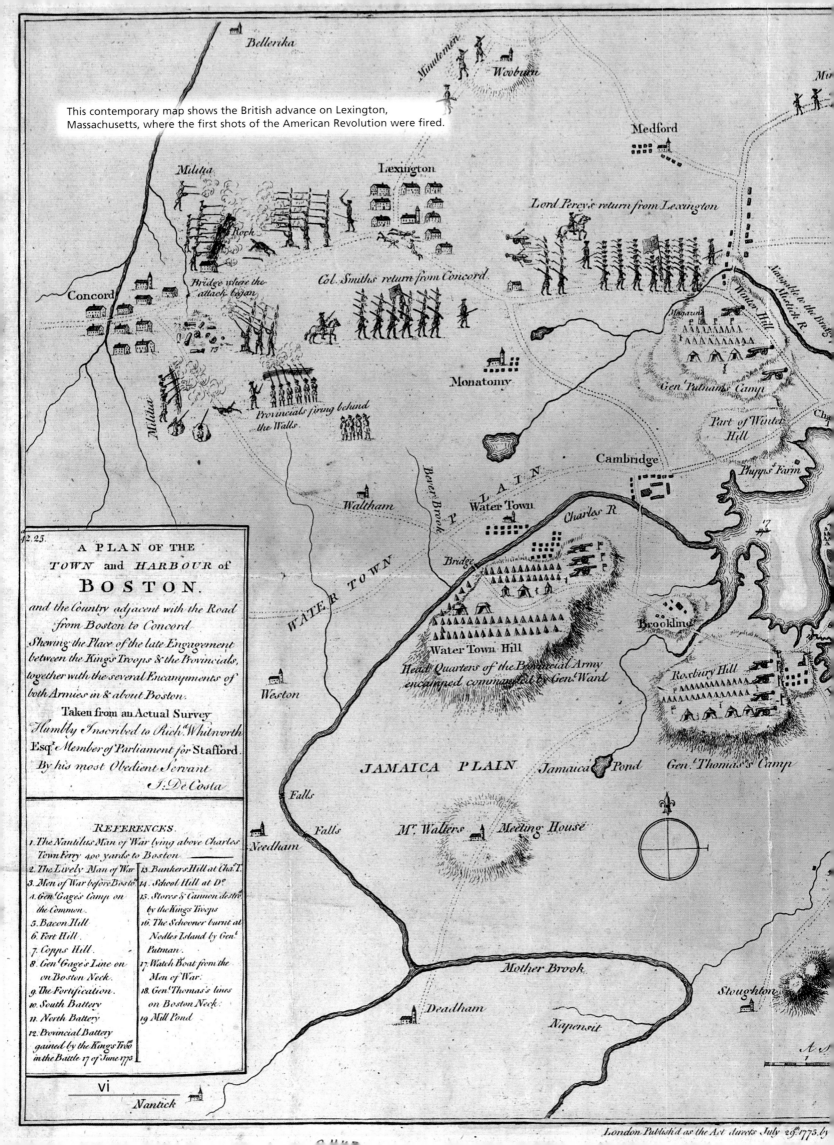

This contemporary map shows the British advance on Lexington, Massachusetts, where the first shots of the American Revolution were fired.

A PLAN OF THE
TOWN and HARBOUR of
BOSTON.

and the Country adjacent with the Road
from Boston to Concord
Shewing the Place of the late Engagement
between the Kings Troops & the Provincials,
together with the several Encampments of
both Armies in & about Boston.

Taken from an Actual Survey
Humbly Inscribed to Rich.ᵈ Whitworth
Esq.ʳ Member of Parliament for Stafford.

By his most Obedient Servant
I: De Costa

REFERENCES.
1. The Nantilus Man of War lying above Charles
   Town Ferry 400 yards to Boston
2. The Lively Man of War
3. Men of War before Boston
4. Gen.ˡ Gage's Camp on
   the Common
5. Bacon Hill
6. Fort Hill
7. Copps Hill
8. Gen.ˡ Gage's Line on
   on Boston Neck
9. The Fortification
10. South Battery
11. North Battery
12. Provincial Battery
    gained by the Kings Troo
    in the Battle 17 of June 1775
13. Bunkers Hill at Cha.T.
14. School Hill at Dᵒ
15. Stores & Cannon destro
    by the Kings Troops
16. The Schooner burnt at
    Nodles Island by Gen.ˡ
    Putman
17. Watch Boat from the
    Men of War
18. Gen.ˡ Thomas's lines
    on Boston Neck
19. Mill Pond

vi
Nantick

London Publish'd as the Act directs July 29.ᵗʰ 1775 by

TABLE OF CONTENTS

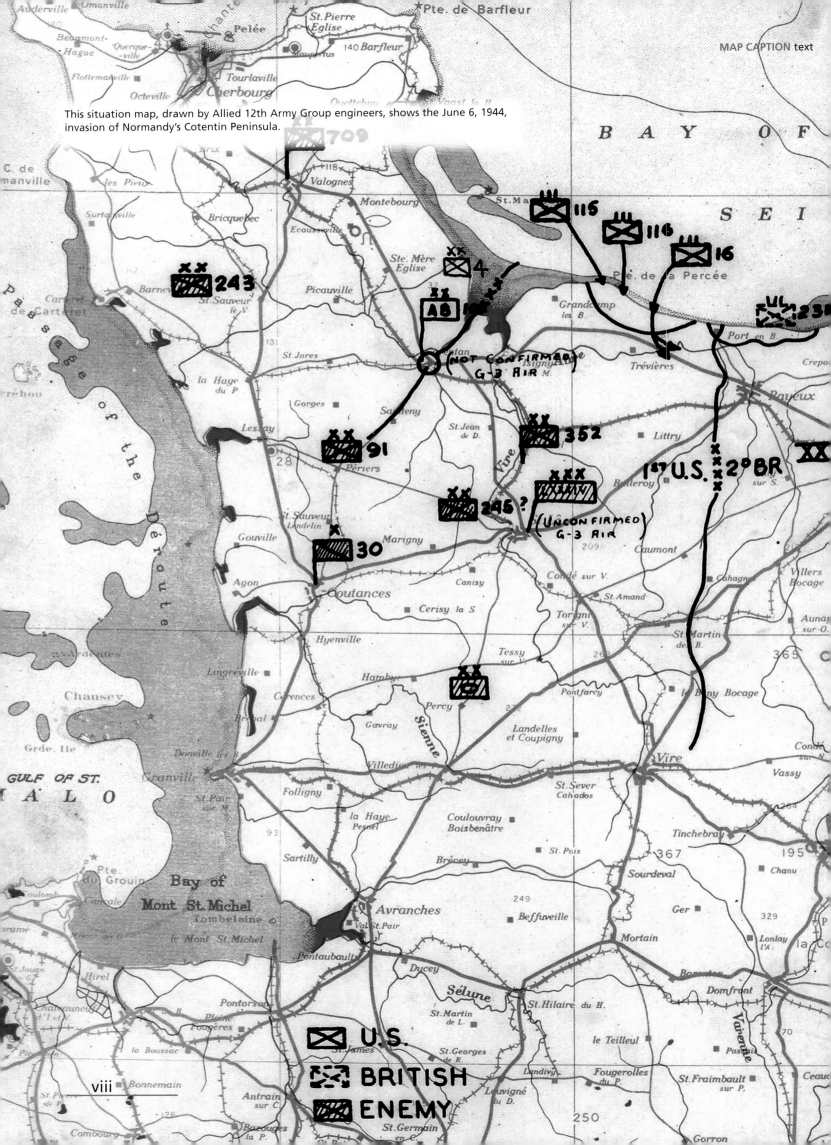

This situation map, drawn by Allied 12th Army Group engineers, shows the June 6, 1944, invasion of Normandy's Cotentin Peninsula.

Introduction
AMERICA'S WARS: A PROFILE

EUROPEAN WARFARE CAME TO NORTH AMERICA in 1565, as age-old hostility between France and Spain brought siege, pillaging, and massacre to Florida. When the Englishman, Sir Francis Drake, sacked Spanish St. Augustine in 1586, the colonial wars were under way. Through the 1600s, native peoples and colonists also often matched strength, and the colonists did not always win. By 1690, however, European powers dominated the Atlantic coast, from Newfoundland to the Carolinas and Florida, and controlled much of the Southwest.

During the mid-1700s, native peoples were important allies of the warring British and French, but when the newly independent United States expanded at the end of the century, the Indians were the losers. The War of 1812's battles intermingled with aggressive operations to remove the native peoples of the Old Northwest and South.

A few decades later, America's belief in her "Manifest Destiny" to conquer the continent brought Texas and much of Mexico under the Stars and Stripes. In 1861, the War Between the States tore the nation in two, but from civil war rose a United States that was stronger than ever, industrializing and on the move. The last decades of the century saw the conquest of the West, with the Indians forced onto reservations.

After defeating Spain in 1898, the United States entered the 20th Century as a colonial empire, an aspiring Great Power that came to the fore during the First World War. Still, Americans were reluctant to be drawn into the foreign intrigues of prime ministers, royalty, and nationalists. Then came World War II, from which the United States emerged the most powerful nation on earth, leader of the "Free World," and bastion of liberty. Next, the adversary was the totalitarian Soviet Bloc, with intrigue, subversion, and the threat of nuclear destruction as the chosen weapons. Near the end of the 20th Century, this "Cold War" dissolved into a confusion of new adversities, dangers, and tensions.

Global politics were now often defined by the hunt for oil reserves, a quest complicated by the resolve of some aggrieved peoples to strive for their rights. Awesome martial technology dominated the conventional battlefield, but the guerrilla fighter—whether patriot or fanatical terrorist—struggled on against immense odds. Thus, the 21st Century opened with the greatest militaries ever known attempting to combat clandestine networks of shadowy enemies who were willing to kill and die for causes they held sacred.

TIMELINE OF AMERICAN MILITARY HISTORY

1541

Oct: De Soto defeats Choctaw at Mabila

1565

Sept 20: French destroy Spanish Ft. Caroline, Fla.

1586

June 6: Drake sacks St. Augustine

1609

Mar 22: Powhattans attack Jamestown: Anglo-Powhattan Wars begin

July 30: Champlain and Algonquins defeat Iroquois

1613

Nov 1: British destroy French Port Royal, Nova Scotia

1622

Anglo-Powhattan Wars resume

1629

July 20: British capture Quebec City; return 1632

1636

July 20: New Englanders massacre Pequots on Block Island: Pequot War (1636–1637)

1637

May 26: Pequot's Mystic River village wiped out

1641

Algonquin war against New Netherland; ends 1645

1642

Iroquois-Huron War; ends after 10 years

1644

April 14: Anglo-Powhattan Wars resume; Jamestown Massacre

1655

Oct 5: Peach War in New Netherlands; ends 1657

1660s

Iroquois war with Ottawa and Abenaki

1664

Sept 7: Dutch New Amsterdam falls bloodlessly to English

1670

July 30: Dutch retake New York (New Amsterdam) bloodlessly; returned 1674

1675

Sept 18: Battle of Bloody Brook: King Philip's War (1675–1678)

Dec 19: Battle of the Great Swamp

1676

Sept 18: Bacon's Rebellion captures Jamestown; ends 1677

1680

Aug 11: Pueblo revolt against Spanish at Santa Fe

1690

Feb 8: Schenectady Massacre: King William's War (1689–1697)

May 19: New Englanders take Port Royal

Oct: New England sieges of Quebec and Montreal fail

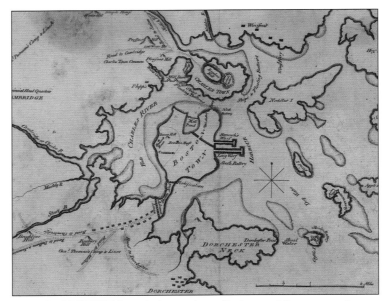

SIEGE OF BOSTON This period map shows Boston and the surrounding area in 1775. Patriot camps besieging the city are indicated.

1702

May: Carolina militia fails to capture St. Augustine: Queen Anne's War (1702–1713)

1704

Feb 29: Deerfield Massacre

1706

May: Spanish and French expedition to Charleston fails

1707

June: British repulsed at Acadia

1710

Oct 13: British take Port Royal

1711

Aug: British repulsed at Quebec and Montreal

Sept: Tuscarora War, Carolinas; ends 1713

1713

Mar 13: Contentnea Creek Tuscarora village massacred

1715

April 15: Yamassee and Creeks uprising

1740

June 5: Oglethorpe campaign against St. Augustine fails: King George's War (1740–1748)

1742

July 7: Battle of the Bloody Swamp

1743

Mar: Oglethorpe campaign against St. Augustine fails

1744

Sept: French repulsed at Annapolis Royal, Nova Scotia

1745

May 30: Siege of Ft. Louisbourg

1754

July 3: Ft. Necessity: French and Indian War (1754–1763)

1755

July 9: Battle of Monongahela

Sept 8: Battle of Lake George

1756

Aug 4: Ft. Oswego falls

1757

Aug 9: Ft. William Henry Massacre

1758

June 2: Siege of Ft. Louisbourg; ends July 26

July 8: Battle of Ft. Ticonderoga

Aug 25: Siege of Ft. Frontenac; ends Aug 27

Nov 25: Ft. Duquesne falls

1759

July 25: Ft. Niagara falls

July 31: Ft. Crown Point falls

Sept 12: Siege of Quebec; ends Sept 18

1760

Sept 8: Montreal falls

1763

May–June: Indians of Northwest capture 9 British posts: Pontiac's Uprising

May 1: Siege of Ft. Detroit; ends July 29

Aug 5: Battle of Bushy Run

1774

Oct 10: Battle of Point Pleasant: Lord Dunmore's War

1775

April 19: Battle of Lexington and Concord: American Revolution

April 19: Rebel army besieges Boston

May 10: Rebels seize Ft. Ticonderoga

May 12: Rebels seize Crown Point

June 12: War's 1st naval battle: sloop *Unity* defeats HMS *Margaretta*

June 14: Congress creates an army

June 15: George Washington, Commander-in-Chief

June 17: Battle of Bunker/Breed's Hill

July 3: Washington arrives at Boston

Aug 24: *Hannah*, 1st armed vessel fitted out by Congress

Oct 13: Congress creates a navy

Nov 9: Benedict Arnold's column reaches Quebec

Nov 10: Marine Corps founded

Nov 13: Rebels occupy Montreal

Dec 2: Rebels besiege Quebec; ends May 6, 1776

Dec 3: *Alfred* commissioned, Continental Navy's 1st ship

Dec 13: Congress authorizes construction of 13 frigates

Dec 31: B. Arnold and Richard Montgomery defeated at Quebec

1776

Mar 3: 1st American amphibious operation: Bahamas

Mar 4: Rebels occupy Dorchester Heights

Mar 17: British evacuate Boston

June 8: Battle of Trois Rivières, Canada

June 9: Americans leave Montreal

June 28: British Navy attacks Ft. Moultrie, S.C.

July 2: British army under Howe lands on Staten Island

July 2: Congress votes to declare the 13 former colonies independent

Aug 27: Battle of Long Island

Sept 16: Battle of Harlem Heights

Oct 11: Battle of Valcour Island, Lake Champlain

Oct 27: 1st Battle of Ft. Washington

Oct 28: Battle of White Plains

Nov 16: Surrender of Ft. Washington

Nov 20: Americans evacuate Ft. Lee

Dec 26: British occupy Newport, R.I.

Dec 26: Battle of Trenton

1777

Jan 3: Battle of Princeton

July 6: Burgoyne takes Ft. Ticonderoga

July 7: Battle of Hubbardton

Aug 3: British besiege Ft. Stanwix; ends Aug 23

Aug 6: Battle of Oriskany

Aug 16: Battle of Bennington

Sept 11: Battle of Brandywine Creek

Sept 19: Battles of Saratoga; end Oct 17

Oct 4: Battle of Germantown

Oct 22: Siege of Ft. Mercer; ends Nov 21

Nov 10: Battle of Ft. Mifflin

1778

June 18: British evacuate Philadelphia

June 28: Battle of Monmouth Court House

Dec 29: British occupy Savannah

1779

Feb 23: Battle of Vincennes

June 18: Sullivan's Expedition

July 16: Battle of Stony Point
Aug 29: Battle of Newtown
Sept 23: USS *Bonhomme Richard* defeats
  HMS *Serapis*
Oct 9: Franco-American force repulsed
  at Savannah
1780
April 1: British besiege Charleston;
  falls May 12
May 29: Battle of Waxhaws
Aug 16: Battle of Camden
Oct 7: Battle of King's Mountain
1781
Jan 17: Battle of Cowpens
Mar 15: Battle of Guilford Court House
April 25: Battle of Hobkirk Hill
July 6: Battle of Green Springs
Sept 8: Battle of Eutaw Springs
Sept 28: Franco-American force
  besieges Yorktown; ends Oct 19
1782
July 11: British evacuate Savannah
Aug 7: Badge of Military Merit
  (Purple Heart) established
Sept 11: Battle of Ft. Henry
Dec 14: British evacuate Charleston
1783
Feb 4: British cease hostilities
April 11: Congress ceases hostilities
Sept 3: Treaty of Paris ends war
Nov 25: British evacuate N.Y. City
Dec 4: British evacuate Staten Island
  and Long Island
Dec 23: Washington resigns as
  Commander-in-Chief
1784
June 2: Congress discharges Continental
  Army
June 3: Congress creates new army:
  1st American Regiment
1789
Aug 7: Congress establishes Department
  of War and Navy
1790
Aug 4: Congress establishes Revenue
  Cutter Service (USRCS)
1791
Nov 4: Battle of the Wabash
1794
May 27: Congress provides for
  construction of six frigates
June 30: Battle of Ft. Recovery
Aug 20: Battle of Fallen Timbers
1797
May 10: *United States* launched
1798
April 30: Congress creates Department
  of the Navy
May 28: Naval war with France begins
  (Quasi-War)
July 7: *Delaware* defeats *La Croyable*
1799
Mar 26: *United States* defeats
  La Tartueffe
June 22: *Eagle* vs. *Revenge*

June 28: *Merrimack* defeats *Magicienne*
1801
May 14: Tripoli declares war on U.S.:
  Barbary Wars
1802
July 4: U.S. Military Academy opens
1803
Oct 31: *Philadelphia* captured by enemy
  in Tripoli harbor
Nov 12: Naval blockade of Tripoli
1804
Feb 16: *Philadelphia* destroyed by U.S.
  raid on Tripoli
Aug 3: Naval bombardment of Tripoli
1805
April 27: U.S. and mercenary troops
  seize Derna
June 4: Peace treaty ends war with Tripoli

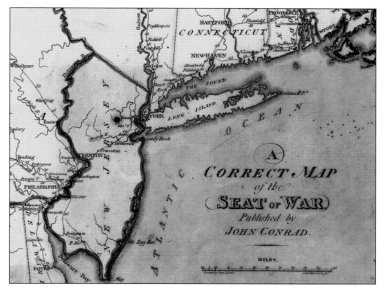

SEAT OF WAR, 1812 Detail taken from a map published in the early 19th Century. Part of the East Coast is shown here. (See large map, p. 42.)

(See large map, p. 42.)

1811
Nov 7: Battle of Tippecanoe Creek
1812
June 18: U.S. declares war on Great
  Britain: War of 1812
Aug 16: Ft. Detroit surrenders to British
Aug 19: *Constitution* defeats *Guerrière*
Sept 12: Battle of Twelve-Mile Swamp
Oct 13: Battle of Queenstown
Oct 25: *United States* defeats *Macedonian*
Nov 9: Naval bombardment: Kingston,
  Ontario
Dec 29: *Constitution* defeats *Java*
1813
Jan 21: Battle of Raisin River
April 27: Army-Navy operation:
  York/Toronto
May 27: Army-Navy operation:
  Queenstown Heights
May 28: Battle of Sackett's Harbor
June 1: *Shannon* defeats *Chesapeake*
July 13: *Essex* captures British Pacific
  whaling fleet
Aug 7: Naval action: Lake Ontario

Aug 30: Ft. Mims Massacre: Creek Wars
Sept 10: Oliver H. Perry defeats British
  on Lake Erie
Oct 5: Battle of the Thames
Oct 25: Battle of Chateauguay
Nov 3: Battle of Tallushatchee:
  Creek Wars
Nov 9: Battle of Talledega: Creek Wars
Nov 11: Battle of Chrysler's Farm
1814
Mar 27: Battle of Horseshoe Bend:
  Creek Wars
June 22: *Independence*, 1st
  ship-of-the-line
July 5: Battle of Chippewa
July 25: Battle of Lundy's Lane
Aug 13: Siege of Ft. Erie; ends Sept 21
Aug 24: Battle of Bladensburg
Aug 24: British occupy Washington, D.C.
Sept 11: Thomas MacDonough defeats
  British on Lake Champlain, British
  attack at Plattsburgh defeated
Sept 13: Battle of North Point
Sept 13: British bombard Ft. McHenry
Oct 29: *Fulton I*, 1st steam-powered
  warship
Dec 24: Treaty ends War of 1812
Dec 28: Battle of New Orleans
1815
Mar 2: U.S. declares war on Algiers
June 17: U.S. vessels *Guerrière*,
  Constellation, *Ontario*, and *Epervier*,
  defeat *Mashouda* of Algiers
July 3: Treaty ends war with Algiers
Dec 10: 1st naval officer school,
  Charlestown, Massachusetts
1817
Nov 30: Apalachicola Massacre:
  Seminole Wars begin
1818
April 7: U.S. forces seize St. Marks,
  Spanish Florida

May 28: U.S. forces seize Pensacola,
  Spanish Florida
1832
Feb 6: U.S. forces land on Kuala Batu,
  Sumatra; punitive action
April 26: Black Hawk War begins
July 21: Battle of Wisconsin Heights:
  Black Hawk War
Aug 2: Battle of Bad Axe River:
  Black Hawk War
1835
June 30: Battle of Anáhuac:
  Texas Independence
Oct 2: Battle of Gonzales:
  Texas Independence
Oct 28: Battle of Mission Concepcion:
  Texas Independence
Dec 28: Dade Massacre: Seminole Wars
Dec 31: Battle of Withlacoochie River:
  Seminole Wars
1836
Jan 14: *Independence* commissioned,
  1st ship, Texas Navy
Feb 23: Battle of the Alamo; ends Mar 6:
  Texas Independence
Feb 28: Battle of Camp Izzard:
  Seminole Wars
April 21: Battle of San Jacinto:
  Texas Independence
1837
Dec 25: Battle of Lake Okeechobee:
  Seminole Wars
1838
Dec 25: *John Adams* bombards Sumatra;
  punitive action
1839
Jan 1: *John Adams* bombards Sumatra;
  punitive action
1840
July 12: U.S. forces land, Fiji Islands;
  punitive action
Aug 12: Battle of Plum Creek:
  Comanche Wars
1841
Feb 25: U.S. forces land, Samoan Islands;
  punitive action
April 9: U.S. forces land, Drummond
  Island; punitive action
1843
Dec 16: U.S. forces land, Liberia;
  punitive action
1846
May 8: Battle of Palo Alto
May 9: Battle of Resaca de la Palma
May 13: U.S. declares war on Mexico:
  Mexican-American War
May 24: Naval bombardment of
  Tampico
July 7: U.S. occupies Monterey, Calif.
Aug 18: U.S. forces occupy Santa Fe
Sept 21: Battle of Saltillo
Sept 21–23: Battle of Monterrey, Mexico
Nov 15: U.S. forces occupy Tampico
Dec 6: Battle of San Pascual
Dec 25: Battle of El Brazito

1847

Jan 8: Battle of San Gabriel
Jan 9: Battle of La Mesa
Jan 10: U.S. forces occupy Los Angeles
Feb 3: Battle of Pueblo de Taos
Feb 22: Battle of Buena Vista
Feb 28: Battle of Sacramento
Mar 10: Siege of Vera Cruz;
ends Mar 27
April 18: Battle of Cerro Gordo
Aug 20: Battle of Contreras
Aug 20: Battle of Churubusco
Sept 8: Battle of El Molino del Rey
Sept 13: Battle of Chapultepec
Sept 14: U.S. forces occupy Mexico City

1848

Feb 2: Treaty of Guadalupe Hidalgo
ends war with Mexico

1850

July 1: U.S. Naval Academy founded
Sept 28: Flogging abolished in USN

1854

July 13: Naval bombardment of
San Juan del Norte, Nicaragua

1855

Mar 3: Congress authorizes purchase of
camels to carry freight in West
April 4: U.S. forces land Shanghai,
China; punitive action

1856

Jan 26: Battle of Seattle: punitive action
April 22: U.S. forces to Kansas for civil
conflict, through 1858
Nov 20: Barrier Forts, Canton, China:
punitive action

1857

May 28: U.S. forces to Salt Lake City,
Utah: punitive action

1858

Oct 6: U.S. forces land, Fiji Islands:
punitive action

1859

Oct 17: Harpers Ferry: John Brown
uprising

1860

Mar 6: U.S. forces land, Anton Lizardo,
Mexico; punitive action

1861

April 12: C.S.A. bombards Ft. Sumter;
Civil War begins
April 15: President Abraham Lincoln
calls for militia to suppress Southern
insurrection
June 3: Battle of Philippi
June 3: CSS *Sumter* 1st Confederate
commerce raider
June 9: U.S. War Department authorizes
use of women nurses
June 10: Battle of Big Bethel
June 22: 1st balloon reconnaissance:
Falls Church, Va.
July 21: 1st Battle of Bull Run/Manassas
Aug 10: Battle of Wilson's Creek
Aug 15: George B. McClellan heads U.S.
Army of the Potomac

Nov 5: Naval action: Hilton Head, S.C.

1862

Jan 19: Battle of Mill Springs
Feb 6: Ft. Henry falls to Ulysses S. Grant
Feb 7: Roanoke Island
Feb 12: Grant besieges Ft. Donelson; falls
Feb 16
Feb 21: Battle of Valverde
Mar 3: New Madrid/Island No. 10;
ends April 8
Mar 7: Battle of Pea Ridge; ends April 8
Mar 9: Battle of Hampton Roads:
USS *Monitor* vs. CSS *Virginia*
Mar 13: New Bern operation
Mar 23: Battle of Kernstown
Mar 26: Battle of Apache Canyon
Mar 28: Battle of Glorieta Pass
April 5: Battle of Yorktown

MEXICAN-AMERICAN WAR This map belonged to Mexican general Mariano Arista. Depicted in red are the positions of Mexican troops during the battle of Resaca de Palma.

April 6: Battle of Shiloh
April 18: Naval action: Fts. Jackson and
St. Philip
April 25: New Orleans surrenders
May 4: Battle of Williamsburg
May 8: Battle of McDowell
May 23: Battle of Front Royal
May 25: Battle of Winchester
May 31: Battle of Seven Pines/Fair Oaks
June 1: Robert E. Lee heads C.S.A. Army
of Northern Virginia
June 8: Battle of Cross Keys
June 9: Battle of Port Republic
June 13: *Alligator*, 1st submarine accepted
by USN
June 25: Battle of Oak Grove
June 26: Battle of Mechanicsville
June 27: Battle of Gaines's Mill
June 29: Battle of Savage's Station
June 30: Battle of Frayser's Farm/White
Oak Swamp
July 1: Battle of Malvern Hill
July 3: Battle of Locust Grove

July 15: Battle of Apache Pass; punitive
campaign
Aug 9: Battle of Cedar Mountain/
Slaughter Mountain
Aug 18: Battle of Ft. Ridgley; Sioux revolt
Aug 24: New Ulm massacre; Sioux revolt
Aug 28: Battle of Groveton
Aug 29: Second Battle of Bull
Run/Manassas
Sept 1: Battle of Chantilly
Sept 14: Battle of Crampton's Gap
Sept 14: Battle of South Mountain
Sept 15: Battle of Harpers Ferry
Sept 17: Battle of Antietam/
Sharpsburg
Sept 27: 1st Louisiana Native Guards:
1st African-American regt
Oct 3: Battle of Corinth

Oct 8: Battle of Perryville
Dec 12: *Cairo*, 1st warship sunk by mine
Dec 13: Battle of Fredericksburg
Dec 20: Battle of Holly Springs
Dec 26: *Red Rover*, 1st USN hospital ship
Dec 27: Battle of Chickasaw Bluffs
Dec 31: Battle of Stones River/
Murfreesboro

1863

Jan 27: Battle of Bear River; punitive
campaign
Mar 3: Congress passes conscription law
Mar 3: Congress extends Medal of Honor
to include army officers; navy & marine
officers added 1915
April 7: Naval action: Charleston
April 9: 1st Red River campaign;
ends May 23
April 17: B. H. Grierson's Raid;
ends May 2
May 1: Battle of Chancellorsville
May 3: Battle of Salem Church
May 14: Battle of Jackson

May 16: Battle of Champion's Hill
May 17: Battle of the Big Black River
May 19: Siege of Vicksburg;
ends July 4
May 27: Battle of Port Hudson;
ends July 9
June 9: Battle of Brandy Station
June 13: Battle of Winchester
June 28: George G. Meade heads Army
of the Potomac
July 1: Battle of Gettysburg; ends July 3
July 10: Charleston siege; ends Feb 18,
1865
July 16: Naval bombardment;
Shimonoseki, Japan
July 17: Battle of Honey Springs
July 24: Battle of Big Mound: Sioux Wars
July 26: Battle of Dead Buffalo Lake:
Sioux Wars
July 28: Battle of Stony Lake: Sioux Wars
Sept 3: Battle of Whitestone Lake:
Sioux Wars
Sept 19: Battle of Chickamauga
Oct 14: Battle of Bristoe Station
Nov 17: Siege of Knoxville; ends Dec 5
Nov 23: Battle of Orchard Knob
Nov 23: Battle of Indian Hill
Nov 24: Battle of Lookout Mountain
Nov 25: Battle of Missionary Ridge

1864

Jan 12: Canyon de Chelly Expedition
Feb 17: Submarine *H.L. Hunley*, 1st
submarine to sink a warship, *Housatonic*
Mar 10: 2nd Red River Campaign; ends
May 22
Mar 12: Grant General-in-Chief of
U.S. armies
April 12: Ft. Pillow Massacre
May 4: Battle of Drewry's Bluff;
ends May 16
May 5: Battle of the Wilderness
May 5: Naval action: Albemarle Sound
May 5: Battle of Rocky Face Ridge
May 7: Battle of Spotsylvania Court
House; ends May 20
May 11: Battle of Yellow Tavern
May 13: Battle of Resaca
May 15: Battle of New Market
May 23: Battle of North Anna; ends
May 27
May 31: Battle of Cold Harbor; ends
June 12
June 9: Battle of Petersburg; ends June 18
June 10: Battle of Brice's Cross Roads
June 18: Siege of Petersburg; ends
Apr 2, 1865
June 19: *Kearsarge* defeats *Alabama*
June 27: Battle of Kennesaw Mountain
July 20: Battle of Peach Tree Creek
July 22: Battle of Atlanta
July 30: Battle of the Crater
Aug 5: Naval action: Mobile Bay
Aug 31: Battle of Jonesboro
Sept 19: Battle of Opequon
Sept 22: Battle of Fisher's Hill

Oct 5: Battle of Allatoona
Oct 19: Battle of Cedar Creek
Oct 23: Battle of Westport
Nov 29: Sand Creek Massacre:
  punitive action
Nov 15: March to the Sea; ends Dec 21
Nov 30: Battle of Franklin
Dec 15: Battle of Nashville
1865
Jan 7: Battle of Julesburg: Sioux Wars
Jan 13: Battle of Ft. Fisher
Mar 7: Battle of Kinston
Mar 19: Battle of Bentonville
Mar 25: Battle of Ft. Steadman
Mar 30: Battle of Five Forks
April 2: Battle of Petersburg
April 2: Battle of Selma
April 6: Battle of Sayler's Creek
April 9: Appomattox Courthouse: Lee
  surrenders to Grant
April 26: C.S.A. Army of Tennessee
  surrenders
May 26: C.S.A. Department of
  Trans-Mississippi surrenders
June 22: CSS *Shenandoah* destroys U.S.
  whaling fleet in Bering Sea
June 23: Stand Watie surrenders, last
  C.S.A. general
1866
July 28: African-American regiments
  authorized: 9th & 10th Cavalry; 38th,
  39th, 40th, and 41st Infantry
Dec 21: Fetterman Massacre:
  Sioux/Cheyenne Wars
1867
Aug 2: Wagon Box Fight:
  Sioux/Cheyenne Wars
1868
Sept 17: Battle of Beecher's Island:
  Sioux/Cheyenne Wars
Nov 27: Battle of Washita River:
  Sioux/Cheyenne Wars
1869
Mar 3: 38th/39th Infantry become 24th
  Infantry & 40th/41st Infantry become
  25th Infantry: African-American
July 11: Battle of Summit Springs:
  Sioux/Cheyenne Wars
1870
Jan 23: Blood River Massacre:
  punitive expedition
Feb 9: Weather Service becomes part
  of Army Signal Service
1871
April 20: Congress establishes
  Life-Saving Service
April 30: Camp Grant massacre:
  Apache Wars
June 10: U.S. forces land Kangwha
  Island, Korea
1873
Mar 27: Battle of Turret Peak: Apache
  Wars
1874
June 27: Adobe Walls: Red River War

1876
Sept 28: Battle of Palo Duro:
  Red River War
June 17: Battle of the Rosebud:
  Black Hills Campaign
June 25: Battle of the Little Big Horn:
  Black Hills Campaign
July 17: Battle of War Bonnet Creek:
  Sioux/Cheyenne Wars
July 31: Revenue Cutter Service School
  of Instruction established
Sept 9: Battle of Slim Buttes:
  Sioux/Cheyenne Wars
Nov 25: Battle of the Tongue River:
  Powder River Expedition
1877
Jan 8: Battle of Wolf Mountain:
  Sioux/Cheyenne Wars
May 7: Battle of Muddy Creek:
  Sioux/Cheyenne Wars
June 17: Battle of White Bird Canyon:
  Nez Percé War
July 11: Battle of Clearwater River:
  Nez Percé War

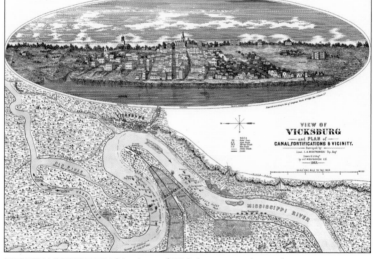

MIGHTY VICKSBURG This view of Vicksburg was drawn by an engineering officer in the Union army in 1863.

Aug 9: Battle of Big Hole River:
  Nez Percé War
Sept 13: Battle of Canyon Creek:
  Nez Percé War
Sept 30: Battle of Snake Creek:
  Nez Percé War
1878
June 12: Mackenzie Expedition
Dec 7: *Ticonderoga*, 1st steam-powered
  warship to circumnavigate globe; returns
  Aug 23, 1881
1879
Sept 29: Battle of Milk Creek: Ute War
1880
July 30: Battle of Tinja de las Palmas:
  Apache Wars
1881
Aug 30: Battle of Cibicue Creek:
  Apache Wars

1882
July 17: Battle of Big Dry Wash:
  Apache Wars
1886
July 19: *Atlanta*, 1st steam-and-sail
  protected cruiser
1889
July 30: U.S. forces land in Honolulu
1890
Dec 29: Massacre at Wounded Knee
1893
Jan 16: U.S. forces land Honolulu
1895
Aug 15: *Texas*, 1st U.S. battleship
1897
Dec 15: *Argonaut*, 1st submarine with
  internal combustion engine
1898
Feb 15: *Maine* explodes in Havana harbor
April 20: U.S. declares war on Spain:
  Spanish-American War
April 27: USN bombard Mantanzas,
  beginning operations against Spain's
  Caribbean installations

May 1: Battle of Manila Bay
May 2: U.S. forces land Cavite,
  Philippines
May 3: U.S. forces land Corregidor
  Island, Philippines
May 11: Naval action: Cienfuegos, Cuba
May 11: Naval action: Cardenas, Cuba
May 19: Spanish squadron arrives
  Santiago, Cuba
May 28: Naval blockade: Santiago, Cuba
June 10: U.S. forces land Guantanamo,
  Cuba
June 14: Battle of Cuzco
June 21: U.S. occupies Guam
June 22: U.S. forces land Daiquiri
June 23: U.S. occupies Siboney
June 24: Battle of Las Guasimas
July 1: Battle of El Caney
July 1: Battle of Kettle Hill

July 1: Battle of San Juan Hill
July 3: Naval action: Santiago, Cuba
July 17: Santiago surrenders to U.S.
  forces
July 17: Battle of Cavite, Philippines
July 25: U.S. forces land Puerto Rico
July 31: Siege of Manila; ends Aug 13
Dec 10: Treaty ends war with Spain
1899
Feb 4: Philippine-American War begins
Feb 4: Manila campaign; ends Mar 17
Feb 8: Iloilo campaign; ends Feb 12
Mar 24: Malolos campaign; ends Aug 16
April 8: Laguna de Bay campaign; ends
  Apr 17
April 10: Battle of Santa Cruz
April 21: 1st San Isidro campaign; ends
  May 30
May 15: Battle of San Isidro
June 13: Zapote River campaign
Oct 7: 1st Cavite campaign; ends Oct 13
Oct 15: Second San Isidro campaign;
  ends Nov 19
Nov 5: Tarlac campaign; ends Nov 20
Nov 6: San Fabian campaign; ends
  Nov 19
Dec 2: Battle of the Clouds
1900
Jan 4: Second Cavite campaign; ends
  Feb 9
May 22: International Relief Expedition:
  Boxer Rebellion
June 20: Boxer siege of legations in
  Beijing; ends Aug 14
July 7: U.S. forces land Tanggu:
  Boxer Rebellion
July 9: Battle of Tienjin; ends July 14
  Boxer Rebellion
Aug 5: Battle of Pei-tsang:
  Boxer Rebellion
Aug 6: Battle of Yang-tsun:
  Boxer Rebellion
Aug 14: U.S. forces enter Beijing:
  Boxer Rebellion
Oct 12: *Holland*, 1st modern submarine
1901
Mar 23: Aguinaldo captured by
  U.S. forces
Sept 28: Battle of Balangiga
Nov 15: Battle of Sohoton River:
  Moro Rebellion, Philippines
1902
April 16: U.S. forces land Panama
May 2: Battle of Pandapatan: Moro Reb.
Oct 1: Battle of Macin: Moro Reb.
1903
April 6: Battle of Bacolod: Moro Reb.
May 2: Lake Lano Expedition: Moro
  Reb.
May 4: Battle of Taraca: Moro Reb.
1905
Oct 22: Battle of Malalag River: Moro
  Reb.
1906
Mar 5: Battle of Bud Dajo: Moro Reb.

Sept 13: U.S. forces land Cuba; ends
Apr 1, 1909
1907
Aug 1: Signal Corps establishes
Aeronautical Division
Dec 16: Great White Fleet departs, returns
Feb 22, 1909
1908
Jan 10: U.S. government contracts with
Wright Bros, for aircraft
1909
May 26: 1st flight, Dirigible No. 1, with
American pilots
1910
Jan 4: *Michigan,* 1st dreadnought
Aug 27: 1st test aircraft-to-ground
radio-telegraphy
Nov 14: 1st aircraft to take off from
a ship
1911
April 11: 1st Army pilot training school,
College Park, Maryland
Dec 22: Siege of Bud Dajo: Moro Reb.
1912
Jan 14: Jolo Expedition: Moro Reb.
July 26: 1st aircraft-to-ship
radio-telegraphy
Aug 4: U.S. forces land Nicaragua; ends
Jan 17, 1913
Mar 5: 1st Aero Squadron activated
April 13: *Jupiter,* 1st electrically propelled
warship
June 11: Battle of Bud Bagsak: Moro Reb.
1914
Mar 1: Battle of Bud Tanu, Moro Reb.
April 9: Tampico Incident, *Dolphin*
April 21: U.S. forces land Vera Cruz;
ends Nov 23
April 25: 1st use of aircraft in combat:
Vera Cruz
1914
April 28: 1st use of aerial photography in
combat: Vera Cruz
May 6: 1st aircraft damaged in action:
Vera Cruz
July 18: Aviation Section of Signal Corps
created
1915
Jan 28: Coast Guard: merges Life-Saving
Service and Revenue-Cutter Service
July 28: U.S. forces land Haiti; ends Aug
15, 1934
Jan 6: U.S. forces land Cuba; ends
Feb 6, 1922
Mar 9: Columbus, N.M., raided by
Pancho Villa's forces
Mar 14: Pershing Expedition enters
Mexico; ends Feb 7, 1917
1916
Mar 29: Battle of Guerreo: Mexican
Intervention
April 10: Battle of La Joya: Mexican
Intervention
April 12: Battle of Parral: Mexican
Intervention

April 22: Battle of Tomochic: Mexican
Intervention
May 5: U.S. forces land Dominican
Republic; ends Sept 16, 1924
May 25: Battle of Alamillo: Mexican
Intervention
June 3: Army Reserve Officers Training
Corps (Navy, 1926; Air Force, 1946)
June 21: Battle of Carrizal: Mexican
Intervention
Aug 29: Naval Flying Corps and Naval
Reserve Flying Corps
Oct 20: *Maumee,* 1st diesel-powered
surface ship
1917
Feb 28: 1st aircraft-to-ground station
voice transmission
April 6: U.S. declares war on Germany,
enters World War I
May 1: Dominican Intervention

THE AEF IN EUROPE This 1932 map shows the movements of the
American Expeditionary Force during World War I. (See large map, p. 132)

May 8: 1st anti-submarine operation
European Theater
May 18: Selective Service Act
May 26: John J. Pershing, Commander in
Chief, American Expeditionary Force
(AEF)
Nov 5: *Alcedo,* 1st U.S. warship sunk by
German submarine
Nov 20: Cambrai: 1st major campaign
involving U.S. forces
Dec 7: U.S. declares war on Austria-Hungary
1918
Feb 18: 103rd Aero Pursuit Squadron
1st operational U.S. Air Service unit
in Europe
Mar 21: Somme Campaign; ends Apr 6
April 9: Lys Campaign; ends Apr 27
May 20: Army aviation separated from
Signal Corps
May 24: U.S. forces land Murmansk:
Russian Intervention

May 27: Aisne Campaign; ends June 5
May 28: Battle of Cantigny
May 31: Battle of Château-Thierry
June 4: Battle of Belleau Wood;
ends June 26
June 8: North Sea Mine Barrage
operation; ends Oct 26
June 9: Montdidier-Noyon Campaign
July 1: Battle of Vaux
July 4: Battle of Hamel
July 15: Champagne-Marne Campaign
July 18: Aisne-Marne Campaign; ends
Aug 6
Aug 3: U.S. forces land Archangel; ends
June 27, 1919: Rian Intervention
Aug 8: Somme Campaign; ends Nov 11
Aug 8: Battles of Gressaire Wood and
Chilpilly Ridge
Aug 15: U.S. forces land Vladivostok;
ends Apr 1, 1920: Rian Intervention

Aug 18: Oise-Aisne Campaign; ends
Nov 11
Aug 19: Ypres-Lys Campaign; ends
Nov 11
Aug 27: Nogales, Texas, border incident
Aug 28: U.S. Army Air Service (USAAS)
Sept 12: St.-Mihiel offensive
Sept 12: 1st combat by armor unit: 304th
Tank Brigade
Sept 12: Air action: St.-Mihiel offensive
Sept 26: Meuse-Argonne Campaign; ends
Nov 11
Oct 3: Naval action: Durazzo, Albania
Oct 24: Vittorio Veneto Campaign; ends
Nov 4
Nov 3: Battle of Ponte della Delizia, Italy
Nov 11: Armistice ends World War I
Nov 11: Battle of Tulga: Rian
Intervention
Dec 30: Battle of Kodish: Rian
Intervention

1919
Jan 19: Battle of Shenkursh: Rian
Intervention
Mar 25: U.S. forces land Murmansk;
ends July 28, 1919: Rian Intervention
1921
July 21: Obsolete battleship sunk with
aerial bombs in test
1922
Oct 2: Air Service Balloon and
Airship School
1923
Jan 24: U.S. forces withdraw from
Germany
May 2: USAAS plane: 1st non-stop
transcontinental flight
1924
April 6: USAAS round-the-world flight
Nov 17: *Langley,* 1st operational carrier
1926
May 6: U.S. forces land Bluefields,
Nicaragua; ends June 5
July 2: Army Air Corps replaces
Army Air Service
1927
Jan 6: U.S. forces land Nicaragua; ends
May 3, 1933
1928
Jan 6: 1st combat aerial resupply:
Nicaraguan Intervention
1936
June 22: Congress designates Coast
Guard as enforcement arm of U.S. laws
on the high seas & inland waters
1937
Dec 12: *Panay* sunk by Japanese aircraft,
Nanking, China
1939
Sept 6: USN Neutrality Patrol established
in Atlantic
1940
Sept 16: Peacetime conscription
authorized
Sept 25: U.S. deciphers Japanese code
1941
June 20: Army Air Force replaces Army
Air Corps
July 7: U.S. forces land Iceland
July 15: USN authorized to attack Axis
ships approaching a convoy
Sept 1: USN authorized to attack Axis
ships anywhere in Atlantic
Oct 17: *Kearny* attacked by German
submarine
Oct 31: *Reuben James* sunk by German
submarine
Nov 1: Coast Guard under USN control
Nov 21: U.S. forces occupy Dutch
Guiana
Dec 7: Japanese air attack on USN base at
Pearl Harbor, Hawaii
Dec 8: U.S. declares war on Japan; enters
World War II
Dec 8: Japanese bomb Clark Field,
Manila, Philippines

Dec 10: Japanese land, Philippines: Northern Luzon

Dec 10: Japanese capture Guam

Dec 11: Battle of Wake Island; ends Dec 23; Germany declares war on U.S.

1942

Jan 7: Siege of Bataan; ends Apr 9

Jan 9: U.S. Joint Chiefs of Staff created

Jan 24: Naval action: Makassar Strait/Balikpapan

Feb 1: Naval air operation: Marshall/Gilbert Islands

Feb 27: Naval action in Java Sea

Feb 28: Naval action in Sunda Strait

Mar 7: Japanese forces land New Guinea

Mar 16: U.S. forces arrive Australia

April 18: Doolittle Raid bombs Tokyo

May 4: Battle of the Coral Sea

May 6: U.S. forces surrender Philippines

June 3: Battle of Midway

June 7: Japanese land Attu and Kiska, Aleutians

June 22: Japanese naval bombardment: Ft. Stevens, Oregon

June 28: Dwight D. Eisenhower assumes command U.S. forces, Europe

July 13: Office of Strategic Services (OSS)

Aug 7: Guadalcanal landing

Aug 8: Savo Island naval action

Aug 17: Eighth Air Force attacks 1st European target

Aug 17: U.S. forces land Butaritari, Makin Atoll

Aug 23: Eastern Solomons: naval action

Aug 30: U.S. forces land Adak, Aleutians

Nov 8: Allies land North Africa: Op. Torch

Nov 8: 1st U.S. combat use of airborne troops: Oran, Algeria

Nov 12: Naval battle of Guadalcanal

Nov 19: Battle of Buna: New Guinea Campaign

1943

Jan 15: Construction of the Pentagon

Feb 19: Battle of Kasserine Pass

Feb 21: Solomon Island Campaign: U.S. takes Russel Islands

Mar 2: Battle of Bismarck Sea

May 11: U.S. forces land Attu, Aleutians

June 28: Women's Army Corps (WACs) established; ends Oct 20, 1978

July 10: U.S. forces land Sicily

Aug 15: U.S. forces land Kiska, Aleutians

Sept 8: Italy surrenders

Sept 9: U.S. forces land Salerno: Italian Campaign

Nov 1: U.S. forces land Bougainville: Solomon Islands Campaign

Nov 20: U.S. forces land Makin and Tarawa, Gilbert Islands

Dec 8: Battle of San Pietro; ends Dec 21: Italian Campaign

Dec 26: U.S. forces land Cape Gloucester: New Britain

1944

Jan 2: U.S. forces land Saidor, New Guinea

Jan 22: U.S. forces land Anzio: Italian Campaign

Jan 31: U.S. forces land Kwajalein: Marshalls Campaign

Feb 17: U.S. forces land Eniwetok: Marshalls Campaign

Feb 18: Truk, 1st night operation by carrier aircraft

Feb 24: 1st use of magnetic airborne detection (MAD) to locate a submerged enemy submarine

April 23: 1st helicopter rescue combat: Burma

VICTORY IN EUROPE A map detail shows the position of American Twelfth Army Group units. Facing them are German units near Dresden, Germany. Positions shown are for May 7, 1945—the day Germany surrendered.

June 4: U.S. forces occupy Rome

June 6: D-Day: Allies land Normandy, Op. Overlord

June 15: U.S. forces land Saipan: Mariana Islands Campaign

June 19: Battle of Philippine Sea

July 21: U.S. forces land Guam: Mariana Islands Campaign

July 24: U.S. forces land Tinian: Mariana Islands Campaign

July 25: U.S. forces break out of Normandy beachhead

Aug 13: Battle of the Falaise Pocket; ends Aug 20

Aug 15: U.S. forces land Southern France, Op. Dragoon

Aug 20: U.S. forces cross Seine River

Aug 25: U.S. forces liberate Paris

Sept 11: 1st U.S. forces enter Germany

Sept 15: U.S. forces land Peleliu: Palau Islands Campaign

Sept 17: Airborne operation, Netherlands: Op. Market Garden

Oct 20: U.S. forces land Leyte: Philippine Campaign

Oct 23: Battle of Leyte Gulf

Oct 25: 1st planned kamikaze attacks by Japanese aircraft on U.S. naval vessels: Leyte Gulf

Dec 1: 1st ballistic missile test

Dec 16: Ardennes II, "Battle of the Bulge"; ends Jan 28, 1945

1945

Feb 3: Battle of Manila; ends Mar 3

Feb 14: Air action: firebombing of Dresden, Germany

Feb 19: U.S. forces land Iwo Jima

Mar 5: Battle of the Rhineland; ends Mar 25

Mar 7: U.S. forces cross Rhine River at Remagen

Mar 9: USAAF incendiary bombing campaign against Japan

April 1: U.S. forces land Okinawa, Ryukyu Islands

April 7: USN sinks *Yamato*, Japanese battleship, world's largest

April 11: U.S. forces reach Elbe River

April 23: 1st combat use of automatic homing missile

April 25: U.S. & U.S.S.R. forces make contact at Torgau, Germany

May 2: German forces in Italy surrender

May 7: Germans in Western Europe surrender at Reims, France

Aug 6: 1st atomic bomb dropped, Hiroshima, Japan

Aug 9: Atomic bomb dropped, Nagasaki, Japan

Aug 15: Japanese government ceasefire

Sept 2: Japanese surrender

Sept 8: U.S. forces enter Korea

Sept 30: U.S. forces land Tanggu, Chinese Civil War

Oct 6: U.S. forces engage Communist People's Liberation Army, Tienjin;

sporadic combat ends May 26, 1949: Chinese Civil War

Nov 19: Eisenhower, Chief of Staff

Dec 3: Lockheed F-80, 1st jet fighter, USAAF

1946

May 22: 1st guided ballistic missile test

July 1: Bikini Atoll nuclear bomb test

1947

Feb 12: 1st test of submarine-launched guided missile

Mar 31: Selective Service ends

Sept 17: Congress creates United States Air Force (USAF)

Oct 14: Charles Yeager, 1st faster-than-sound flight

1948

June 12: Women in the Air Force (WAF)

June 22: Selective service reestablished

June 26: Berlin Air Lift; ends Sept 30, 1949

July 20: 1st jet transit of Atlantic

1949

June 29: U.S. occupation forces withdraw from S. Korea

1950

June 25: N. Korea invades S. Korea: Korean War

June 26: President Truman approves air and naval operations in Korea

June 27: UN Security Council imposes sanctions on N. Korea

July 2: Naval action: Chumunjin

July 3: Naval air action: Pyongyang

July 5: Battle of Osan

July 9: Battle of Choui

July 11: Battle of Chochiwon

July 13: Air action: Wonson

July 14: Battle of Kum River & Taejn

July 26: Battle of Hadong

Aug 2: Battle of Chindong-ni

Aug 4: 1st helicopter medical evacuation

Aug 5: Battle of Naktong Bulge; ends Aug 26

Aug 16: Taegu carpet bombing

Aug 26: Battle of Pusan Perimeter; ends Sept 10

Sept 3: Second Battle of Naktong Bulge

Sept 5: Battle of Yongchon; ends Sept 13

Sept 15: Amphibious assault Inchon, Op. Chromite

Sept 19: Pusan Breakout Offensive

Sept 29: UN forces occupy Seoul

Oct 19: UN forces capture Pyongyang

Oct 20: Airborne assault – Sukchon and Sunchon

Oct 25: U.S. forces land Wonsan

Oct 25: Chinese 1st Phase Offensive

Oct 29: U.S. forces land Iwon

Oct 29: U.S. forces land Chinnampo

Nov 8: 1st all-jet aerial combat

Nov 8: Bombing, Yalu River bridges

Nov 25: Chinese Second Phase Offensive

Dec 1: UN forces at Chosin and Pujon Reservoirs withdraw

Dec 3: Wonson evacuation; ends Dec 10
Dec 5: UN forces leave Pyongyang
Dec 31: Chinese Third Phase Offensive
1951
Jan 4: UN forces leave Seoul
Jan 15: UN counter-offensives begin
Jan 21: 1st Chinese-U.S. air engagement
Feb 13: Battle of Chipyong
Mar 14: UN forces occupy Seoul
July 10: Armistice talks begin, Kaesong
Aug 18: Battle of Bloody Ridge;
    ends Sept 5
Aug 23: Armistice talks suspended
Aug 25: Air operation: Rashin
Sept 13: Battle of Heartbreak Ridge;
    ends Oct 15
Sept 21: 1st helicopter lift of combat unit:
    Op. Summit
Oct 25: Armistice talks resume,
    Panmunjom
Nov 12: UN forces cease offensives
1952
June 26: Battle of Old Baldy;
    ends Mar 26, 1953
Aug 27: Air operation: Pyongyang
Oct 14: Battle of Triangle Hill; ends Nov 5
Oct 26: Battle of the Hook
Nov 1: 1st hydrogen bomb test—
    on Eniwetok
1953
Mar 21: 2nd Battle of the Hook
Mar 23: Battle of Pork Chop Hill;
    ends July 11
May 25: 1st artillery shell with nuclear
    warhead fired
July 13: Battle of the Kumsong Salient
July 27: Korean Armistice Agreement
1954
July 26: USN aircraft from Philippine Sea
    engage Chinese People's Republic
    aircraft: Hainan Incident
Sept 30: *Nautilus,* 1st nuclear-powered
    submarine
1955
July 11: U.S. Air Force Academy
Aug 17: Military Code of Conduct
Nov 1: *Boston,* 1st guided missile cruiser
Nov 1: Military Assistance Advisory
    Group, Vietnam, established
1958
July 15: U.S. forces land Lebanon
1959
July 8: 1st advisors KIA in S. Vietnam:
    Bien Hoa
1960
Feb 24: *Triton,* 1st submerged
    circumnavigation; ends Apr 10
July 20: 1st ballistic missile launch
    by submerged submarine
1961
Sept 9: *Long Beach,* 1st nuclear-powered
    surface warship
Oct 11: President Kennedy authorizes
    USAF training unit for S. Vietnamese
    Air Force

Nov 25: *Enterprise,* 1st nuclear-powered
    carrier
1962
Jan 13: Op. Ranch Hand, defoliation;
    ends Jan 7, 1971
Feb 6: Military Assistance Command,
    Vietnam (MACV) established
May 15: U.S. forces land Bangkok,
    Thailand; ends Aug 7
1964
Aug 2: Naval action: Tonkin Gulf,
    Maddox
Aug 5: Naval air action against
    N. Vietnam
Nov 1: Viet Cong guerrillas attack air
    base at Bien Hoa, S. Vietnam
Dec 2: President Johnson authorizes
    limited air operations against
    N. Vietnam
Dec 24: Air/naval air action-Laos

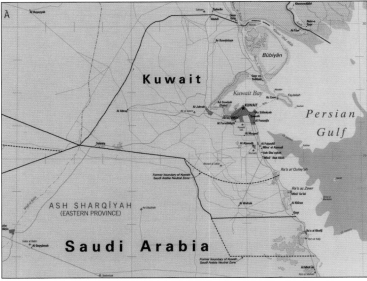

WARS IN THE GULF This detail from a 1991 CIA map shows Kuwait and its strategic access to the Persian Gulf. (See large map, p. 225.)

1965
Mar 2: Air campaign over N. Vietnam:
    Op. Rolling Thunder
Mar 8: 1st overt U.S. combat forces land
    S. Vietnam
April 25: U.S. forces land Dominican
    Republic; ends Sept 27
July 4: Battle of Ba Gia
Nov 14: Battle of Ia Drang Valley
1966
May 1: U.S. forces bomb VC positions
    in Cambodia
June 29: Air/naval air action: Hanoi &
    Haiphong, N. Vietnam
1967
Jan 8: Op. Cedar Falls; ends Jan 26
Feb 22: Op. Junction City; ends May 14
June 8: *Liberty* attacked by Israeli aircraft
June 22: Battle of Dak To
Sept 10: Battle of Con Thien; ends Oct 4
Oct 29: Battle of Loc Ninh
Nov 4: Second Battle of Dak To

1968
Jan 23: *Pueblo* seized by N. Korea
Jan 30: VC and N. Vietnamese Tet
    Offensive; ends Feb 24
Mar 16: My Lai Massacre
Mar 31: Johnson suspends N. Vietnam
    bombing above 20th parallel
April 29: Battle of Dong Ha
Nov 15: Air/naval air action: Laos
1969
May 10: Battle of Hamburger Hill; ends
    May 20
June 8: 1st combat units withdraw from
    S. Vietnam
1970
May 1: Cambodian incursion; ends
    June 29; Op. Binh Tay
Nov 21: Son Tay POW raid
1971
Jan 30: Op. Dewey Canyon II

1972
May 9: North Vietnamese harbors
    mined
May 10: Linebacker I: air/naval air
    action; ends Oct 23
May 13: Air action-Thanh Hoa Bridge,
    N. Vietnam: 1st combat use of
    laser-guided bomb
Dec 18: Linebacker II: Air/naval air
    action; ends Dec 29
1973
Jan 23: Cease-fire agreement between
    U.S. and N. Vietnam
Jan 27: President Richard M. Nixon halts
    all hostile acts by U.S. forces in N. and
    S. Vietnam
Feb 21: Air actions Laos end; resume Feb
    24–26 and Apr 16–17
Mar 29: Last organized units leave S.
    Vietnam
July 1: Congress ends inductions under
    Selective Service Act

1975
April 29: U.S. Saigon evacuation
May 14: U.S. forces land Cambodia:
    Mayaguez incident
1980
April 24: Iranian hostage rescue aborted
1981
Aug 19: Naval air action: Gulf of Sidra
1982
Aug 25: U.S. forces land Beirut, Lebanon;
    ends Sept 10
Sept 26: U.S. forces land Beirut, Lebanon;
    ends Feb 26, 1984
1983
Oct 23: USMC Headquarters in Beirut
    destroyed by truck bomb
Oct 25: U.S. forces land Grenada
Dec 4: Air action: Bekka Valley,
    Lebanon
Dec 18: USN bombardment: Beirut
1984
Jan 15: USN bombardment: Beirut
Feb 8: USN bombardment: Beirut
1986
Mar 24: Naval/naval air action:
    Gulf of Sidra
April 15: Air action: Libya
1987
May 17: *Stark* attacked by Iraqi aircraft
Sept 21: Air action: Persian/Arab Gulf
Oct 8: Air action-Persian/Arab Gulf
Oct 19: Naval action: Persian/Arab Gulf
Nov 1: Naval action: Persian/Arab Gulf
1988
April 14: *Samuel B. Roberts* mines
    Persian/Arab Gulf
April 18: Naval action: Persian/Arab Gulf
July 3: *Vincennes* shoots down
    Iran Air Flight 655
1989
Jan 4: Air action: Gulf of Sidra, Libya
1989
Dec 20: U.S. forces land Panama
1990
Aug 5: Monrovia, Liberia evacuation;
    ends Aug 21
Aug 8: U.S. aircraft land Saudi Arabia,
    Op. Desert Shield
Aug 9: U.S. forces land Saudi Arabia,
    Op. Desert Shield
Nov 29: UN authorizes force to compel
    Iraq to withdraw from Kuwait
1991
Jan 4: Mogadishu, Somalia, evacuation
Jan 16: Naval action: Persian/Arab Gulf
Jan 17: Air action: Iraq
Jan 24: Air action: Persian/Arab Gulf
Jan 29: Battle of Khafji
Feb 24: Op. Desert Storm; ends Feb 28
Feb 27: Allied forces occupy Kuwait City
1992
Dec 9: U.S. forces land Somalia;
    ends Mar 25, 1994
Dec 27: Air/naval air action: Iraq;
    continues through 2002

1993

April 12: Air action: Bosnia, against Bosnian Serbs to stop civil war

Oct 3: Battle of Mogadishu

1994

Sept 19: U.S. forces land Haiti to stop election violence

Dec 19: NATO-led SFOR (Stabilization Force) of 30,000 men begins Op. Joint Guard to keep peace in former Yugoslavia

1995

Aug 30: Op. Deliberate Force: NATO bombs Bosnian Serbs to compel them to make peace; ends Sept 21

Dec 20: Op. Joint Endeavor: NATO IFOR (Implementation Force) deploys 20,000 Americans with troops from other nations to keep peace in Bosnia-Herzegovina; ends Dec 20, 1996

1996

June 25: Radical Saudi Shiite group's truck bomb devastates Khobar Towers, U.S. military residence in Dhahran, killing 19 servicemen

1998

Aug 7: U.S. embassies in Tanzania and Kenya bombed by terrorists

Aug 20: U.S. missiles strike Afghanistan and Sudan facilities in reprisal

Dec 16: 1st of three successive Coalition air strikes on Iraq to prevent military moves against Kurds

1999

Mar 23: Op. Allied Force: NATO bombing campaign to make Serbia accept Kosovo peace plan; ends June 10, as Serbs withdraw from Kosovo

Dec 31: U.S. returns Panama Canal to Panama

2000

Oct 12: Terrorists attack *Cole*, Aden

2001

Sept 11: Suicide hijackers fly two domestic airliners into World Trade Center, killing 2,600; another hits Pentagon, and a fourth crashes in a Pennsylvania field; total deaths approach 3,000

Oct 7: Afghanistan invasion, Op. Enduring Freedom, to oust Taliban regime

Dec 6: Kandahar falls, Taliban's last major stronghold

2002

Mar 7: Special forces attack Taliban and al-Qaida in Afghanistan mountains; operations continue

2003

Mar 19: Third Persian Gulf War: Op. Iraqi Freedom

May 1: Major conflict declared over in Op. Iraqi Freedom; Coalition occupation continues

2004

Feb: U.S. troops lead Haiti intervention during coup that deposes President Jean Bertrand Aristide

U.S.-led Coalition occupation of Iraq continues with more than 160,000 troops; as many as 140,000 are Americans

Hostile resistance continues with daily attacks by Iraqi guerrillas

NATO forces occupy parts of Afghanistan, including the capital, Kabul

Taliban resistance is sporadic, but persists

U.S. Special Forces hunt for al-Qaida leaders in mountains along Afghanistan-Pakistan border

MAP KEY

Washington / Cornwallis	Commanding officer of army
Infantry	Infantry
Cavalry	Cavalry
Naval forces (battleships, gunboats, firing battleship)	Naval forces (battleships, gunboats, firing battleship)
Artillery	Artillery
Troop position	Troop position
Troop advance	Troop advance
Troop retreat	Troop retreat
Redoubt	Redoubt
Field works, trenches	Field works, trenches
Fort	Fort
Encampment	Encampment
American Indian encampment	American Indian encampment
Battle	Battle
Airfield	Airfield
Airborne drop zone	Airborne drop zone
Cities (national capital, state or province capital, city)	Cities (national capital, state or province capital, city)
American Indian village	American Indian village
Bridge	Bridge
Building	Building
Levee	Levee
Mountain pass	Mountain pass
Pontoon bridge	Pontoon bridge
Railroad	Railroad
Road	Road
Trail	Trail
Elevated area	Elevated area
Forest	Forest
Swamp	Swamp
City or urban area	City or urban area

Note: In most instances, blue symbols are used to denote the United States, Patriot, or Union forces. Red symbols are used to denote the British, Confederate, French, Mexican, American Indian, German, Japanese, and other forces.

TREATY OF PARIS This detail is taken from a contemporary map created by a London cartographer around 1774. Shown here is eastern North America after the Treaty of Paris, 1763, which ended the French and Indian War. With Britain's victory, the vast land of New France, from the Great Lakes to Newfoundland, became British Canada. France also ceded Louisiana (shown in yellow to the west) to Spain, which in turn transferred Florida to Britain.

PART ONE

Wars of the Colonial Period

BEFORE THE ARRIVAL OF EUROPEANS, most wars of the North American Indians were limited affairs of honor and tradition. The object was to display courage, to chase away the enemy, perhaps to inflict one or two deaths, but there was no intent to wreak total destruction. Warmaking changed soon after the first Europeans settled on the continent.

As the French in the North, the British and Dutch in the mid-Atlantic region, and the Spanish in the South established colonies that grew and expanded, friction developed with the native peoples. Resulting hostilities were brief but bloody, and massacres were common on both sides. American warfare was no longer about honor and tradition, but about total victory or utter defeat. The Europeans were not to be driven out, however, and American Indians came to depend on them for trade goods, including guns and ammunition.

The wars of Europe were brought to the colonies of the New World, and many native warriors fought for one side or the other. Then colonial forces were reinforced by the arrival of professional regiments, and wars recurred again and again in the colonies. The British finally defeated the French in the Seven Years' War, which ended in 1763.

The American Revolution that began in 1775 was the last colonial war in British North America. It was an eight-year struggle that ended with the new United States of America coming into the world.

Washington's troops cross the Delaware, Christmas 1776.

1: FUR TRADE, COLONIES, AND FIREARMS

The 1513 landing of Spain's Juan Ponce de León in Florida was the beginning of European conquest of North America. Spanish adventurers clashed with native peoples in the South and Southwest, and in 1541 Hernando de Soto won a major victory against the Choctaw at Mabila, on the Gulf Coast. Spain was challenged in 1564 when the French built Fort Caroline in northeastern Florida. The Spanish destroyed the fort the following year and established Saint Augustine, which was sacked by Englishman Sir Francis Drake in 1586.

Early in the 1600s, French, English, and Dutch began to settle along the eastern seaboard. For the most part, European explorers and settlers were peacefully received by the natives, who were eager to trade furs for manufactured goods. In 1609, France's Samuel de Champlain allied with Algonquins against Iroquois in the Battle of Lake Champlain, an early victory of modern firepower over native bows and spears.

NATIVE WARRIOR This Virginia Indian was portrayed in a 1587 watercolor by Englishman John White, the leader of the colony at Roanoke, Virginia. White sailed back to England that year. When he returned the colony had mysteriously disappeared, perhaps wiped out by Indian raids. It became known as the "Lost Colony of Roanoke."

"Starving Time" at Jamestown

Also in 1609, the two-year-old English colony of Jamestown, on the Virginia coast, was attacked by the Powhatans, who were angry at the settlement's expansion. The Powhatans destroyed outlying communities and laid siege to Jamestown itself, bringing on famine, so that the winter of 1609–1610 was known as the "Starving Time." More than two-thirds of the 600 colonists had died when ships arrived in the spring, lifting the siege.

Trouble persisted for another four years, when a truce was made, but two more Anglo-Powhatan wars erupted in 1622 and 1644. More than 400 Jamestown settlers were massacred in the latter conflict. The Virginians then wiped out the entire Powhatan nation to finally end hostilities.

A war breaks out over peaches

To the north, the Dutch colony of New Netherland had its share of warfare with the Indians. New Netherland was founded as a commercial enterprise by the Dutch West India Company. Peace with the Indians was essential to the colony's main mission: the fur trade.

Yet peace was not easy to maintain, for the growing colony encroached on Indian holdings. At various times, the Dutch fought the Mohawks, Delawares, and Esopus. Deadly strife between a settler and Indians who were stealing his

TRIBES OF THE CHESAPEAKE REGION, EARLY 1600s

Maryland

New Jersey

Potomac R.

Delaware Bay

Wicomiss

Anacostanh
Mattapanicut
Piscataway
Pamunkey
Naogemeick
Potapaco
Acquintanaesuck
Yaocomaco
Potomac R.

Delaware

Nanticoke

Pocomoke

Virginia

Chesapeake Bay

ATLANTIC OCEAN

Acohanock

Gingaskin

N

0   50 miles
0   50 km

Note: Map shown with modern boundaries for reference.

POWHATAN CONFEDERACY The settlers of Jamestown, Virginia, warred with the tribes of the Chesapeake region, but also depended on them for trade in times of peace. Without food from the Indians, white settlements could not survive. Many tribes were part of the loosely organized Powhatan Confederacy, ruled by Wahunsonacock, also known as "King Powhatan." His daughter, Pocahontas, married settler John Rolfe, promoting peaceful relations between the peoples.

THE PEQUOT WAR, 1636–1637

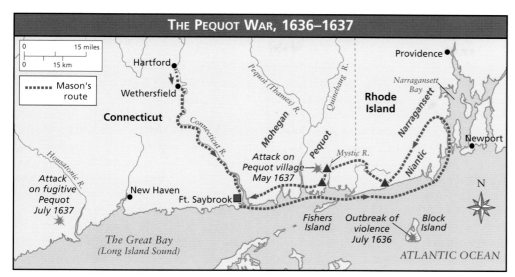

DESTRUCTION OF THE PEQUOT New England colonists considered the powerful Pequot a threat and conspired with the Narragansett of Rhode Island and the Mohegan of Connecticut to destroy them. In May 1637, an army of colonists and warriors, led by Major John Mason of Connecticut, made a surprise night attack on a Pequot village, slaughtering 600 inhabitants.

"My heart breaks; now I am ready to die. . . ."

—METACOMET, ALSO CALLED KING PHILIP, IN 1676, WHEN HIS WIFE AND SON WERE CAPTURED BY MASSACHUSETTS PURITANS AND THREATENED WITH EXECUTION

peaches brought on the full-scale "Peach War" of 1655–1657. At the same time, the Dutch had troubles with the Swedes, who had planted the colony of Fort Christina in New Netherland territory. New Netherland governor-general, Pieter Stuyvesant, led an expedition southward to capture the fort in 1554.

Pequot and King Philip's wars

At this time, Stuyvesant's Puritan neighbors in New England were between major Indian conflicts. In the Pequot War of 1636–1637, the Puritans had attacked and utterly destroyed the powerful Pequots, who were accused of planning an uprising against the colonists. By the mid-1600s, New England whites numbered 40,000, compared to 20,000 Indians of tribes such as the Wampanoag, Narragansett, Nipmuc, and Abenaki.

In 1675, renewed friction resulted in clashes that caused several Indian deaths, and full-scale hostilities broke out. Wampanoag chief Metacomet, known to the settlers as "King Philip," destroyed a dozen communities, but the better-armed colonists were victorious. Metacomet was killed in 1676, and Indian resistance dwindled to an end. The war cost the lives of 1,000 colonists and unknown thousands of Indians, but whites now controlled most of New England.

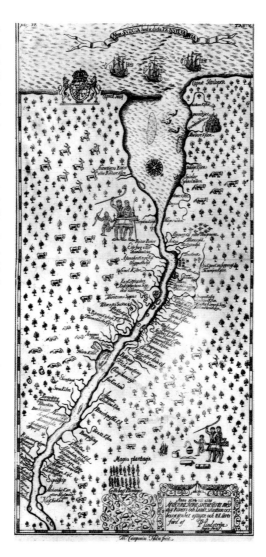

WARRIOR NATION
IROQUOIS WARS

Iroquois warrior, carrying a decorated tomahawk and globe-headed club.

The Iroquois League was a powerful alliance of the Seneca, Onondaga, Cayuga, Oneida, and Mohawk tribes that controlled fur trading routes between Lake Erie and the Hudson River. The Iroquois benefited from trade with the colonies, and the firearms they acquired made them a dominant force.

Peoples such as the Huron, Ottawa, and Abenaki competed with the Iroquois in the fur trade. To defeat this competition, the Iroquois attacked the Hurons in 1642, starting ten years of conflict that drew in the settlers of New France as Huron allies. Peace found the Iroquois in a strong position of power, and in the mid-1660s, they next attacked the Ottawa and Abenaki. By now, however, these nations were armed with guns provided by the French, who fought alongside them. The war ended in an Iroquois defeat, and French influence rose dramatically among the eastern Indian nations.

THE COLONY OF NEW SWEDEN This map of New Sweden shows the Delaware River, then called the South River—the Hudson was the North River. Swedish settlements are along the Delaware, which flows into Delaware Bay. Swedish settler Thomas Campanius Holm drew this map, based on an earlier version.

EUROPEAN WARS BRING CONFLICT TO AMERICA

The English and Dutch empires went to war in 1652, setting off a world-wide naval struggle for control of sea routes, fishing grounds, and maritime trade. This first in a series of Anglo-Dutch wars was felt in America, where New Englanders considered the time ripe to move against the Dutch colony of New Netherland.

Colonial rivalry for rich land

There was considerable trade and social intercourse between the colonies, but New Netherland blocked populous New England's western expansion. Only 12,000 New Netherlanders occupied a vast and fertile region, while more than 40,000 New Englanders were hemmed in, unable to migrate. Thousands of them had been allowed to settle on eastern Long Island, where they prospered. Yet most of these settlers were eager to end the rule of New Netherland's governor-general, Pieter Stuyvesant, and the Dutch West Indian Company he served. The war ended in 1654, before blood was shed between the colonies, but continued commercial rivalries stimulated the Second Anglo-Dutch War by 1664.

An attack on New Netherland

An English fleet sailed to America and landed 400 soldiers on Long Island that September. Stuyvesant might have fought off the enemy troops, but he found himself vastly outnumbered when hundreds of English settlers from Long Island joined the invaders. Stuyvesant was prepared to resist, but his subordinate officers persuaded him to surrender. New Amsterdam became New York in honor of the Duke of York, brother of England's King Charles II.

The Third Anglo-Dutch War began in 1670, and the Dutch navy retook New York without a fight in 1672. The treaty of 1674 then returned the city to England, exchanging New York for the colony of Madras, India.

King William's War

In 1689, King William III of England and several European allies went to war against France to prevent King Louis XIV from gaining too much power in Europe. In Quebec City, the governor of New France, Louis de Baude, Comte de Frontenac, was desperate to stop bloody Iroquois attacks on his settlements. One raid destroyed the village of Lachine, across the river from Montreal, massacring 200 men, women, and children and capturing another 120. Many Indian nations were doubting French power.

Frontenac considered the British and Iroquois to be allies in competition with New France for the fur trade. He took advantage of the war in Europe to strike at British frontier settlements. On February 8,

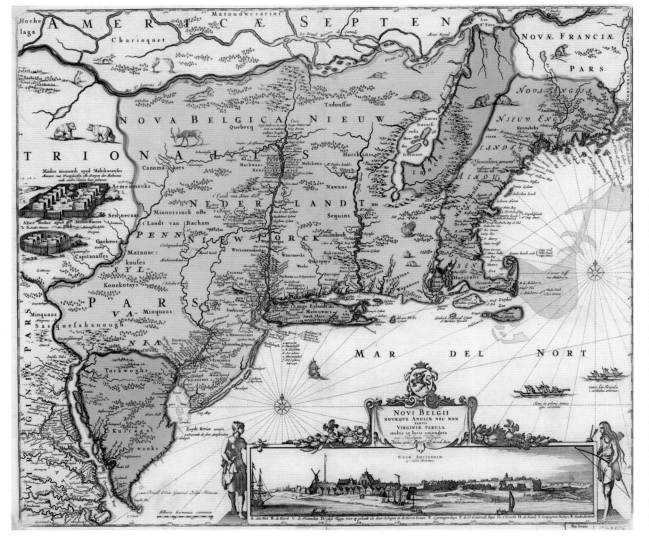

NEW WORLD COLONIES This Amsterdam cartographer's map shows New Netherland and the colonies around it. New Netherland, in yellow, takes in territory to the east also claimed by the New England colonies, shown in red. To the west are longhouses of the powerful Iroquois Confederacy. At bottom right is the growing city of New Amsterdam on Manhattan Island. Governor-general Pieter Stuyvesant surrendered New Amsterdam to English forces in 1664.

1690, an expedition of 300 French Canadians and Indian allies surprised unguarded Schenectady, New York, and wiped it out. Other raids destroyed remote settlements in New England and along the coast.

In retaliation, New Englanders allied with New Yorkers to attack French-Canadian coastal towns and raid close to Montreal. That fall, a British fleet of 35 vessels and 1,300 colonial militia sailed into the St. Lawrence River to besiege Quebec City. Frontenac mounted an effective defense, although there was little actual fighting. The onset of cold weather and a smallpox epidemic among the troops forced the invaders to withdraw.

Known in America as King William's War, the conflict dragged on for seven years in a series of skirmishes and raids that set the stage for future struggles between the British and French in North America.

SCHENECTADY MASSACRE: In 1690, during King William's War, a raiding party of Indians led by French officers swooped down from Canada to attack the unsuspecting frontier settlement of Schenectady, New York.

"I assure you, Sir, if my Master gives me leave, I will be as soon at Quebec as you shall be at Albany...."

—NEW YORK GOVERNOR, THOMAS DONGAN, TO MARQUIS DE DENONVILLE, FRENCH GOVERNOR OF CANADA, DEMANDING THE RETURN OF ENGLISH AND DUTCH CAPTIVES TAKEN IN A 1687 FRENCH AND INDIAN RAID, JUST BEFORE THE OUTBREAK OF KING WILLIAM'S WAR

OLD SILVERNAILS
PIETER STUYVESANT

In 1664, the governor-general of New Netherland was a soldier who, for 18 years, had ruled the colony with a heavy hand. Pieter Stuyvesant had absolute control of the Dutch West India Company's territory and the rowdy seaport town of New Amsterdam. Stuyvesant's wooden leg, lost fighting in Dutch wars for empire in the Caribbean, was proof of his martial spirit. The glittering studs in his wooden leg earned him the name, "Old Silvernails." Now in his sixties, Stuyvesant had directed frequent warfare against the Indians, faced down threats from hostile New Englanders, and marched out to capture the Swedish colony of Fort Christina. After New Amsterdam fell in 1664, he spent his last years at his beloved city estate, "The Bouwerij," later known as "The Bowery."

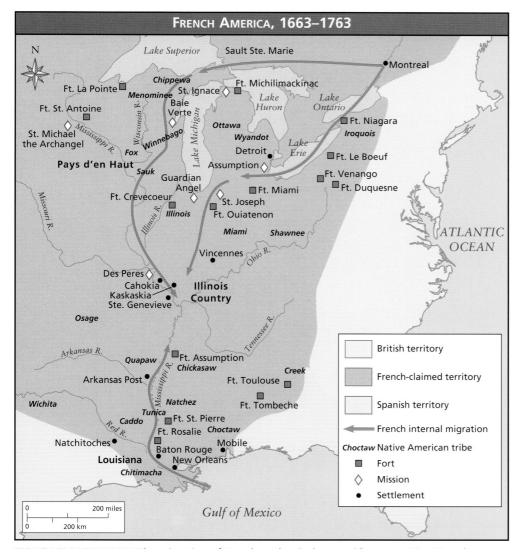

FRENCH AMERICA, 1663–1763

Legend:
- British territory
- French-claimed territory
- Spanish territory
- → French internal migration
- *Choctaw* Native American tribe
- ■ Fort
- ◇ Mission
- • Settlement

FRENCH FRONTIERSMEN The migration of French settlers is shown with arrows. Most French were fur traders, boatmen, or former soldiers, and many took Indian wives, adopting native ways of life.

NEW FRANCE COLLIDES WITH BRITISH AMERICA

British and French colonies in America entered the 18th century under a cloud of worsening hostility. The legacies of King William's War—raids and counter raids, massacres and destruction—had generated enduring hatred between New France and British America.

New France was vastly outnumbered, however. By mid-century, there were fewer than 80,000 French colonists, while British America's population approached a million and was steadily growing. That population would soon turn westward, toward territory claimed by France.

Queen Anne's War

In Europe, the War of the Spanish Succession (1701–1714) pitted the British and their allies against France and Spain in a struggle to decide the next king of Spain. The fighting in colonial America was called Queen Anne's War, after the British queen.

In 1702, Carolina militia and Indian allies sacked Spanish St. Augustine. In reprisal, the Spanish and French mounted a seaborne attack on Charleston, South Carolina, in 1706, but the expedition failed and withdrew. A year later, the British moved against the Spanish at Pensacola, but French reinforcements drove them off.

The winter of 1703–1704 saw surprise raids by the French-allied Indians, who destroyed remote New England communities, including Deerfield, Massachusetts. New England and New York militias, along with Iroquois warriors, conducted their own raids against the French towns. A combined British and colonial expedition captured Port Royal on the island of Acadia (Nova Scotia) in 1710. This opened the way for an invasion up the Saint Lawrence in 1711, when a 64-vessel fleet with 5,000 troops sailed toward Quebec. The fleet was devastated by a storm that drowned more than 900 men, aborting the invasion.

The war's peace terms left Nova Scotia in British possession, so New France was somewhat smaller. Hostility between French and British colonies had deepened, and another war was only a matter of time.

THE DEERFIELD MASSACRE Abenaki Indians paddle away with prisoners after destroying the settlement of Deerfield, Massachusetts, in the winter of 1704. Adults taken in raids were frequently sold to French Canadians as indentured servants or held for ransom, while children often were adopted by the tribe. French Jesuit priests often tried to convert them to Catholicism.

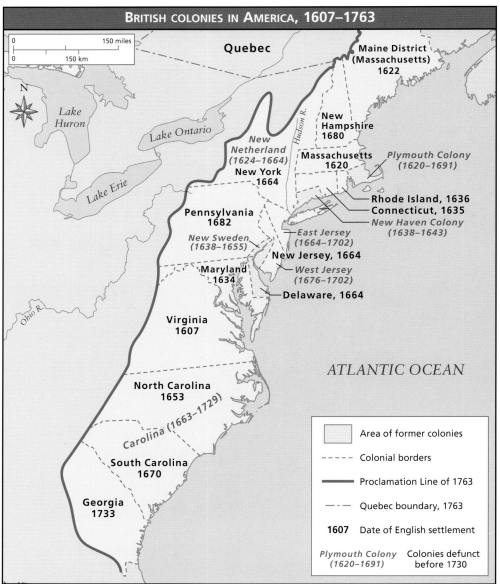

BRITISH COLONIES IN AMERICA, 1607–1763

Quebec

Maine District (Massachusetts) 1622

Lake Huron

Lake Ontario

Lake Erie

New Netherland (1624–1664)

New York 1664

New Hampshire 1680

Massachusetts 1620

Plymouth Colony (1620–1691)

Rhode Island, 1636

Connecticut, 1635

New Haven Colony (1638–1643)

Pennsylvania 1682

New Sweden (1638–1655)

East Jersey (1664–1702)

New Jersey, 1664

West Jersey (1676–1702)

Delaware, 1664

Maryland 1634

Ohio R.

Virginia 1607

North Carolina 1653

Carolina (1663–1729)

South Carolina 1670

Georgia 1733

ATLANTIC OCEAN

Hudson R.

	Area of former colonies
	Colonial borders
	Proclamation Line of 1763
	Quebec boundary, 1763
1607	Date of English settlement
Plymouth Colony (1620–1691)	Colonies defunct before 1730

THIRTEEN COLONIES IN 1763 Britain's American colonies grew rapidly from the early 1600s to 1763. Settlements that had struggled to survive in the early years became thriving colonies pushing ever westward. The Proclamation Line of 1763 strictly controlled settlement on the new frontier.

LOUISBOURG BESIEGED New England militia row ashore to attack the French fortress of Louisbourg on Cape Breton. Designed on the principles of French military engineer Sébastien Vauban and mounting 250 guns, the newly built Louisbourg was thought impregnable.

"Aminidab is just come home,
His eyes all smeared with bacon,
And all the news that he could tell
Is Cape Breton is taken."

—A verse of "Yankee Doodle," referring to New England troops, smeared with grease against Cape Breton mosquitoes, boasting of capturing Louisbourg

King George's War

The next cause of trouble between French and British America sprang from the War of the Austrian Succession (1740–1748). In North America, this struggle was named after the British king, George II.

Britain and Spain had been fighting intermittently since 1739, and engagements in the Caribbean spilled over to the southern colonies. In 1742, British forces repelled a Spanish attack on Georgia's St. Simon's Island in the Battle of the Bloody Swamp. The next year, southern colonial forces failed in an attack on Saint Augustine.

In 1744, the French were repulsed attempting to recapture Nova Scotia, but they were building massive Fort Louisbourg on Cape Breton. Considered one of the world's strongest fortresses, Louisbourg dominated fishing grounds and merchant traffic in the North Atlantic. British colonists asked Parliament to capture Fort Louisbourg but the government refused, claiming it would be too difficult. Undaunted, in 1745 New England and New York militias launched their own expedition, supported by a British naval squadron that blockaded Louisbourg. The colonials astounded Parliament by capturing the fort that June.

This triumph made colonists proud, but to their dismay, the 1748 peace treaty handed Louisbourg back to the French. Many colonials never forgave this undoing of their great victory. This bitterness fostered anti-Parliament hostility that helped bring on the American Revolution in 1775.

DEFENDING GEORGIA In 1742, soldiers such as this kilted Scots Highlander and British grenadier repelled a Spanish assault on St. Simons Island, Georgia.

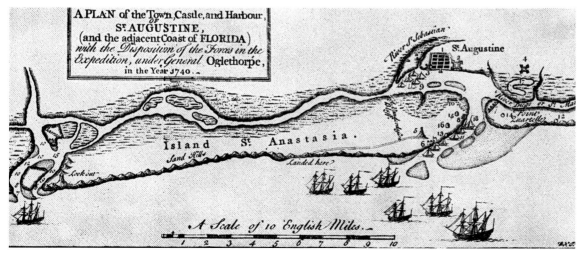

SIEGE OF ST. AUGUSTINE James Oglethorpe, founder and governor of Georgia, led two failed expeditions, 1740 and 1743, against the Spanish stronghold of St. Augustine, Florida, shown on this contemporary map.

2: THE SEVEN YEARS' WAR IN AMERICA

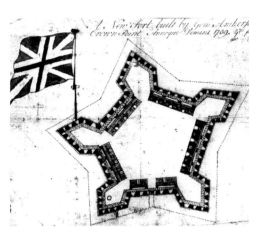

A KEY POST French Fort St. Frédéric guarded strategic Lake Champlain, until British general Jeffrey Amherst captured it in 1759. The French demolished the fort before retreating, and it was rebuilt as Fort Amherst. Its name was soon changed to Crown Point.

The end of the last French-British colonial conflict was less than seven years past when Virginia colonel George Washington led a small force toward Fort Duquesne, the French stronghold defending the forks of the Ohio River. The Virginians, who had come to lay claim to the region, built a small stockade they called Fort Necessity in July 1754. The French and their native allies soon surrounded Washington, who had no choice but to surrender and go back to Virginia. This minor altercation over ownership of the Northwest's lands was a first spark in the French and Indian War, which became part of a worldwide struggle for dominance known as the Seven Years' War (1756–1763).

The North American phase of the Seven Years' War ended generations of strife over control of the wilderness between New France and British America. The French had more allies among the native peoples than did the British, who had hoped for Iroquois support but received little. The Iroquois lived between the white combatants, and they preferred to stay out of the fighting rather than risk their communities to rampaging armies.

The French and Indian War

The French and their Indian allies won a spectacular victory in 1755, a disastrous year for the British. General Edward Braddock's 2,000-strong expedition was ambushed and destroyed while marching against Fort Duquesne. Half the men were killed, including Braddock. Washington was a key leader on this campaign, although Braddock disregarded

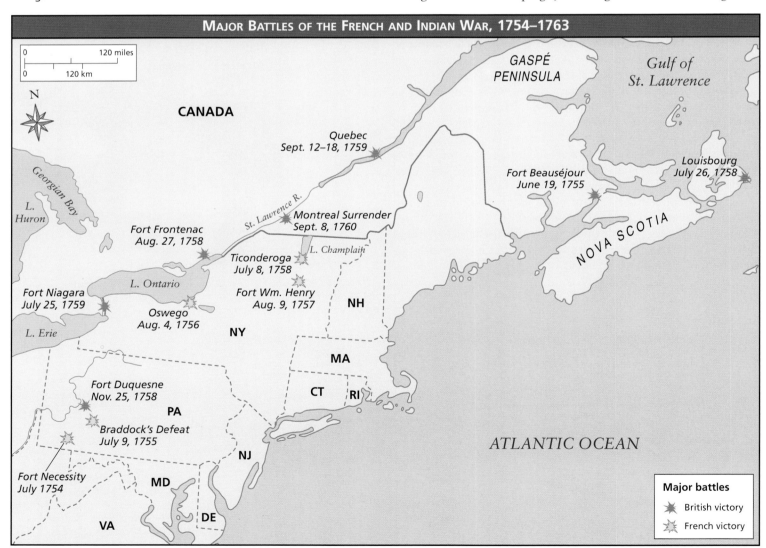

FRONTIER WAR Much of the French and Indian War was waged in bloody wilderness clashes and raids. American troops, such as Rogers' Rangers, won fame for making forced marches through the enemy country to scout and harass the French and Indians.

most colonial advice. The Virginian won fame by conducting a fighting retreat that saved many troops. In this year, the British army in America seemed impotent. Only a colonial force under New York's William Johnson was victorious, defeating French and Indians at the Battle of Lake George.

Raids drove thousands of settlers from the frontiers, filling cities such as Philadelphia with refugees. Backcountry settlements were abandoned to a depth of 200 miles from the original frontiers. British arms met two more disasters in 1757, when Fort Oswego on Lake Ontario and Fort William Henry on Lake George fell after sieges. French commanding general Louis de Montcalm won a key victory in taking Fort William Henry, but his triumph was soiled by massacre. Montcalm's Indian warriors fell on the unarmed captives of Fort William Henry and killed hundreds of soldiers and civilians before the French could intervene.

Montcalm made his base at mighty Fort Carillon (later named Ticonderoga by the British), defending the water route down Lake Champlain toward Quebec. The following summer, in 1758, he and 3,200 troops were besieged by an army of 15,000 under General James Abercrombie. Abercrombie had one of the finest armies ever assembled in North America, with excellent regular troops and fine commanders as well as the crack scouts of Rogers's Rangers. Instead of surrounding and starving out Montcalm, however, Abercrombie launched foolhardy frontal attacks that left hundreds of his men dead before Carillon's defensive works. The incompetent Abercrombie soon withdrew in defeat.

The changing fortunes of war

By now, the tide of war was turning in Britain's favor. That same July, Fort Louisbourg on Cape Breton fell to General Jeffrey Amherst and his able subordinate, General James Wolfe. Fort Duquesne and Fort Frontenac also were taken by the British, endangering Montreal and Quebec. Wolfe would lead an invasion up the Saint Lawrence against Quebec, while Amherst went to New York to command operations against Fort Carillon.

WESTERN PENNSYLVANIA In June 1755, British troops under General Edward Braddock were defeated attempting to take Fort Duquesne, part of a chain of French frontier posts. A year earlier, George Washington had built Fort Necessity, which was captured by the French.

AMBUSH! Marching on Fort Duquesne, General Braddock did not understand wilderness warfare. His troops moved in a long column, vulnerable to ambush. French and Indians surprised his army, almost wiping it out, and Braddock was shot off his horse, fatally wounded.

BRITISH VICTORY AND THE END OF NEW FRANCE

By mid-1759, British and colonial forces captured Fort Oswego and Fort Niagara to seize control of Lake Ontario. Montcalm was needed to command at Quebec, and he left Lake Champlain, which Amherst reached by July with a force of 11,000 British and colonials. Within a few days, the last French defenders abandoned and blew up Fort Carillon and burned its satellite fort at Crown Point. The way was now open for Amherst to strike at Montreal.

For the last few weeks, Wolfe's army of 9,000 had been before Quebec, where Montcalm commanded a mixed garrison of 14,000 regulars, Canadians, and Indians. The city stood above the Saint Lawrence River, protected by high cliffs, although its landward defenses were relatively weak. Near the end of July, Wolfe launched an ill-fated attack to take the top of the cliffs, but he was repulsed with more than 440 killed and wounded. Montcalm could afford to wait out the British, who would have to depart before cold weather. Wolfe, however, had to bring on an open battle. His artillery pounded the city as he desperately sought a way to get to the level land known as the Plains of Abraham, beyond the cliffs.

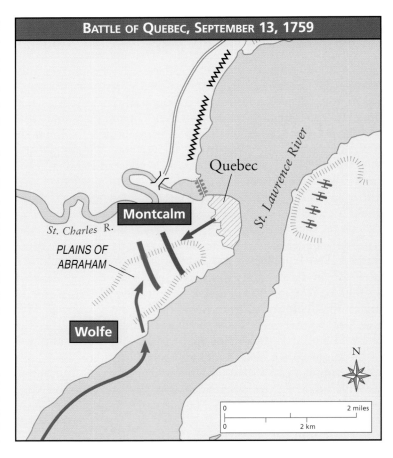

BATTLE OF QUEBEC, SEPTEMBER 13, 1759

BOLD WOLFE On the night of September 13, 1759, James Wolfe daringly led troops up an undefended path onto the flats before Quebec. French commander Louis de Montcalm was soon defeated, losing the city, the capital of New France.

PLAINS OF ABRAHAM British infantry at Quebec had the advantage in firepower and training, and they routed the French. Wolfe, commanding near the front lines, was killed. Montcalm was mortally wounded while trying to hold his troops together.

"There is such a choice of difficulties, that I own myself at a loss how to determine."

—JAMES WOLFE, IN A 1759 REPORT ABOUT ATTACKING QUEBEC

By mid-September, Wolfe's men had found an undefended pathway to the top. On the night of September 13, he led his troops to the crest, unchallenged. Sunrise revealed thousands of redcoated British troops arrayed for battle on the Plains of Abraham. With the British now across his main supply line and Quebec under bombardment, Montcalm was compelled to meet Wolfe in the open field. Each force numbered approximately 4,000 Regulars, but superior British firepower and tactics won the day. Quebec surrendered, but both Wolfe and Montcalm died from their wounds.

The fall of Montreal

Ever the cautious leader, General Amherst was slow to move against Montreal, the last French stronghold. He planned for three armies to advance on the city in the coming year. One force would come from the west, another from the south over Lake Champlain, and a third from Quebec. In the early spring of 1760, the French managed to rally an army and attack Quebec, briefly laying their own siege to the city. The arrival of a British fleet ended the siege, however, and the campaign against Montreal soon began.

By September 1760, overwhelming force compelled Montreal's surrender to Amherst, ending the fighting in North America. Final peace terms were approved in 1763, as the French ceded Canada and a vast territory along the Ohio River and east of the Mississippi. After 70 years of war, French power in North America was broken, and the British ruled supreme. Britain was master of the seas, and her American colonies grew richer with every passing year. Soon, they were too powerful to remain colonies subordinate to Britain, and they demanded equal rights, respect, and eventually independence.

PONTIAC'S UPRISING

With the defeat of New France, British troops occupied French forts in the region known as the Northwest. Posts such as Fort Detroit and Fort Pitt were centers of the fur trade and key points of contact with the Indians. These nations had fought and lost as allies of the French, so they had no love for the British. In 1763, an Ottawa war chief named Pontiac masterminded a coordinated surprise attack on British forts. Detroit and Pitt were besieged and smaller forts captured. Hundreds of frontier communities were attacked and farms destroyed, with more than 2,000 settlers killed or made captive.

The largest battle of "Pontiac's Uprising" occurred in August 1763 at Bushy Run, Pennsylvania, where a British expeditionary force under Colonel Henry Bouquet was ambushed and surrounded for two days. Bouquet outmaneuvered the Indians on the second day, drawing them into a devastating crossfire followed by a counterattack that won the battle. Pontiac's Uprising was suppressed by expeditions that relieved the forts—and also by a smallpox epidemic that killed hundreds of Indians.

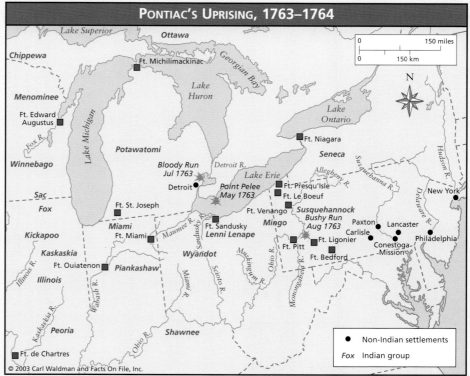

WARPATH In 1763, Chief Pontiac of the Ottawa led Northwest nations in coordinated attacks on British forts and settlements. The uprising was shaken by a decisive British victory at Bushy Run in western Pennsylvania.

3: THE AMERICAN REVOLUTIONARY WAR

"JOIN OR DIE" In Benjamin Franklin's sketch the American colonies are represented by a snake cut into pieces; to survive, the colonies, like the snake, must join together.

"If we take a determined stand now, Boston will submit and all will end in victory without carnage."

—LORD MANSFIELD, A MEMBER OF LORD NORTH'S GOVERNMENT

The 13 original British colonies in America grew rapidly in population and wealth thanks in part to profits from supplying the military during the French and Indian War. These million and a half American colonists also benefited from worldwide trading opportunities in the newly dominant British Empire. Parliament and King George III, facing an immense national debt as a result of the Seven Years' War, resolved to have Americans pay for administration of their colonies. New taxes and duties were levied on the colonies in the 1760s, but many Americans angrily objected, declaring that since they had no representation in Parliament, the government had no right to tax them.

Conflict escalated, with open clashes between radical and conservative colonials and attacks on royal governors and tax collectors. The British Army was called in to keep the peace, and several regiments were sent to America. The colonies of Canada, Nova Scotia, and East and West Florida—all acquired by victory in the Seven Years' War—showed no interest in similarly defying the British government.

Arming for resistance

The 13 colonies expanded their militia establishments, making sure the companies were led by adherents to the cause of resistance—Patriots, they were termed, while pro-government colonists were called Loyalists.

Boston was a hotbed of opposition to the government, and not even the governor of Massachusetts was safe from attack by the mob. In 1768, as punishment for the colony's defiance of Parliament's rule, several thousand troops occupied Boston to maintain order. Until then, New York had been the headquarters of the British Army in North America. Now, most of the king's American troops were based in Boston, where they were unable to cope with other disturbances, riots, and tea-dumping that occurred in places such as New York and Charleston, South Carolina.

Military occupation of Boston made many colonials even more furious with the government.

Opposition to military rule

Colonial resistance to Parliament had gathered strength by the spring of 1775. The previous year, the colonies had sent delegates to Philadelphia for a Continental Congress, which demanded the troops leave Boston and pledged not to import British goods until the crisis was ended. Massachusetts delegate John Adams schemed for Congress to create a united military force to prove the colonies would fight. Adams would nominate, as overall commander, the best-known colonial field officer: Virginia colonel George Washington.

The 4,500 government troops in Boston were under General Thomas Gage, who had led British Regulars in wilderness fighting during the French and Indian War. Gage's regiment had been clad in brown jackets and saw action in the forests of New York and Canada. In Boston, his force was far different. Gage's red-coated Regulars were, for the most part, inexperienced in American service and not familiar with colonials. This, in itself, often caused hostility between soldiers and civilians. Gage's duty was to protect government officials and ensure that loyal citizens would be safe from increasingly violent resistance to Parliament's policies. His soldiers had the task of finding and confiscating munitions being stockpiled by anti-British New England militia.

When a hidden cache of arms was suspected, expeditions hurried out of Boston to capture them. Gage soon learned that the militia were watching him closely, for they mustered under arms to shadow and insult his troops on the march. Seldom were any arms caches actually found, but it was clear there might be a clash between Regulars and militia some day.

That day came on April 19, 1775, at Lexington Green, about a dozen miles from Boston.

THE BOSTON MASSACRE British soldiers in occupied Boston were often harassed by rowdy anti-Parliament mobs. In March of 1770, soldiers fired on a taunting crowd, killing five Bostonians. Engraver Paul Revere created this illustration, which depicts troops firing on helpless citizens. Lawyer John Adams defended soldiers brought up on charges and won them virtual acquittals.

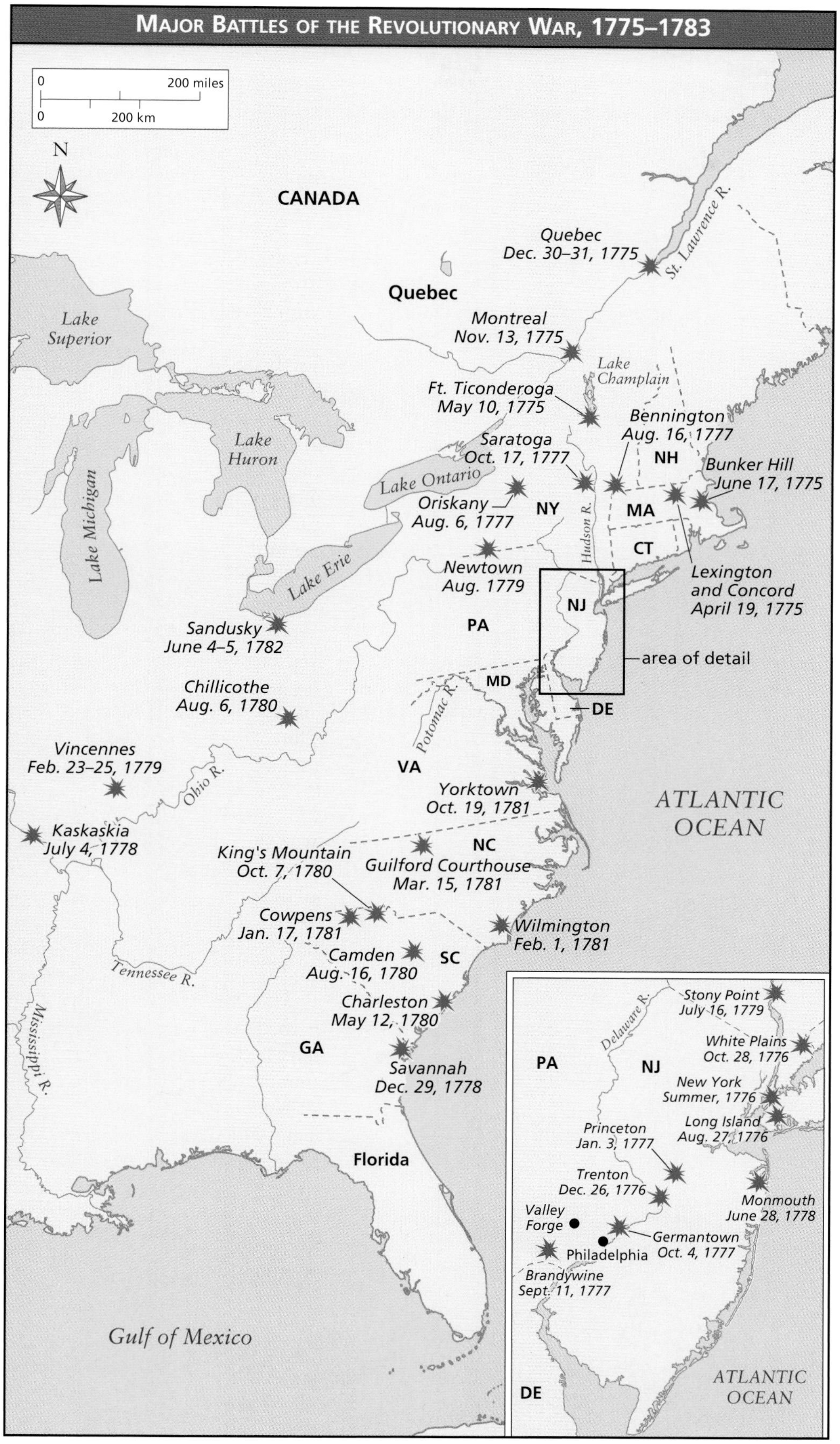
MAJOR BATTLES OF THE REVOLUTIONARY WAR, 1775–1783
0 200 miles
0 200 km
N
CANADA
Quebec
Quebec Dec. 30–31, 1775
St. Lawrence R.
Montreal Nov. 13, 1775
Lake Champlain
Ft. Ticonderoga May 10, 1775
Bennington Aug. 16, 1777
Saratoga Oct. 17, 1777
NH
Bunker Hill June 17, 1775
Lake Superior
Lake Huron
Lake Michigan
Lake Ontario
Lake Erie
Oriskany Aug. 6, 1777
NY
MA
Hudson R.
CT
Newtown Aug. 1779
Lexington and Concord April 19, 1775
NJ
PA
area of detail
Sandusky June 4–5, 1782
Chillicothe Aug. 6, 1780
MD
DE
Potomac R.
Vincennes Feb. 23–25, 1779
VA
Ohio R.
Yorktown Oct. 19, 1781
ATLANTIC OCEAN
Kaskaskia July 4, 1778
NC
King's Mountain Oct. 7, 1780
Guilford Courthouse Mar. 15, 1781
Cowpens Jan. 17, 1781
Wilmington Feb. 1, 1781
Camden Aug. 16, 1780
SC
Tennessee R.
Charleston May 12, 1780
Mississippi R.
GA
Savannah Dec. 29, 1778
Florida
Gulf of Mexico
Stony Point July 16, 1779
Delaware R.
White Plains Oct. 28, 1776
PA
NJ
New York Summer, 1776
Long Island Aug. 27, 1776
Princeton Jan. 3, 1777
Trenton Dec. 26, 1776
Monmouth June 28, 1778
Valley Forge
Germantown Oct. 4, 1777
Philadelphia
Brandywine Sept. 11, 1777
ATLANTIC OCEAN
DE

BATTLES OF THE AMERICAN REVOLUTION The war began in 1775 in the northern colonies, where the British were driven from New England and upper New York. In 1777, Philadelphia fell to Sir William Howe; British grand strategy of cutting off New England from the other colonies was stopped when General John Burgoyne surrendered at Saratoga, north of Albany. The war shifted to the South in 1779, and the British won victories in Georgia and South Carolina. Nathanael Greene's campaign won back the South, and when Washington was victorious at Yorktown, the Americans began negotiations to gain acknowledgment of their independence.

COMMANDER-IN-CHIEF
GEORGE WASHINGTON
1732–1799

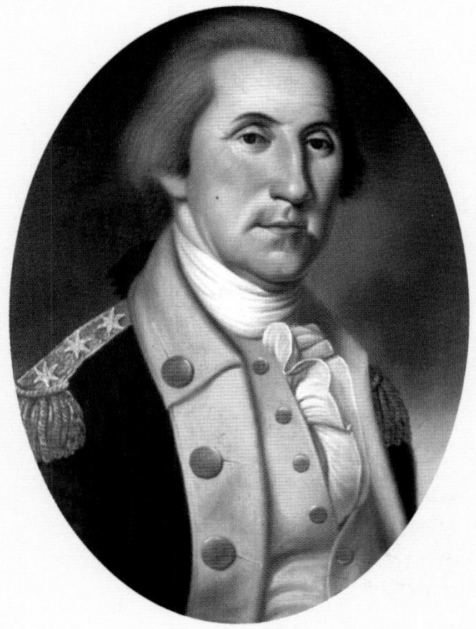

Heir to Mount Vernon, his family's plantation in Virginia, Washington was a 22-year-old lieutenant colonel of militia when his colony sent him to prevent the French from establishing forts in the Ohio River region. He won a victory over the French and Indians at Great Meadows that spring, but by July was surrounded and forced to surrender.

The next year, as General Edward Braddock's aide-de-camp, Washington was key to saving part of Braddock's army, which was wiped out near Fort Duquesne. He then took overall command of Virginia's militia, guarding the frontiers against French and Indian raids.

Resigning in 1759, Washington married the wealthy widow, Martha Dandridge Custis, and lived the life of a successful planter and member of Virginia's House of Burgesses. As troubles with Parliament developed, he joined the Patriot cause and became a delegate to the Continental Congress in Philadelphia. In the spring of 1775, Congress chose Washington as its army's commander-in-chief, and by mid-June he was riding north to take charge of the New Englanders besieging Boston.

FIRST BLOOD, FIRST VICTORY IN NEW ENGLAND

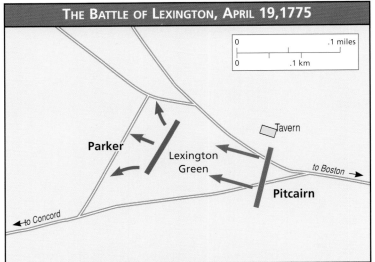

THE BATTLE OF LEXINGTON, APRIL 19, 1775

Parker

Lexington Green

Tavern

Pitcairn

to Boston →

← to Concord

THE SHOT HEARD ROUND THE WORLD British officers claimed someone near the Lexington Green tavern fired at them, starting the engagement. Whoever began it, the first shot sparked a revolution that was observed from every corner of the British Empire.

On the night of April 18, 1775, express riders alerted militia companies around Boston that Gage had secretly sent Colonel Francis Smith with an 800-man expedition to Concord to confiscate Patriot cannon, arms, and ammunition stored there.

At sunrise, 70 militiamen commanded by French and Indian War veteran, Captain John Parker, met the British on Lexington Green, six miles from Concord. Seeing the overwhelming numbers against him, Parker ordered his men to disperse rather than bring on an engagement. Suddenly, a shot rang out—from whom is not clear—and in response the soldiers fired volleys, then charged with the bayonet. Eight militia were killed, 10 wounded, with one Regular injured.

A HARRIED RETREAT This contemporary map shows the route of the British advance on Lexington, where the first American dead are shown in blue, then on to Concord, where Regulars and militia fire on each other. The militiamen are depicted shooting from behind walls. American reinforcements are shown in red, as they march toward the fighting. After chasing the Regulars back to Boston, the militia camped around the city, laying siege to it.

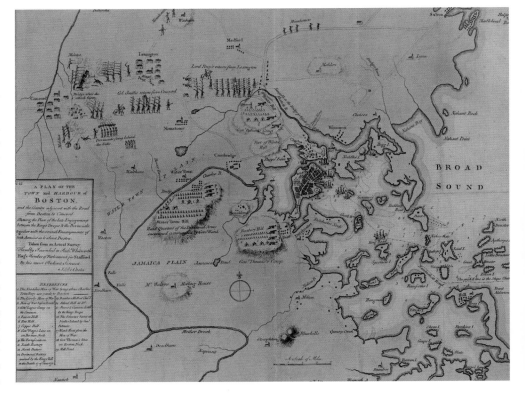

"BATTLE ROAD" Retreating British Regulars were harassed by militiamen firing from behind stone walls and from inside houses along the road. The British often counterattacked and routed small groups of militia. In these charges, enraged Regulars took bloody revenge, mercilessly bayoneting those they caught.

A fighting retreat from Concord to Boston

Smith's troops hurried on to Concord, six miles away, only to find much of the munitions had already been removed. By now, thousands of angry militia were marching toward Concord, and at mid-morning shooting began at nearby North Bridge. Regulars stationed there were driven back, and Smith's withdrawal started, becoming a 20-mile running battle all the way to Charlestown.

Militia appeared at bends in the road or in nearby houses and opened fire on the troops. Light infantry squads made bayonet charges to drive the militia away or kill them, but other ambushes were waiting farther down the road. More than 1,000 British reinforcements, led by Lord Hugh Percy, met Smith's expedition at Lexington, but the entire British force was compelled to retreat. They fought all the way to Charlestown, arriving at dusk, exhausted and bloodied.

The British suffered 269 casualties, the Americans about 95. Up to 20,000 militia had mustered that day, with about 3,700 getting into the fight. Gage now found himself under siege in Boston.

Earthworks thrown up on Breed's Hill

Two months after Lexington and Concord, a Patriot army numbering 17,000 hemmed in Gage's 6,500 troops. On the night of June 16, the colonials moved onto the Charlestown Peninsula and occupied Breed's Hill, overlooking Boston. Gage resolved to drive them out of earthworks they were hastily digging on Breed's Hill, and also farther back on Bunker Hill. The main American force of about 1,200 men was under the command of Massachusetts colonel William Prescott. As were many American officers, Prescott was a veteran of previous colonial wars.

Led by General Sir William Howe, the British rowed across the Charles River under cover of heavy naval cannon fire and landed on the peninsula. More than 2,200 Regulars would be brought into action, each man carrying a full pack and gear weighing 60 pounds. Patriot defenses consisted of a redoubt and earthworks on Breed's Hill, and an extended line eastward along a rail fence. New Hampshireman John Stark, a former French and Indian War ranger, commanded at the fence.

When 11 British companies attacked early that afternoon, Stark's militia shattered their ranks with disciplined volley fire. Howe personally directed a simultaneous assault on Breed's Hill, but was likewise driven back by heavy musketry.

Regulars win victory at great cost

Howe immediately launched a second attack, but with the same deadly results. Now the Regulars threw off knapsacks and extra gear and returned to the attack. The Americans fired their last rounds and began to retreat. The main Patriot force escaped from the peninsula but suffered 441 casualties, including 141 killed. The British had 1,150 casualties, with 226 killed—shocking losses that infuriated Parliament, which soon demanded Gage's recall.

It was apparent that Regular British troops were not invincible if Americans were led by good commanders. George Washington soon reached Boston to take charge of this blooded New England army, which was proud of its accomplishments and suspicious of any officers but its own.

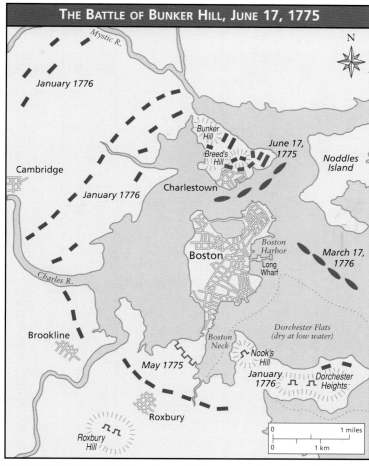

THE BATTLE OF BUNKER HILL, JUNE 17, 1775

BATTLE OF BUNKER HILL American militia surrounding Boston in June 1775 heard the British planned to occupy the Charlestown peninsula, across the Charles River from the city. On the night of June 16, the Americans fortified Breed's Hill on the peninsula, and the next day Regulars rowed across to dislodge them. The British frontal assault cost almost half the attacking force.

"My Reg't, being one of the first that entered the redoubt, is almost entirely cut to pieces: there are but 9 men left in my co, & not above 5 in one of the others."

—British officer Lord Hugh Percy, writing after the Battle of Breed's (Bunker) Hill

GRENADIERS Each British regiment had a grenadier company, distinguished by tall fur caps with embossed metal plates and considered their regiment's elite troops.

INDEPENDENCE, RETREAT—AND RISE TO FIGHT AGAIN

HESSIAN FLAG captured at the Battle of Trenton.

Washington found an unruly Patriot army besieging Boston. From the start, the commander-in-chief had to be a strict taskmaster, teaching officers and privates alike the need for order and military discipline.

One by one, able leaders appeared at Washington's side: Samuel Webb of Connecticut; Nathanael Greene of Rhode Island; John Sullivan of New Hampshire —good soldiers as well as good organizers. Two other outstanding commanders were off on a campaign against Canada: Benedict Arnold of Connecticut and Richard Montgomery of New York.

Failure at Quebec; Boston taken

Arnold had already proved his abilities that spring by aiding Ethan Allen in the capture of strategic Fort Ticonderoga on Lake Champlain. In the fall, Arnold led a march through the Maine wilderness toward Quebec City. Montgomery, a former British officer, captured Montreal in November and joined Arnold at Quebec, which Sir Guy Carleton, the British governor general, had fortified and was determined to defend. The Patriots launched their attack on December 31, but were repulsed, and Montgomery was killed.

Meanwhile, General Henry Knox hauled 60 of Fort Ticonderoga's cannon 300 miles to Boston. On the night of March 4, 1776, those guns were placed on Dorchester Heights, threatening the city and forcing General William Howe, who was now in command, to evacuate. Washington's brilliant siege of Boston was soon overshadowed by the news that Howe had been reinforced and intended to take New York City.

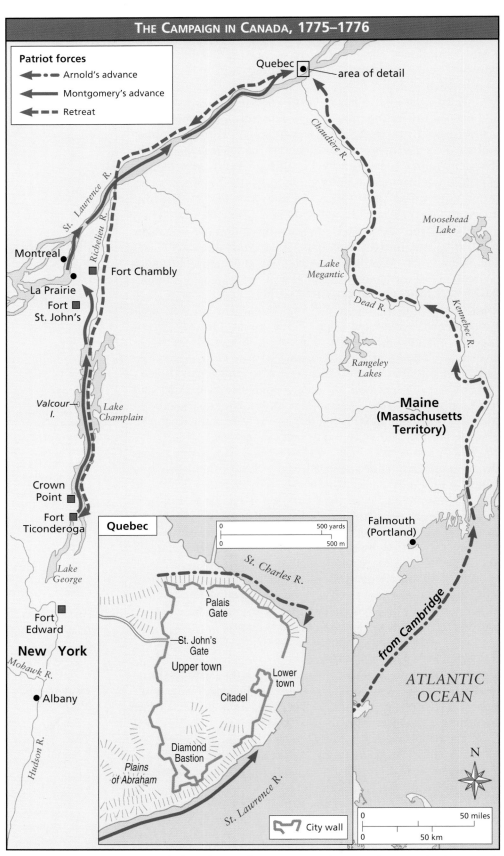

THE CAMPAIGN IN CANADA, 1775–1776

Patriot forces
- Arnold's advance
- Montgomery's advance
- Retreat

SEIZING THE INITIATIVE In 1775, before the British were prepared to stop them, Patriot forces took Ticonderoga and Crown Point on Lake Champlain. Montgomery then captured Fort St. John's and Montreal and—with 300 troops—moved on Quebec as Arnold's 600-man force made a brutal winter march through Maine's wilderness to join him there. The Patriots were defeated at Quebec, and in spring of 1776 began a retreat from Canada. The reinforced British followed close behind.

STRUGGLE FOR NEW YORK Howe defeated Washington at the Battle of Long Island in August 1776, but the Patriot army escaped to White Plains, where it was again beaten by Howe, who took Fort Washington and Fort Lee. Washington retreated through New Jersey, pursued by Cornwallis.

New York falls to Howe; Washington retreats

Washington hurried southward to organize New York's defenses. Meanwhile, the Canadian campaign was failing, as British reinforcements broke the siege and drove the Patriots out.

Patriot triumphs this year included the defeat in February of a Loyalist uprising at Moore's Creek Bridge, North Carolina, and the repulse of a seaborne attack on Charleston, South Carolina, in June. On July 4th, the 13 former colonies proclaimed their Declaration of Independence, a moment of great inspiration to Patriot forces.

Still, Washington had much to worry about. His untrained army of 28,000 was dispersed in various garrisons and posts because he was unsure where Howe—with his powerful naval capabilities—would launch his attack. The untrained Americans were no match for Howe's 32,000 troops, who landed on Staten Island in July 1776. On August 26, Howe outflanked Washington from the east, pinning his force against the East River at Brooklyn Heights, apparently defeated. Yet, Washington escaped under cover of darkness and continued to fight on. In September, he was driven from Manhattan, and in October lost at White Plains, New York.

Good news came from the north, where Benedict Arnold had fought a delaying action against Carleton's fleet at Valcour Bay on Lake Champlain. Carleton had to withdraw because of approaching cold weather.

Counterstrike on Christmas day

Disasters continued as Hudson River forts Washington and Lee fell to Howe. Washington's army melted away, and the enlistments were almost up for many of those who remained. What he could hold together reeled southward, just ahead of enemy pursuit, and crossed the Delaware into Pennsylvania. With winter closing in, Howe called a halt to his campaign. On Christmas Day, Washington made a perilous crossing of the ice-choked Delaware with 2,400 men and surprised Hessian troops garrisoning Trenton. He captured more than 900 men, with little Patriot loss.

One of Howe's top generals, Lord Charles Cornwallis, hurried to trap Washington near Trenton, but Washington again slipped away. After a forced march, he crushed Cornwallis's rear guard at Princeton, another victory that lifted Patriot spirits.

Washington soon positioned his army in the hills near Morristown, New Jersey. There, he could hold out all winter, then renew the fight in the springtime.

"I think the game is pretty well up. . . .
You can form no idea of the perplexity of
my situation. No man, I believe, ever had a
greater choice of difficulties. . . ."

—WASHINGTON, TO HIS BROTHER JOHN, DECEMBER 18, 1776

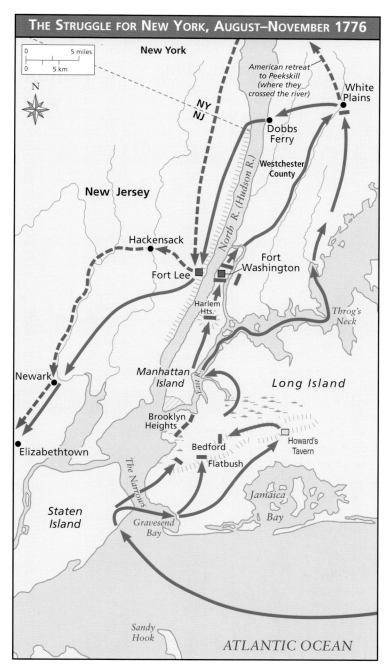

THE STRUGGLE FOR NEW YORK, AUGUST–NOVEMBER 1776

CHRISTMAS ATTACK Washington's surprise assault on Trenton in the early morning of December 26, 1776, caught the Hessians unprepared. Fallen Hessian soldiers, in their pointed "mitre" hats, lie around a captured cannon as American soldiers push past them.

IN THE NORTH: CONQUEST OVER BURGOYNE'S INVASION

Patriot fortunes were at a low ebb in mid-1777, with ferocious attacks by Indians and Loyalists on frontier settlements, and three British armies on the move. The first was John Burgoyne's crack force of 7,000 British, Germans, Loyalists, and Indians, which swept down from Canada and compelled outnumbered Patriots to abandon Fort Ticonderoga early in July.

Burgoyne's advance guard was surprised by a sharp clash with the Patriot rear guard at Hubbardton, Vermont, and other of his detachments also met unexpectedly stubborn resistance. Yet, the general was confident about taking Albany. He had not, however, counted on Albany Dutch general, Philip Schuyler, who rallied fighting men to contest every foot of Burgoyne's advance.

FRASER IS KILLED Daniel Morgan's riflemen were deadly sharpshooters who made officers their special targets. Here, sniper Timothy Murphy perched in a tree at Freeman's Farm picks off British general Simon Fraser, who falls from his horse in the clearing. One of Burgoyne's best officers, Fraser was loved by his men and admired by the Americans.

BURGOYNE'S GRAND PLAN The Saratoga Campaign was part of a three-pronged invasion of New York, with Burgoyne striking south from Canada to Albany, Lieutenant Colonel Barry St. Leger moving east from Fort Oswego, and General Howe coming north from New York City. The grand plan failed: St. Leger was stopped at Fort Stanwix; Howe failed to cooperate, instead moving against Philadelphia; and Burgoyne was surrounded and forced to surrender at Saratoga.

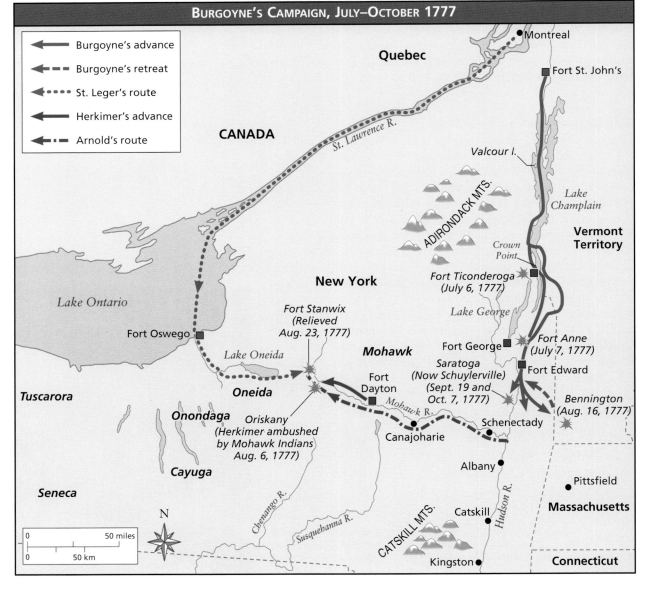

BURGOYNE'S CAMPAIGN, JULY–OCTOBER 1777

Legend:
- Burgoyne's advance
- Burgoyne's retreat
- St. Leger's route
- Herkimer's advance
- Arnold's route

Montreal
Quebec
Fort St. John's
CANADA
St. Lawrence R.
Valcour I.
Lake Champlain
ADIRONDACK MTS.
Crown Point
Vermont Territory
New York
Fort Ticonderoga (July 6, 1777)
Lake George
Fort Stanwix (Relieved Aug. 23, 1777)
Lake Ontario
Fort Oswego
Lake Oneida
Mohawk
Fort George
Fort Anne (July 7, 1777)
Tuscarora
Fort Dayton
Saratoga (Now Schuylerville) (Sept. 19 and Oct. 7, 1777)
Fort Edward
Oneida
Mohawk R.
Bennington (Aug. 16, 1777)
Onondaga
Oriskany (Herkimer ambushed by Mohawk Indians Aug. 6, 1777)
Schenectady
Canajoharie
Cayuga
Albany
Pittsfield
Seneca
Chenango R.
Catskill
Massachusetts
N
CATSKILL MTS.
Hudson R.
Susquehanna R.
0   50 miles
0   50 km
Kingston
Connecticut

"That man on the grey horse is a host in himself and must be disposed of."

—BENEDICT ARNOLD TO DANIEL MORGAN DURING THE BATTLE OF BEMIS HEIGHTS, CALLING FOR A SHARPSHOOTER TO PICK OFF SIMON FRASER

A second British force from Canada, under Colonel Barry St. Leger, had been moving from the west toward Albany but was delayed by Fort Stanwix, holding out in the Mohawk Valley. Burgoyne had a major setback when a detachment of 700 German troops he sent toward Bennington to gather supplies was defeated by Patriots under John Stark. The third British army in the field was Sir William Howe's force from New York, which sailed into Chesapeake Bay in August and landed within striking distance of Philadelphia. Washington hurried his troops to block the way as Congress evacuated the capital.

Burgoyne's plans suffered yet another blow when 800 Mohawk Valley farmers marched to relieve Stanwix and, on August 6, fought St. Leger's Loyalists and Indians at Oriskany. The Patriots, under General Nicholas Herkimer, suffered heavily and had to withdraw, but the ferocity of the battle sapped their enemy's fighting spirit. Hearing that Benedict Arnold and fresh troops were approaching, St. Leger's Indian allies abandoned him, compelling his retreat. Burgoyne now was alone to face a growing Patriot army under former British officer Horatio Gates.

The Battles of Saratoga

General Gates met Burgoyne at Saratoga, a village above Albany, on the west side of the Hudson River. The armies fought their first battle at Freeman's Farm on September 19, where Burgoyne held the field, but lost 600 men, compared to 319 American casualties. Benedict Arnold was a key Patriot commander, while Gates remained at his headquarters tent, often unable to influence the course of battle. Burgoyne advanced again on October 7, his thrusts met by Arnold and ranger commander Daniel Morgan. Patriot general Enoch Poor held the American center, while Arnold led the brigade of Ebenezer Learned on the attack. Burgoyne's tactical plan was thrown off by the aggressive Arnold and Morgan. Key British officers were lost, along with 600 troops, and at the end of the day Burgoyne withdrew from the battlefield. The Patriots suffered 150 casualties.

Burgoyne dug in, expecting an American attack at any moment. When escape routes to the north were cut off by John Stark's rangers, Burgoyne was doomed. On October 17, Gates accepted his surrender, a shocking defeat to the British, and a victory that proved to France that the revolution in America could succeed.

FIRST BATTLE OF SARATOGA (FREEMAN'S FARM), SEPTEMBER 14, 1777

FIRST BATTLE OF SARATOGA Gates fortified Bemis Heights, blocking Burgoyne's advance. The British attacked near Freeman's Farm, hoping to capture high ground, but Arnold and Morgan counterattacked, driving them back. German commander Baron Von Riedesel came to Burgoyne's rescue, and the British held the field.

SECOND BATTLE OF SARATOGA (BEMIS HEIGHTS), OCTOBER 7, 1777

SECOND BATTLE OF SARATOGA Burgoyne again advanced on the American works and was attacked by Morgan and Arnold. Leading one assault after another against the British lines, Arnold captured a redoubt on the British right, outflanking Burgoyne and forcing him to retreat to Saratoga.

PHILADELPHIA CAPTURES HOWE, PATRIOTS FIGHT ON

In the summer of 1777, Washington expected Howe to strike northward, up the Hudson River, to cooperate with Burgoyne. Instead, Howe sailed to the Chesapeake Bay, moving against the American capital city of Philadelphia.

American Defeat at Brandywine

As he had on Long Island, Howe outgeneraled Washington when they met at Brandywine Creek, west of Philadelphia. A feint against the American center was led by Hessian commander Baron von Knyphausen. This attack diverted Patriot attention from a flank march by Howe and Cornwallis around the American right. The British hit hard and won the field, but the Patriots had fought well. Washington's army withdrew in good order, having survived again.

After Brandywine, Washington could not prevent the fall of Philadelphia. The Continental Congress escaped to York, Pennsylvania, and continued to govern, proving that even the loss of the capital would not end the Revolution.

Germantown: A near-victory

In October, a confident Continental army attacked 9,000 Regulars camped outside Philadelphia at Germantown. The assault was made in four columns of 11,000 men, hitting the British at dawn.

The center column burst from the fog, surprising the Regulars and forcing a retreat. Victory seemed near, but resistance by 120 British under Colonel Thomas Musgrave in a stone mansion slowed the Americans. Confusion struck as Nathanael Greene's late-arriving col-

umn collided with other Americans in the fog, causing Patriots to fire on one another. Seeing their opportunity, the British counterattacked, and Washington was forced to retreat. Yet the Americans remained confident, knowing they had almost won a major victory.

Winter at Valley Forge

Howe's army was quartered comfortably in Philadelphia while Washington's men suffered in cold huts at nearby Valley Forge. Supply problems plagued the Patriots until Nathanael Greene took over as quartermaster general this winter, drastically improving that department.

Hope came to Valley Forge in February 1778, with news that France had made an alliance with America. As they prepared for the spring campaign,

"No, Philadelphia has captured Howe!"

—Benjamin Franklin, upon being told Howe had taken Philadelphia, which Franklin considered a bad move strategically

AMERICA'S GREATEST CITY For its capital, the Continental Congress chose Philadelphia, the British Empire's second-largest city after London. Howe won a great victory by capturing Philadelphia in the fall of 1777, but he could not destroy Washington's army, allowing the Revolution to survive.

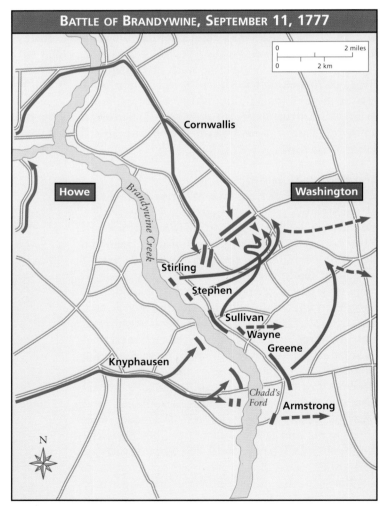

BATTLE OF BRANDYWINE, SEPTEMBER 11, 1777

HOWE'S SKILLFUL TACTICS At Brandywine, Howe outmaneuvered Washington, sending General von Knyphausen to feint directly against the overextended Patriot army while marching his main force around the American right. The assault rolled back the American flank, threatening disaster, but Washington and his officers held their men together in a fighting retreat. He soon would return to the attack.

BATTLE OF GERMANTOWN, OCTOBER 4, 1777

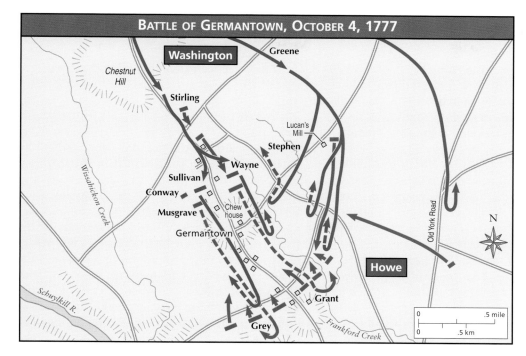

A NEAR VICTORY Washington sent four columns against the British army at Germantown, marching them through the night to attack at dawn. The center columns made the British retreat, but the Patriot advance was stopped when Regulars occupied a stone mansion and made a stand. A British counterattack drove the Americans back, and Washington was forced to withdraw.

"His presence stopped the retreat . . . his fine appearance on horseback, his calm courage, roused to animation by the vexations of the morning, gave him the air best calculated to excite enthusiasm."

—LAFAYETTE'S DESCRIPTION OF
WASHINGTON AT MONMOUTH

Washington's troops were strictly trained in battle tactics by newly arrived Prussian officer Baron Friedrich von Steuben. This training paid off that spring in a hard-fought engagement at Monmouth Court House, New Jersey.

Standoff at Monmouth

Angry that Howe had not destroyed the Patriot army, the British government replaced him with General Sir Henry Clinton. Now some of the troops in Philadelphia were needed for the coming world-wide war with France, so Clinton was ordered to abandon the city.

On June 28, as Clinton marched across New Jersey toward New York, Washington attacked his rearguard. Clinton launched a counterattack. Washington's second-in-command, General Charles Lee, did not believe Continentals could hold against Regulars, and he ordered a retreat.

Dismayed at seeing his veterans pulling back, Washington furiously ordered Lee to the rear and took charge. The Americans formed a line that met the British offensive, and fighting swayed back and forth all that blisteringly hot day, ending at nightfall in a draw. That night, Clinton withdrew to Sandy Hook, where his troops were ferried to New York. Washington proceeded to lay siege to the city.

BATTLE OF MONMOUTH, JUNE 28, 1778

LEE'S FOLLY Recently exchanged after being a prisoner for more than a year, Lee had not seen the improvement in the Patriot army. Lack of confidence caused him to retreat at Monmouth until Washington rallied the troops and fought the British to a standstill.

WASHINGTON STEMS RETREAT Enraged at seeing his Continentals leaving the battle, Washington confronts Lee and demands an explanation. Lee said the Americans were no match for Clinton's crack troops, but Washington knew better and ordered Lee to the rear. Lee was later courtmartialed and left the army.

A WIDENING WAR BETWEEN COLONIAL EMPIRES

From the start, France closely studied the American Revolution, hoping to strike a blow at Great Britain. At first, the French would not openly support the Patriots and bring on another war with the British. Yet, as early as 1776, French military supplies were secretly sent to Washington, helping to keep him in the field after the defeats in New York that year.

The decisive victory at Saratoga in 1777 was made possible by supplies from France. Soon afterwards, the French foreign minister, the Comte de Vergennes, convinced the government of King Louis XVI to establish a formal alliance, ratified by Congress in May 1778. Now Britain was engaged in a world-wide war with France, also a great naval power. The first engagements were at sea, as every colony of these sprawling empires was fair game. Britain, herself, was only lightly defend-ed by 10,000 Regulars in 1778, but her navy and the English Channel served as her main line of defense.

French ambitions centered on Britain's rich West Indies islands, but by the end of the war, fleets and armies were bat-tling around the world, with merchant shipping vulnerable on every ocean. The British merchant fleet, alone, lost more than 6,000 ships during the war.

American privateer John Paul Jones, based in France, won a reputation for capturing merchant vessels and for raiding the British coast. Commodore Jones's fame was assured in September 1779, when he defeated the HMS *Serapis*, even though his own flagship, *Bonhomme Richard*, was damaged and sinking.

Franco-American setbacks

The first French expedition to America set off in mid-1778, under Admiral Comte d'Estaing, but resulted in early failure. D'Estaing's slow crossing of the Atlantic to New York was too late to attack Clinton's army, which was withdrawing from Philadelphia. That summer, a force of 10,000 Patriots under John Sullivan and D'Estaing's fleet offshore failed to attack the 3,000-man British garrison at Newport, Rhode Island, before the arrival of a British fleet. D'Estaing put out to sea to meet the enemy, but a violent storm swept both navies before it, with much damage done to the ships.

D'Estaing's withdrawal from Newport caused the Patriot army to suffer many desertions, and Sullivan withdrew. The British followed, and on August 29 attacked Sullivan in the Battle of Rhode Island. Each army suffered more than 200 casu-alties, and the Americans retreated. One notable incident was the performance of a recently raised Rhode Island regiment of black troops. Fighting with "desperate valor," this regiment repelled three determined assaults by Hessian troops, according to Patriot leaders, who were impressed. Few black regiments were raised during the Revolution, but thousands of blacks

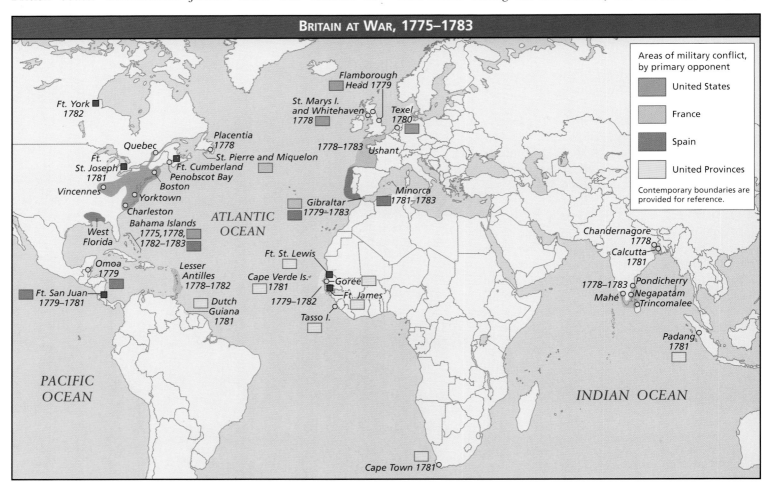

BRITAIN AT WAR, 1775–1783

Areas of military conflict, by primary opponent

- United States
- France
- Spain
- United Provinces

Contemporary boundaries are provided for reference.

A WORLD WAR When France, Holland (United Provinces), and Spain entered the war on the Patriot side, Britain's military resources were stretched thin. The empire had to be defended, not only in North America, but also in the Caribbean, India, and Africa.

A GRUELING CAMPAIGN In the winter of 1778–1779, Clark journeyed to the Falls of Ohio, near present-day Louisville, Kentucky. There he gathered backwoods fighters for a campaign against British forts at Kaskaskia and Vincennes, which he captured.

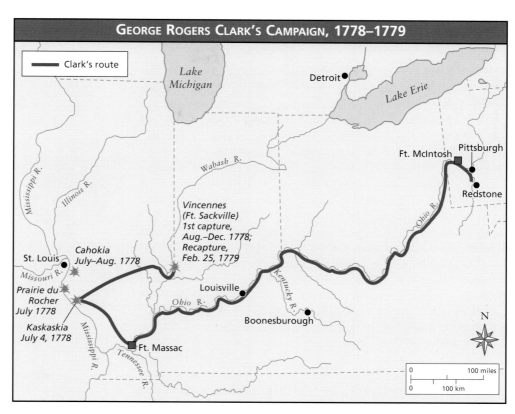

GEORGE ROGERS CLARK'S CAMPAIGN, 1778–1779

served as volunteers in regiments of the Patriot army.

Clark in the Northwest

Virginian George Rogers Clark brought the war to British outposts of the vast Northwest, which stretched from the original colonial frontier beyond the Great Lakes and the Mississippi River. From June 1778 to February 1779, Clark led 200 frontiersmen in an arduous campaign that required 180-mile marches through flooded swamps to capture posts on the Mississippi and Wabash rivers.

Clark's greatest triumph was taking Fort Sackville at Vincennes, which British regional commander, Colonel Henry Hamilton, surrendered in February 1779. Clark's victories, almost bloodless, helped establish future American claims to the Northwest when final peace terms were negotiated.

"Colonel Clark's Compliments to Mr. Hamilton and begs leave to inform him that Col. Clark will not agree to any other terms than that of Mr. Hamilton's Surrendering himself and garrison, prisoners at Discretion—."

—GEORGE ROGERS CLARK'S MESSAGE DEMANDING THE SURRENDER OF THE BRITISH FORT AT VINCENNES, COMMANDED BY COLONEL HAMILTON

FRONTIER FIGHTERS Colonel George Rogers Clark, left, accepts British commander Henry Hamilton's surrender of Fort Sackville at Vincennes in February 1779.

J.P. JONES CIRCUMNAVIGATES BRITAIN Jones left from the French naval port L'Orient to sail around Britain, raiding all along the coast and capturing merchant vessels. Jones engaged and defeated the British warship HMS *Serapis* off Flamborough Head, England, in September 1779.

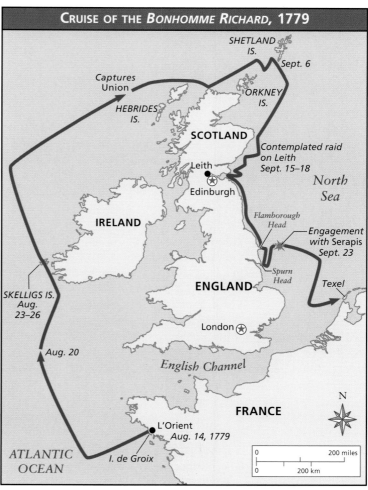

CRUISE OF THE *BONHOMME RICHARD*, 1779

WAR FOR THE SOUTH

Results on the battlefield were still indecisive by late 1779, but the good news for Patriots included Spain and The Netherlands entering the war alongside the United States and France. New England was too strong for the British to attack, as was New York outside occupied New York City. In July, Clinton had sent a force up the Hudson River to wreak havoc and threaten fortresses at Stony Point and West Point. Stony Point fell, but was retaken with a night bayonet charge led by General Anthony Wayne. Clinton soon recalled his expedition.

British prospects in the North dimmed, but the South was said to be teeming with Loyalists. In September 1779, British-held Savannah, Georgia, was besieged by 2,500 Americans under Benjamin Lincoln and a 4,000-man French expeditionary force commanded by Admiral Comte d'Estaing. Savannah's 2,400 defenders held out until the hurricane season threatened the French warships. D'Estaing abandoned the siege, while Lincoln withdrew to Charleston.

The British take the offensive

Now Henry Clinton laid siege to Charleston, which Lincoln surrendered in May, along with 5,500 troops. This devastating Patriot loss was compounded in August at Camden, South Carolina, when Horatio Gates, the victor of Saratoga, was resoundingly defeated by Lord Charles Cornwallis. Gates had 3,000 men, Cornwallis 2,200.

Gates was replaced by Washington's best commander, General Nathanael Greene, but Patriot fortunes ebbed in the South, as Loyalist supporters rallied to Cornwallis's banner. The situation improved when 900 Loyalists were defeated at King's Mountain, South Carolina, in October.

The year 1781 opened with another Patriot victory, this one over the flamboyant dragoon commander, Banastre Tarleton, in January. Drawn into battle at The Cowpens in South Carolina by veteran Daniel Morgan, Tarleton attacked Morgan's 1,000 men with an equal number—most British were Regulars. Tarleton was outfought, his army completely destroyed, and he barely escaped with his life.

Cornwallis pursues Greene through Carolinas

In March, Cornwallis went after Nathanael Greene, trying to bring on a decisive battle. As long as Greene could operate freely, the Patriot cause would dominate the South, and Loyalists would be intimidated. After months of eluding Cornwallis, Greene turned to face him at Guilford Court House, North Carolina.

Greene had 4,300 men, mostly militia, against Cornwallis's 1,900 seasoned veterans. Cornwallis attacked, breaking through two lines of militia, but his men were thrown back by lethal volleys from Continentals in the third line. He launched another attack, but Greene had slipped away, leaving the battlefield strewn with more than 500 British dead and wounded. Greene suffered about 260 casualties.

After withdrawing to Wilmington, North Carolina, on the coast, Cornwallis headed into Virginia for reinforcements and supplies. Harrying his flanks were 1,200 Continentals commanded by the Frenchman, General Marquis de Lafayette. As with Greene, Cornwallis tried unsuccessfully to snare Lafayette.

"Sir, there are enough for our purpose."

—HORATIO GATES'S REPLY UPON LEARNING THAT HIS ARMY, SOON TO FACE CORNWALLIS'S VETERANS AT CAMDEN, WAS LESS THAN HALF THE SIZE HE HAD IMAGINED

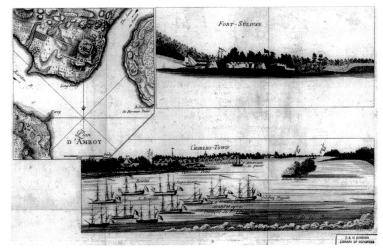

SOUTH'S GREATEST CITY FALLS This contemporary French map shows views of Charleston Harbor during British general Sir Henry Clinton's 1780 siege of Charleston, which he captured.

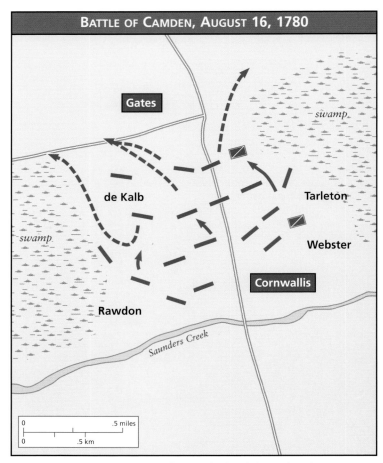

A DISASTROUS DEFEAT Cornwallis attacked with his right wing at Camden in August 1780, smashing through the American militia. Continental troops fought bravely, but were finally overwhelmed. Gates fled the field with the rout of the militia.

The road to Yorktown begins

By late July, Cornwallis was on his way to Yorktown, on the Virginia coast. There, he was further reinforced until he had a powerful army of more than 8,000 veterans.

Future British strategy was unclear, but Cornwallis could strike north for Philadelphia or resume campaigning in the South. Whatever Clinton planned for the American rebels, Cornwallis's men needed rest to recover from a fast-moving campaign that had earned the British nothing but casualties. The stubborn enemy was still in the field.

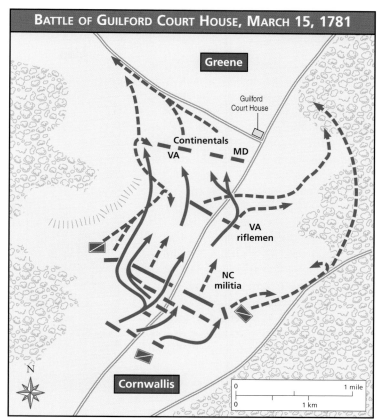

BATTLE OF GUILFORD COURT HOUSE, MARCH 15, 1781

CORNWALLIS WINS HOLLOW VICTORY As had Morgan at Cowpens, Greene put his militia in front to slow Cornwallis's attack at Guilford Court House in March 1781. Behind the militia, waiting Continentals repulsed the British attack. Cornwallis later won the field, but with irreplaceable losses, while Greene withdrew to fight again.

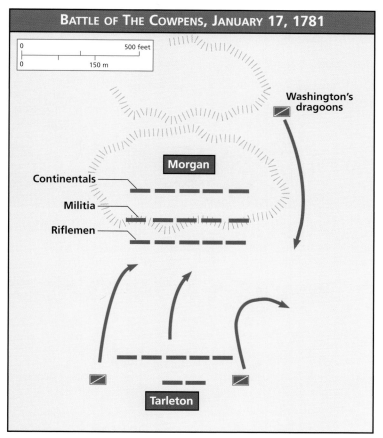

BATTLE OF THE COWPENS, JANUARY 17, 1781

TARLETON IS WHIPPED At The Cowpens, Morgan placed his militia in front, supported by Maryland and Delaware Continentals. Tarleton's men broke through the militia, which made a short retreat and soon returned to the fight. The British hit the Continental line and were driven back. William Washington's dragoons galloped in to complete the victory.

"If they fight, you beat Cornwallis, if not, he will beat you. . . . Put the militia in the center with some picked troops in their rear to shoot down the first man that runs."

—MORGAN'S ADVICE TO GREENE REGARDING THE USE OF "THE GREAT NUMBER OF MILITIA" ON THE AMERICAN SIDE PRIOR TO THE BATTLE OF GUILFORD COURT HOUSE.

MASTER STRATEGIST: NATHANAEL GREENE 1742–1786

Greene's reputation as a Patriot general was second only to Washington's. The Rhode Islander's Revolutionary service went beyond the battlefield, however, as he also undertook for a time the difficult task of supplying the army. After the hungry winter of 1777–1778 at Valley Forge, Washington appointed Greene quartermaster general. A key commander in all Washington's campaigns until then, Greene would rather have been leading troops in the field.

Nevertheless, he successfully reorganized the quartermaster's department, which was crucial to the Patriot cause. In December 1780, Greene took command of the Southern theater, where Patriot armies had been routed. He skillfully maneuvered against Cornwallis, never winning a battle, but inflicting heavy casualties and preserving his own army. After Yorktown, Greene stayed in the South until the last British soldiers were withdrawn.

YORKTOWN AND THE LAST BATTLES

In the summer of 1781, George Washington longed to attack Henry Clinton at New York. The American army's fortifications had kept the British bottled up in the city since 1778. Other than the 1779 Stony Point expedition, Clinton had done little more than conduct forays in strength to test Patriot defenses or find food for his livestock. By 1781, the 10,000-man garrison in New York was essentially out of the war, which continued in the South.

Comte de Rochambeau, with a French army of 4,000 at Newport, Rhode Island, was reluctant to go along with Washington's wish to attack New York. The city was too well defended and could be supported by the warships of the royal navy. Hearing the fleet of Admiral François de Grasse would be in American waters at the end of the summer, Rochambeau and Washington devised another plan, one that was daring and fraught with risk. They resolved to march south to Yorktown and attack

DEFEAT FOR THE ROYAL NAVY Admiral De Grasse's French warships, at left, trade salvos with ships of the Royal Navy under admirals Thomas Graves and Samuel Hood in September 1781. The British were defeated in this, the Battle of the Chesapeake Capes, which left Cornwallis blockaded at Yorktown. The royal fleet limped back to British-controlled New York City.

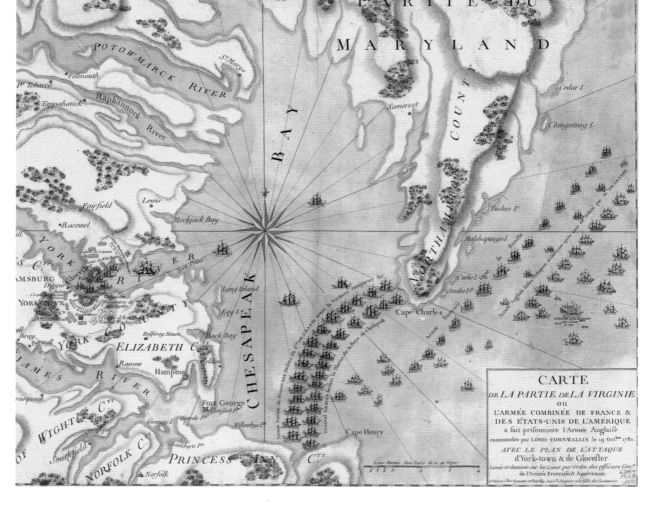

YORKTOWN, LAND AND SEA This contemporary French map of Yorktown shows De Grasse's fleet guarding the entrance to the Chesapeake Bay. The British fleet is in line of battle outside the bay. British defenses around Yorktown are hemmed in by the French and American camps.

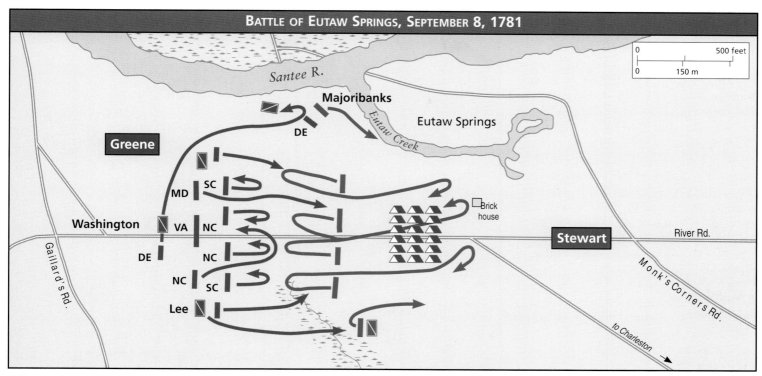

BATTLE OF EUTAW SPRINGS, SEPTEMBER 8, 1781

EUTAW SPRINGS Greene's attack surprised the Regulars and forced them to retreat. A stand by John Marjoribanks prevented total disaster, and British commander Alexander Stewart rallied his men, counterattacking and beating the Americans back. Stewart held the field, but his force was badly mauled. The British retreated to Charleston, South Carolina, and Nathanael Greene's army began a siege of the city.

"At the close of the war, we fought the enemy with British soldiers; and they fought us with those of America."

—NATHANAEL GREENE COMMENTING ON THE LARGE NUMBER OF DESERTERS FOUND IN THE RANKS OF THE ARMIES OF BOTH BRITAIN AND THE UNITED STATES

CONTINENTAL SOLDIER
A Continental infantryman loads his musket. The core of Washington's army, well-trained Continentals often stood firm against elite British soldiers, who were considered among the world's best troops.

Cornwallis. At the same time, De Grasse would sail to Chesapeake Bay and blockade Yorktown, preventing the British Navy from reaching Cornwallis.

If De Grasse did not appear, however, or if British warships got through to Yorktown first, the complexion of the campaign would change drastically for the worse. Either Cornwallis would be strongly reinforced and become a formidable adversary, or he would be transported away by the navy. Both scenarios would allow Clinton to sally from New York against weakened Patriot positions and break the siege. Washington and Rochambeau took the gamble and in August started their armies on a month-long forced march of more than 350 miles to Yorktown.

Greene carries on the Fight

Meanwhile, Nathanael Greene ably led Patriot forces in the South, attacking Colonel Alexander Stewart's 2,000-man army at Eutaw Springs, South Carolina, on September 8. Greene won early suc-cess, but the assault faltered when his hungry men stopped to loot captured British tents and supplies. Stewart's counterattack won the field, though at the heavy cost of more than 840 British killed, wounded, and captured. Greene had 520 casualties.

Stewart withdrew his shattered force to Charleston, one of the few remaining British strongholds in the South—Yorktown, Savannah, and Wilmington, North Carolina, were the others, all seaports. The Patriots now had virtual control of the region.

French sea power triumphs

It was not until September 14, with their armies approaching Yorktown, that Washington and Rochambeau heard the welcome news of De Grasse defeating the British Navy near the entrance to Chesapeake Bay. Cornwallis and his 8,300 British and German troops were now blockaded and could not be reinforced if the Americans and French successfully laid siege to Yorktown.

French heavy artillery arrived by sea to support Allied operations, and Cornwallis came under massive and non-stop bombardment. The Allies dug trenches and built earthworks that brought their guns steadily closer to the British works, and Cornwallis was forced to reduce his defensive perimeter. Washington and Rochambeau had a powerful force of 17,000 troops—7,800 French Regulars and 6,000 Continentals, the rest militia—but they avoided full-scale frontal assaults that would cause unnecessary slaughter. Instead, they tightened the noose on Cornwallis, who hoped Clinton somehow would get reinforcements past the French naval blockade.

On the night of October 15, American and French troops attacked and captured two crucial redoubts, then turned the guns there to fire pointblank on the town. Cornwallis had no choice but to surrender. He did so on October 19, 1781, ending the last campaign of the Revolutionary War with a Franco-American victory that promised an ultimate Patriot triumph.

Washington did not allow himself to be euphoric, however, because he knew the military might of the British Empire could prolong the war. The Patriots must be prepared to fight on in case the British came back in force. Soon returning to the siege of New York, Washington swore not to leave his command until the last British Regular departed from the city.

ASSAULT WITH BAYONETS The British infantry were famous for unstoppable bayonet charges. By 1781, American Continentals had also become skilled with that weapon. Led by Captain Alexander Hamilton, a daring American bayonet attack captured a British redoubt at Yorktown.

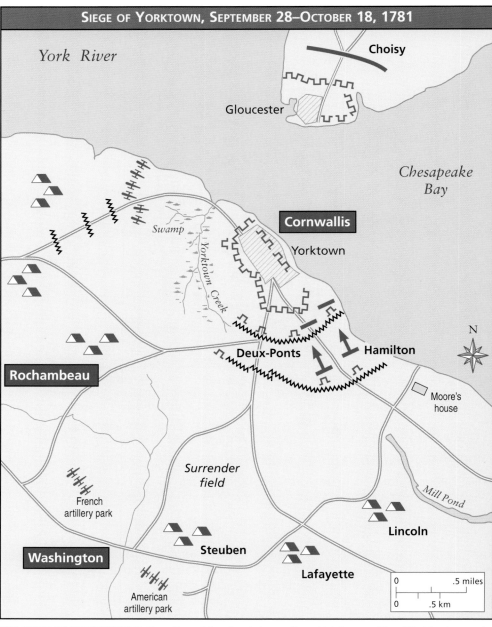

SIEGE OF YORKTOWN, SEPTEMBER 28–OCTOBER 18, 1781

THE SIEGE OF YORKTOWN Rather than risk a frontal assault and high casualties, Washington and Rochambeau laid siege to Yorktown, moving their lines closer each day as Allied artillery reduced the town to rubble. On October 14, a night attack captured two key redoubts. When the cannon in these redoubts were turned around to fire into Yorktown, Cornwallis had to surrender.

"My situation now becomes very critical; we dare not show a gun to their old batteries, and I expect that their new ones will open to-morrow morning. . . . The safety of this place is, therefore, so precarious that I cannot recommend that the fleet and army should run great risque in endeavouring to save us."

—LORD CORNWALLIS WRITING TO SIR HENRY CLINTON IN NEW YORK, REGARDING THE SITUATION OF HIS ARMY BESIEGED IN YORKTOWN, OCTOBER 15, 1781

TWO LINGERING YEARS TO A FINAL PEACE

Peace negotiations moved slowly in Paris and London, and George Washington maintained an army at Newburgh, north of occupied New York City. Clinton was replaced by Sir Guy Carleton, governor of Canada. In the winter of 1782–1783, with peace terms virtually agreed upon, Carleton ordered a complete British withdrawal from the South.

Still, Washington did not go home to Virginia. His army would be kept at the ready until the British evacuated New York. Washington had to be with the troops to maintain morale and to prevent mutiny by embittered officers who were owed years of back pay by Congress. That spring of 1783, officers at Newburgh held meetings to discuss marching on Congress in Philadelphia to demand their rightful pay. Some had been bankrupted by years of service in the Revolution. Washington realized the ringleaders of the growing insurrection might march on Congress and attempt to bring about its overthrow.

At a crucial meeting before the officers marched, Washington rose to speak and convinced them not to throw away the victory they had won as Patriots. Love and respect for Washington kept them to their duty, and they did not mutiny. Word soon came of a final peace treaty, and the army was disbanded, sent home with Congress's promise to pay them some day.

On November 25, 1783, the last British soldier left New York, and Washington arrived to celebrate triumph in the American War for Independence.

NORTH AMERICA AFTER THE TREATY OF PARIS, 1783

ARCTIC OCEAN

ALASKA

Baffin Bay

Baffin Land

NEWFOUND-LAND

Hudson Bay

LABRADOR

RUPERT'S LAND

Area disputed by Spain, England, and Russia

Area disputed by England and U.S.

PACIFIC OCEAN

Columbia R.

Snake R.

ST. PIERRE and MIQUELON (FRANCE)

QUEBEC

St. Lawrence R.

NOVA SCOTIA

UNITED STATES

Mississippi R.

Area disputed by Spain and U.S.

ATLANTIC OCEAN

N

E W

Rio Grande

S P A I N

FLORIDA

Bahamas (ENGLAND)

Gulf of Mexico

CUBA

ST. DOMINGUE

BRITISH HONDURAS

JAMAICA

Caribbean Sea

MOSQUITO COAST PANAMA

0 — 500 miles

0 — 500 km

French possessions

Russian claims

Spanish possessions and claims

Disputed areas

United States

Area unexplored by non-Indians

British possessions

TRIUMPH AND PEACE The Treaty of Paris in 1783 ended the Revolution and brought independence for the 13 United States. Spanish-held territory hemmed in the new country to the west and south.

WASHINGTON'S DRILLMASTER
FRIEDRICH WILHELM VON STEUBEN
1730–1794

One of Washington's most dependable commanders, Von Steuben had been a member of the Prussian general staff, attached to Frederick the Great's headquarters during the Seven Years' War. Soon after arriving at Washington's winter encampment in Valley Forge with a letter of introduction from Benjamin Franklin, Von Steuben began drilling a company of 100 picked men in the manual of arms and maneuver. They, in turn, instructed the rest of the troops. By springtime, the Continental army was transformed, capable of complex battlefield and parade maneuvers and skilled with the bayonet. Von Steuben remained in service with Washington until the very end of the war in 1783.

Military Weaponry in Colonial Times

When Europeans began to settle the Americas in the 1500s, edged and pole weapons often were preferred over less-dependable firearms. European soldiers still wore iron helmets and armor on breast and thighs. Some firearms used wheel-lock mechanisms—an improvement over the matchlock, but expensive and relatively fragile. By the 1700s, the sturdy flintlock musket replaced the matchlock, and edged weapons gave way to firearms on the battlefield.

Through the Revolutionary War, most soldiers used smoothbore, muzzle-loading flintlock muskets, while frontiersmen took up the rifle. Although far more accurate than the smoothbore, the rifle was slower to load and could not accept a bayonet, a great disadvantage. In a pitched battle, trained infantry could fire and load smoothbore muskets three times faster than rifles.

The main weapon of the Revolutionary-era army was the smoothbore musket, and American battle tactics were much like the British or French—close-rank volleying and charging. By the end of the war, American Regulars displayed considerable proficiency in bayonet charges, a fundamental tactic of infantry of the day.

At sea, cannons ruled—mainly those made of iron. Though heavier than bronze, and more susceptible to bursting, iron cannon were one-third as expensive as bronze cannon. More guns meant greater firepower, which was now the requirement for military success on sea or on land.

ELABORATE PAINT This warrior from a colonial-period tribe in Florida is decorated with symbolic patterns and carries a stout bow and poison-tipped arrows.

TRADE TOMAHAWK Prized by native peoples, British-made "pipe tomahawks" also served as tobacco pipes. The head had a bowl and the handle was hollowed out.

MATCHLOCK MUSKET The standard infantry firearm for almost 200 years, matchlocks were clumsy but simple to operate and maintain. A glowing matchcord—thin rope treated to smolder—was positioned in the lock, and the lit match was dropped onto the priming powder, firing the gun. Wet weather rendered matchlocks virtually useless.

HELMETS Triple-bar "lobsterback" helmets were typical for the 1640s. Most soldiers wore cheaply made "munition" armor, often discarded by soldiers in America's dense forests.

FIELD CANNON Artillery was heavy and cumbersome to maneuver, but steady progress was made throughout the 18th Century to make field guns lighter and more effective. Implements needed to serve the guns included handspikes, rammers, sponges, brushes, and worms.

ROUNDSHOT AND SHELL Cannon fired ammunition of two kinds: solid iron balls, or shell. Solid iron balls were designed to plow through enemy units or to batter walls and earthworks. Shell was a hollow iron ball, filled with gunpowder and fitted with a fuse. When the shell burst, fragments could kill and wound enemy soldiers. Shell was unpredictable in use, and was often ineffective.

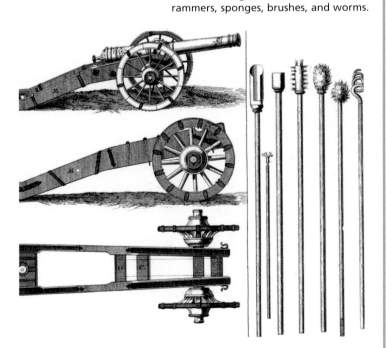

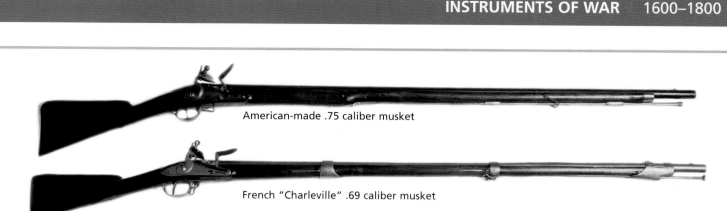

American-made .75 caliber musket

French "Charleville" .69 caliber musket

English Short Land Pattern or "Brown Bess" .75 caliber musket

FLINTLOCK MUSKETS These three firearms are typical of those used during the American Revolution by American, French, and British forces. The Americans manufactured copies of French and British muskets, and used high-quality captured or imported muskets whenever possible.

BRITISH SOCKET BAYONET Musket-armed soldiers needed to be defended against swarms of cavalry on the battlefield. Long pikes were made unnecessary by the invention of the bayonet in the late 17th Century. At first bayonets fit into the muzzle of the musket, rendering them unable to fire. Eventually a bayonet was designed with a socket that fitted over the barrel, making it possible to load and fire with the bayonet in place.

MUSKET CARTRIDGE This was a paper tube holding a one-ounce lead musket ball and the correct amount of gunpowder. Soldiers normally carried 40 to 60 cartridges in leather boxes. Cartridges were torn open with the teeth. Priming and loading the musket was then done according to a series of specific motions, taking about 20 seconds.

BRITISH CAVALRY SABER Swords, used since ancient times, continued to serve as infantry and cavalry weapons. Infantry carried short swords called "hangers," and cavalry used a variety of straight or curved blades. Swords formed a part of every officer's equipment on both land and sea. In the close-quarters fighting, swords were fearsome weapons.

AMERICAN RIFLE Developed to meet the needs of the American frontier—economical in their use of powder and ball, and deadly accurate in skilled hands—rifles found little favor in the regular armies of the American Revolution because they were too slow to load. Units of rifle-armed, sharpshooting militia did operate effectively, however, especially in the South.

SHIP-OF-THE-LINE These were the most powerful sailing warships, so-called because they were big enough to form in a fleet's line of battle. Carrying 50 to 120 muzzle-loading cannon on two or three decks, ships-of-the-line had crews of 500 to 1,000 sailors and marines. Smaller frigates, with one gun deck, served to scout and also to protect merchant convoys.

THE SEAT OF WAR This 19th-century map shows the main regions of conflict during the War of 1812: most fighting was along the United States-Canadian border, with a British attack on Washington, D.C. in 1814.

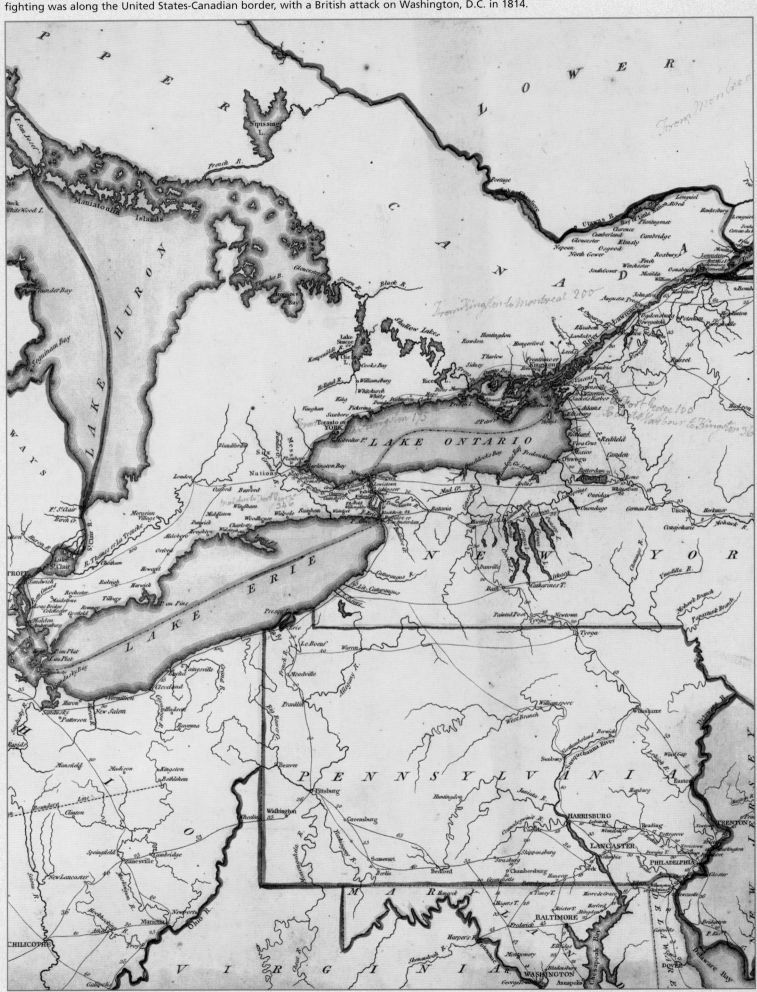

PART TWO

Wars of the Young Republic

AFTER THE REVOLUTION, THE UNITED STATES was not looking for a foreign war, but she was forced into more than one as the 18th Century closed. The Barbary states of North Africa sent corsairs against American merchant shipping, no longer protected by the mighty British Navy. Revolutionary France, desperate in her war with Britain, demanded that the United States honor the past Franco-American alliance and forsake trade with the British. When the United States stood up to the Barbary pirates and the French, American merchant vessels were captured, the flag insulted, and undeclared war began.

The story was different in America's western lands, possessed by tenacious native peoples and disputed by the presence of British garrisons. Here, America chose to make war: first against the Indians, and with disastrous results, then against the British in the War of 1812, which brought more defeats. In time, American arms triumphed, preparing the way for the Mexican-American War's victories, which annexed half a million square miles of territory to the United States.

Immense migrations across these newly acquired lands made the Indian nations uneasy, but America was on the move, spurred on by belief in her "Manifest Destiny" to dominate the continent from sea to sea. American growth in territory, population, and wealth seemed unstoppable. Then came civil strife that a few prosperous decades earlier had played out in Congress, but not yet on the battlefield.

1812 brig *Niagara* with "Don't Give Up the Ship" flag

4: AMERICAN WARSHIPS ON THE HIGH SEAS

THE USS *CONSTITUTION* This woodcut was done in 1833 on a piece of oak from the superstructure of the frigate, nicknamed "Old Ironsides" because her stout hull withstood most cannon fire. After the warship became obsolete, she was preserved for posterity.

Seeking to minimize the national budget after the Revolutionary War, Congress disbanded its navy of 13 frigates so that by 1794 there was no naval force other than a few small revenue cutters patrolling the coasts to prevent smuggling. Though lacking a navy, Americans had traditionally played an important role in international seafaring. Not only did some of the finest wood for shipbuilding come from America, but the new nation had top-flight ship builders and designers. American vessels were among the best in the world, and American seamen, especially from New England, were highly regarded.

The "Quasi-War" with France
By the early 1790s, President Washington and Congress were working to keep the country out of the French revolutionary wars and also trying to improve relations with Great Britain. Napoleonic France, struggling for survival against Britain and a host of enemies, demanded that the United States limit her commercial ties with the British Empire. Americans, however, were determined to trade where and with whom they wished. The subsequent strain in relations led to the so-called "Quasi-War" between the United States and France, an undeclared con-

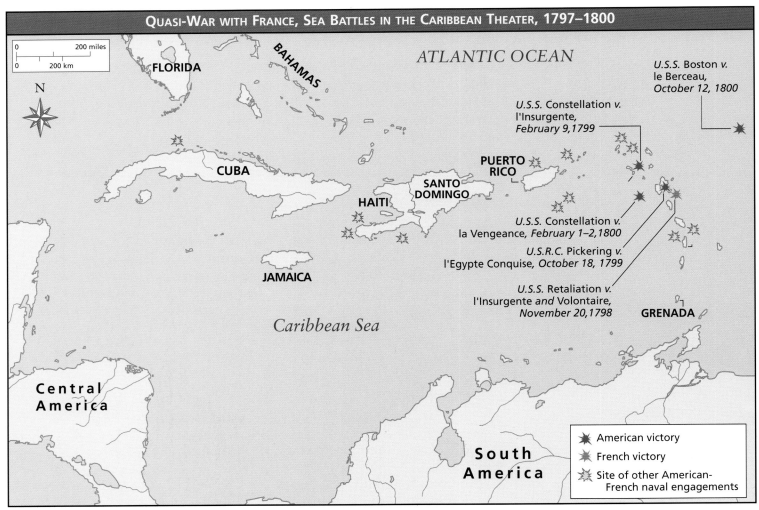

QUASI-WAR WITH FRANCE, SEA BATTLES IN THE CARIBBEAN THEATER, 1797–1800

0   200 miles
0   200 km

N

FLORIDA
BAHAMAS
ATLANTIC OCEAN

U.S.S. Boston *v.* le Berceau, *October 12, 1800*

U.S.S. Constellation *v.* l'Insurgente, *February 9, 1799*

CUBA
PUERTO RICO
SANTO DOMINGO
HAITI

U.S.S. Constellation *v.* la Vengeance, *February 1–2, 1800*

U.S.R.C. Pickering *v.* l'Egypte Conquise, *October 18, 1799*

JAMAICA

U.S.S. Retaliation *v.* l'Insurgente *and* Volontaire, *November 20, 1798*

GRENADA

Caribbean Sea

Central America

South America

✹ American victory
✸ French victory
✺ Site of other American-French naval engagements

NAVAL ENGAGEMENTS Most action in the Quasi-War with France was in the eastern Caribbean, where American merchant vessels had been falling prey to French privateers. The new American war fleet's successes forced the French to agree to peace terms.

"Millions for defense, but not one cent for tribute!"

—United States Minister to France, Charles Cotesworth Pinckney, to the French government, which had asked him for a bribe to avoid hostilities

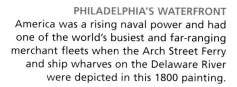

PHILADELPHIA'S WATERFRONT
America was a rising naval power and had one of the world's busiest and far-ranging merchant fleets when the Arch Street Ferry and ship wharves on the Delaware River were depicted in this 1800 painting.

flict on the high seas. Hostilities started in 1797 as French warships and privateers captured hundreds of American vessels said to be trading with British seaports. In response, the United States authorized its armed merchant vessels to attack French shipping.

At this time, there was trouble with the states of the Barbary Coast of northern Africa, who were plundering American merchant vessels and holding crews and passengers for ransom. The United States had built three new frigates by now, but she needed a larger navy, and President John Adams took the initiative to create one.

The rebirth of the U.S. Navy

The first American fighting ships were frigates, heavily timbered and armed with as many guns as they could carry. Secretary of the Navy Benjamin Stoddert put into action offensive operations in the Caribbean, where French cruisers were taking American merchant vessels. In June 1798, only one American naval vessel was deployed at sea, but within six months 20 American warships were convoying merchant ships and cruising against the enemy. The American navy seized 19 French privateers over the winter of 1798-99 alone.

The French challenge was met by bold American captains whose warships won fine reputations, especially the *Constitution* and *Constellation,* the best known naval vessels. One noteworthy American success involved a naval force under Lieutenant Isaac Hull, which in May 1800 captured a French privateer moored in Santo Domingo harbor and spiked the fort's guns.

Before the Quasi-War ended in 1800 by mutual agreement, the American navy had almost 30 fighting vessels at sea, with 700 officers and 5,000 sailors. During the two-and-a-half years of the Quasi-War, Americans made prizes of approximately 85 French vessels and recovered 70 captured merchant ships, a performance that compelled France to seek peace terms. The subsequent agreement freed the United States from previous treaties with France and left Americans with a new confidence in their growing sea power.

THE USS *CONSTELLATION,* left, engages a French frigate.

A SMALL BUT GALLANT FLEET OF FRIGATES

The USS *Constitution,* launched in 1797, was one of six frigates authorized by Congress to establish an American naval force. The *Constitution* had 56 cannon and stout oaken sides, making her formidable on the high seas. She captured nine French vessels during the Quasi-War and later improved her reputation in the War of 1812, when her thick hull earned the nickname "Old Ironsides." She was more powerful than most foreign frigates—intermediate-size warships that were smaller than ships-of-the-line, which carried between 70–100 guns.

The other American frigates of this era were the 44-gun *Constellation, United States,* and *President,* and the 36-gun *Chesapeake* and *Congress.* The vessel that gained most fame in the conflict with France was the *Constellation,* which captured the *L'Insurgente* and outfought the *Vengeance,* both frigates. Over the following decades, these American warships rendered invaluable service against the pirate states of the Barbary Coast and in the War of 1812. America's navy was in its infancy at the start of the 19th Century, but it already had won the grudging respect of its opponents.

FIGHTING PIRATES ON THE HOSTILE SHORES OF TRIPOLI

"I hope I shall never again be sent to Algiers with tribute, unless I am authorized to deliver it from the mouth of our cannon."

—CAPTAIN WILLIAM BAINBRIDGE AFTER DELIVERING TRIBUTE TO THE DEY OF ALGIERS IN 1800

For generations the states of North Africa's Barbary Coast had raided foreign shipping in the Mediterranean Sea or had exacted payments of tribute not to do so. With independence in 1783, the former British colonies no longer had the protection of the Royal Navy, resulting in a rising number of attacks on American merchant vessels by the Barbary states. Crews and passengers often were held captive for years until ransoms were paid.

America fights the Barbary Wars

The Barbary states included Tripoli, Tunis, Algiers, and Morocco, who sent cruisers as far as the Atlantic to take prizes. In 1794, Congress authorized the building of six frigates as the foundation of a navy. At first intended to make a show of force in the Mediterranean, these warships were needed in the Quasi-War with France from 1797–1800. In the meantime, treaties were negotiated with the Barbary states, which promised not to attack American

FIGHT TO THE DEATH American naval commander Stephen Decatur, lower right, kills an enemy as his men do battle with the crew of a Tripolitan gunboat during the Barbary Wars.

BARBARY POWERS, EARLY 1800s

BARBARY COAST The North African states of Tripoli, Tunis, Algiers, and Morocco made up the Barbary Powers, shown shaded. These Muslim peoples fought the Spanish for centuries, vying for control of the Mediterranean. By the early 19th Century, piracy was the main source of revenue in the Barbary States.

shipping if the United States paid a yearly tribute in naval stores.

At the end of the Quasi-War, the United States was left with an effective and experienced navy, which came into use when the pasha who ruled Tripoli demanded increased tribute. The demand was refused, and in 1800 Tripoli declared war on the United States.

The Tripolitan War

President Jefferson sent warships to patrol the Barbary Coast and protect American interests. Morocco also declared war, and Tunis was threatening the same. By 1802, nine American naval vessels were operating as the Mediterranean Squadron, based at Gibraltar, and under the command of Commodore Richard V. Morris. The squadron was ordered to aggressively defend American shipping and seize hostile vessels. Morris had little success, however, and was recalled in mid-1803, when the Mediterranean Squadron was reinforced by a fleet under the command of Commodore Edward Preble.

Preble set about blockading Tripoli and cruised off Tangiers and Tunis. His warships frequently sailed into Tripoli harbor to sink vessels and bombard the city, but the pasha refused to agree to negotiations favoring the United States. During this campaign, the frigate *Philadelphia* ran aground in the harbor and was captured along with her crew. In February 1804, Lieutenant Stephen Decatur led volunteers into the harbor,

EATON'S CAMPAIGN, 1805

SICILY
Syracuse
GREECE
OTTOMAN EMPIRE
MALTA
CRETE
Argus, Hornet and Nautilus bombard Derna, April 27, 1805
CYPRUS
Eaton resupplied by Argus, April 16, 1805
Mediterranean Sea
Tripoli
Surrenders to Eaton, April 28, 1805
Derna
Bomba
Gulf of Sirte
Alexandria
Eaton's line of march
N
TRIPOLI
LIBYAN DESERT
Eaton leaves Alexandria March 8, 1805
Nile R.
0   250 miles
0   250 km
EGYPT

A DESERT MARCH Former Revolutionary War soldier William Eaton led Marines and mercenaries through the Libyan Desert to threaten the pasha of Tripoli in 1805; Eaton was resupplied by the U.S. Navy at Bomba before the combined land and sea attack on Derna.

boarded the *Philadelphia*, and set her ablaze to prevent Tripoli from using the frigate in its own fleet.

Eaton's desert march

Jefferson sent more warships to the Mediterranean that summer, until the squadron numbered 23, but the Tripolitan War continued sporadically and inconclusively. Then, in March 1805, the former American consul to Tunis, William Eaton, led several officers and eight Marines along with a hired force of almost 400 mercenaries—mainly Arabs and Greeks—on a 1,000-mile march

across the desert from Alexandria, Egypt, to Tripoli. Eaton planned to overthrow Tripoli's pasha and recognize the pasha's brother as rightful ruler.

Supported by effective American naval attacks, Eaton's expedition captured the city of Derna in April. Now, the American navy was off Tripoli, prepared to cooperate with a land assault. In June, the pasha agreed to peace terms, which included the release of American prisoners. The Barbary Wars were essentially over, and the United States Navy was firmly established.

BOMBARDMENT OF TRIPOLI
A fleet of powerful American frigates under Commodore Edward Preble bombards the North African city of Tripoli as enemy gunboats dash out to attack the squadron.

5: NATIVE DEFENSE OF THE NORTHWEST

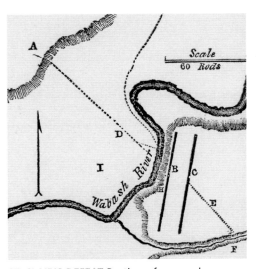

ST. CLAIR'S DEFEAT Portion of a map drawn from descriptions by officers who were present: A, militia camp; B, C, encampment of main army; D, retreat of militia; E, route of St. Clair's retreat; F, burial-place of soldiers; I, site of cannon unearthed in 1830. (This period map skips over the letters G and H.)

The 1768 British-Indian Treaty of Fort Stanwix had established frontier boundaries that limited white settlement in the region known as the Northwest, but after the Revolution, the United States rejected the treaty's terms. The government was desperately in need of funds, and sale of lands in the Northwest Territory promised to be profitable. Also, thousands of prospective settlers were eager to move into Indian country—many already had settled illegally there.

War on the frontier

Native Americans asserted that the United States did not have the right to settle the Northwest Territory. Though the new republic claimed the region in accord with peace terms of the Revolution, native peoples asserted that they had never given their lands over to the British —therefore the British had no authority

to bargain them away in the treaty. For decades the Indians had been able to count on guns and ammunition provided by the British at posts such as Detroit, which still had not been turned over despite the 1783 American victory in the Revolution. Native peoples had the hope that the British would fight alongside the Indians to prevent American invasions.

Little Turtle takes command

By 1786, Algonquian-speaking peoples of the region were organizing into a powerful alliance that included the Shawnee, Miami, Ottawa, Wyandot, Chippewa, Delaware, Sac, Potawatomi, Mingo, and Fox. Their war chief was Little Turtle—*Mishikinakwa* to his own people, the Miami.

An experienced leader who had participated in many attacks on white settlements in the Ohio and Kentucky frontiers, Little Turtle defeated an invad-

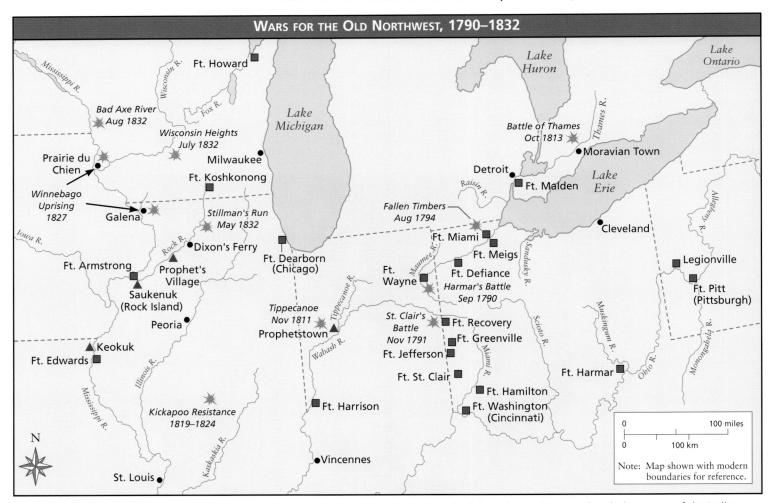

WARS FOR THE OLD NORTHWEST, 1790–1832

A STRUGGLE FOR POSSESSION In the early years of the republic, the United States launched several expeditions to break the power of the Indian nations in what later became known as the "Old Northwest"; the first campaigns often ended in Indian victories.

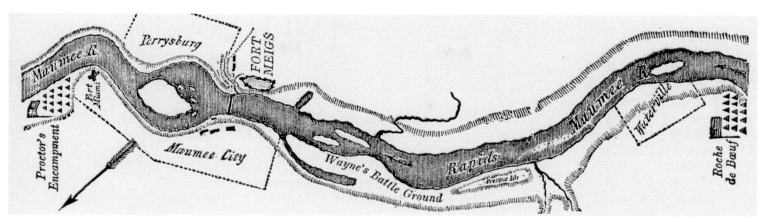

ing army under General Josiah Harmar in October 1790. Harmar's 350 Regulars and 1,100 frontier militia were burning abandoned Miami towns in the Maumee River valley when Little Turtle struck and routed the Americans. Many of the militia panicked and ran, while most of the Regulars, who stood their ground, were killed. Harmar was driven out of the region.

St. Clair's Expedition

A year later, an even more disastrous defeat crushed a 1,450-man army led by former Revolutionary War general Arthur St. Clair, now governor of the Northwest Territory. St. Clair's camp on the Maumee River was surprised and attacked on November 3, 1791, by Little Turtle and his Shawnee lieutenant, Blue Jacket. Most of St. Clair's troops were undisciplined militia, who once again broke and fled. More than 630 Americans were killed or missing in what was one of the greatest native victories of the Indian wars.

This triumph was short-lived. Another invasion followed in 1794, led by Revolutionary War hero General Anthony Wayne, who for two years had trained and disciplined his 2,000 troops. Then he followed a methodical plan to build supply depots and strongpoints to support his advance. Little Turtle observed the strength of the invasion and advised his people to make peace rather than fight. He was overruled, and Blue Jacket took command. When Blue Jacket attacked Wayne, Little Turtle fought alongside his own Miami.

The battlefield was called Fallen Timbers, a place where trees had been downed by a storm. Casualties were relatively light on both sides—fewer than 175 in both forces—but the defeat was made all the more decisive by the refusal of a nearby British fort's commander to offer the Indians military support or even refuge within the fort's walls.

Without British aid, the nations of the Northwest could not resist future American invasions. The Treaty of Greenville in 1795 ceded native lands in southern Ohio to the United States.

WAYNE'S VICTORY General Anthony Wayne advanced from Roche de Boeuf to defeat Blue Jacket, whose warriors retreated toward Fort Miami, a British post within United States territory. Fort Meigs, shown at left center, was a later American construction.

A GENERAL AND HIS LEGION In full-dress uniform with general's epaulets, Wayne and an officer study enemy positions through telescopes during the Fallen Timbers campaign; troops of his "Legion of the United States," wearing hats with bearskin crests, await orders.

"Picked up and recruited from the offscourings of large towns and cities . . . it was impossible they could have been made competent to the arduous duties of Indian warfare."

—St. Clair's adjutant on the men raised to fight Indians in the Northwest

FORT HARMAR Built on the Ohio River by American troops in 1785, this frontier post was sketched in 1790, looking southward; the Muskingum River enters at lower left, and farm buildings stand on the Virginia shore, across the Ohio.

U.S. GOVERNMENT DEFEATS THE NORTHWEST NATIONS

After 1795, whites continued to settle on Indian lands despite the terms of various peace treaties. Resentment and fury built up among many young warriors, whose peoples were being dispossessed by the influx of white settlers and the maneuvers of American officials. Government policy was to make individual treaties with the tribes, picking pliable leaders who were willing to sell lands—even though they might not have the right to do so. One outstanding young Shawnee believed the land belonged communally to all the nations and tribes. Therefore, he said, the selling or ceding of lands required the consent of all the native peoples in order to be legitimate. This Shawnee was Tecumseh, who was determined to promote Indian nationhood in the face of American resolve to break the resistance of the tribes in the Northwest Territory.

The Battle of Tippecanoe

Tecumseh was an excellent warrior as well as a skilled organizer of native peoples. He joined with his half-brother, Tenskwatawa—known as "The Prophet" for his mysticism—to build an alliance of the nations in order to prevent the piecemeal loss of land to whites. Tecumseh became a bitter enemy of Governor William Henry Harrison, who was trying to make separate treaties with tribes. In a meeting at Vincennes, Tecumseh's pro-Indian oratory infuriated Harrison, and they almost fought with each other.

In the early morning of November 7, 1811, while Tecumseh was visiting native communities in the Southeast, his brother Tenskwatawa led an attack against invading American forces under Harrison on the Wabash River. Named for nearby Tippecanoe Creek, the battle involved 700 warriors against about 1,000 Regulars and volunteers. This defeat for Tenskwatawa caused approximately 70 white and 50 Indian casualties.

Immediately, Harrison accused the British of militarily supporting the native fighters, and the resultant outcry in Congress helped spur a declaration of war

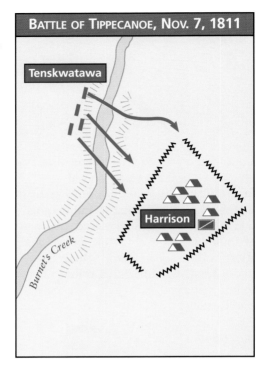

BATTLE OF TIPPECANOE, NOV. 7, 1811

THE PROPHET'S DOOMED ASSAULT In 1811, warriors led by the holy man, Tenskwatawa, attempted to defend their nearby village by attacking William Henry Harrison's stronger force near the Wabash River; the Indians were driven off and abandoned their village, which was soon destroyed.

HARRISON'S POSITION AT TIPPECANOE The army's camp on Burnett Creek was just two miles from Tenskwatawa's village, called Prophetstown; the main Indian force attacked the perimeter while a few slipped into camp in a failed attempt to kill Harrison, whose tent was at center.

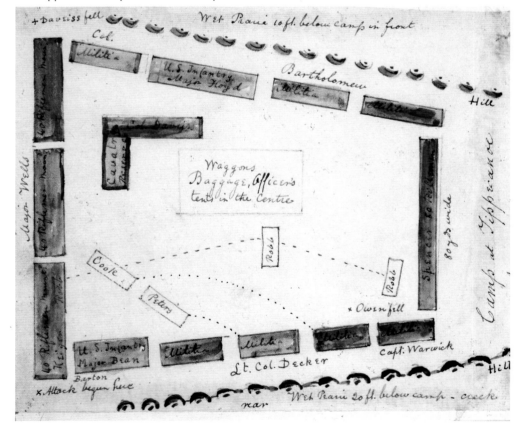

TENSKWATAWA (1775–1836) "Shawnee Prophet," Tenskwatawa, led a movement to return Native Americans to traditional lifestyles; defeated by Harrison at Tippecanoe, he fled to Canada, later returning to cooperate in the Shawnee removal west of the Mississippi.

against Britain. Now, Tecumseh and the Indian nations of the Northwest became firmly allied with the British.

War of 1812; Battle of the Thames

Tecumseh's able leadership of native forces was instrumental in the capture of Fort Detroit in August 1812. Operating with British colonel Henry Procter, Tecumseh also laid siege to Fort Meigs, on the Maumee River, in May 1813. The fort was strongly defended by 2,000 men under William Henry Harrison, who held out, even though Tecumseh destroyed a reinforcement expedition of 600 Kentucky militiamen.

Other forts were attacked or came under siege by British and Indian forces, as inconclusive, but bloody, fighting raged across the region. One native offensive cap-

tured Fort Dearborn, where Potawatamies massacred more than 50 soldiers and civilians who had been left behind after the main American body abandoned the post.

When the situation turned in favor of the United States in late 1813, Tecumseh urged the British not to retreat from the Northwest, but they did. This compelled him to abandon his homeland and join their withdrawal to Upper Canada. There, at Moraviantown on the Thames River, Harrison's 3,300 men defeated the combined force of Procter's 450 British and Tecumseh's 750 Indians. Most British troops escaped, but Tecumseh made a last stand that cost his life.

The Battle of the Thames shattered the Indian cause in the Northwest, helping clear the way for westward pioneer expansion.

> *"The behavior of both regulars and militia troops was such as would have done honor to veterans."*
>
> —WILLIAM HENRY HARRISON, ON THE BATTLE OF TIPPECANOE

ORATOR AND WARRIOR
TECUMSEH 1768?–1813

The son of a Shawnee father and a Creek mother, Tecumseh symbolized Native Americans of both the Northwest and South, who were hard-pressed by American desire for their land.

Born in the Ohio region, Tecumseh was in his mid-twenties when he fought in the defeat at Fallen Timbers in 1794. He rejected the Treaty of Greenville that ended hostilities and annexed Indian lands. For the next few years, he traveled from village to village, as far away as Florida, calling for native unity and self-determination. He joined the British in the War of 1812, hoping to establish an Indian state. In recognition of Tecumseh's abilities, the British made him a brigadier general.

Tecumseh was defeated at the Battle of the Thames in October, and reportedly killed, although his body was never found. Tecumseh's death marked the virtual end of native resistance in the Northwest.

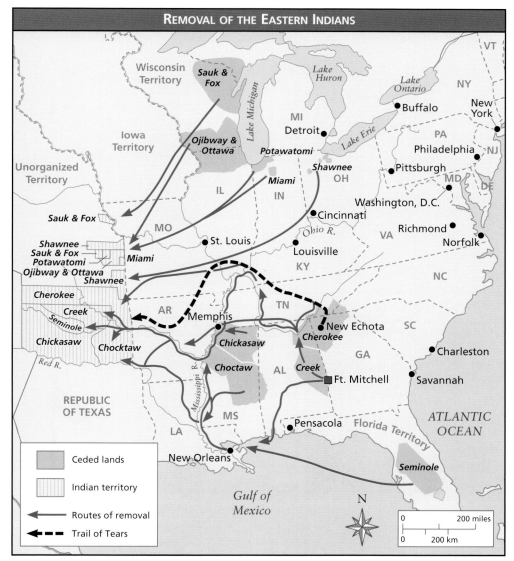

REMOVAL OF THE EASTERN INDIANS

Legend:
- Ceded lands
- Indian territory
- Routes of removal
- Trail of Tears

ESTABLISHING "INDIAN TERRITORY" The government negotiated treaties and also used force to move Native Americans west of the Mississippi. The removals continued for decades, as Indian families trekked long distances, under escort, to settle in arid lands beyond the frontier.

6: THE WAR OF 1812: AN UNWANTED CONFLICT

1812 AMERICAN ARTILLERYMEN Gunners in this idealized woodcut are ready to do battle.

Tensions between the United States and the British Empire mounted throughout the first decade of the 19th Century, as the Napoleonic Empire Wars (1803–1815) raged, catching Americans in the middle. The Quasi-War with France had rebuffed French attempts to compel Americans not to trade with the British Empire, but the young republic next faced heavy-handed British policies geared to dominate United States commerce with Europe. At the same time, the Royal Navy impressed American seamen, stopping vessels on the high seas and forcing sailors into the crews of British warships.

American anger stirred up war fever in part of the population, but the majority of the nation did not favor war. New England's seafaring community, for example, opposed war with Britain because the inevitable losses of American shipping and commercial profits would be devastating. For her part, Britain was too mired in the European conflict to want another war with America. Feelings were different in the American West, where frontier communities were eager to dislodge the

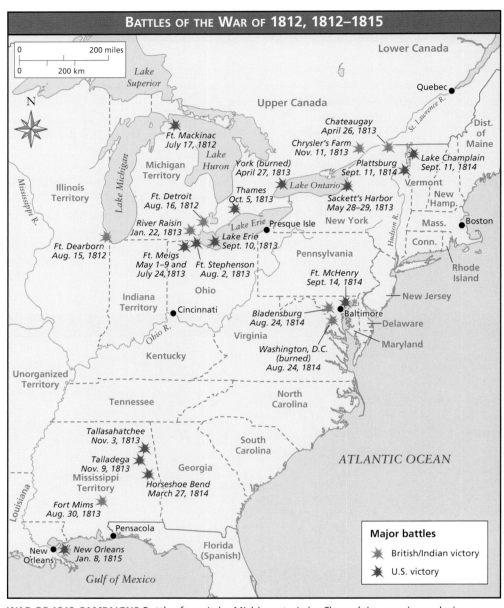

BATTLES OF THE WAR OF 1812, 1812–1815

Lower Canada

Upper Canada

0 _____ 200 miles
0 _____ 200 km

Lake Superior

Quebec

Ft. Mackinac
July 17, 1812

Michigan Territory

Lake Huron

Chateaugay
April 26, 1813

Chrysler's Farm
Nov. 11, 1813

Dist. of Maine

Lake Champlain
Sept. 11, 1814

York (burned)
April 27, 1813

Plattsburg
Sept. 11, 1814

Illinois Territory

Lake Michigan

Mississippi R.

Ft. Detroit
Aug. 16, 1812

Thames
Oct. 5, 1813

Lake Ontario

Sackett's Harbor
May 28–29, 1813

Vermont

New Hamp.

River Raisin
Jan. 22, 1813

Lake Erie Presque Isle

New York

Hudson R.

Mass.

Boston

Ft. Dearborn
Aug. 15, 1812

Lake Erie
Sept. 10, 1813

Conn.

Pennsylvania

Rhode Island

Ft. Meigs
May 1–9 and
July 24, 1813

Ft. Stephenson
Aug. 2, 1813

Ft. McHenry
Sept. 14, 1814

New Jersey

Indiana Territory

Ohio

Cincinnati

Bladensburg
Aug. 24, 1814

Baltimore

Delaware

Ohio R.

Virginia

Maryland

Unorganized Territory

Kentucky

Washington, D.C. (burned)
Aug. 24, 1814

Tennessee

North Carolina

Tallasahatchee
Nov. 3, 1813

South Carolina

ATLANTIC OCEAN

Talladega
Nov. 9, 1813

Georgia

Mississippi Territory

Horseshoe Bend
March 27, 1814

Louisiana

Fort Mims
Aug. 30, 1813

Pensacola

New Orleans

New Orleans
Jan. 8, 1815

Florida (Spanish)

Gulf of Mexico

Major battles

✳ British/Indian victory

✳ U.S. victory

WAR OF 1812 CAMPAIGNS Battles from Lake Michigan to Lake Champlain were inconclusive, as was Washington's fall in 1814. Victories over southern tribes prepared the way for further Indian removal, and the 1815 triumph at New Orleans helped bolster America's military reputation.

"The acquisition of Canada this year as far as the neighborhood of Quebec will be a mere matter of marching."

—THOMAS JEFFERSON'S OPINION ON CONQUERING CANADA IN 1812

FORT NIAGARA Strategically located between lakes Erie and Ontario, Niagara —pictured in an 1821 woodcut—was a jumping off point for an American invasion of Canada in the War of 1812.

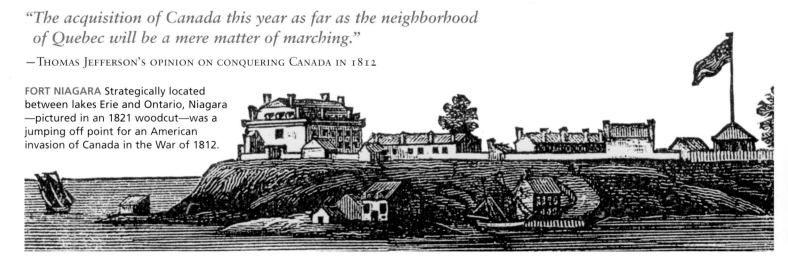

Indian nations, who looked to British Canada for support. Westerners had influential "war hawks" representing them in Congress, and they successfully maneuvered President James Madison's government into declaring war on June 18, 1812.

United States attacks Canada

The American population was eight million, Canada's only 300,000. The Americans had 7,000 Regular troops, compared with 10,000 British Regulars in Canada, but there were 700,000 militia in the United States and only 86,000 Canadian militia.

American military movements aimed to take over Upper Canada, the region between Lake Huron and Lake Ontario. These attempts failed, as the British captured Detroit and 2,000 American soldiers in August 1812. Other offensives failed, and moves on Montreal also were driven back.

One outstanding American officer was young Colonel Winfield Scott, who led well-disciplined Regulars into action. Scott was soon promoted to general. Most American commanders performed ineptly in 1813, and militia forces often refused to cross into Canada—stating that their terms of enlistment only required them to fight on American soil. A notable victory in the Canadian theater was scored by Commodore Oliver H. Perry in September. "We have met the enemy, and they are ours," was Perry's oft-quoted report of the Battle of Lake Erie. He captured a British squadron and established American control of water routes, compelling the British to abandon Detroit.

Another victory destroyed a British-Indian force in Upper Canada that October at the Battle of the Thames, won by General William Henry Harrison.

1814 northern campaigns

The war tipped back and forth, with the British usually prevailing. When Napoleon was defeated in the spring of 1814, the British sent reinforcements to North America. The United States renewed its offensives on the Niagara frontier, with Winfield Scott's Regulars winning the Battle of Chippewa in July. Later that month, Scott joined forces with General Jacob Brown to take on General Gordon Drummond at Lundy's Lane. In a five-hour fight to a draw, Lundy's Lane was one of the war's bloodiest battles, costing both sides more than 850 casualties. Scott was wounded twice.

British power threatened northern New York State's Lake Champlain region in September, as 11,000 Regulars and a war fleet moved on Plattsburgh. The fleet was defeated by Commandant Thomas Macdonough in a hard-fought battle on September 11, stopping the invasion force, which withdrew to Canada.

OLIVER HAZARD PERRY (1785–1819) Perry became a national hero after winning the September 1813 naval Battle of Lake Erie. He died of yellow fever after serving in the Mediterranean and Caribbean.

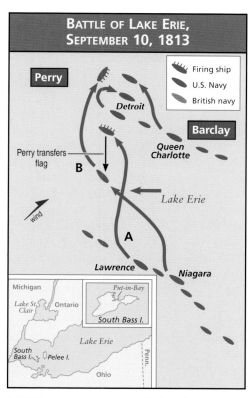

BATTLE OF LAKE ERIE, SEPTEMBER 10, 1813

Firing ship
U.S. Navy
British navy

Perry · Detroit · Barclay · Queen Charlotte · Perry transfers flag · B · Lake Erie · wind · A · Lawrence · Niagara

Michigan · Lake St. Clair · Ontario · Put-in-Bay · South Bass I. · South Bass I. · Pelee I. · Lake Erie · Penn. · Ohio

BATTLE OF LAKE ERIE Perry built a fleet on Lake Erie to oppose British captain Robert H. Barclay, veteran of the 1805 Battle of Trafalgar. Battered by the longer-range guns of Barclay's *Detroit*, Perry abandoned his flagship, *Lawrence*, and fought on from the *Niagara* until Barclay lowered his flag in surrender.

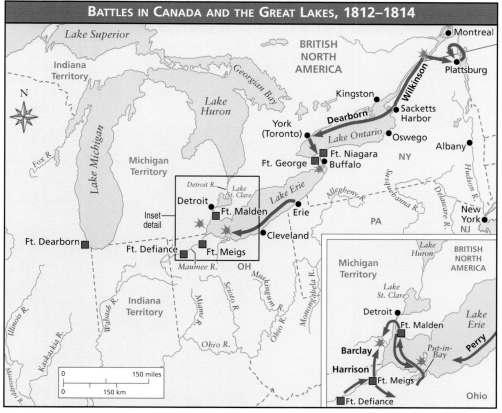

BATTLES IN CANADA AND THE GREAT LAKES, 1812–1814

Lake Superior · Indiana Territory · BRITISH NORTH AMERICA · Montreal · Georgian Bay · Lake Huron · Kingston · Plattsburg · Wilkinson · Dearborn · Sacketts Harbor · York (Toronto) · Lake Ontario · Oswego · Albany · Ft. Niagara · NY · Ft. George · Buffalo · Fox R. · Lake Michigan · Michigan Territory · Detroit R. · Lake St. Clare · Detroit · Ft. Malden · Erie · Lake Erie · Allegheny R. · Susquehanna R. · Hudson R. · Delaware R. · New York · NJ · Inset detail · Cleveland · PA · Ft. Dearborn · Ft. Defiance · Ft. Meigs · Maumee R. · OH · Scioto R. · Muskingum R. · Monongahela R. · Lake Huron · BRITISH NORTH AMERICA · Michigan Territory · Lake St. Clare · Detroit · Ft. Malden · Lake Erie · Put-in-Bay · Perry · Illinois R. · Wabash R. · Miami R. · Barclay · Harrison · Ft. Meigs · Kaskaskia R. · Indiana Territory · Ohio R. · Ft. Defiance · Ohio · Mississippi R. · N · 0 150 miles · 0 150 km

WAR OF 1812 NORTHERN CAMPAIGNS In August 1812 Fort Detroit fell to the British, who also won at nearby Frenchtown. Other engagements were indecisive, but in September 1814 Macdonough took firm control of Lake Champlain for the United States, blocking a major British offensive, which included veterans of Wellington's army that had defeated Napoleon.

WASHINGTON BURNED, VICTORY AT NEW ORLEANS

Adding to the hostilities, Creek Indians in the South rose up and fought American troops under General Andrew Jackson, who decisively defeated them in March 1814 at the Battle of Horseshoe Bend, Alabama. On the mid-Atlantic coast, there was ignominious defeat for the United States, as British seaborne raiders struck again and again at undefended coastal towns. The American navy could do little to stop powerful British warships from leading expeditions against ports in northern Maine and along the Chesapeake shores. These strikes led to an invasion in August, when 4,000 veteran Regulars landed to attack Washington, D.C. Only raw militia were on hand to meet the enemy, who swept them aside at the Battle of Bladensburg on August 24. The British entered Washington and burned most of the public buildings, including the White House, in retaliation for Americans burning York, Ontario.

They next sailed against Baltimore, but American forces were organized and halted the invasion. The Royal Navy tried unsuccessfully to blast the harbor's Fort McHenry into submission with a 25-hour bombardment. Watching from a British ship, where he was a prisoner, Francis Scott Key was moved to see the fort hold out. He wrote the verses of "The Star-Spangled Banner," which eventually became the national anthem. Failing at McHenry and Baltimore, the British expedition withdrew, and the war's land action moved south.

United States warships win victories

At first, the American navy did well, as British naval strength was concentrated against France. In August 1812, the frigate *Constitution* defeated the British frigate *Guerrière* and earned the name "Old Ironsides." That October, the *United States*, commanded by Barbary Wars naval hero Stephen Decatur, captured the *Macedonia*. In December, the *Constitution* next took the *Java*. By the end of the war, the *Constitution* had defeated four British warships and taken eight merchant vessels, adding to America's growing naval reputation.

Yet the navy was not strong or new. Most of its 18 vessels had been built before 1802, and there was a shortage in naval ordnance. British naval units tightly blockaded the United States coastline. Elusive American privateers slipped in and out, but few other vessels were able to pass the blockade. American trade was virtually stopped by the war.

For all Great Britain's naval prowess, American privateers inflicted severe damage on her merchant fleet, taking at least 1,000 vessels. This loss, and the defeat of Napoleon, persuaded the British to negotiate peace with the United States.

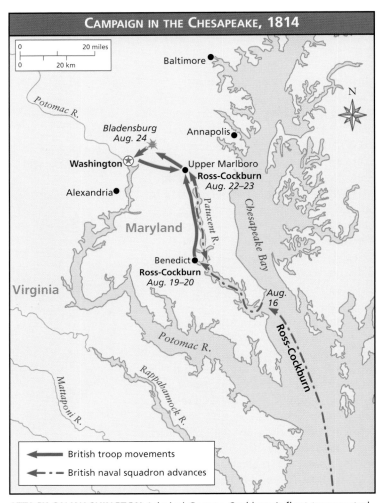

CAMPAIGN IN THE CHESAPEAKE, 1814

ATTACK ON WASHINGTON Admiral George Cockburn's fleet transported British troops under General Robert Ross into the Chesapeake for a campaign that defeated the Americans at Bladensburg on August 24, 1814, and captured the capital. The British burned public buildings and withdrew the following day.

BATTLE OF NORTH POINT The 5th Maryland Infantry Regiment in action at North Point, Maryland, a British victory during the campaign against Baltimore in September 1814. The battle cost the British their commanding general, Robert Ross, killed by a sharpshooter.

CONSTITUTION VS. GUERRIÈRE American frigates won 12 of 16 early War of 1812 sea battles. One victory was by Captain Isaac Hull's *Constitution* over the *Guerrière* on August 19, 1812.

WAR OF 1812 AT SEA In some early naval engagements, the United States triumphed, but for much of the war, American warships were blockaded by overwhelming British sea power. In January 1815, Barbary Wars hero Stephen Decatur was captured with his frigate, *President*.

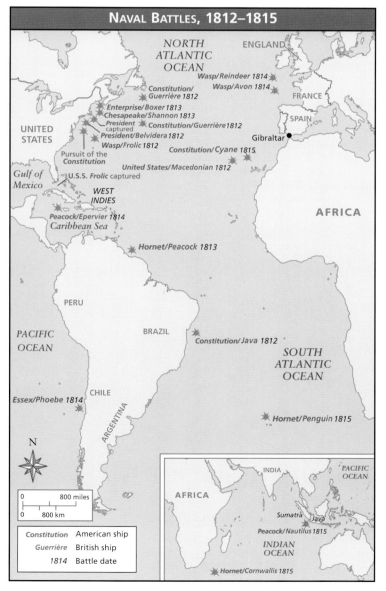

NAVAL BATTLES, 1812–1815

Constitution	American ship
Guerrière	British ship
1814	Battle date

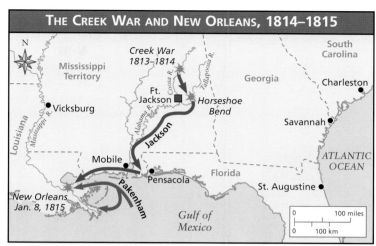

THE CREEK WAR AND NEW ORLEANS, 1814–1815

JACKSON SAVES NEW ORLEANS After defeating the Creeks, General Andrew Jackson marched to the Gulf Coast to repulse a British invasion of West Florida, Mississippi Territory, and Louisiana. In this last campaign of the war, Jackson won enduring fame as the hero of New Orleans.

The Battle of New Orleans

A powerful expeditionary force under General Sir Edward Pakenham struck at New Orleans on January 8, 1815. The combatants were unaware the Treaty of Ghent had been signed on December 24—also known as the Peace of Christmas Eve.

Pakenham's 14,000 troops and a fleet of 60 warships were met by General Andrew Jackson's 5,000 entrenched defenders, made up of Regulars, Tennessee frontiersmen, local militia, Choctaw, free blacks, and artillerymen from pirate Jean Lafitte's nearby lair. When an attempt to turn the Americans out of their position failed, the British sent about 5,000 men on frontal assaults that were smashed by murderous defensive fire. More than 2,000 British fell in just over an hour of fighting, and Pakenham, himself, was killed rallying his men. Jackson suffered fewer than 70 casualties. This last campaign of the War of 1812 ended on January 25, as the British reembarked and sailed away. In all, the war cost the lives of 1,877 Americans, with another 4,000 wounded.

"Oh, the Yankee boys for fighting are the dandy-O!"

—FROM A POPULAR 1812 SONG, "THE CONSTITUTION AND THE GUERRIÈRE," CELEBRATING THE AMERICAN VICTORY

DEATH OF PAKENHAM In January 1815, massed ranks of British frontally attack Andrew Jackson's defenses at New Orleans, only to be repelled with heavy loss. British general Edward Pakenham lies mortally wounded.

7: DESTROYING RESISTANCE OF EASTERN NATIONS

CREEK CHIEFS TAKE SIDES William MacIntosh, left, of mixed Scottish and Creek blood, fought alongside Jackson at Horseshoe Bend; in 1825, he was murdered by other Creeks. Menauway, right, an Upper Creek, was a Red Stick chieftain who fought in the battle.

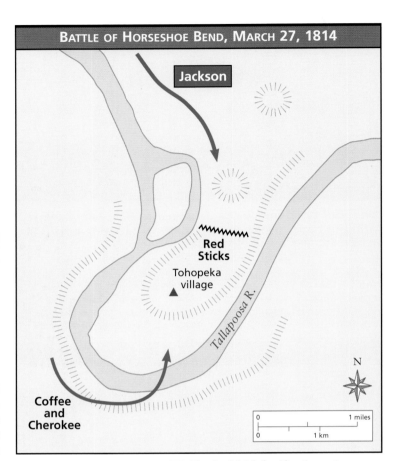

BATTLE OF HORSESHOE BEND, MARCH 27, 1814

THE BATTLE OF HORSESHOE BEND The Red Stick fortifications at Horseshoe Bend—protecting Tohopeka Village—withstood bombardments by Jackson's six-pounder artillery. General John Coffee of the Tennessee militia made a diversion with troops and Cherokee allies, setting fire to the village. Jackson then assaulted the distracted defenders, most of whom fought to the death.

The Creek tribes of Alabama and Georgia—the Southwest —were divided into the Upper Creeks and Lower Creeks. The Lower Creeks were mainly farmers, living like whites, with whom they intermarried. The Upper Creeks largely rejected white culture and opposed American incursions into their country. Civil strife developed among the Creeks, with a warlike anti-American faction taking the name Red Sticks. Early in 1813, conservative Creeks executed several Red Sticks found guilty of killing white settlers. The executions caused a deep rift in the nation, with Red Sticks attacking their own council headquarters.

Struggle in the Southwest

That spring, with the War of 1812 under way, the Red Sticks struck at white settlements in Alabama and Georgia. Led by William Weatherford, a mixed-blood known as Red Eagle, they captured Fort Mims on the Alabama River in August, killing almost all 550 whites there.

Tennessee militia general Andrew Jackson campaigned against the Red Sticks, leading militia and Creek and Cherokee allies. Jackson's force sometimes numbered 5,000 men. Other military expeditions, from Mississippi and Georgia, operated against the Red Sticks, whose villages were burned. Jackson defeated 700 Red Sticks at Talladega, killing 300. William Weatherford then withdrew to the Talapoosa River, where he fortified a peninsula at Horseshoe Bend, in Alabama. Jackson followed, but in January 1814 was defeated in several engagements. Reinforced, he attacked the Red Stick stronghold on March 27, 1814, in the Battle of Horseshoe Bend. More than 500 Creek men and many women and children died, while Jackson's force lost 70 dead and more than 200 wounded. Weatherford escaped, but later surrendered.

The resulting Treaty of Fort Jackson cost both hostile and peaceful Creeks 23 million acres, ceded to the states.

WEATHERFORD SURRENDERS Creek chief William Weatherford, also called Red Eagle, survived the destruction of the Red Sticks at Horseshoe Bend and escaped, but with his followers defeated, he eventually surrendered to Jackson. Weatherford was permitted to return to his people.

TERRITORY OF THE CREEK CONFEDERACY, 1800s

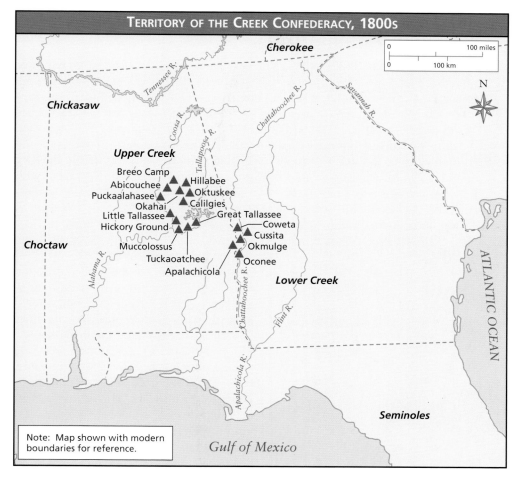

Note: Map shown with modern boundaries for reference.

CREEK CONFEDERACY In 1813, the Upper and Lower Creek communities began a civil war that became a conflict with whites. The anti-assimilation faction known as Red Sticks mustered 4,000 warriors to oppose white settlers and the army, who had Lower Creek, Cherokee, and Choctaw allies.

BLACK HAWK (1776–1838) Furious when his nation ceded 50 million acres to the government, Sauk and Fox chief Black Hawk fought alongside the British in the War of 1812. In the late 1820s, his failed attempts to organize new resistance ended in defeat and captivity.

The Black Hawk War

The Sauk and Foxes of northern Illinois had accepted a treaty in 1804 that ceded their lands to the United States. They were allowed to remain until the late 1820s, when settlers begin to appear, and the government arranged with leading chief Keokuk to move the Sauk and Foxes into Iowa. A group led by the elderly Chief Black Hawk refused to go.

In the summer of 1831, Illinois militia mustered against Black Hawk, who fled with 1,000 people across the Mississippi. After a hungry winter, Black Hawk's folk returned to their homeland to reap corn they had planted before leaving. Now, more than 1,600 troops marched against these "hostiles," but Black Hawk again led his people to safety. American troops pursued them, bringing on small engagements that cost a few lives and created the false impression that Black Hawk had large numbers of hostile warriors on the loose. In fact, some of his men did join with other renegades to attack settlers, killing more than 200.

Army Regulars struck the Sauk and Foxes at the Battle of Wisconsin Heights, which cost 70 Indian lives, only one American. As Black Hawk's people again fled, they offered several times to surrender. The whites refused to accept, however, and attacked in the Battle of Bad Axe River, as the Indians were trying to cross the Mississippi. With an armed steamboat firing grape shot, 300 Sauk and Foxes were slaughtered, half of them women and children. The Americans suffered only 27 dead and wounded. Black Hawk got away, but later was captured and imprisoned.

This was the last Indian war fought east of the Mississippi.

"I will lead you on one condition — that before we go we kill our old men and our wives and our children to save them from lingering death by starvation."

— CHIEF KEOKUK, EXHORTING HIS SAC PEOPLE NOT TO JOIN IN THE 1832 BLACK HAWK WAR

MERCILESS DESTRUCTION After refusing to accept the surrender of Black Hawk's people, white troops massacred them as they attempted to flee across the Bad Axe River in mid-1832. Only 150 of the original 1,000 followers of Black Hawk survived their year-long ordeal.

FLORIDA'S SEMINOLES ARE DEFEATED IN THREE WARS

For decades before 1817, relations had been uneasy between southern whites and the Seminoles of southern Georgia and Spanish-owned Florida. Seminoles were accused of raiding white settlements and farms and of harboring escaped slaves. "Seminole" was a name given by whites to a mix of Lower Creek peoples and smaller tribes such as the Apalachicola and Tallahassee. They often intermarried with African-Americans who had fled the plantations. Southern slave owners demanded the federal government send a military expedition against the Seminoles. In early 1816, General Edmund P. Gaines led troops against Negro Fort, on the Apalachicola River, a stronghold built by runaway slaves. The fort was taken, with almost 300 blacks dying in the assault. The First Seminole War soon began, as both sides launched border raids.

The First Seminole War

Major David Twiggs was sent to burn the Seminole village of Fowltown in November, and soon afterwards Seminoles massacred a boatload of soldiers and their families on the Apalachicola, killing 46 persons.

Fresh from victories in the Creek War and against the British at New Orleans, General Andrew Jackson invaded Spanish Florida early in 1818. He led 4,000 men, including Creek fighters. Jackson was unofficially given a free hand by the federal government to attack and capture Spanish posts during his campaign to destroy Seminole and free black villages. In late May, he took Pensacola, meeting little Spanish resistance, and installed an American government. After Jackson departed Florida that spring, America negotiated the purchase of Florida for $5 million. Jackson became territorial

FLORIDA IN 1839 This military map, commissioned by General Zachary Taylor, shows the "seat of war" of the Seminole conflicts, involving major clashes in central Florida and at Lake Okeechobee, right.

REGULARS IN FLORIDA The steamy climate and dense, swampy wilderness of Seminole country brought hardship to these United States Regulars, who wear light "undress," or "fatigue" uniforms and soft leather forage caps as they consult with a Seminole scout.

BATTLE OF LAKE OKEECHOBEE
In the largest engagement of the Second Seminole War, Indian and African-American fighters attack a blockhouse at Lake Okeechobee. Outnumbered, they melted into the swamps after the battle and kept on fighting.

"They could not capture me, except under a white flag. They cannot hold me, except with a chain."

—OSCEOLA, CAPTURED IN VIOLATION OF A FLAG OF TRUCE

governor of Florida and was positioned to become president in 1828. A major legacy of his presidency would be the Indian Removal Bill that forced native peoples west of the Mississippi.

The Second and Third Seminole Wars

In the 1830s, the federal government determined to send the Seminoles beyond the Mississippi along with most other native peoples. Treaties were signed, but Seminoles often claimed they were coerced. Violence broke out in 1835, and the Seminoles turned to war chief Osceola.

Born in 1804 of a Creek mother, Osceola either had a Creek father or was the son of a Scottish trader who married his mother. In December 1835, his warriors wiped out 108 soldiers under Major Francis L. Dade, and the native fighters controlled most of Florida. More United States troops invaded, and Seminoles fought bitterly. A force of 1,100 soldiers led by General Gaines was besieged for eight days at the Withlacooche River before being relieved. Government forces kept pressure on the Seminoles, but Osceola led effective hit-and-run attacks as he took on General Thomas Jesup and Colonel Zachary Taylor.

Jesup tricked Osceola into meeting under a flag of truce in October 1837, then arrested him. Osceola died in captivity that January. The Seminoles fought on. In a major engagement at Lake Okeechobee in December, Taylor led 1,000 troops against 400 Seminoles in an inconclusive battle that cost 24 Seminole and 150 American casualties. Jesup campaigned successfully in 1837, capturing 2,000 Seminoles and killing 300. Fighting continued until 1842, followed by negotiations that allowed Florida's few hundred remaining Seminoles to live in peace.

A Third Seminole War began in December 1855, as the military routed out the last survivors in a series of sharp clashes. By 1858, most Seminoles were removed to the West.

OSCEOLA (ca. 1804–1838) Known as Billy Powell during childhood, Osceola spurned his allegedly mixed blood and asserted he was a full-blooded Muskogee. Opposing the government's removal policy, Osceola became a war chief who led guerrilla resistance against 8,000 soldiers until he was captured. He died at Fort Moultrie, Charleston.

8: TEXAS WRESTS INDEPENDENCE FROM MEXICO

"Great God, Sue, the Mexicans are inside our walls!"

—CAPTAIN ALMERON DICKENSON TO HIS WIFE ON THE MORNING OF MARCH 6, 1836, AS SANTA ANNA'S MEN STORMED THE ALAMO

THE ALAMO'S FALL Tennessee's Davy Crockett, in coonskin cap, fights alongside Texas rebels defending the Alamo against Mexican troops, whose sudden attack in predawn darkness quickly penetrated the defenses.

Americans had been allowed to settle in Texas, Mexico's northeastern state, since 1820. By 1835, they were a numerous and influential portion of the population. Then Mexican president and commanding general, Antonio Lopéz de Santa Anna, began consolidating his power in the federal government at Mexico City, threatening Texan liberties under Mexico's 1824 constitution. A coalition of Hispanic Texans—*Tejanos*—and American immigrants formed to defy Santa Anna.

Known as "Texians," insurgents led by Colonel William B. Travis occupied the port town of Anáhuac in June, and in October others drove off 100 Mexican cavalrymen from Gonzales. The Texans held a convention to establish a state government loyal to the federal system, but with its own army, militia, and even a navy. From October to early December they laid siege to 600 Mexican troops at San Antonio, commanded by General Martin de Cos. The city fell to a Texian assault that cost the attackers 30 casualties and Cos 150.

The Texas army commander was immigrant Sam Houston, a former Regular officer who had been a representative to Congress from Tennessee as well as governor of the state. In January of 1836 Houston found himself facing an invasion by General Santa Anna and upwards of 6,000 government troops.

The fall of the Alamo

Santa Anna first moved against 200 Texans occupying the Alamo, a former mission at San Antonio. The defenders, led by Colonel Travis, included newly arrived volunteers from the United States, one of whom

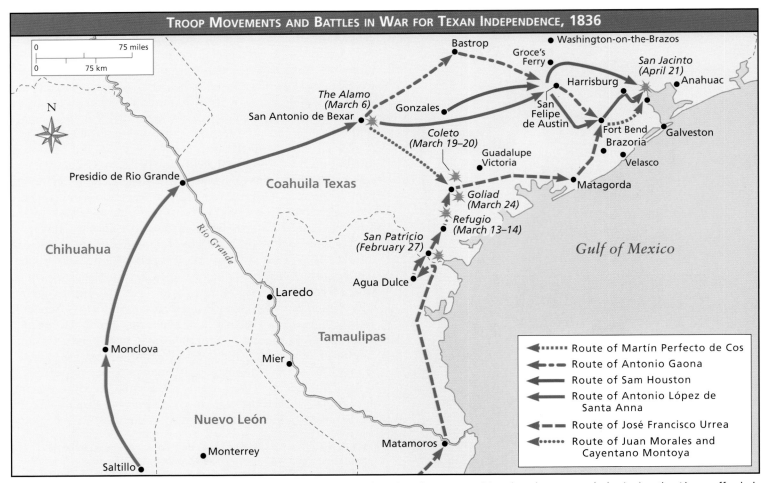

TROOP MOVEMENTS AND BATTLES IN WAR FOR TEXAN INDEPENDENCE, 1836

- ◄┈┈┈ Route of Martín Perfecto de Cos
- ◄┅┅ Route of Antonio Gaona
- ◄— Route of Sam Houston
- ◄— Route of Antonio López de Santa Anna
- ◄┅┅ Route of José Francisco Urrea
- ◄┈┈┈ Route of Juan Morales and Cayentano Montoya

TEXAS WAR OF INDEPENDENCE Early in 1836, General Santa Anna moved against the Texas uprising, but the two weeks besieging the Alamo afforded time for the rebels to gather their forces. To pursue the retreating Texans, Santa Anna divided his army, only to be defeated at San Jacinto in April.

was famous frontiersman and Tennessee politician Davy Crockett.

On February 23, Santa Anna laid siege to the Alamo, but soon grew impatient at being delayed while Houston organized an army to oppose him. On March 6, Santa Anna sent 1,800 troops in an assault that overran the defenders in an hour and a half, killing all of them. Several, including Crockett, were allegedly captured alive and summarily executed. The Mexicans suffered 600 casualties.

The Battle of San Jacinto

In mid-March, Mexican troops captured approximately 400 Texans stationed at Goliad. The prisoners were executed, although about 25 escaped.

Meanwhile, Houston's 900-man army withdrew eastward in the face of Santa Anna's advance. The provisional Texas government was also on the run, and Santa Anna divided his forces to go after both the delegates and Houston at the same time. Santa Anna closed in on Houston at the San Jacinto River, west of Anáhuac in mid-April.

Expecting the rebels would wait to be attacked by the superior force of 1,400 government troops, the overconfident Santa Anna did not bother to post sentries to guard his camp. On April 21, Houston attacked, taking the Mexicans by surprise. Shouting the battle cries "Remember the

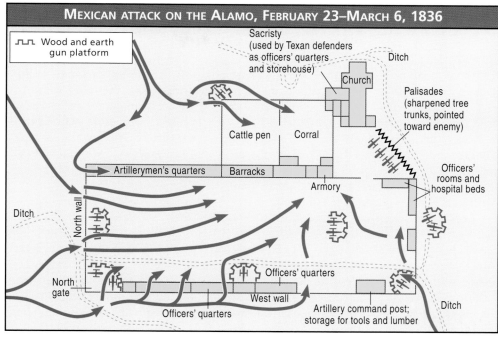

MEXICAN ATTACK ON THE ALAMO, FEBRUARY 23–MARCH 6, 1836

THE BATTLE OF THE ALAMO Santa Anna's 1,800 attackers burst through the fortifications under cover of darkness and overran the 200 Texas defenders, who made a final stand at the interior walls.

Alamo!" and "Remember Goliad!" the Texans wiped out Santa Anna's army, killing 630 and capturing more than 700. Texan losses were fewer than 40. Santa Anna, himself, was captured and forced to sign peace terms that required all Mexican troops to withdraw south of the Rio Grande.

The Republic of Texas was founded that December, with Houston as its first president. The central government at Mexico City refused to accept Santa Anna's treaty, however, and a state of open hostility between Mexico and Texas lasted for another decade.

BATTLE OF SAN JACINTO, APRIL 21, 1836

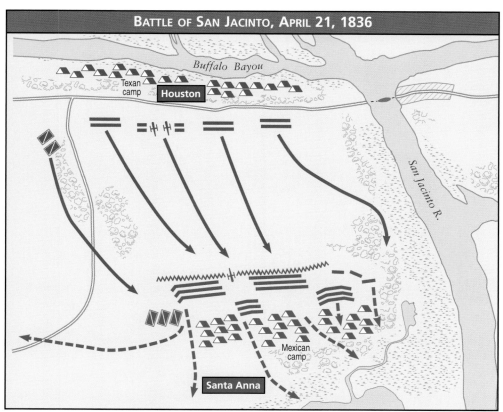

SAM HOUSTON (1793–1863) A Virginian, Houston fought in the War of 1812 and with Jackson against the Red Sticks before becoming a lawyer in Tennessee. He settled in Texas in 1832, soon to command the rebel army. Houston was the republic's first president and later a senator and governor for the State of Texas.

THE BATTLE OF SAN JACINTO Outnumbered Texians at San Jacinto in April 1836 had their backs to Buffalo Bayou, expecting Santa Anna to attack. Instead, Sam Houston led them in an assault—undetected, though the charge crossed a mile of open ground—to catch the Mexicans during afternoon siesta.

9: TEXAS AND THE MEXICAN-AMERICAN WAR

The conflict between Mexico and the Republic of Texas, which Mexico still claimed, was an excuse for America to start a war of western conquest. In 1845, Congress admitted Texas to the Union, in keeping with the doctrine of Manifest Destiny, which asserted a God-given American right to occupy the continent.

Ever since Texan independence from Mexico in 1836, there had been border clashes between the republic and Mexican forces. Both claimed disputed territory north of the Rio Grande, a region the American Congress intended to include in the Texas annexation of 1845. When President James K. Polk proposed that Mexico sell its northern regions, including California, to the United States, Mexicans were insulted and infuriated.

In January 1846, Polk sent General Zachary Taylor to occupy the disputed territory. In response, Mexican cavalry clashed with Taylor, creating the pretext for war Polk wanted.

The Mexican War begins

In April, before war was officially declared, General Mariano Arista crossed the Rio Grande to lay siege to American-held Fort Texas, across the river from Matamoros. Taylor immediately moved to break the siege. Though outnumbered, his 4,300 troops won the first battles—at Palo Alto on May 8, and Resaca de la Palma on the 9th. Fast-moving American field artillery was key to the victories. At Resaca, Arista tried to fight defensively, but Taylor's "flying artillery," as it was known, cooperated closely with infantry and dragoons to overwhelm the Mexicans. Taylor had approximately 140 casualties; Mexican losses were estimated to be more than 500. The United States Military Academy at West Point had turned out hundreds of well-trained artillerymen and military engineers who gave the Americans a crucial advantage.

Congress overwhelmingly supported the declaration of war on May 13, 1846, authorizing 50,000 volunteers to augment

MEXICAN-AMERICAN WAR, 1846–48

THE MEXICAN-AMERICAN WAR
Fighting began in early 1846 with a cavalry skirmish near the Rio Grande, as Taylor moved into disputed territory. He won several victories, climaxing with Buena Vista in February 1847. American army and naval forces invaded California, meeting little resistance, while Scott captured Mexico City after a series of bitterly fought battles.

American military advances
- ◄━·━·━ Alexander Doniphan
- ◄·············· Stephen Kearny
- ◄━ ━ ━ Winfield Scott
- ◄═════ John Sloat
- ◄─·─·─·─ Robert F. Stockton
- ◄━━━ Zachary Taylor
- ◄━··━··━ John Wool

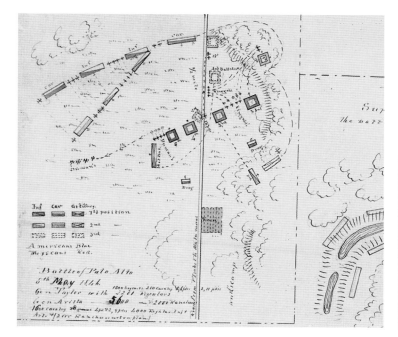

THE BATTLE OF PALO ALTO Troop deployments and movements on May 8, 1846, are shown in this detail from a sketch map by New Orleans mapmaker Charles R. Glynn, who was at the battle; Taylor's forces are depicted in blue, and General Arista's Mexican troops are shown in red.

BOMBARDMENT OF VERACRUZ After an amphibious landing, Scott's campaign against Mexico City began with the siege of Gulf Coast city Veracruz in mid-March 1847. Protected by strong walls, the defenders endured two weeks of bombardment by heavy guns before surrendering.

the Regular Army's 7,300 men. The army would eventually increase to 32,000, joined by 72,000 volunteers and militia. Mexico's 32,000 men were poorly equipped and scattered over a vast region. Americans could pick and choose targets to attack. An expedition from Fort Leavenworth under General Stephen Kearny invaded Mexican territory, moving westward through lightly defended New Mexico and into California. To the south, Taylor was reinforced to 6,500 troops as he advanced on Monterrey, in northeastern Mexico. Starting on September 21, General Pedro de Ampudia's 10,000 men fought for four days to defend the city house by house. Ampudia withdrew on the 25th, under an armistice.

That December, General Antonio Lopéz de Santa Anna advanced northward with 15,000 troops. A decisive battle took place at Buena Vista on February 22, against Taylor's 5,000 men. This bitter fight, which cost Santa Anna 3,400 casualties, was again largely won by American artillery. Taylor suffered 660 killed and wounded.

Scott's coastal assault

In early March, the United States Navy carried the 10,000 troops of War of 1812 hero, General Winfield Scott, on an amphibious invasion of Mexico's Gulf Coast. Virtually unopposed, the Americans struck at several seaports, finally landing and laying siege to Veracruz on the 9th.

Scott faced 4,000 enemy troops with scores of cannon in powerfully fortified Veracruz. Firing heavy naval guns that had been brought ashore, and aided by the firepower of a warship, Scott forced the city's surrender on March 27. Mexican casualties were estimated at between 200 and 1,000, while the Americans lost fewer than 70 men. Scott's invasion and Taylor's operations in northern Mexico were the two main campaigns of the war.

"Give them a little more grape, Captain."

—TAYLOR'S ORDER AT BUENA VISTA TO CAPTAIN BRAXTON BRAGG, WHOSE CANNON FIRED INTO THE WAVERING MEXICAN LINES, FORCING A RETREAT

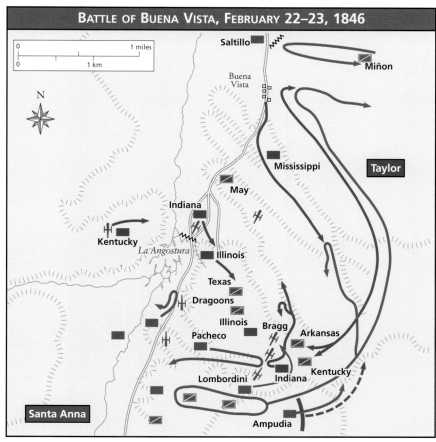

BATTLE OF BUENA VISTA, FEBRUARY 22–23, 1846

TAYLOR TRIUMPHS OVER SANTA ANNA In one of the great victories of the war, Taylor's 5,000 men defeated Santa Anna's 15,000; "flying artillery" moved quickly to repulse Mexican attacks, and inflicted heavy casualties. A Mexican flanking maneuver was defeated by hastily assembled Americans at Buena Vista.

CALIFORNIA FALLS, AND SCOTT MOVES ON MEXICO CITY

CALIFORNIA GUERRILLA Squadrons of *Californio* volunteer lancers fought fiercely against the American invaders, but there was little organized resistance to oppose United States army and navy invasions.

While Winfield Scott and Zachary Taylor fought pitched battles against Mexican armies, vast tracts of territory to the north were falling under United States control with little bloodshed. General Stephen Kearny's 1,700-man expedition in New Mexico took the important trading center of Santa Fe in mid-August 1846. Kearny had 300 dragoons, a battalion of Mormon infantry, and a force of Missouri volunteers led by their colonel, Alexander Doniphan. By now, American naval forces had moved against the California coastal cities of Los Angeles, San Francisco, and Monterey, landing marines and sailors to occupy them.

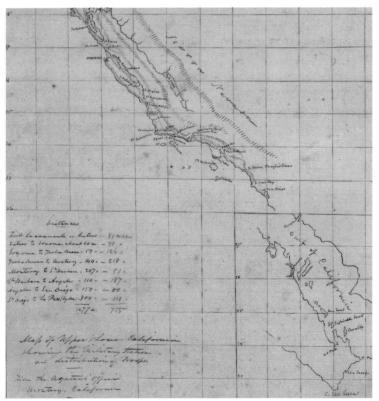

THE CALIFORNIA COAST IN 1847 Towns, military stations, and the distribution of American troops are shown on this period map of California population centers.

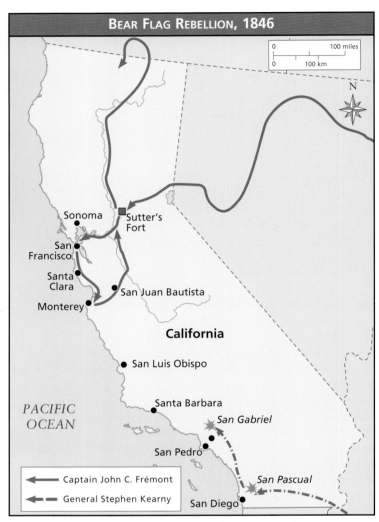

BEAR FLAG REBELLION, 1846

Captain John C. Frémont
General Stephen Kearny

THE CALIFORNIA CAMPAIGN A company of dragoons under Kearny approached from the southeast, joining with a navy expedition to win battles at San Pasqual and San Gabriel. American adventurers supporting Frémont carried a flag with a bear image, calling their insurrection the "Bear Flag Rebellion."

Conquering New Mexico and California

Kearny detached 1,000 troops under Doniphan, who swung south to capture El Paso at the end of December and Chihuahua in March. Meanwhile, Kearny and 100 dragoons pushed on to California, where he met a few Regulars under Captain John C. Frémont of the army's topographical corps. Kearny joined Commodore Robert F. Stockton, whose naval squadron had occupied Los Angeles. Another squadron, under Commodore John D. Sloat, had landed marines at Monterey.

Although Kearny was the highest ranking field officer, he conceded command to Stockton as the Mexicans rose to fight the American occupation and recaptured Los Angeles. Kearny and Stockton won a battle at San Pasqual, in December. On January 8, 1847, they defeated 450 *Californio* mounted volunteers and government cavalry at the Battle of San Gabriel, east of Los Angeles. The Mexicans tried to regroup to defend the city, but Stockton and Kearny overran them at the Battle of the Rio Los Angeles. The Americans retook Los Angeles on January 10, ending the California campaign, which had caused few casualties on either side. The Southwest, from the Pacific to the Mississippi, was now under American control.

Scott drives on Mexico City

With the capture in March 1847 of Veracruz, Mexico's main port on the Gulf of Mexico, General Scott could supply his offensive toward Mexico City, more than 200 miles to the west. First he renewed the struggle with Santa Anna, who had 12,000 men at Cerro Gordo, on the national road to Mexico City.

Scott led his 8,500 men toward Cerro Gordo, while West Point officers, Captain Robert E. Lee and Lieutenant P.G.T. Beauregard, conducted reconnaissance to find routes around the enemy flanks. The officers were successful, and the Americans advanced undetected until they attacked on April 17. The surprise assaults forced the Mexicans to retreat, but the battle resumed the following day and included fierce hand-to-hand fighting. Scott drove Santa Anna from Cerro Gordo, inflicting 1,100 Mexican casualties and capturing more than 3,000. American losses were 417, including 64 killed. Scott continued his advance.

The direct route on the national road to the capital city was strongly defended at mountain passes, where Santa Anna prepared to mount stubborn resistance. In the mountains, American artillery would not be as effective as in open battle. Scott, always reluctant to risk unnecessary casualties, faced a decision when his army reached Puebla at the end of May. Here, the road forked, with one branch

RUGGED HILL COUNTRY American troops, artillery, and supply wagons toiled through difficult terrain with rocky slopes and deep ravines to attack the dug-in Mexicans in the Battle of Cerro Gordo during Scott's 1847 Mexico City campaign.

leading through Mexican defenses protecting the city, and the other going southward for 50 miles before turning toward Mexico City.

Scott waited two months for his depleted army to be reinforced with fresh troops to 10,000 men, then took the longer route to outflank Santa Anna's defenses.

ZACHARY TAYLOR'S SOLDIERS
On the march in northern Mexico, an American infantry lieutenant in a dark blue frock coat stands before a mounted dragoon, while a column of infantry wearing light blue fatigue jackets and trousers passes by.

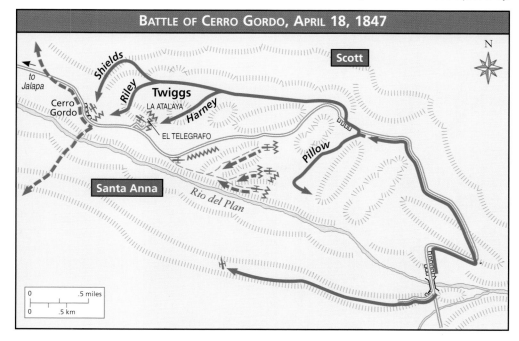

BATTLE OF CERRO GORDO, APRIL 18, 1847

Shields
to Jalapa
Riley
Cerro Gordo
Twiggs
LA ATALAYA
Harney
EL TELEGRAFO
Scott
Pillow
Santa Anna
Rio del Plan
N
0   .5 miles
0   .5 km

"I . . . to this day regard the war . . . as one of the most unjust ever waged by a stronger against a weaker nation."

—Ulysses S. Grant, Memoirs, on the Mexican War

A RELENTLESS ADVANCE Strong Mexican positions on high ground at Cerro Gordo blocked Scott's march on Mexico City in April 1847. Finding obscure trails that flanked the Mexican left, the Americans attacked unexpectedly and gained an advantage that won the field after two days of hard fighting.

65

CHAPULTEPEC AND THE CAPTURE OF MEXICO CITY

Winfield Scott's rapid march on Mexico City proceeded without setback, and his advance guard was within striking distance by August 12. Santa Anna had concentrated 20,000 troops to defend the capital, but many were kept in defensive positions, unable to enter the fight unless it came to them.

The first American attack was at Contreras on August 19, which ended with the rout of General Gabriel Valencia's forces. Scott took possession of strategic road intersections and immediately advanced on enemy positions at the convent of Churubusco, which he assaulted frontally. For three hours the defenders fought fiercely until they ran out of ammunition and were compelled to surrender. Scott lost almost 1,000 men, while Santa Anna lost eight generals among his 3,000 casualties.

The Mexican captives included 72 Irish-Americans who had deserted the American army and joined the Mexican army. Mainly Roman Catholic immigrants, these men believed the mostly Protestant American troops were out to destroy Catholicism in Mexico. They formed the *San Patricio* (Saint Patrick) battalion and fought valorously for Mexico at Monterrey and Buena Vista. Those captured at Churubusco were tried as deserters and condemned to death. Scott regretfully authorized their execu-

tions, which took place in September. On September 8, an unexpected major battle developed at Molino del Rey, southwest of Mexico City. Scott had sent 3,000 men to raid a suspected cannon foundry there, but Santa Anna was present with 12,000 troops.

Molino del Rey and Chapultepec
The Americans suffered severe losses and withdrew. Once again, field artillery swung into action and blasted Mexican

THE STRUGGLE FOR MEXICO'S CAPITAL
On September 13, American troops stormed lofty Chapultepec Castle, the cornerstone of Mexico City's western defenses, then immediately fought their way into the city, which surrendered on the 14th.

"Brave rifles, veterans, you have been baptized in fire and blood and have come out steel!"

—Scott, to the Regiment of Mounted Rifles after Contreras, August 20, 1847

BATTLE OF CHAPULTEPEC AND TAKING MEXICO CITY, SEPTEMBER 12–14, 1847

(Map showing: Worth, San Cosme Causeway, Mexico City, Cathedral, Palace, Citadel, Chapultepec, Quitman, Worth, Casa de Mata, Pillow, Yacubaya Causeway, Scott, Molino del Rey, Quitman, San Antonio Causeway, Twigg, Tacubaya; scale 1 mile / 1 km; N compass)

THE BATTLE OF CHURUBUSCO
Hard-fighting Mexican defenders in this key battle were let down by their supply department, which delivered the wrong caliber ammunition to the front lines. After victory, Scott expected Santa Anna to surrender, but the Mexico City campaign was not yet over.

"I believe if we planted our batteries in Hell the damned Yankees would take them from us."

—GENERAL ANTONIO LOPÉZ DE SANTA ANNA

A TRIUMPHANT GENERAL Shown here reviewing his infantry, artillery, and cavalry parading on Mexico City's Grand Plaza, Winfield Scott was the first American commander to raise the Stars and Stripes over a captured foreign capital.

defenses and gun batteries. American infantry and marine assaults brought on hand-to-hand fighting, and after two hours the Mexicans retreated. They lost 2,000 killed and wounded and 685 captured. American losses were almost 800.

Five days later, on September 13, Scott attacked Santa Anna's lines, which were anchored on Chapultepec Castle, a hilltop fort and site of the Mexican military academy. Almost 8,000 Mexicans defended the castle and its approaches. Scott sent 7,000 men forward, supported by an artillery barrage that devastated the castle and its defenders. Using scaling ladders, and under heavy musket fire, the Americans climbed the walls and broke into the castle's compound to win the victory. This defeat cost Santa Anna another 1,800 men, while Scott's army lost 450. Santa Anna fled, leaving Mexico City undefended. The city's leaders surrendered on the 14th, and for the first time, the Stars and Stripes flew over a captured foreign capital.

The aftermath
The Mexican-American War cost 17,435 American casualties, including 1,733 battle deaths and 11,550 deaths from illness and other causes.

The American military had proved extremely effective, and its professional officer corps was hailed for its ability and gallantry. Decorated officers such as Lee and Beauregard continued with prominent careers in the peacetime army, and others such as Ulysses S. Grant and Jefferson Davis entered private life. In 1861, Mexican War veterans would again meet on the battlefield, some still in the uniform of the United States, others in that of the newly formed Confederacy.

TREATY OF GUADALUPE HIDALGO
THE UNITED STATES SPANS A CONTINENT

The end of the Mexican-American War came with the Treaty of Guadalupe Hidalgo on February 2, 1848. The United States acquired approximately 40 percent of Mexico, which also officially ceded Texas. The Americans paid Mexico $15 million for territory that became the states of California, New Mexico, Colorado, Utah, Nevada, and Arizona. The United States also assumed $3 million worth of claims reputedly owed by Mexico to American citizens. With possession of vast new lands, difficult questions arose for Americans. The most pressing of all was whether those lands would permit expansion of the South's "peculiar institution": slavery.

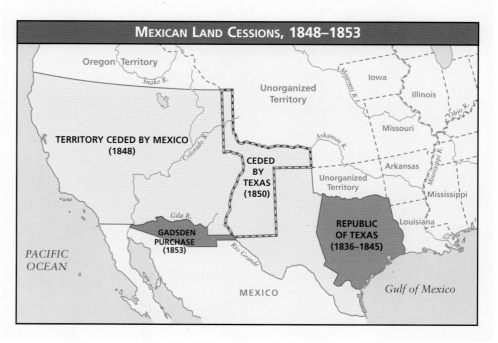

MEXICAN LAND CESSIONS, 1848–1853

10: A SMALL ARMY ON A VAST FRONTIER

The United States Army was reduced after the War of 1812 to seven infantry regiments and four artillery battalions. As decades passed and the nation grew in size and population, more troops were needed to guard northern borders, man coastal fortifications under construction, and garrison forts on the frontiers. The army gradually increased in size.

There were schools for the army's several branches. Officers, many specializing in engineering, studied at the United States Military Academy at West Point, New York, founded in 1802. The Artillery School at Fortress Monroe, Virginia, was established in 1823; the Infantry School, at Jefferson Barracks, St. Louis, in 1826. The Cavalry School opened at the Carlisle Barracks in Carlisle, Pennsylvania, in 1835, and officers were sent to Europe to study cavalry systems. West Pointers were also trained in cavalry tactics. In 1845, the United States Naval Academy was founded at Annapolis, Maryland.

The Indian lands

With the removal of most native peoples into the West, the government established a vast trans-Mississippi region known as the "Indian Frontier." This unofficial

demarcation between Indian nations and whites was expected to guarantee peaceful coexistence, but any plans for stability were dashed by the new territorial acquisitions of the Mexican War and the 1849 discovery of gold in California.

Thousands of emigrants, often termed "overlanders," journeyed westward on the Oregon Trail to California or to the Pacific Northwest. Another major migration followed the Mormon Trail to Utah's Salt Lake Valley, where the Church of Jesus Christ of Latter Day Saints—"Mormons"—were

FORT SNELLING, MINNESOTA Established in 1819, this was among the earliest forts on the new frontier; work on the massive fortifications began in 1840.

OVERLAND ROUTES In the mid-19th century, the emigrants' long wagon train journey across the West usually began in Missouri, from St. Joseph, Independence, or Fort Leavenworth, Kansas. Military posts were constructed at strategic points to patrol portions of the wagon roads, such as the 2,400-mile Oregon Trail from Independence to Oregon City.

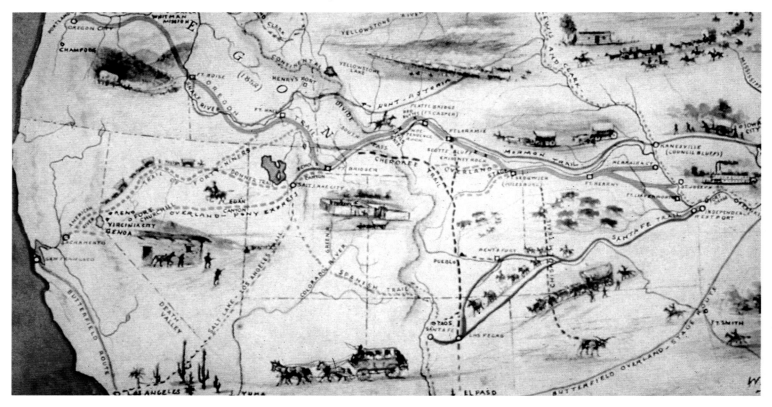

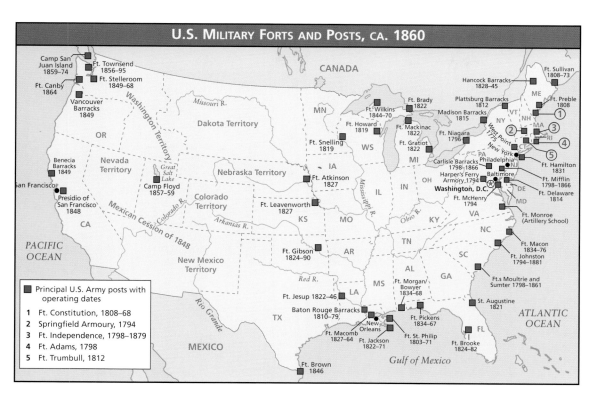

U.S. MILITARY FORTS AND POSTS, CA. 1860

Principal U.S. Army posts with operating dates
1 Ft. Constitution, 1808–68
2 Springfield Armoury, 1794
3 Ft. Independence, 1798–1879
4 Ft. Adams, 1798
5 Ft. Trumbull, 1812

FORTRESSES, BARRACKS, AND OUTPOSTS By 1860, the 17,000-man United States Army was scattered far and wide across the continent, with most active duty troops serving in the trans-Mississippi West and in border and coastal forts.

"Many were told . . . they would have nothing to do but to ride on horseback, over the country, to explore the western prairies and forests . . . in delightful and inspiring occupations."

— JAMES HILDRETH, FIRST REGIMENT OF DRAGOONS, ON 1830S RECRUITING PROMISES

creating settlements and farms. Army posts kept watch on the Indian nations along these routes, but as the wagon trains multiplied in number and size, this brought trouble with the warriors. Wagon trains muddied rivers, their hunters shot the game, and the wide swaths trampled down by wagons and herds of livestock intruded on native lands. Further, the overlanders' herds were a temptation to young warriors, who often ran off horses or slaughtered cattle. Armed clashes between overlanders and native peoples made parts of "Indian country" hostile to pioneers, requiring cavalry patrols to keep the peace.

Dragoons and cavalry

In 1832, the First Regiment of Dragoons was established to serve on the frontier. Dragoons were originally infantry who rode to the battlefield, but usually fought on foot. By the Mexican War, a second dragoon regiment and the Regiment of Mounted Rifles had been formed.

Although most of the army was disbanded after the war, the dragoons and Mounted Rifles remained in service, needed to enforce the law on the frontier, protect wagon trains, and pursue renegade Indians, who rode fast ponies. Two more mounted units, later officially designated as the 1st and 2nd Regiments of United States Cavalry, were created in 1855.

Until the Civil War, there were no major battles between cavalry and Indians in the West, but frontier soldiering was a hard and lonely life. Each regiment was stretched thinly across the trans-Mississippi West, stationed in remote forts from which troopers patrolled an enormous and often inhospitable territory.

WEST POINT IN WAR AND PEACE

Many early graduates of the United States Military Academy at West Point saw their first action fighting Indians. West Point provided most of the Regular Army's junior officers for the wars against Creeks and Seminoles. Later, West Pointers fought with distinction in the Mexican War. Among them were Robert E. Lee, Ulysses S. Grant, Thomas J. Jackson, George H. Thomas, P.G.T. Beauregard, Albert Sydney Johnston, Joseph E. Johnston, William T. Sherman, and Jefferson Davis.

In peacetime, West Pointers were America's best civil and military engineers, their service essential to the growing new country. West Pointers led expeditions to explore and map unknown regions and gather scientific information, including geological samples. Major civil engineering tasks also were directed by West Point engineers, including railroad construction, flood control, and harbor improvements. Army and navy officers sat on the Board of Engineers for Fortifications, whose master plans were carried out by the Army Corps of Engineers. Coastal fortifications were massive military engineering projects that often went on for decades.

AN IDYLLIC VIEW OF WEST POINT IN 1834 This painting looks south, down the Hudson River, which is guarded by the United States Military Academy, on the bluff at right.

AMERICAN NAVAL POWER GAINS PROMINENCE

After 1820, Congress was reluctant to bear the expense of a navy, so when the economy turned down, ship-building and maintenance programs often were neglected. Yet, the navy proved invaluable to the nation, both for Indian conflicts and on the high seas.

During recurring hostilities with the Seminoles and free blacks in Florida, flat-bottomed naval barges and shallow dugouts carrying marines penetrated the watery wilderness to supply army troops and make amphibious landings.

Naval operations against the Creeks extended to southern Alabama and Georgia, where steamers plied the rivers, keeping open supply routes and lines of communication.

Pirates, slavers, and the U.S. Navy

Through the first decades of the 19th Century, the United States Navy fought to suppress pirates, who committed thousands of ruthless attacks on merchant vessels. The West India Squadron, created in 1822, aggressively attacked pirate lairs infesting the uncharted bays and lagoons of the Caribbean and Gulf of Mexico.

Enduring fierce close-quarter combat as well as storms, tropical heat, and fevers, American sailors and marines had crushed piracy by the early 1830s.

Another duty that fell to the navy was battling the outlawed slave trade. From 1820–1860, a squadron known as the African Slave Trade Patrol operated off West Africa and South America, and especially in waters near Cuba, where thousands of slaves were illegally disembarked every year. The patrol captured more than 100 slave ships.

COMBATING THE SLAVE TRADE From the 1820s to the 1860s, the American navy's West India Squadron operated from the coast of Africa to the Caribbean, patrolling the sea lanes and investigating remote coves to find slave ships and stop this internationally prohibited trade. This detail from an 1820s map shows the Caribbean region.

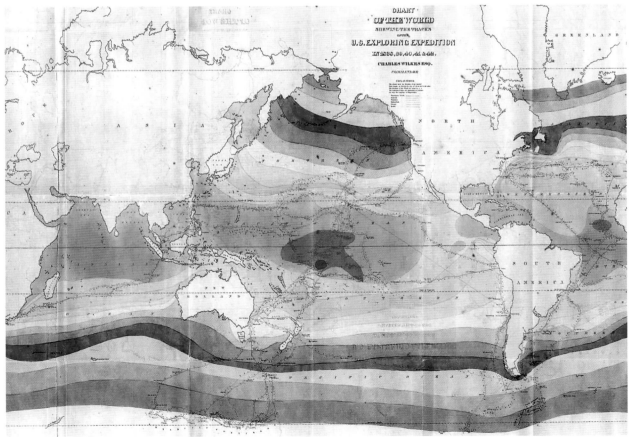

NAVAL EXPLORATION The United States Exploring Expedition of 1838–1842 was known as the Wilkes Expedition after its leader, navy lieutenant Charles Wilkes. The expedition surveyed 200 Pacific islands, mapped 800 miles of the Oregon coast and more than 1,500 miles of Antarctica.

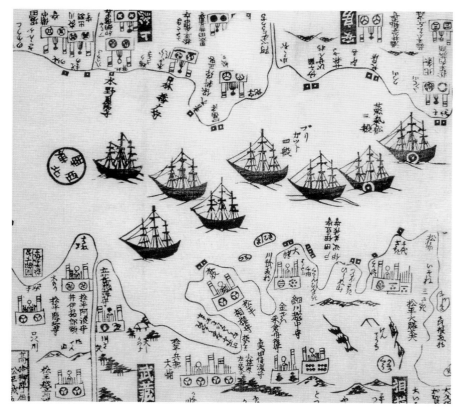

THE AMERICAN NAVY IN TOKYO HARBOR This 19th Century Japanese print depicts the 1854 arrival in Tokyo Bay of Commodore Perry's fleet of black-painted, steam-powered warships. Perry had first visited Tokyo a year earlier. His 1854 exhibition of American military power strongly impressed Japan's rulers.

In the Mexican War, naval operations were crucial to victory. Warships blockaded Mexico's coasts, seized seaports, and landed troops. The city of Veracruz fell after the navy put ashore 12,000 troops in a single day, preparing for the march on Mexico City itself. In California, marines and sailors from the Pacific Squadron landed at Monterey, San Francisco, and San Diego, joining with small army detachments to win that campaign decisively.

Foreign ports and domestic duties

Naval officers commanded cruises of exploration that journeyed as far as the South Pacific and Antarctica. The navy also conducted an ongoing coastal survey of American waters, its ships touching the Oregon coast and strengthening United States claims to the region.

Intrepid commanders sailed to ports where the American flag had seldom been seen. In the early 1850s, Commodore Matthew C. Perry led a powerful fleet of seven modern steamers into Tokyo's harbor and convinced the Japanese to sign a treaty that opened their ports to American vessels and trade.

In 1859, one particular land assignment for a company of marines turned out to be pivotal to the nation's future. They were called upon to put down John Brown's anti-slavery insurrection at Harpers Ferry, Virginia. The marines, who stormed Brown's position, were under the command of United States Army colonel Robert E. Lee.

THE ACADEMY AND NAVAL INVENTION

The need to standardize the navy and train young officers led to the 1845 founding of the United States Naval Academy at Annapolis, Maryland. Prominent senior officers, such as Commodore Matthew Perry, advised the navy on a choice of curriculum for midshipmen at the Academy.

In these years, progressive naval leadership adopted the most modern warship designs, as the service changed from sail to steam. Modern firepower, too, was developed, as naval yard ordnance officer John A. B. Dahlgren invented hard-hitting new naval artillery. By 1861, the United States Navy had some of the finest, best-armed warships afloat, with a pool of well-trained and educated officers to command them. Within a year, American innovation would create ironclad gunboats and change the face of naval warfare forever.

THE CIVIL WAR YEARS The Naval Academy at Annapolis ca. 1860

Musketry to Minié Rifles

The 19th Century ushered in the "industrialization of warfare," as fast-developing mechanics and manufacturing produced more powerful firearms and ammunition, better explosives, and the first warships propelled by steam.

During the War of 1812, steamboat inventor Robert Fulton built the first steam warship for the United States, but the conflict ended before she saw action. Steam propulsion options further improved after 1829, when the screw propeller was invented to replace the less maneuverable paddle wheel, which was vulnerable to gunfire. The conservative naval establishment at the time was slow to incorporate these innovations into warships.

The early 1800s saw the first use of the exploding canister shell, invented by Henry Shrapnel, a British artillery officer. Until the Civil War, however, little practical improvement was made to field and naval artillery.

The flintlock mechanism, which had served for well over 150 years, remained in use through the 1840s. Meanwhile, experiments in improved firearm ignition led to the adoption of the reliable percussion cap mechanism in the 1850s.

Bullets had to tightly fit the rifle barrel's grooves to ensure a proper seal. Therefore, ramming home a rifle bullet was slower than loading a smoothbore musket ball. In 1849, the conical Minié ball was invented in France. The base of the Minié expanded when fired and fit into the grooves of the rifle barrel. The Minié ball was smaller than the barrel bore, so it could be muzzle-loaded as quickly as a smoothbore musket. The Minié rifled musket with percussion lock soon became the principal firearm of the American military—a truly formidable weapon.

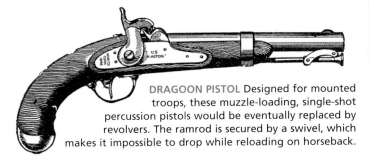

DRAGOON PISTOL Designed for mounted troops, these muzzle-loading, single-shot percussion pistols would be eventually replaced by revolvers. The ramrod is secured by a swivel, which makes it impossible to drop while reloading on horseback.

COASTAL FORTIFICATIONS The United States built a number of massive masonry forts to protect important harbors with large-caliber muzzle-loading cannon housed in tiers of casemates. Mounted on "barbette" carriages, these huge guns could be loaded, traversed and fired in relative safety.

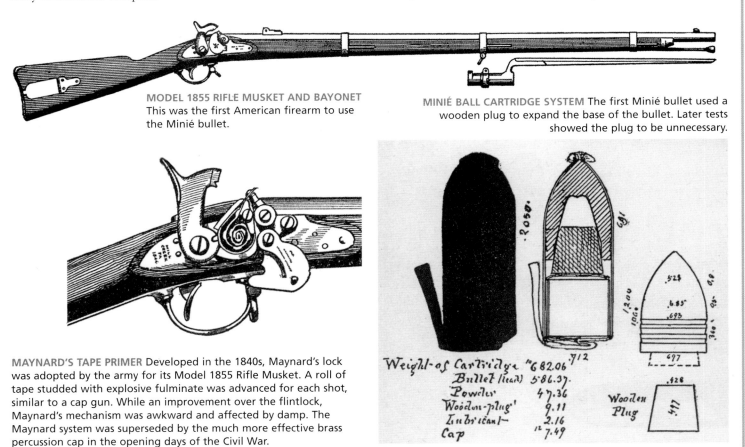

MODEL 1855 RIFLE MUSKET AND BAYONET This was the first American firearm to use the Minié bullet.

MINIÉ BALL CARTRIDGE SYSTEM The first Minié bullet used a wooden plug to expand the base of the bullet. Later tests showed the plug to be unnecessary.

MAYNARD'S TAPE PRIMER Developed in the 1840s, Maynard's lock was adopted by the army for its Model 1855 Rifle Musket. A roll of tape studded with explosive fulminate was advanced for each shot, similar to a cap gun. While an improvement over the flintlock, Maynard's mechanism was awkward and affected by damp. The Maynard system was superseded by the much more effective brass percussion cap in the opening days of the Civil War.

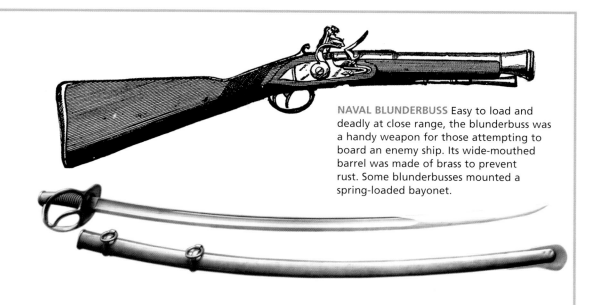

NAVAL BLUNDERBUSS Easy to load and deadly at close range, the blunderbuss was a handy weapon for those attempting to board an enemy ship. Its wide-mouthed barrel was made of brass to prevent rust. Some blunderbusses mounted a spring-loaded bayonet.

SAILOR WITH BOARDING PIKE During the War of 1812 few ships were sunk in battle—they either surrendered or were captured by boarding. Crews were armed with cutlasses, pikes, and pistols. Boarders stormed onto the enemy ship, hoping to overwhelm the opposing crew in a short but sometimes vicious hand-to-hand fight.

"LONG TOM" NAVAL CANNON ca. 1812 Sized to fire a 12- or 18-pound ball, these cannons were accurate and powerful additions to a frigate's armament, able to engage enemy ships at longer range than most naval guns.

MODEL 1840 CAVALRY SABER AND STEEL SCABBARD Issued to dragoon and cavalry regiments, this somewhat heavy sword was called "Old Wristbreaker" by soldiers who used it. Although this model saw extensive service into the early years of the Civil War, the lighter Model 1860 Light Cavalry saber was much more popular.

STEAM FRIGATE USS *MISSISSIPPI* Side paddle-wheel steam warships suffered from several problems. The paddle wheels did not perform well in heavy seas, putting considerable strain on the steam engine. Also, the room needed for boilers, steam engine, and driving mechanisms limited the number of cannon carried broadside; and coal bunkers took up room needed for crew and stores.

BIRDS EYE VIEW
OF THE
SEAT OF WAR AROUND RICHMOND

SHOWING THE BATTLE ON CHICKAHOMINY RIVER 29 JUNE 1862

PART THREE

The War Between the States

THE UNITED STATES WAS PROSPEROUS IN 1860, with thousands of immigrants arriving each year, eager to build new lives in booming cities or on the frontier, and there was plenty of open land to accommodate the most ambitious and restless of her people.

The nation grew in confidence and pride, protected by the oceans from foreign aggression and profiting from international trade as her bounty, natural resources, and manufactures found ready markets around the world. Yet success and growth also bred hostility between regions of the country. The North's population now far surpassed that of the South, which felt its political power diminishing. At the same time, bitter hatred of Southern slavery on the part of Northern Abolitionists fed the flames of intersectional strife.

The question seethed in Congress, in newspapers, and in parlors: how were the lands of the West to be settled and governed? As slave states or free? Slavery and states' rights were hotly contested issues, causing resentments that became hatreds, and hatreds became open enmity. By April 1861, Northerners and Southerners were ready to wage war— civil war—to resolve their differences. Few could imagine the violence of the storm being called down upon the nation.

The Civil War cost the lives of more than 620,000 Americans, who died in battle or from disease. Slavery, too, died in the war. Thenceforth, though at such a price, the United States truly was the land of the free.

Longstreet's attack at Gettysburg (detail), by A.R. Waud, 1863

11: FREE STATES, SLAVE STATES, AND DISUNION

Tensions between North and South mounted through the 1850s, with anti-slavery forces opposing slavery's expansion to new states or territories. Pro-slavery advocates asserted that each state had the right to determine its own laws without Federal interference. In the halls of Congress and on the frontiers, antagonism deepened, poisoning relations between North and South. In both regions, there was increased talk of dissolving the Union if matters became worse.

The United States Regular Army, scattered across the West and along the borders, numbered fewer than 17,000, although it had a disproportionately large officer corps—structured to build up a fighting force rapidly in case of war. The navy was small, but many of its 90 vessels were modern, steam-powered warships. Inadequate military spending, however, left the best vessels languishing in dry dock, needing maintenance. In both services, hundreds of Southern officers were prepared to resign if their states actually seceded from the Union.

The population of the free states grew rapidly in this decade, as millions of immigrants came from Europe to flood the North's fast-growing cities. Settlers moved westward to populate the newly formed states that made up the "Border Section"— Michigan, Minnesota, Iowa, and Wisconsin. By 1860, the free states had 22.3 million people, the slave states 9.1 million, including 3.6 million slaves or free blacks. The North had 85 percent of the nation's

A SLAVE FAMILY Several generations of African-American slaves are seen on a plantation in South Carolina shortly before the Civil War.

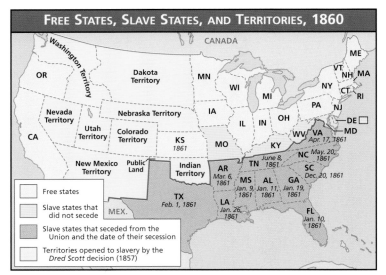

FREE STATES, SLAVE STATES, AND TERRITORIES, 1860

Free states

Slave states that did not secede

Slave states that seceded from the Union and the date of their secession

Territories opened to slavery by the *Dred Scott* decision (1857)

DIVIDING LINES OF WAR Militarily, the Confederacy held a central defensive position while the Union had to send its forces long distances around the South's perimeter.

TROUBLES IN THE WEST

"Bleeding Kansas," 1855–1859

In the mid-1850s, two opposing political forces moved into Kansas Territory, a candidate for entry into the Union. One force was composed of eastern abolitionists sworn to making Kansas a free state. The other was mainly Missouri border toughs, who were just as resolved to make Kansas a slave state.

Armed conflict was frequent and often deadly, as pro-slavery forces destroyed anti-slavery communities, and fanatic abolitionists such as John Brown murdered pro-slavery settlers. The federal government could do little to prevent this civil war, fought by privately armed battalions that earned their territory the name "Bleeding Kansas."

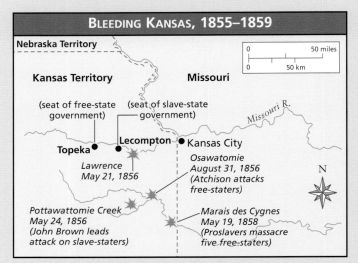

BLEEDING KANSAS, 1855–1859

OPEN WARFARE Civil war raged in Kansas Territory after the 1854 Kansas-Nebraska Act left residents to decide on slavery's status. Pro- and anti-slavery parties established territorial capitals, and abolitionist fanatic John Brown took part in several murders.

Utah War of 1857–1859

Also known as the "Mormon Expedition," this brief confrontation brought 2,500 Regular Army troops into Utah Territory to enforce Federal authority over the members of the Church of Jesus Christ of Latter Day Saints, the "Mormons." In July 1857, President James Buchanan ordered soldiers to Salt Lake City to remove appointed governor Brigham Young and install a new governor more pliable to Washington.

In previous decades, the Mormons had endured expulsion and violent bigotry, so they feared the worst. At first they resisted, capturing and destroying two wagon trains with military supplies. This thwarted the expedition, which was stranded and hungry throughout the winter of 1857–1858. In February 1858, the new governor persuaded the officials at Salt Lake City to accept his authority and avoid bloodshed. Thus, the "Mormon War" ended peacefully.

This strife was a prelude to the Civil War.

industry, while the South depended on cash-crop farming—cotton, rice, and tobacco—grown on large-scale plantations.

Sectional and political strife

Attempts at compromise failed again and again to resolve differences over slavery. The powerful Democratic Party was riven by these differences, and in 1854 anti-slavery Democrats broke off to form the Republican Party. They unsuccessfully ran John C. Frémont in the 1856 presidential election, won by Democrat James Buchanan, whose party became even more split over slavery and states' rights.

Buchanan's administration was not able to prevent open clashes between pro- and anti-slavery forces, especially in Kansas Territory, where armed companies fought over its admission to the Union as a free or slave state. Buchanan was ineffectual in pacifying Kansas, but he asserted Federal authority in Utah Territory. There, Mormon settlers were accused of open hostility to the national government. In mid-1857, Buchanan sent troops into Utah in a show of force that was also meant to warn Southern extremists that the government would not permit rebellion.

Many Americans saw military action as the inevitable solution to the nation's problems. Almost everywhere, the militia system was revived, reinvigorated as it had not been since the War of 1812. Smartly uniformed young men drilled on village greens and paraded down city streets, learning how to maneuver by company and regiment and to use their muskets. War fever heightened, and increasingly contentious politics fired the national disposition for a bloodletting.

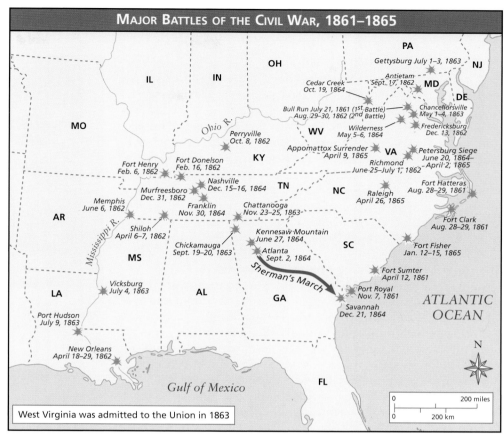

MAJOR BATTLES OF THE CIVIL WAR, 1861–1865

Gettysburg July 1–3, 1863
Antietam Sept. 17, 1862
Cedar Creek Oct. 19, 1864
Bull Run July 21, 1861 (1st Battle) Aug. 29–30, 1862 (2nd Battle)
Chancellorsville May 1–4, 1863
Fredericksburg Dec. 13, 1862
Perryville Oct. 8, 1862
Wilderness May 5–6, 1864
Appomattox Surrender April 9, 1865
Petersburg Siege June 20, 1864– April 2, 1865
Fort Henry Feb. 6, 1862
Fort Donelson Feb. 16, 1862
Richmond June 25–July 1, 1862
Nashville Dec. 15–16, 1864
Fort Hatteras Aug. 28–29, 1861
Murfreesboro Dec. 31, 1862
Raleigh April 26, 1865
Memphis June 6, 1862
Franklin Nov. 30, 1864
Chattanooga Nov. 23–25, 1863
Fort Clark Aug. 28–29, 1861
Shiloh April 6–7, 1862
Kennesaw Mountain June 27, 1864
Chickamauga Sept. 19–20, 1863
Atlanta Sept. 2, 1864
Fort Fisher Jan. 12–15, 1865
Sherman's March
Fort Sumter April 12, 1861
Vicksburg July 4, 1863
Port Royal Nov. 7, 1861
Port Hudson July 9, 1863
Savannah Dec. 21, 1864
New Orleans April 18–29, 1862
Gulf of Mexico
ATLANTIC OCEAN

West Virginia was admitted to the Union in 1863

0 — 200 miles
0 — 200 km

PATHS OF WAR The Civil War's heaviest fighting took place around Richmond and Washington, and crucial campaigns were fought for control of the Mississippi River and Tennessee.

Lincoln elected, South secedes

The Republicans ran Abraham Lincoln of Illinois in the presidential election of 1860. Lincoln's opposition to extending slavery to the territories put him squarely at odds with pro-slavery Southerners. When he was elected, emergency state conventions were called to decide on leaving the Union.

In December, South Carolina adopted an ordinance of secession, followed in January by Mississippi, Florida, Alabama, Georgia, and Louisiana. Texas seceded in February.

The Confederate States of America was immediately established with former West Pointer and secretary of war, Jefferson Davis, as president. As one of his first acts, President Davis demanded that Federal troops evacuate all their posts in the Confederacy, including Fort Sumter in Charleston harbor. Without hesitation, President Lincoln refused. The stage was set for war.

"There were early morning drills, before breakfast, forenoon drills, afternoon drills and night drills, besides guard mounting and dress parades."

—A SOLDIER IN THE UNION "IRON BRIGADE OF THE WEST," COMPOSED OF WISCONSIN, INDIANA, AND MICHIGAN TROOPS

UNION INFANTRY DRILL As their band plays a tune, lower right, the thousand men of a volunteer regiment parade with fixed bayonets at their encampment near Washington in 1861.

THE GUNS OF CIVIL WAR OPEN AT FORT SUMTER

The government will not assail you," Lincoln told secessionists in his inaugural address on March 4, 1861. "You can have no conflict without being yourselves the aggressors." Although the Federal government would not begin the conflict, Lincoln refused to surrender Federal forts and installations in the Confederacy. In turn, secessionists were determined to take over all symbols of Federal authority, such as Fort Sumter at the entry to Charleston Bay. Occupying an artificial island, Sumter was commanded by Major Robert Anderson of Kentucky, whose 84 officers and men were low on ammunition and food. The C.S.A.'s President Davis intended to force Sumter's surrender before Lincoln could resupply and reinforce the fort.

The American Civil War begins at Fort Sumter

On April 12, Confederate batteries under the command of General P.G.T. Beauregard opened fire on Sumter. Thousands of Charlestonians gathered to watch the bombardment, which continued through the night, lasting 34 hours. When fires broke out in the fort, Anderson had to give up. The only death occurred on April 14, when a Union soldier was killed by the explosion of a Federal cannon that had been firing in salute as the flag was lowered.

Four more states soon seceded from the Union: Virginia, Arkansas, North Carolina, and Tennessee. Davis called for 82,000 volunteers to serve in the Army of the Confederate States of America, and Lincoln called for 75,000 three-month volunteers for the United States. Hundreds of militia companies that had been drilling in the North and South rallied to their cause.

Battle of First Bull Run

On July 16, Union general Irvin McDowell advanced into Virginia with 30,000 men, moving toward a Confederate force of 20,000 under Beauregard. A second Confederate force of 9,500, led by General Joseph E. Johnston, began boarding railroad trains to journey 50 miles to Manassas Junction, where McDowell and Beauregard would meet. Both armies were green, although many officers were West Point graduates who had served in the Mexican War.

Also heading for Manassas were hundreds of civilians from Washington, expecting to enjoy watching the battle.

On July 21, McDowell attacked, driving Beauregard's troops back, although not those of Virginian Thomas J. Jackson, whose regiment stopped the Federal

FIRST BATTLE OF BULL RUN On July 21, McDowell attacked, attempting to crush Beauregard's left flank, which began to crumble until Johnston arrived with reinforcements and counterattacked, throwing much of the Union army into headlong retreat.

GUNS OF SECESSION The palmetto flag of seceded South Carolina flutters above the state artillery pounding Fort Sumter in Charleston harbor on April 12, 1861, beginning the Civil War.

"There stands Jackson like a stone wall"

— CONFEDERATE GENERAL BARNARD BEE, AT THE FIRST BATTLE OF BULL RUN; BEE WAS KILLED SOON AFTERWARDS

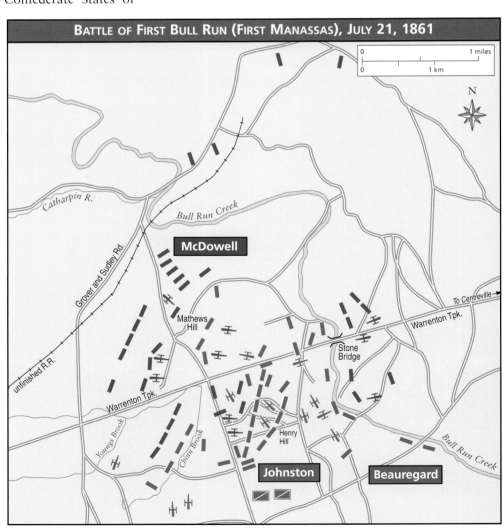

BATTLE OF FIRST BULL RUN (FIRST MANASSAS), JULY 21, 1861

Catharpin R.

Bull Run Creek

McDowell

Grover and Sudley Rd.

To Centreville →

Warrenton Tpk.

Mathews Hill

Stone Bridge

unfinished R.R.

Warrenton Tpk.

Youngs Brook

Chinn Brook

Henry Hill

Bull Run Creek

Johnston

Beauregard

THE "ANACONDA PLAN" This 1861 cartoon depicts Scott's plan to crush the Confederacy as a great snake; Scott, however, saw control of the Mississippi as key to the strategy.

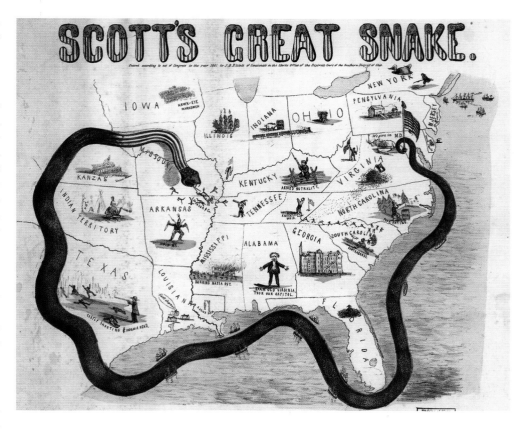

assault. Jackson earned the enduring name "Stonewall" that day, and the tide turned against McDowell. When Johnston's railborne reinforcements arrived, the Union troops began to retreat, and then panic suddenly swept them. Many rushed headlong from the field and were caught up with the terrified civilians mobbing roads and bridges, everyone fleeing desperately for the safety of Washington.

McClellan takes command

The Union was dismayed, the Confederacy overjoyed, with this first battle, known to the North as Bull Run and to the South as Manassas. Both sides were shocked by the unexpectedly heavy casualties: an estimated 3,334 Union and 1,982 Confederate.

Now General George B. McClellan took charge of the Union army, and General Johnston became commander of Confederate forces in northern Virginia. As the armies trained, the Union suffered yet another embarrassing defeat, this time at Ball's Bluff, on the Virginia side of the Potomac. A Union force that crossed there was counterattacked and crushed on October 21, with 921 casualties, more than 700 of whom were captured or missing. The Confederates suffered only 149 casualties.

The Union had one notable success when a joint army-navy expedition captured weakly defended Port Royal, South Carolina, early in November. This move was part of a grand strategy prepared by retiring General-in-chief Winfield Scott, who proposed blockading the Southern coast and capturing the Mississippi Valley. Many objected to this strategy as being too slow, nicknaming it the "Anaconda Plan," after the snake that slowly crushes its prey. In time, however, Scott's strategy proved the key to ultimate Union victory.

TWO PRESIDENTS: LINCOLN AND DAVIS

Jefferson Davis

Abraham Lincoln

The 16th president of the United States, Abraham Lincoln (1809–1865), and Confederate president Jefferson Davis (1808–1889), were both born in southern Kentucky, less than a year apart.

Davis attended college, then entered West Point, eventually serving as an officer in the 1832 Black Hawk War and on the Northwest frontier. In 1845, he was elected as a Democratic congressman for Mississippi, resigning to serve in the Mexican War, which began that year. When he left the military in 1847, Davis was appointed senator from Mississippi, and in 1853 was secretary of war in the Franklin Pierce administration. Returning to the Senate in 1857, he was a staunch advocate of states' rights, and by 1860 favored secession and the establishment of the Confederacy.

Lincoln's youth was spent mainly in frontier Indiana, with little formal education. As a young man he moved to Illinois, where he briefly volunteered as a militiaman in the Black Hawk War. Lincoln worked in a grocery while he studied law, soon becoming a successful lawyer. He served several terms as a Whig member of the Illinois state legislature and was a congressman for one term, 1847–1849. His outspoken opposition to the Mexican War cost him reelection to Congress. In 1858, Lincoln won a national reputation for debating Stephen A. Douglas, promoter of the 1854 Kansas-Nebraska Act, which allowed the residents of those territories to decide whether they would become slave or free states.

As the Republican candidate, Lincoln won the November 1860 presidential election. The Confederate congress appointed Davis its provisional president in February 1861.

GRANT TAKES THE OFFENSIVE IN THE WEST

As the war in the East awaited the arming and training of Johnston's and McDowell's raw regiments in mid-1861, conflict erupted in Missouri, where Union forces faced an ever-growing army of pro-secessionists. Union men under General Nathaniel Lyon drove the secessionist governor out of St. Louis. Next, Lyon and 6,000 men advanced on a force twice his size under General Sterling Price, a former governor and Mexican War general. Lyon was killed in the Battle of Wilson's Creek that August, and Price took control of Springfield, the state capital.

The Union had to go on the attack down the Mississippi Valley, which linked the Confederacy with the West. Taking control of the Mississippi Valley would cut the South in half. That November, a small Union force failed in attacking Belmont, Missouri, but its commander, General Ulysses S. Grant of Ohio, proved both able and aggressive.

Grant bursts onto the stage

A West Point graduate who had retired after the Mexican War, Grant led 15,000 men against Confederate forts on the

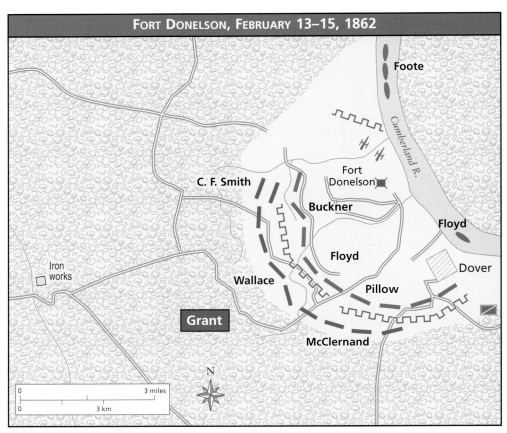

FORT DONELSON, FEBRUARY 13–15, 1862

THE FALL OF FORT DONELSON In February 1862, Grant's army invested Donelson while Foote's gunboats attacked from the Cumberland River. Though the gunboats were driven off and Foote wounded, Donelson was doomed; Floyd and 3,000 troops escaped across the river.

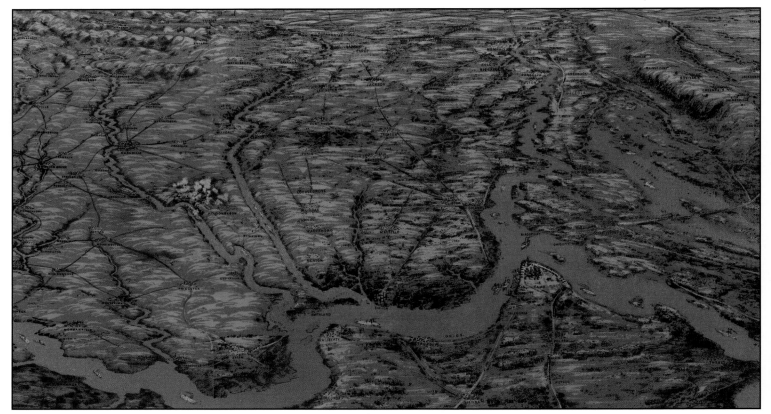

A **BIRD'S-EYE VIEW** This early-1862 panorama looks south, over Cairo, Illinois, and the Kentucky-Tennessee "seat of war"; smoke shrouds Confederate-held Fort Donelson as Union gunboats ply the Cumberland's waters. The Mississippi is at right, the Ohio in the foreground.

> "Men of Arkansas! They say you boast of your prowess with the Bowie Knife. Today you wield a nobler weapon—the bayonet. Employ it well."
>
> —CONFEDERATE GENERAL ALBERT SIDNEY JOHNSTON TO THE MEN OF THE 9TH ARKANSAS REGIMENT AT THE BATTLE OF SHILOH

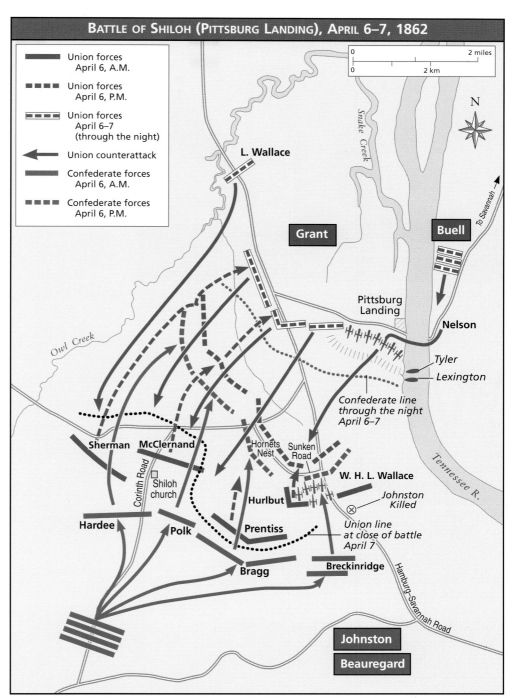

BATTLE OF SHILOH (PITTSBURG LANDING), APRIL 6–7, 1862

THE BATTLE OF SHILOH Johnston's Confederates drove back Grant's troops with a surprise attack on April 6, but the Union lines reformed and held near Pittsburg Landing. Reinforced by General Don Carlos Buell, Grant counterattacked on the 7th and forced the enemy to withdraw. Americans on both sides were shocked by news of this bloody battle, which foreshadowed the long and difficult conflict to come.

Cumberland and Tennessee rivers in February 1862. Cooperating with gunboats under Flag Officer Andrew H. Foote, Grant captured weakly garrisoned Fort Henry on the Tennessee, after a brief artillery bombardment on February 6.

Reinforced to 27,000 men, Grant laid siege to Fort Donelson on the Cumberland, where 15,000 troops were commanded by General John B. Floyd, a former secretary of war. Fearing execution as a traitor if captured, Floyd escaped, and command devolved on General Simon B. Buckner. Surrounded and greatly outnumbered, Buckner surrendered on February 16.

Another Union victory: Pea Ridge

With Grant prying open invasion routes into Tennessee, Kentucky was virtually abandoned by Confederates. West of the Mississippi, in northern Arkansas, General Earl Van Dorn led 17,000 Confederates against General Samuel Curtis, who had 11,000 troops. They engaged at Pea Ridge in March in a battle known to Southerners as Elkhorn Tavern. Curtis held the field, though he lost almost 1,400 men compared to 800 Southern casualties.

Missouri was firmly in Union hands.

Grant holds on at Shiloh

Positioned for a new offensive, Grant's army of more than 40,000 men was camped along the Tennessee River at Pittsburg Landing, Tennessee, on Sunday, April 6. With Grant was General William T. Sherman, also from Ohio and a former Regular officer who had returned to the army when war began.

Grant and Sherman thought the main Confederate force was 25 miles or more distant. It numbered 40,000 troops under

General Albert S. Johnston, a regular army general who had turned down high rank in the Union army to serve the Confederacy. The Union camp was taken by surprise that morning when Johnston's soldiers burst from the woods and sent Sherman's regiments reeling. The Union men rallied, battle lines swaying back and forth around the crossroads at Shiloh Church. Johnston was shot and died of his wounds. He was succeeded by General Beauregard, his second-in-command.

By nightfall, Grant's men had held, and he was reinforced to more than 60,000 troops. Beauregard was unable to bring up reinforcements in time, so he withdrew from the field. Known as the Battle of Pittsburg Landing to Southerners, the Battle of Shiloh was claimed as a victory by both sides. Now, Union forces were positioned to advance down the Mississippi Valley and divide the Confederacy.

BATTLE OF HAMPTON ROADS: CLASH OF IRONCLADS

MONITOR VS. VIRGINIA The more maneuverable *Monitor,* foreground, closes with the Confederate ram *Virginia* at Hampton Roads, Virginia, in March 1862, for the world's first battle between warships protected by iron armor.

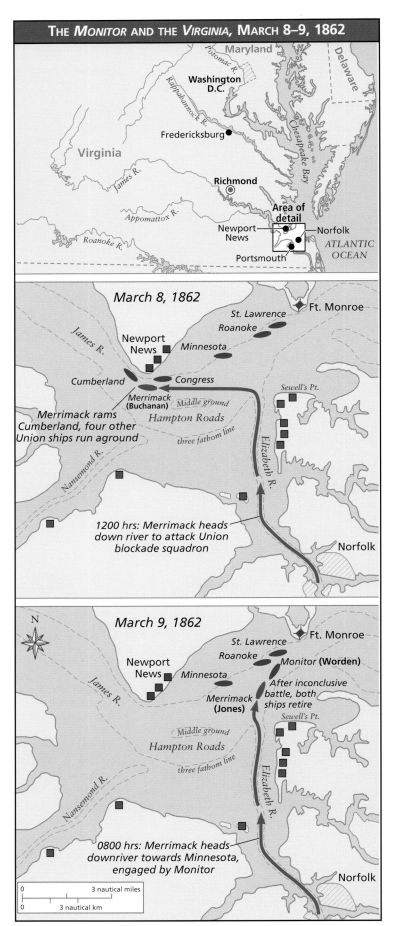

THE *MONITOR* AND THE *VIRGINIA*, MARCH 8–9, 1862

March 8, 1862

Merrimack rams Cumberland, four other Union ships run aground

1200 hrs: Merrimack heads down river to attack Union blockade squadron

March 9, 1862

After inconclusive battle, both ships retire

0800 hrs: Merrimack heads downriver towards Minnesota, engaged by Monitor

When the South seceded, 236 of the United States Navy's 1,457 officers resigned to join the new Confederacy, which could count 50 captains and commanders but had no fleet. The Union navy was small and in need of repair, for government neglect had allowed its 90 ships to deteriorate. Though the navy's five modern steam frigates matched the best warships of the day, they were all out of commission. Half the navy's vessels were steam-powered and serviceable, but most of the sailing ships were obsolete.

The navy's great yard at Norfolk, Virginia, was seized by the Confederates on April 20, 1861, although the Federals had destroyed many buildings and scuttled most vessels there. One of the warships scuttled at its dock was the five-year-old steam frigate *Merrimack.*

Confederacy and Union build first ironclads

The *Merrimack* was raised, its hull cut down to the water line and fitted with a four-foot cast-iron prow for ramming. A sloping superstructure was built and clad with iron bars laid upon oak 22 inches thick—appearing like a floating barn roof. Renamed CSS *Virginia,* this ironclad was 263 feet long, armed with 10 guns, and although slow and ponderous was virtually impregnable to artillery.

Meanwhile, a completely new ironclad was being built in New York, with a circular, revolving turret that was armored with eight one-inch iron plates. The turret, with two cannon, sat on a low, 172-foot deck, like a "Yankee cheese box on a raft." Named USS *Monitor,* she set out on March 6, 1862, for Hampton Roads, Virginia—under tow because she was not very seaworthy.

Two days later, the *Virginia* steamed into Hampton Roads, where the Federal fleet, Union shore batteries, and soldiers watched with wonder. *Virginia* fatally rammed the frigate

DOORWAY TO VIRGINIA Hampton Roads was a strategic opening to eastern Virginia and Richmond, and the aptly named ironclad, *Virginia,* seemed an ideal guardian on March 8, 1862, when she threw the Union blockading fleet into chaos. The *Monitor* arrived in the nick of time to defend the fleet, and Hampton Roads and Norfolk soon fell under Union control.

Cumberland, whose guns did little damage to her armor, although a fluke shot penetrated the wheelhouse and wounded her commander, Commodore Franklin Buchanan. While goring the *Cumberland*, which sank, the *Virginia* fired on the *Congress*, driving her aground. The Union fleet was helpless, but with the tide ebbing, the *Virginia* had to break off the action. That night, the *Monitor* arrived in Hampton Roads. At 9 a.m. the next day, March 9, 1862, the world's first battle of ironclad warships began.

The brief debut of ironclads

This three-hour Battle of Hampton Roads, also known as the Battle of the *Monitor* and *Merrimack*, was a thunderous, awkward, close-quarters bombardment that both vessels stoutly endured. When the *Monitor* took a direct hit on the pilothouse sight-hole, temporarily blinding Lieutenant John L. Worden, her master, she had to withdraw. By noon the battle was over. The *Virginia*, commanded now by Lieutenant Catesby ap Roger

Jones, seemed the winner, though she was battered and taking on water.

Returning to Norfolk, the *Virginia* saw no more action because the Union Army soon invaded, and in May she was scuttled rather than allowed to be captured. The *Monitor* sank in a gale off Cape Hatteras on December 31, with some loss of life.

Both the Union and Confederacy quickly set about building more ironclads, which caught the eye of navies around the world. Warship design was changed forever.

New Orleans falls to Farragut

In April 1862, Flag Officer David G. Farragut boldly led a Union fleet past the guns of two enemy forts protecting the mouth of the Mississippi below New Orleans.

Through the night of April 24, Farragut's 24 warships and 19 mortar boats dashed upriver, blasting the forts while losing only one vessel. His fleet arrived at undefended New Orleans, the

South's greatest city and most important seaport. Fearing a ruinous bombardment, New Orleans authorities surrendered to Farragut without a shot on April 25. The Mississippi with all its commerce was now tightly sealed.

"Whereas, we had one hundred and forty-nine first-class warships, we have now but two."
— The *London Times*, after Hampton Roads, declaring the day of wooden warships to be over

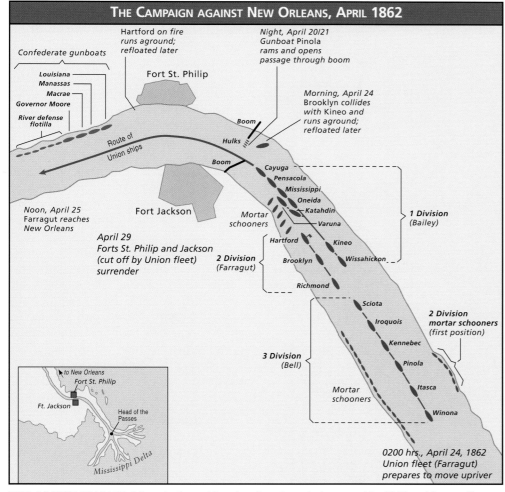

THE CAMPAIGN AGAINST NEW ORLEANS, APRIL 1862

Confederate gunboats
Louisiana
Manassas
Macrae
Governor Moore
River defense flotilla

Hartford on fire runs aground; refloated later

Fort St. Philip

Night, April 20/21 Gunboat Pinola rams and opens passage through boom

Morning, April 24 Brooklyn collides with Kineo and runs aground; refloated later

Route of Union ships

Boom

Hulks

Boom

Cayuga
Pensacola
Mississippi
Oneida
Katahdin
Varuna

Noon, April 25 Farragut reaches New Orleans

Fort Jackson

Mortar schooners

1 Division (Bailey)

April 29 Forts St. Philip and Jackson (cut off by Union fleet) surrender

2 Division (Farragut)

Hartford
Brooklyn
Richmond

Kineo
Wissahickon

Sciota
Iroquois

2 Division mortar schooners (first position)

Kennebec

3 Division (Bell)

Pinola

Itasca

to New Orleans
Fort St. Philip

Ft. Jackson

Head of the Passes

Mortar schooners

Winona

Mississippi Delta

0200 hrs., April 24, 1862 Union fleet (Farragut) prepares to move upriver

FALL OF NEW ORLEANS After six days of bombarding Forts Jackson and St. Philip without effect, Farragut rushed his fleet between them and captured New Orleans, the South's busiest seaport. Confederate commerce was drastically reduced, and Union conquest of the Mississippi Valley began.

McCLELLAN SUFFERS DEFEAT ON THE PENINSULA

GEORGE B. McCLELLAN (1826–1885) A West Pointer honored for gallantry in the Mexican War, McClellan was an excellent military organizer, but was accused of lacking aggressiveness.

In March 1862, Union commander-in-chief George B. McClellan used his advantage in naval power and landed an army on the peninsula formed by the York and James rivers of eastern Virginia. By April, McClellan commanded 112,000 men facing 60,000 C.S.A. troops under Joseph Johnston. Faulty intelligence, however, led McClellan to believe Johnston had 120,000 strongly fortified troops. In early May, he prepared to assault what he thought were extensive enemy defensive works at Yorktown. Overnight, those works were evacuated by the Confederates, and McClellan found many dummy guns made of wood.

Known as the Peninsular Campaign, McClellan's advance on Richmond, 70 miles away, was slow and halting, though there was little resistance after Yorktown. He established a supply base at White House, on the Pamunkey River, and hoped his assault on Richmond would be supported by McDowell's 40,000 troops in northern Virginia.

Jackson's Valley Campaign

Lincoln wanted McDowell to protect Washington from attack by Stonewall Jackson's fast-moving army in the Shenandoah Valley. With General Robert E. Lee advising President Davis, Jackson had been ordered to create a diversion in the valley and draw off Union troops that could have reinforced McClellan.

Instead of merely making a diversion, Jackson defeated his enemy again and again, marching swiftly up and down the valley and earning his men the nickname "foot cavalry." From May to June, Jackson's force, varying from 10–17,000 men, shattered Union armies five times. The combined Union strength was 50,000 but—because Jackson was too elusive—that number was never brought against him in a single battle.

Lee assumes command

By mid-May, McClellan's army was moving through the formidable barrier of rain-swollen rivers and swamps on the route to Richmond. The Chickahominy River divided Union forces, leaving the Fourth Corps isolated south of the river. On May 31, Johnston pounced on this corps, attacking at Fair Oaks and Seven Pines.

Maneuvering and fighting in a driving rainstorm, the Confederate offensive ground to a halt as the Fourth Corps was reinforced by troops who crossed the dangerously flooded Chickahominy. Each side threw 42,000 men into the battle, which became a standoff—the Union losing approximately 5,000 men, the Confederacy 6,100. Johnston, himself, was severely wounded, and Lee arrived to take charge. As Lee withdrew his forces to

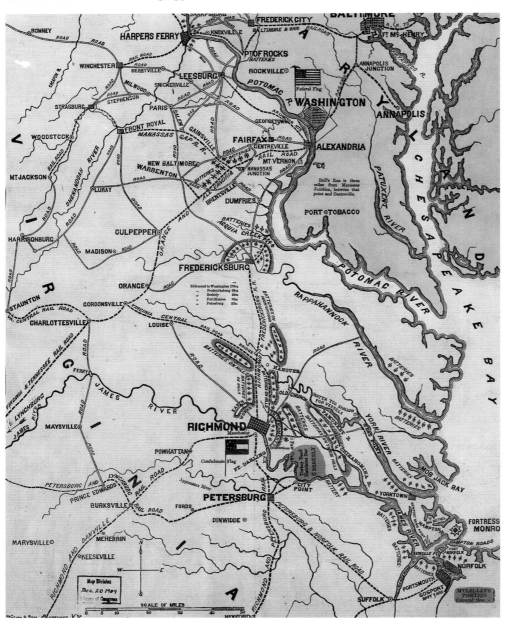

THE PENINSULA This English period map of the eastern Virginia "seat of war" during McClellan's 1862 Virginia campaign shows forts and gun batteries from Washington, D.C., to Richmond. The area controlled by the Union army is shaded.

defensive positions, McClellan crossed the Chickahominy with most of his army and approached Richmond's gates.

The Seven Days' Battles

McClellan moved on Richmond by attacking at Oak Grove on June 25, opening a series of engagements known as the Seven Days' Battles. The next day, Lee took the offensive, striking the Union Fifth Corps at Mechanicsville, north of the Chickahominy. Lee lost heavily, but McClellan feared his right flank was exposed and ordered the Fifth Corps to withdraw. The next day, Lee again attacked, driving Union defenders from Gaines's Mill and persuading McClellan to hastily abandon his supply base at White House.

Lee pursued, hoping to inflict a decisive defeat. On the 29th, he hit McClellan's rear guard at Savage's Station, but the Union troops fought hard, refusing to be routed. Lee next attacked at Frayser's Farm on the 30th, but still could not break through. Again, McClellan withdrew, and on July 1 Lee attacked at Malvern Hill, launching frontal assaults that were repulsed with severe losses. McClellan continued retreating, and the Peninsular Campaign became another Union humiliation. Lee lost 20,000 men, but saved Richmond. McClellan lost 16,000 and also his position in charge of the main Union field force.

THE SIEGE OF YORKTOWN Overestimating the numbers of troops and the strength of Confederate defensive works at Yorktown in the spring of 1862, McClellan was delayed in his advance up the Peninsula toward Richmond.

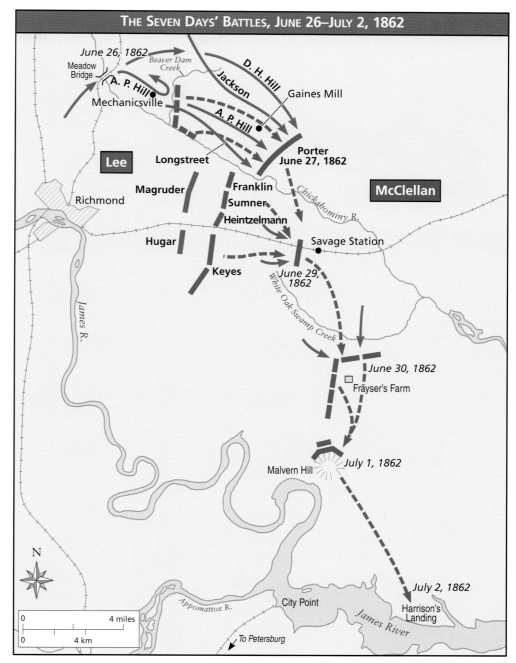

THE SEVEN DAYS' BATTLES, JUNE 26–JULY 2, 1862

June 26, 1862
Meadow Bridge
Beaver Dam Creek
A. P. Hill
Mechanicsville
D. H. Hill
Jackson
A. P. Hill
Gaines Mill
Lee
Longstreet
Porter June 27, 1862
Magruder
Franklin
Richmond
Sumner
Heintzelmann
McClellan
Chickahominy R.
Hugar
Savage Station
Keyes
June 29, 1862
White Oak Swamp Creek
June 30, 1862
Frayser's Farm
July 1, 1862
Malvern Hill
July 2, 1862
Appomattox R.
City Point
Harrison's Landing
James River
To Petersburg
James R.
N
0   4 miles
0   4 km

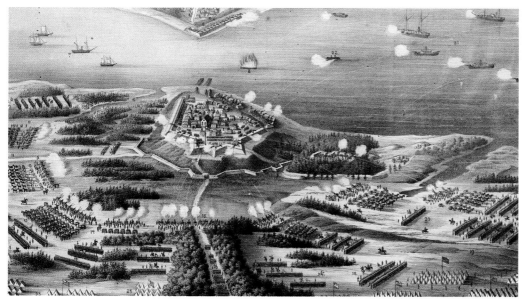

LEE OUTGENERALS McCLELLAN With his army on Richmond's doorstep and a supply base on the nearby Pamunkey River, McClellan was poised for a decisive attack. Lee struck instead, throwing McClellan off balance in a series of battles known as the "Seven Days," which convinced the Union commander to abandon his offensive.

"Praying and fighting appeared to be his idea of the whole duty of man."

—Brigadier General Richard Taylor on Stonewall Jackson's eccentric personality

12: LEE'S VICTORIES THREATEN THE NORTH

UNION CHARGE A Civil War era woodcut depicts perfect ranks, bayonets sloped, on the attack.

General John Pope had achieved some success in the West—enough to impress General Henry W. Halleck, Lincoln's new commander-in-chief. Halleck persuaded Lincoln to give Pope command of a new force in northern Virginia.

In August, a detachment of 8,000 troops under Nathaniel P. Banks was defeated at Cedar Mountain by Jackson and General A.P. Hill, with 16,800 men. Cautiously withdrawing his main army northward, Pope awaited reinforcements from McClellan, which would double his numbers to 130,000 and overwhelm Lee's 55,000. Lee did not allow Pope time, however, and in mid-August sent Jackson and 25,000 men with J.E.B. "Jeb" Stuart's cavalry through Thoroughfare Gap and behind Pope's army.

Marching more than 60 miles in just two days, Jackson destroyed Pope's supply base at Manassas. Also, Stuart raided Pope's headquarters when the general was away. Pope turned to attack Jackson on August 29, unaware Lee and General James Longstreet were closing in. For the better part of two days, Jackson repelled attack after attack, and on the second day Lee and Longstreet joined the battle, driving Pope across Bull Run.

Union casualties numbered more than 16,000, and the Confederates lost 9,000. Pope was removed from command, and Lincoln recalled McClellan to the front, giving him the task of stopping Lee from invading Maryland.

McClellan repels Lee's invasion

On September 15, Jackson and A.P. Hill captured Harpers Ferry, Virginia, after a brief artillery bombardment, taking 10,000 prisoners. On this day, Lee and 19,000 men were at Sharpsburg, Maryland, with McClellan approaching, about to bring on battle.

Lee called his forces together, and Jackson made a forced march to reach him on the 16th, bringing the army to about 30,000 men. Hill's division had not yet arrived. With the Potomac River at his back, and his front partly protected by Antietam Creek, Lee made a stand. McClellan attacked on the 17th with approximately 40,000 troops, hammering at Jackson's corps on Lee's left. The troops of Union general Ambrose E. Burnside captured a stone bridge over the creek and rushed across, threatening Lee's right. Just then, A.P. Hill arrived and counterattacked, saving Lee's army.

The battle broke off that night, after the bloodiest single day of the war. McClellan lost more than 12,000, Lee almost 14,000. When McClellan did not

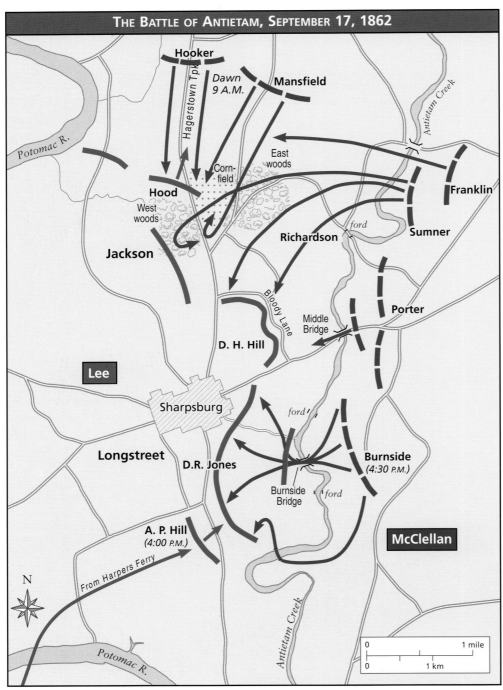

THE BATTLE OF ANTIETAM, SEPTEMBER 17, 1862

Hooker

Hagerstown Tpk

Dawn 9 A.M.

Mansfield

Potomac R.

Antietam Creek

East woods

Corn-field

Hood

West woods

Franklin

Jackson

ford

Sumner

Richardson

Bloody Lane

Porter

Middle Bridge

D. H. Hill

Lee

Sharpsburg

ford

Longstreet

D.R. Jones

Burnside
(4:30 P.M.)

Burnside Bridge

ford

A. P. Hill
(4:00 P.M.)

From Harpers Ferry

McClellan

N

Antietam Creek

Potomac R.

0   1 mile

0   1 km

STANDOFF AT ANTIETAM CREEK McClellan attacked piecemeal on a broad front, sending his strongest force against Lee's left, where the "Corn Field" entered history as the site of heroic charges. The attack across "Burnside's Bridge" also won fame, but Hill's arrival stopped a near-breakthrough on that flank.

resume the attack, the Confederate army withdrew on the night of the 18th. McClellan chose not to follow immediately, though Lincoln urged him to do so.

Frustrated, Lincoln replaced McClellan with Burnside, who took command in November.

Slaughter at Fredericksburg

Burnside planned to surprise Lee with a crossing of the Rappahannock River at Fredericksburg in December, a time of year when armies normally were in winter quarters. The strategy was imaginative, but the bridges across the river had been destroyed. Burnside's 116,000-man army stopped at the banks of the Rappahannock, facing lightly defended Fredericksburg, and waited two weeks until pontoon bridges arrived. The delay gave Lee time to fortify Fredericksburg's heights with 72,000 men.

On the 13th, Burnside attacked the Confederates, attempting unsuccessfully to turn their right flank. Wave after Union wave was mowed down. The heaviest fighting was for Marye's Heights, held by Longstreet's veterans positioned along a sunken road. The Federals were massacred, losing more than 12,600 men in several hopeless assaults; Lee lost 5,300. On the 14th, Burnside wanted to continue attacking, but his generals persuaded him against it. He withdrew, soon to resign his brief, but disastrous, command.

CONFEDERATE GENERAL
ROBERT E. LEE
1807–1870

Second in his 1829 class at West Point, Lee came from a distinguished Virginia family. An engineer by training, he served gallantly in the Mexican War, and from 1852–1853 was superintendent of West Point.

In 1859, Lee led the Marines who put down John Brown's insurrection at Harpers Ferry, but in 1861 he declined command of the Federal armies. Lee took over Virginia's troops, leading a campaign in western Virginia before going on to organize Confederate coastal defenses. Called to Richmond as Davis's military advisor, Lee took field command when Johnston was wounded at Fair Oaks in June 1862.

Lee won brilliant victories until his defeat at Gettysburg in July 1863. He was daring in critical situations, especially when dividing his army in the face of a much superior enemy. This tactic succeeded at Second Bull Run and Chancellorsville, where Lee kept the initiative against powerful Union armies. After Gettysburg, he conducted stubborn defensive operations while Grant held the initiative.

Lee officially took command of all Confederate armies in February 1865, two months before surrendering at Appomattox. He later served as president of Washington College in Lexington, Virginia—in 1871 renamed Washington and Lee.

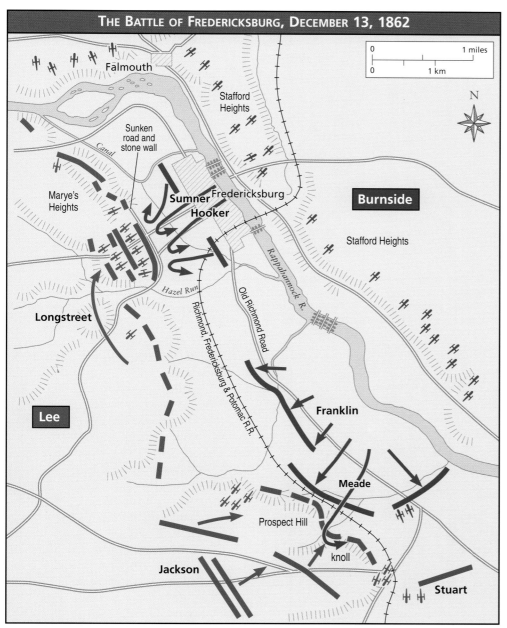

THE BATTLE OF FREDERICKSBURG, DECEMBER 13, 1862

Falmouth
Stafford Heights
Sunken road and stone wall
Canal
Marye's Heights
Sumner
Hooker
Fredericksburg
Burnside
Stafford Heights
Rappahannock R.
Hazel Run
Longstreet
Old Richmond Road
Richmond, Fredericksburg & Potomac R.R.
Lee
Franklin
Meade
Prospect Hill
knoll
Jackson
Stuart

STORMING MARYE'S HEIGHTS Burnside launched his main attack against Marye's Heights, the strongest point of Lee's works. The Union attackers were under constant fire and had little hope against such determined defenders. Other assaults breached Confederate lines but were repulsed by counterattack.

THE UNION FIGHTS ON; LEE PLANS INVASION

"Tell Old Jack we're all a–comin. Don't let him begin the fuss till we get thar."

—A SOLDIER, TO ONE OF JACKSON'S STAFF OFFICERS, WHILE ON A FLANK MARCH AT CHANCELLORSVILLE

The year 1862 ended with the Battle of Stones River in Tennessee, an inconclusive, bloody clash between the South's Braxton Bragg and the North's William Rosecrans. Bragg, with almost 35,000 troops, had retreated from Kentucky after the battle at Perryville in October. He took positions near Murfreesboro, Tennessee, blocking the way to Chattanooga, a strategic rail junction. Rosecrans, with the 41,000-man Army of the Cumberland, moved from Nashville and prepared to take on Bragg.

At dawn on December 31, Bragg attacked Rosecrans, and a desperate day-long fight ensued, ending with darkness. Bragg attacked again on New Year's Day, but his assault was shattered by Federal artillery fire. Bragg withdrew two days later, yet still defended the route to Chattanooga. The Union lost almost 13,000 at Stones River, also known as the Battle of Murfreesboro, while the Confederates lost more than 11,700.

The Battle of Chancellorsville

General Joseph Hooker replaced Burnside as commander of the Union Army of the Potomac. "Fighting Joe," as he was known, was expected to bring the battle to Lee and threaten Richmond. This he did, at the end of April 1863, crossing the Rappahannock west of Fredericksburg with half his 136,000-man army. A Union force under General John Sedgwick crossed the river at Fredericksburg, intending to hold Lee in place while Hooker made the decisive blow from the west.

Leaving General Jubal Early and 10,000 men at Fredericksburg to contest Sedgwick's crossing, Lee led 50,000 troops to meet Hooker, who dug in at

FEDERAL CANNON With Stones River and the Nashville railroad in the distance, massed Union artillery prevents a Confederate breakthrough in January 1863. Union reinforcements, foreground, move in for a counterattack.

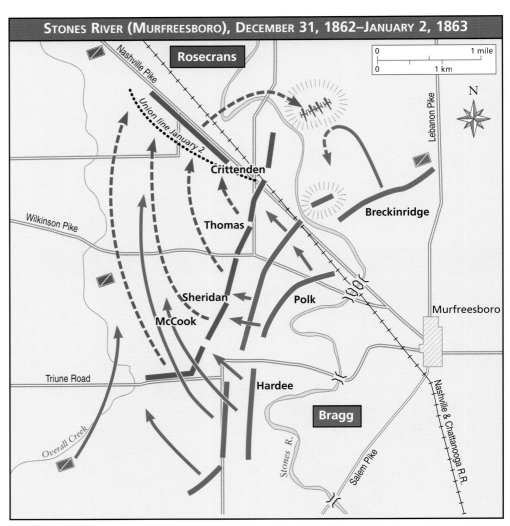

STONES RIVER (MURFREESBORO), DECEMBER 31, 1862–JANUARY 2, 1863

ROSECRANS CHECKS BRAGG The Confederates forced back the Union right wing at Stones River, but the Federals stubbornly kept fighting and inflicted heavy losses. The Southerners attacked on January 2, sending Northern troops reeling, but Union artillery soon shattered this assault.

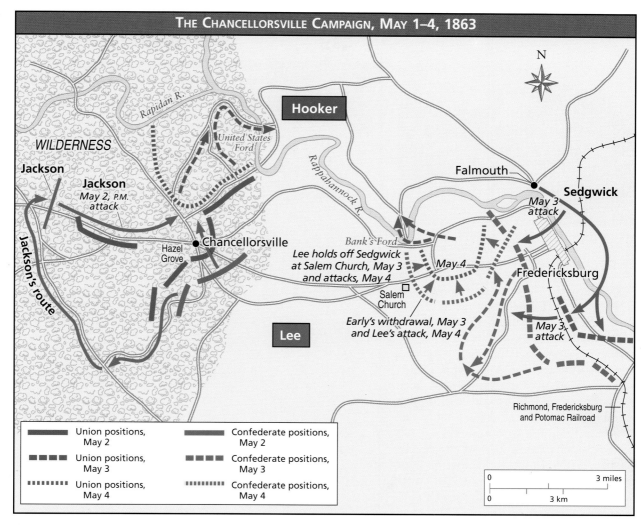

THE CHANCELLORSVILLE CAMPAIGN, MAY 1–4, 1863

VICTORY AND LOSS
Hooker gave up the initiative at Chancellorsville, and Jackson made the most of it—marching around the Union right and delivering a crushing blow. During the battle Hooker was stunned and nearly killed by a Confederate cannon ball smashing into his headquarters building. Riding through darkness that evening, Jackson was accidentally shot by his own men and died eight days later.

Lee holds off Sedgwick at Salem Church, May 3 and attacks, May 4

Early's withdrawal, May 3 and Lee's attack, May 4

Richmond, Fredericksburg and Potomac Railroad

—— Union positions, May 2	▬▬ Confederate positions, May 2
■■■ Union positions, May 3	■■■ Confederate positions, May 3
▪▪▪ Union positions, May 4	▪▪▪ Confederate positions, May 4

0 ——— 3 miles
0 ——— 3 km

Chancellorsville to await the Confederate attack. On May 2, concealed by dense woods, Jackson and 26,0000 troops made a 16-mile march around Hooker's right. That evening, Jackson's surprise assault routed the Union wing, forcing Hooker to withdraw toward the Rappahannock. Then Jackson was accidentally shot by his own pickets, and he soon died, a profound loss for the Confederacy.

Sedgwick's assaults at Fredericksburg were successful, but on May 4 he was counterattacked by the combined forces of Lee and Early. Hooker's 75,000 men remained in position as Sedgwick was forced to retire back across the river. Hooker withdrew north of the river on May 6. He was shortly replaced by veteran general George G. Meade.

Brandy Station: the cavalry's fight

This largest cavalry battle of the Civil War was also the first true cavalry engagement. The Battle of Brandy Station, also known as Beverly Ford, took place on June 9, 1863, when an 11,000-strong Union force—mostly cavalry—went looking for Lee's main army. About to invade the North, Lee's army was screened by Jeb Stuart's cavalry to keep troop movements secret as long as possible.

When the powerful Union force under cavalry general Alfred Pleasonton dashed across the Rappahannock before dawn, Stuart was taken by surprise. Confederate cavalry regiments were driven back as Pleasonton pushed toward Brandy Station, just a few miles northwest of Culpeper, where Lee's army was gathered. Stuart rallied his troopers and counterattacked, and both sides made charge after charge in a battle that raged for 12 hours. Union troopers fought skillfully and bravely, earning Confederate respect. Stuart held possession of the battlefield, but it was a close struggle, and he had been embarrassed by being unprepared for Pleasonton's attack. The South lost 523, the North about 930, including almost 500 taken prisoner.

Pleasonton had succeeded in finding Lee's army, and Union commanders now knew the invasion was under way.

THOMAS J. JACKSON (1824–1863) A Virginian and West Pointer, Jackson was austere and religious, often secretive to the point that his top officers were unaware of his plans. By 1863, he was Lee's right hand: "I know not how to replace him," Lee said after Jackson was killed.

CONFEDERATE STRONGHOLDS BESIEGED BY THE UNION

UNDERGROUND Confederate soldiers and civilians sheltered in hillside dugouts during the long siege of Vicksburg, Mississippi.

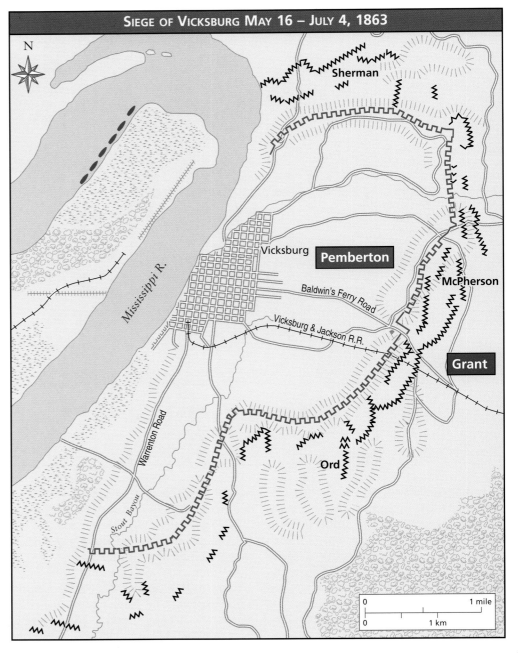

SIEGE OF VICKSBURG MAY 16 – JULY 4, 1863

N

Sherman

Mississippi R.

Vicksburg

Pemberton

Baldwin's Ferry Road

McPherson

Vicksburg & Jackson R.R.

Grant

Warrenton Road

Ord

Stout Bayou

0   1 mile
0   1 km

There was hope in Richmond, seat of the Confederate government, that Lee's invasion of the North in mid-1863 would help relieve the ongoing siege of Vicksburg, the key fortress on the Mississippi River. Since December 1862, Grant had been campaigning to capture the city, which stood on high bluffs commanding the river. By the end of June 1863, in a series of successful battles, he had driven the army of General John C. Pemberton back within its fortifications. Grant had cooperated with Admiral David Porter's gunboat fleet to invest Vicksburg, but several direct Union infantry assaults had been bloodily repulsed.

Since May, Pemberton had been cut off from supplies, and his 20,000 troops were starving. A Confederate army of 30,000 under Joseph Johnston, now in overall command in the region, was unable to fight its way past Grant. By the first days of July, Pemberton knew he would never be rescued. On the 4th, he surrendered, and the Confederacy was virtually cut in half.

Pemberton's men were paroled, in accordance with the surrender terms, but many soon violated their agreements and returned to the battlefield.

The fall of Port Hudson

Another siege was going on downriver at Port Hudson, Louisiana, where Union troops under Nathaniel Banks had been unable to force a surrender after weeks of struggle. C.S.A. general Franklin Gardner and his 7,200 defenders had fought off several heavy Union assaults.

In the Union force were two black regiments, part of the new "native guards" establishment composed of Southern black volunteers led by white officers. The 2nd and 3rd Louisiana Native Guards were among the first black fighting regiments brought into the Union army. The Louisiana Native Guards were in the thick of the heaviest assaults at Port Hudson, suffering severe losses. Their excellent performance in battle confirmed the potential of a new Federal plan to enlist thousands of black troops for the war effort.

Hearing Vicksburg had fallen, Gardner surrendered Port Hudson, the last of the Confederate fortresses on the Mississippi River, on July 9.

GRANT'S IRON RING The fine generalship of Ulysses S. Grant was manifest in the 1863 campaign for Vicksburg. Grant risked his career by disregarding orders to march on Port Hudson, and instead brilliantly defeated enemy field forces and drove on Vicksburg.

"Hardly any part of the city was outside the range of the enemy's artillery. . . ."

—A DESCRIPTION OF CONDITIONS INSIDE VICKSBURG, BESIEGED BY GRANT

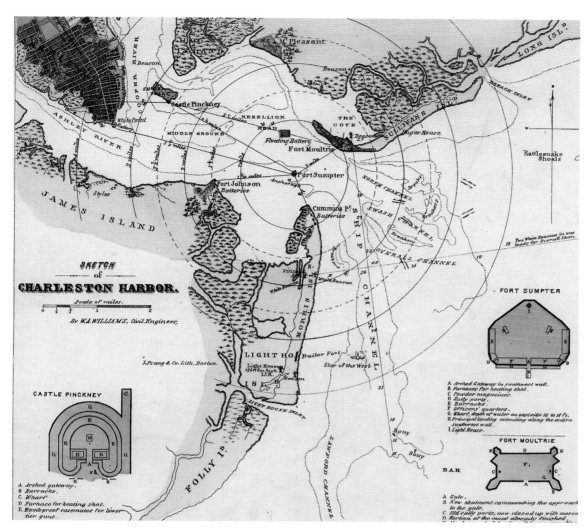

"They've as much right to fight for themselves as I have a right to fight for them."

—A Pennsylvania soldier's opinion of black troops being recruited for the Union army

Besieged Charleston fights on

By July 1863, the port city of Charleston, South Carolina, had been under siege from Union land and naval forces for more than a year. Her great harbor was blockaded by ironclads that blasted her forts and gun batteries, and Union infantry invaded the coastal islands to attack Confederate positions.

The North especially wanted to regain Fort Sumter, lost on that first day of the Civil War. By now, Sumter was an utter ruin, battered to rubble by the first Confederate bombardment and later by Union guns. Still, the Confederate flag flew over the fort, and artillery fired from behind her wrecked walls. Commanding Charleston's defenders was General P.G.T. Beauregard, the officer who had bombarded Sumter in 1861.

On July 10 and 18, Union troops were sent on reckless assaults against Fort Wagner, an important coastal battery strongly defended by 1,200 infantry and field guns. Charging along a narrow front, the Union regiments were cut to pieces before the Confederate ramparts. The attack on the 18th was led by the 54th Massachusetts, the first black regiment raised in the North. The combined assaults on Wagner cost almost 1,800 Union casualties, while the Confederates lost fewer than 190.

The Union then conducted a siege of Wagner, which was abandoned in early September. In this time, Fort Sumter endured a fierce naval bombardment that destroyed its artillery, but its infantry fought off a Union amphibious attack on September 8. The siege of Charleston would continue until February 1865.

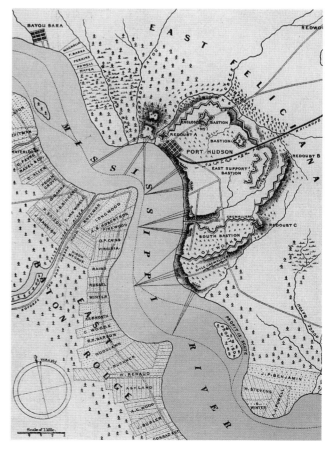

PORT HUDSON'S DEFENSES This 1863 map of the last Mississippi River stronghold shows Port Hudson's high ground with nearly impregnable fortifications.

GETTYSBURG: FORTUNES OF WAR FAVOR THE UNION

"I think this is the strongest position by nature upon which to fight a battle that I ever saw."

—UNION GENERAL WINFIELD S. HANCOCK, COMMENTING ON HIS ARMY'S POSITION AS THE BATTLE OF GETTYSBURG BEGAN

Robert E. Lee's resounding victory at Chancellorsville in May held out hope that another such success would break the North's will to continue the war. If the Union were beaten on its own soil, the effect would be even more dramatic, and even Britain and France might be prepared to support the Southern cause. In late June, the Army of Northern Virginia, 89,000 strong, marched unopposed through Maryland and into Pennsylvania.

The 122,000-man Army of the Potomac was still under Hooker, who clashed bitterly with Halleck on strategy and requested to be relieved. On June 28, Lincoln replaced Hooker with George Meade, a West Pointer and a veteran of the Mexican War. On July 1, Meade faced a battle with Lee at the crossroads of Gettysburg, Pennsylvania.

Early in the day, Union cavalry under General John Buford occupied the town and fought with A.P. Hill's advance guard. Both sides were reinforced in strength, and General John Reynolds took command of the Union troops but was killed by a sharpshooter. Lee arrived that afternoon and ordered a general advance. The Federals lost heavily, with thousands captured, and they withdrew to the high ground of Cemetery Hill and Cemetery Ridge. Commanded by General Winfield S. Hancock, they dug in as darkness fell. Meade appeared at midnight to array his forces in the form of a fishhook, awaiting Lee's attack. Meade had more than 85,000 men for the battle, and Lee 75,000.

July 2: Union wings under assault

Late the next afternoon, Longstreet struck Meade's left, where Union troops had moved forward to occupy a peach orchard and a wheat field. The fighting was fierce, as the Federals slowly gave ground. A near-breakthrough at Little

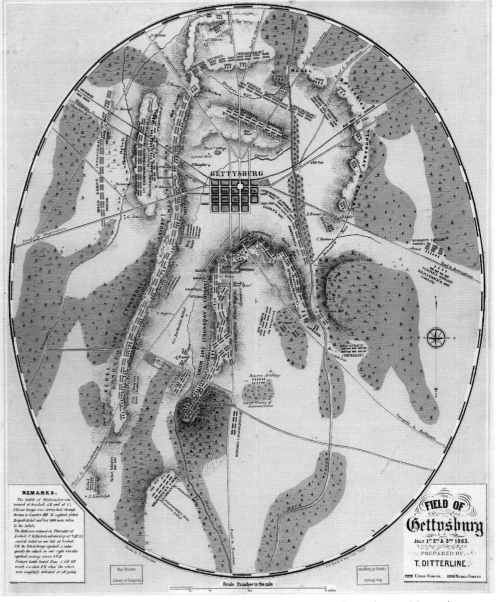

THE "FIELD OF GETTYSBURG" This 1863 map shows the advantage of Meade's position, where Union troops and guns could be shifted rapidly to reinforce threatened sectors. Lee's smaller army had to deploy along outer lines extending a much greater distance, which sometimes caused considerable delays in mounting attacks.

Round Top by the Confederates was counterattacked by a force hastily gathered by General Gouverneur K. Warren, the army's chief engineer. On Meade's right flank—Culp's Hill at the barb of the fishhook—another Confederate attack was stopped and driven back. The day ended with the South holding the initiative.

Although his original plan for the campaign had been to take a strong position and maneuver the Federals into attacking him, Lee now changed tactics—though his chief subordinate, Longstreet,

disagreed with him. Believing the center of Meade's position to be weak, Lee resolved to hurl a massive assault against the Union center occupying Cemetery Hill and Cemetery Ridge and commanded by Hancock. Between 12–15,000 men would make the assault, with General George E. Pickett as the lead commander.

July 3: Lee's doomed charge

The mile-long approach to the Union lines was rolling and open, without cover for attacking troops. Starting the offen-

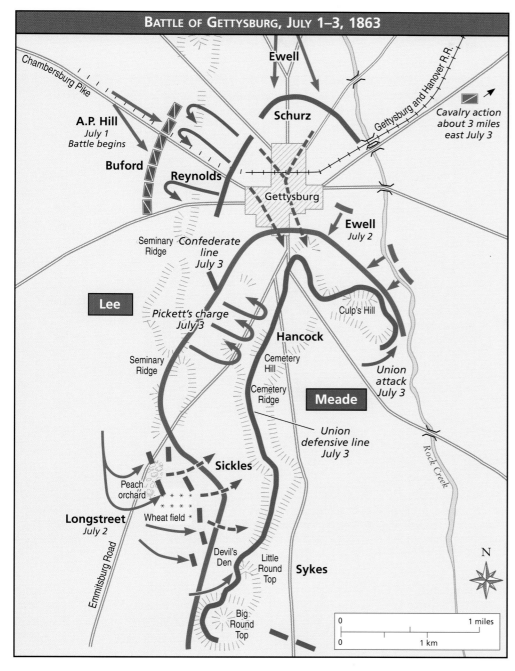

BATTLE OF GETTYSBURG, JULY 1–3, 1863

Chambersburg Pike

Ewell

Schurz

Gettysburg and Hanover R.R.

Cavalry action about 3 miles east July 3

A.P. Hill
July 1
Battle begins

Buford

Reynolds

Gettysburg

Ewell
July 2

Seminary Ridge

Confederate line July 3

Lee

Pickett's charge July 3

Culp's Hill

Seminary Ridge

Hancock

Cemetery Hill

Cemetery Ridge

Meade

Union attack July 3

Union defensive line July 3

Rock Creek

Sickles

Peach orchard

Wheat field

Longstreet
July 2

Emmitsburg Road

Devil's Den

Little Round Top

Sykes

N

Big Round Top

0 — 1 miles
0 — 1 km

sive at 1 p.m., 160 Confederate guns began a duel with 100 Union guns. This greatest artillery engagement of the war did little damage to the Union guns, which stopped firing in order to conserve ammunition for the coming attack.

Battle flags flying, regiment after Southern regiment moved out of the woods, formed rank upon rank, and charged, the keen "Rebel Yell" carrying them forward through a storm of lead and iron. Union guns and muskets cut them down in swaths, but the Confederates kept coming. Although many attackers broke off and withdrew, hundreds of others reached the Union positions, where they were killed, captured, or driven back. "Pickett's Charge" utterly failed, with 6,500 casualties—especially costly in officers, although Pickett survived.

Lee and Longstreet reorganized the shattered army and waited through July 4 for Meade's attack, which did not come. A rainstorm began that afternoon and helped cover Lee's retreat. He had suffered an estimated 28,000 casualties. Meade had lost more than 23,000 and was too badly battered to oppose Lee's withdrawal. The tide of war began to turn against the Confederacy at Gettysburg. The South's war for independence was now a struggle for survival.

PICKETT'S CHARGE Seen from behind the Federal position, Union troops pour in heavy fire as infantry and artillery reserves rush up amid the chaos of battle. Several Confederate generals were killed or wounded leading their men during the attack.

THREE DAYS OF BATTLE Union cavalry and infantry bought time for Meade's army to come up to Gettysburg on July 1. Lee attacked the Union wings on July 2, but was thrown back, convincing him the enemy center was the most vulnerable. He underestimated the number of Union troops before him.

"Come on boys! Give them the cold steel! Who will follow me?"

—CONFEDERATE GENERAL LEWIS ARMISTEAD, AS HIS MEN REACHED FEDERAL LINES DURING PICKETT'S CHARGE; ARMISTEAD WAS KILLED MINUTES LATER

13: A CONTEST BITTERLY FOUGHT TO THE END

After the Battle of Stones River, William Rosecrans took the initiative against Braxton Bragg. In June 1863, Rosecrans's Army of the Cumberland outmaneuvered the Confederate Army of the Tennessee, forcing Bragg to withdraw south of Chattanooga. Known as the Tullahoma Campaign, Rosecrans's brilliant movements put Bragg on the defensive at every turn, although there was little actual fighting.

On September 19, Longstreet arrived from Virginia with reinforcements for Bragg. That same day, Bragg, with more than 66,000 men, attacked Rosecrans's 58,000 near Chickamauga Creek. Fighting raged until darkness, ending without advantage to either side. The battle resumed on the 20th. Late that morning, confused orders on the Union right created an opening in the line at the very moment Longstreet's corps attacked. The Confederates broke through, shattering the Union right and center. The left held, however, inspired by the leadership of General George H. Thomas, thereafter known as "The Rock of Chickamauga." Thinking his army destroyed, Rosecrans fled toward Chattanooga, unaware Thomas was still fighting and had prevented Bragg from exploiting his success.

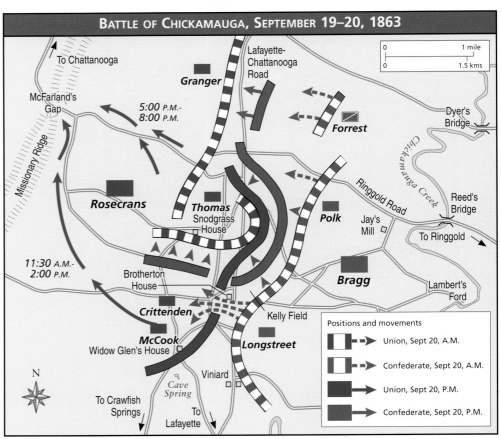

BATTLE OF CHICKAMAUGA, SEPTEMBER 19–20, 1863

Positions and movements

	Union, Sept 20, A.M.
	Confederate, Sept 20, A.M.
	Union, Sept 20, P.M.
	Confederate, Sept 20, P.M.

THE "ROCK OF CHICKAMAUGA" Longstreet's corps attacked the Union right near Chickamauga Creek and broke through, starting a near rout—except that General George Thomas refused to retreat, earning him the nickname, "Rock of Chickamauga." Thomas's stand allowed the Union army to withdraw to Chattanooga.

BRAXTON BRAGG (1817–1876) As a West Pointer with Mexican War experience, the temperamental Bragg was admired by Jefferson Davis, but was despised by some of his top commanders.

After nightfall, Thomas withdrew to rejoin Rosecrans at Chattanooga, which soon came under siege by Bragg's army. The Union lost more than 16,100 casualties at Chickamauga, the Confederacy more than 18,400. Rosecrans was soon replaced by Thomas as commander of the Army of the Cumberland.

The Chattanooga campaign

To strengthen Union forces in Tennessee, Lincoln sent out Joseph Hooker and two corps by railroad. Starting in late September, 20,000 men and 3,000 mules and horses were transported more than 1,100 miles in about two weeks.

In mid-October, Ulysses Grant was appointed overall commander in the region, and he made his way into Chattanooga to take charge. He soon captured important ferry crossings and reestablished supply lines to the city. With experienced officers such as William T. Sherman, Thomas, Philip H. Sheridan,

and Hooker leading his forces, Grant proceeded to attack Bragg's formidable positions on fortified heights overlooking Chattanooga. On November 24, Hooker's men stormed mist-wreathed Lookout Mountain, capturing it in what was called the "Battle Above the Clouds." The next day, Thomas's attacking troops pressed on beyond their first objective and swiftly reached the crest of Missionary Ridge, driving the surprised Bragg from his position and causing a full retreat.

Thus, the year 1863 ended with yet another Confederate defeat, one that prepared the way for an invasion of the South. Union casualties at Chattanooga numbered more than 5,800, Confederate approximately 6,600.

Red River Campaign

Early in 1864, Lincoln ordered an expedition up the Red River to eliminate enemy forces west of the Mississippi. He also intended to show the flag to Napoleon

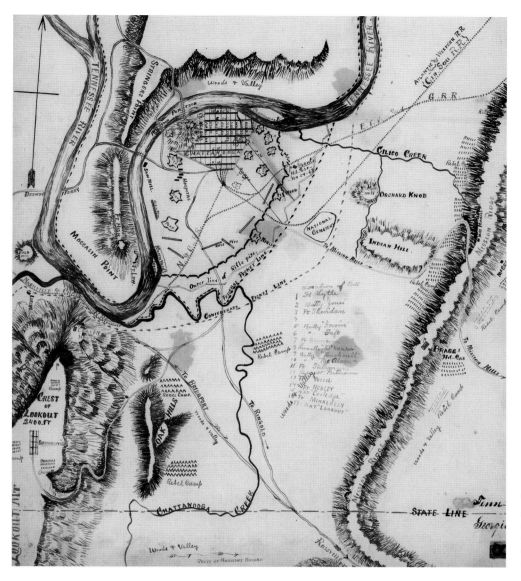

CHATTANOOGA UNDER SIEGE This period map shows fortifications around the city of Chattanooga in autumn 1863, with Union and Confederate picket lines, rifle pits, and Confederate encampments. Bragg occupied high ground that dominated the city, positions that Grant captured in November, ending the siege.

"Madam, are you mad? There are not enough Yankees in Chattanooga to come up here. Those are all my prisoners."

—BRAXTON BRAGG, REASSURING AN ANXIOUS CIVILIAN BYSTANDER ON THE STRENGTH OF HIS POSITIONS OVERLOOKING BESIEGED CHATTANOOGA

FAILED MARCH ON TEXAS Aiming to threaten Texas and wipe out Confederate forces west of the Mississippi, Banks's troops and Porter's gunboat fleet advanced along the Red River in the spring of 1864. Tenacious enemy resistance foiled the invasion, and low water almost trapped the vessels during the withdrawal.

III's French troops occupying Mexico in support of Emperor Maximilian. The expedition aimed to capture Shreveport, Louisiana, and strike a blow at Texas.

In command was Nathaniel Banks, who had captured Port Hudson the previous summer. Setting out in mid-March, Banks had 17,000 troops and the 18-vessel fleet of Admiral David Porter. There was strict time pressure, because many of Banks's troops were scheduled to leave in a month and join Sherman's march on Atlanta. As the expedition advanced, Confederate resistance steadily mounted, led by generals Edmund Kirby Smith and Richard Taylor. Their attacks cost Banks heavily, and he found himself running out of time, forced to conduct a fighting withdrawal.

Porter had his own troubles, as the river fell and his vessels became stranded at a rapids. For more than two weeks, the Union men labored to build a series of dams that raised the water level so the Union fleet could float downriver to safety. Banks and Porter narrowly escaped annihilation.

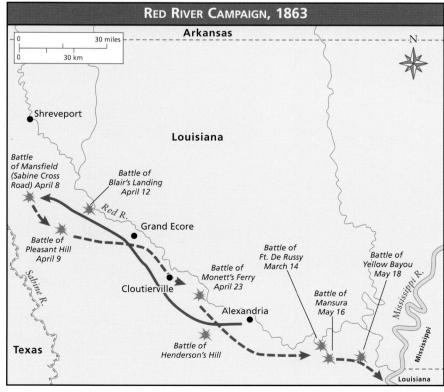

RED RIVER CAMPAIGN, 1863

BLOCKADES, BLOCKADE RUNNERS, AND COMMERCE RAIDERS

OUTSAILING THE BLOCKADE The Confederate blockade runner *Sumter* dashes past the patrolling Union warship, *Brooklyn;* blockade runners brought $200 million worth of goods into the Confederacy and exported 1.25 million bales of cotton.

The Confederacy desperately needed trade with foreign countries, especially because so much of her commerce had gone through New York City before the war. She required markets for staple crops such as cotton, tobacco, and rice, and in return had to purchase armaments and manufactured goods that were not produced in the South. The best market was Great Britain, which needed Southern cotton to feed her booming textile industry and could offer the Confederacy armaments in payment.

In 1864, even though the Federal naval blockade had stifled most Southern seaborne commerce, hundreds of fast vessels risked the dangers of blockade-running for the sake of patriotism or profit.

Blockade runners regularly slipped past naval patrols, often to Bermuda, where their cargoes were unloaded and new ones loaded. With holds full of guns, ammunition, medicines—and also luxury goods—blockade runners dashed homeward to slip into a secluded Southern cove. As many as 1,650 blockade-runners made a total of 8,000 round trips, bringing goods which were essential to the Confederacy's survival.

Yet, the Confederacy did not have a real navy to match the Union fleet, because the South did not have the industrial capacity to build one. At first, she attempted to build a navy overseas, especially in Britain.

Liverpool cruisers, C.S.A. warships

One way to challenge the Federal navy on the high seas was privateering, by which a government authorizes vessels to attack enemy shipping, naval or merchant. Although privateers—also termed "commerce raiders"—had been made illegal by recent international treaties, the Confederacy licensed several privately owned vessels to raid Northern shipping.

Early in the war, secret contracts were arranged for fast cruisers to be built in Liverpool and sold to bogus buyers, not directly to the Confederacy. They then would be armed and fitted out as Confederate warships in other ports, such as Nassau, the Bahamas. Liverpool shipyards launched the cruiser *Florida* in March 1862, and the *Alabama* in July. These vessels began to prey on Northern shipping, and whenever ships were taken or sunk the United States responded angrily by presenting the British government with bills for reparations. These bills, of course, were ignored.

In mid-1863, two powerful ironclad rams were under construction in Liverpool, ostensibly for foreign buyers, but destined for the Confederacy. The United States ambassador warned that such a transaction would be considered an act of war. The great Federal victories at Gettysburg and Vicksburg that summer helped persuade

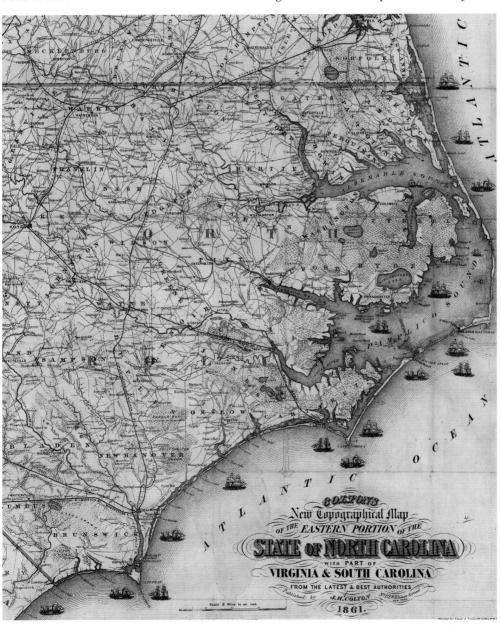

NORTH CAROLINA'S COAST Confederate coastal forts and the Union naval blockade are seen in this detail from an 1860s map of eastern North Carolina, where secluded coves could shelter blockade runners.

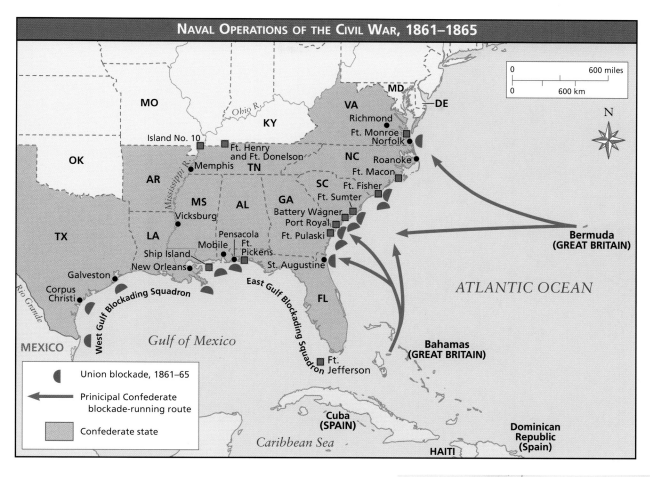

NAVAL OPERATIONS OF THE CIVIL WAR, 1861–1865

MO

Ohio R.

KY

VA
Richmond
Ft. Monroe
Norfolk

MD
DE

Island No. 10
Ft. Henry
and Ft. Donelson
Memphis
TN
AR
OK

NC
Roanoke
Ft. Macon

SC
Ft. Fisher
Ft. Sumter
Battery Wagner
Port Royal
Ft. Pulaski

MS
AL
GA

Vicksburg

TX
LA
Pensacola
Mobile   Ft.
Pickens
Ship Island
New Orleans
Galveston
Corpus
Christi

West Gulf Blockading Squadron

Rio Grande

MEXICO

St. Augustine

East Gulf Blockading Squadron

FL

Gulf of Mexico

Ft.
Jefferson

ATLANTIC OCEAN

Bermuda
(GREAT BRITAIN)

Bahamas
(GREAT BRITAIN)

Cuba
(SPAIN)

Caribbean Sea

HAITI

Dominican
Republic
(Spain)

N

0   600 miles
0   600 km

◗ Union blockade, 1861–65

← Prinicipal Confederate
blockade-running route

▢ Confederate state

THE UNION STRANGLEHOLD Lincoln proclaimed a blockade on 3,550 miles of Southern coastline in April 1861, when 6,000 vessels used Southern ports annually. In the next year, only 800 vessels penetrated the blockade, and cotton exports fell from $191 million to $4 million, a severe blow to the Confederacy.

the British government to seize the rams before they were sent to the South. Still, British-built commerce raiders continued to ravage Union shipping around the world.

The *Alabama* and *Kearsarge* duel

In her two-year career as a commerce raider, the *Alabama* destroyed more than 60 merchant vessels and one Union warship. Commanded by Captain Raphael Semmes, she won great fame and was considered the finest cruiser of the day.

On June 19, 1864, the *Alabama* met the Federal sloop *Kearsarge* off the French port of Cherbourg. The ships were equal in size and firepower and both wooden-hulled, but the *Kearsarge* was protected by a layer of iron chains hung over her sides. Captain John A. Winslow had learned this tactic while serving as a gunboat commander under David Farragut. The *Alabama's* crew lacked the skill of the *Kearsarge's* navy gunners, and within two hours, the raider was sinking. Semmes and his crew leaped into the sea, most of them picked up by a passing British steam yacht. Semmes went on to become a Confederate rear admiral and served for the rest of the war.

That October, the *Florida*, which had destroyed or taken more than 50 vessels, was sunk by the Federal navy. In June 1865, two months after the war ended, the commerce raider *Shenandoah* was still destroying American whaling ships, unaware the conflict was over.

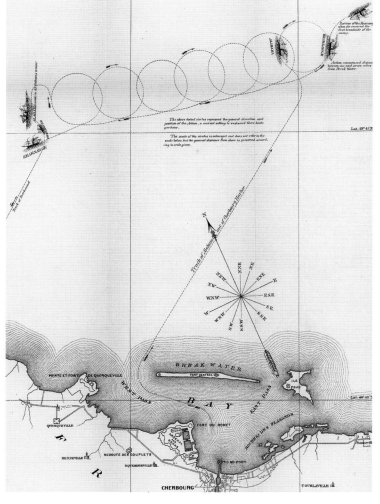

KEARSARGE DEFEATS THE *ALABAMA* This 1864 map shows the "Position of the *Kearsarge* when she received the first broadside of the enemy," the movement of the ships, and where the *Alabama* sank in 45 fathoms of water. Citizens of Cherbourg gathered on shore, trying to watch the fight, only a few miles from their city.

GRANT'S RELENTLESS ASSAULTS IN NORTHERN VIRGINIA

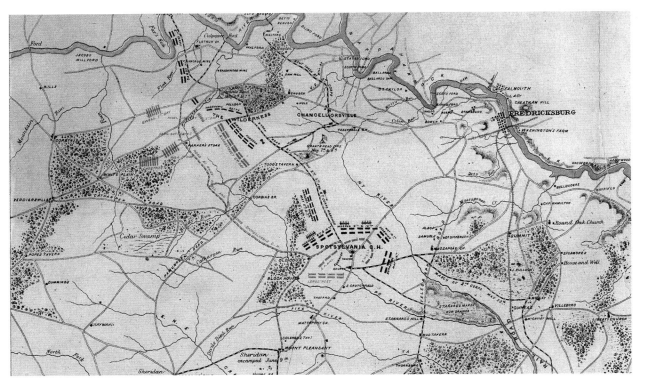

ARMIES AT THE WILDERNESS
This contemporary military topographical map shows troop positions and routes of march for the May 1864 Battle of the Wilderness in northern Virginia. Meade led the Union's Army of the Potomac, although Grant was overall commander, with the rank of lieutenant general.

Early in March 1864, Lincoln brought Grant east and appointed him commander in chief of the Union armies, with Henry Halleck as chief of staff. Grant would personally lead the troops in Virginia while Meade continued to command the Army of the Potomac. The new Union strategy was to defeat Confederate armies rather than attempt to capture cities or regions. That spring, all Union armies were to engage the enemy, thus preventing the deployment of Confederate reinforcements from one theater to another.

With 120,000 men against Lee's 70,000, Grant planned to turn Lee's flank and force him to launch attacks where the Union had the advantage. At the beginning of May, Grant tried to get between Lee and Richmond, but Lee moved decisively, and on May 5 forced a battle in the tangled, gloomy Wilderness west of Chancellorsville. For two days, fighting raged in close combat that cost 17,000 Union and more than 7,000 Confederate casualties, including Longstreet, who was mistakenly wounded by his own men.

Spotsylvania Courthouse

On the 7th, Grant moved again, trying to flank Lee and beat him to the crossroads at Spotsylvania Courthouse. Again Lee was able to block the Union move. Another

ferocious battle developed at Spotsylvania, continuing from May 8–19. Each side charged and countercharged, threw up earthworks, and hastily dug rifle pits, often finding themselves entrenched just a few yards from the enemy. One of the best-loved Union generals, John Sedgwick, was killed by a sharpshooter. Confederate cavalry commander Jeb Stuart died in a clash at Yellow Tavern.

On the 12th, Grant launched a massive assault at a salient known as the "Mule Shoe." The Union troops broke through, but Lee immediately counterattacked, bringing on some of the worst hand-to-hand fighting of the war. One grimly contested part of the Confederate defenses earned the name "Bloody Angle." The Union assault, under Hancock, had partial success, but stubborn Southern

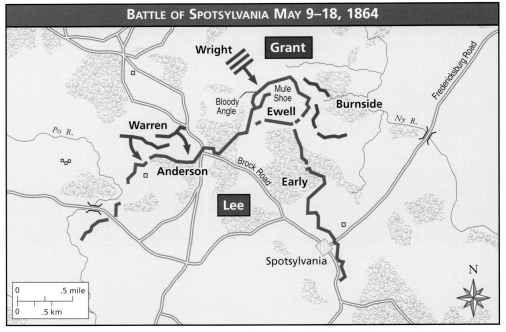

BATTLE OF SPOTSYLVANIA MAY 9–18, 1864

ORDEAL AT SPOTSYLVANIA Between May 8–19, the armies of Grant and Lee were locked in a deadly grip, struggling hand-to-hand at Spotsylvania Court House.

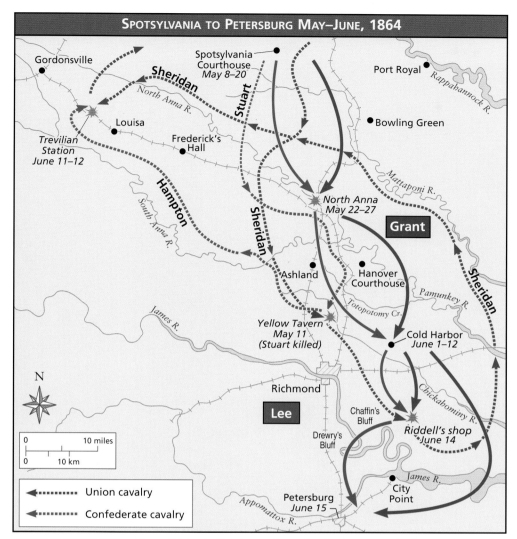

SPOTSYLVANIA TO PETERSBURG MAY–JUNE, 1864

Union cavalry
Confederate cavalry

GRANT FLANKS LEE Breaking off bloody fighting at Spotsylvania, Grant marched around Lee, who countered to block his enemy's path to Richmond. Subsequent battles—the most ferocious at Cold Harbor—brought Grant's army to Petersburg in June.

"They couldn't hit an elephant at this distance."

—GENERAL JOHN SEDGWICK'S LAST WORDS BEFORE BEING KILLED BY A CONFEDERATE SHARPSHOOTER AT SPOTSYLVANIA

CHAMPION OF THE UNION
ULYSSES S. GRANT
1822–1885

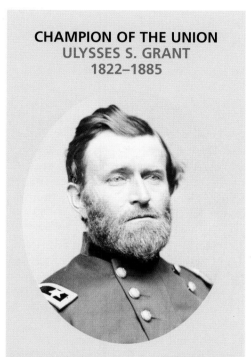

A West Pointer from Ohio, Grant won citations for gallantry in the Mexican War. In the peacetime army, he served in a lonely outpost on the West Coast and began drinking too much. Accused of neglect of duty, he resigned in 1854, avoiding a court martial. Grant's subsequent civilian life was financially unsuccessful.

When the Civil War began, Grant was given command of an Illinois regiment and soon after became a brigadier general. His triumphs at Forts Henry and Donelson brought him to national prominence, and his campaign to capture Vicksburg in mid-1863 made him a hero. After the Chattanooga campaign later that year, Lincoln named Grant commander of all the Union armies.

After defeating Lee, Grant went to to become secretary of war and in 1868 was elected 18th President of the United States. Sadly for Grant, his two-term administration was plagued with scandal. In his retirement, as he was dying of throat cancer, he wrote much-admired memoirs.

defenders fought for every inch. Heavy rain stopped further major fighting at Spotsylvania.

The Union lost almost 11,000 troops, the Confederates fewer, although the precise figure is unknown.

Hopeless charge at Cold Harbor
Through the end of May, in extremely hot weather, elements of the the two armies engaged in skirmishes and small battles as Lee kept moving to prevent Grant from outflanking him.

By May 31, the armies were close to Richmond, with Lee again strongly entrenched. The Union had 108,000 troops, the Confederates 59,000. Grant attacked Lee's defenses, testing and probing for a vulnerable spot to assault. Finding none, he resolved on an overwhelming mass charge at Cold Harbor, hoping to smash through Lee's defenses with a frontal attack. A general assault

was launched on June 3, but the Union troops were cut to pieces, 7,000 falling in half an hour. Lee lost 1,500 men. Cold Harbor earned Grant a reputation as "The Butcher," an epithet that haunted him because he profoundly regretted his tactics that day. Still, he could bring in replacements, which Lee could not.

Again Grant maneuvered around Lee, in mid-June crossing the James River on pontoon bridges to rapidly advance on the railroad city of Petersburg, south of Richmond. General P.G.T. Beauregard was there with only a few thousand defenders, but he stalled Grant's advance guard long enough for Lee's main army to arrive. Grant was forced to lay siege to Petersburg, giving his weary army a much-needed rest. In more than a month of campaigning, he had lost 50,000 men, or 41 per cent of his original force. Lee had lost 32,000, or 46 percent.

SHERMAN AND JOHNSTON FIGHT A WAR OF MANEUVER

In early May 1864, Sherman's 100,000 troops began to push their way past Joseph Johnston's 62,000 men blocking the route to Atlanta. Sherman attempted to outflank the Confederates, while Johnston played for time, avoiding full-scale engagements. The Lincoln-McClellan presidential election that November would be influenced by whether the Union was winning the war. If Johnston prevented Sherman from taking Atlanta, then Northern impatience with the war's progress could cause Lincoln's defeat. McClellan as president might make peace, and the Confederacy would be secure.

To that end, Johnston countered Sherman's moves but did not commit to a do-or-die battle.

Sherman's Atlanta Campaign

Grant had ordered Sherman to "break up" Johnston's army while "inflicting all the damage you can against their war resources" and advancing as deeply as possible into the South.

The plan was sound, except that the tenacious Johnston stood in the way. Sherman and his generals brought their superior numbers to bear, threatening Johnston's flanks, and driving him ever southward. While Sherman pressed for a decisive battle, only inconclusive actions resulted, and Johnston continued his retrograde through Georgia. At Dalton, Resaca, Adairsville, and Kingston, the Confederates fought and withdrew, staying between Sherman and Atlanta. In late June the armies clashed at Kennesaw Mountain, with 16,000 Federals attacking 17,700 Confederates. Sherman suffered 2,000 casualties, Johnston fewer than 500.

Johnston again withdrew, this time to the Chattahoochee River, just north of Atlanta. Sherman outflanked him once more, and Johnston crossed the river to the outskirts of Atlanta.

By now, C.S.A. President Jefferson Davis had decided Sherman was being permitted to advance too far and too fast. Davis relieved Johnston and replaced him with John Bell Hood, a West Pointer whose philosophy was attack and attack again. Hood did just that, suffering heavy casualties on July 20. An offensive two days later, known as the Battle of Atlanta, cost 8,500 Southern troops compared with a Union loss of 3,700. Sherman later

CHATTANOOGA TO ATLANTA This postwar bird's-eye view titled, "Western and Atlantic R.R., the great Kennesaw route from Atlanta to the north and north-west," shows the section of Tennessee and Georgia, where Sherman and Johnston fought during the Atlanta campaign in spring and early summer, 1864.

wrote that by replacing Johnston, Davis had "rendered us a great service."

With 85,000 men, Sherman laid siege to Hood's 42,000-man army in Atlanta from mid-July to September 1st. Hood was compelled to evacuate Atlanta to keep his army alive.

In this same time, Admiral David Farragut and the Union Navy defeated the harbor batteries and warships of

"I beg to present you, as a Christmas gift, the city of Savannah."

—SHERMAN'S TELEGRAM TO PRESIDENT LINCOLN UPON THE CAPTURE OF SAVANNAH, DECEMBER 21, 1864

IN THE HEART OF GEORGIA From May to December 1864, Sherman relentlessly pushed through Georgia, capturing Atlanta on September 1 and Savannah on December 21.

Mobile, Alabama, one of the last ports open to blockade runners. Farragut's victory in the Battle of Mobile Bay on August 5 helped seal the fate of the Confederacy, now virtually unable to import armaments or manufactured goods.

The Franklin-Nashville Campaign

As Sherman's army rested and recuperated in Atlanta, Hood led his men in an offensive north to Tennessee, toward Nashville. Sherman's plan was to march to Savannah, so Hood faced the armies of George Thomas and John M. Schofield. Hood could count on fewer than 40,000 men, while about 80,000 Federal troops were in the region.

Schofield, with 32,000 men, and Hood fought a major battle at Franklin on November 30. As before, Hood's aggressiveness cost him dearly, and he lost 7,000 troops. Still, he pressed on, hoping for an uprising of Confederate supporters, which did not develop. Near Nashville on December 1, Hood's 25,000 weary and hungry men were attacked by Thomas's 50,000. Hood suffered 6,700 casualties, while Thomas lost 5,300. The shattered Confederate army retreated southward.

Meanwhile, Sherman's "March to the Sea" devastated Georgia. Meeting little organized resistance, his 60,000-strong army destroyed railroads and plantations, confiscating or ruining any property that could be of military value to the South. Sherman captured undefended Savannah on December 21.

SHERMAN'S MARCH TO THE SEA 1864

BOMBARDING ATLANTA Sherman observes his artillery firing heavy barrages on Atlanta during the month-long siege of Hood's army holding the city.

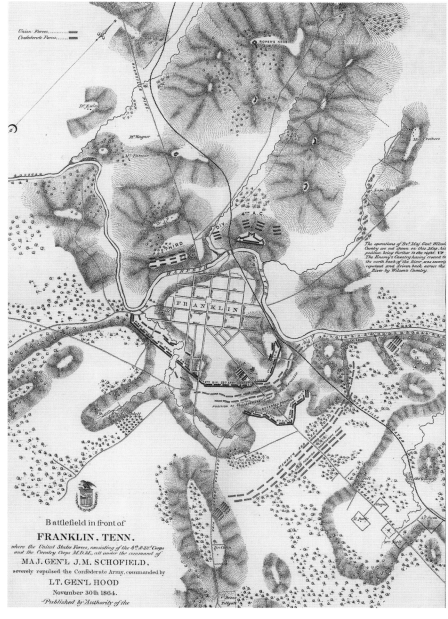

THE BATTLE OF FRANKLIN In 1874, the war department's topographical engineers published this map of troop positions during the November 30, 1864, fighting at Franklin, Tennessee, when Schofield repulsed frontal assaults launched by Hood.

A HUNGRY CONFEDERATE WINTER, A SPRINGTIME OF DEFEAT

SHERIDAN'S RIDE TO VICTORY Sheridan galloped 20 miles to rally his troops and win the Battle of Winchester in October 1864.

General Philip Sheridan conducted a successful Shenandoah Valley Campaign in late 1864, defeating General Jubal Early and helping increase the hardship for the defenders of Richmond and Petersburg. Sheridan laid waste the fertile Shenandoah, killing or running off livestock, ruining farms—burning more than 2,000 barns—and destroying flour mills. Without the Shenandoah's food, besieged Confederate civilians and soldiers suffered intense hunger that winter.

Sheridan's aggressive subordinate, General George A. Custer, wiped out the tattered remainder of Early's force in March 1865. Sheridan conducted a bold cavalry raid with 10,000 men across northern Virginia then joined Grant for an attack on Lee's right wing at Five Forks on April 1. The Union inflicted 8,000 casualties on General George Pickett's Confederates—approximately 4,000 were taken prisoner—while losing only 1,000 men.

Grant grows stronger

Well-supplied from river depots, the army under Grant increased in size and strength during the nine-month siege of Petersburg. Though starving and poorly equipped, Lee's forces held on, and late in March launched a failed attack at Fort Stedman, a Union strongpoint. Lee lost 5,000 men, Grant 2,000.

Grant broke the Petersburg siege on April 2 by forcing an opening in Lee's defenses. Lee had to abandon his position, so there was no holding Richmond now. The Confederate government evacuated the city, setting fire to military facilities and inadvertently causing much of Richmond to become an inferno. Lee conducted a fighting retreat to the southwest, planning to unite with Joseph Johnston, who in February had taken command of 21,000 troops in the Carolinas. These included the remnants of his former army, which had been destroyed when under Hood at Atlanta and Nashville.

Sherman in the Carolinas

The odds against Johnston were daunting. Sherman with 60,000 men was advancing north from Savannah, while Schofield commanded another army operating near the coast, where Beauregard fought on resolutely.

Known now as the Grand Army of the West, Sherman's force grew to 80,000. It marched and fought constantly for 50 days, covering 425 miles from Savannah and through the Carolinas with little rest. As in the Atlanta campaign, Johnston had to maneuver to keep his ragged army alive, yet he dared go on the offensive in mid-March, attacking two Union corps at Bentonville, North Carolina. When

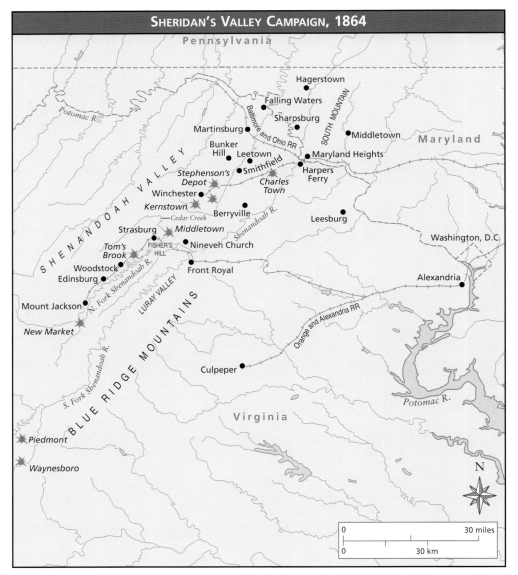

SHERIDAN'S VALLEY CAMPAIGN, 1864

Pennsylvania

Potomac R.

Hagerstown

Falling Waters

Sharpsburg

SOUTH MOUNTAIN

Martinsburg

Baltimore and Ohio RR

Middletown

Maryland

Bunker Hill

Leetown

Maryland Heights

Stephenson's Depot

Smithfield

Harpers Ferry

SHENANDOAH VALLEY

Winchester

Charles Town

Kernstown

Cedar Creek

Berryville

Shenandoah R.

Leesburg

Strasburg

Middletown

Washington, D.C.

Tom's Brook

FISHER'S HILL

Nineveh Church

Woodstock

N. Fork Shenandoah R.

Front Royal

Alexandria

Edinsburg

LURAY VALLEY

Mount Jackson

Orange and Alexandria RR

New Market

BLUE RIDGE MOUNTAINS

S. Fork Shenandoah R.

Culpeper

Virginia

Potomac R.

Piedmont

Waynesboro

N

0   30 miles
0   30 km

THE UNION TAKES THE SHENANDOAH As the main armies became mired down in the siege of Petersburg, Sheridan triumphed in the Shenandoah Valley, defeating Early and ravaging farmland. Though a ruthless scourge to the valley and its people, Sheridan was a top field commander.

UNION VICTORY IN VIRGINIA 1864–1865

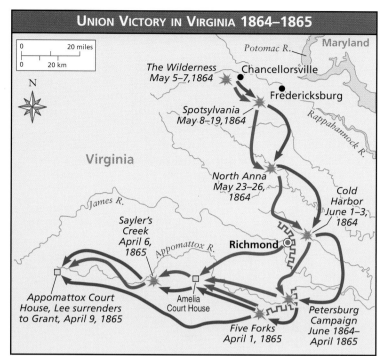

GRANT CONQUERS LEE The long journey to Union victory began in the spring of 1864, as Grant opened his campaign in the Wilderness. Lee fought against heavy odds until he had no choice but to surrender his starving army at Appomattox on April 9.

Sherman appeared with his full force, Johnston withdrew. In Virginia, Lee was retreating before Grant, who intended that the Union vise would soon crush both Confederate forces.

Lee and Johnston surrender

Lee had 50,000 troops, who would be formidable numerically if combined with Johnston's army. Grant was determined to prevent that, and he pursued closely with his 112,000 men, striking at Lee's columns, lopping off units, capturing thousands at a time, including generals.

On April 7, after destroying a Confederate supply train, Sheridan blocked Lee's line of retreat. Two days later, on April 9, Grant and Lee met at Appomattox Court House and agreed to surrender terms. Johnston, who faced a similarly hopeless situation near Goldsboro, North Carolina, surrendered to Sherman on April 26.

A few diehard Confederates in the West fought on for weeks to come, but the final triumphs of Grant and Sherman brought the American Civil War to an end, after four long years.

"Let the thing be pressed."

—PRESIDENT LINCOLN'S STATEMENT TO GENERAL GRANT AFTER HEARING SHERIDAN'S SUGGESTION THAT IF PRESSED, LEE MIGHT SURRENDER HIS ARMY

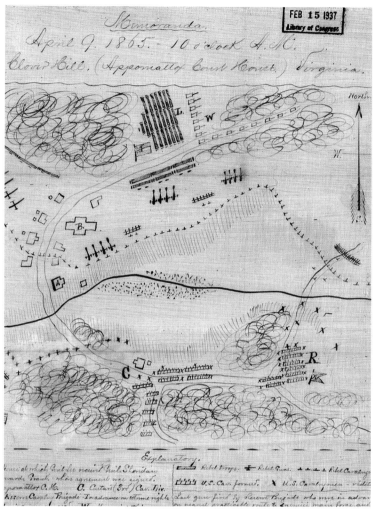

THE FINAL SCENE Showing Appomattox Court House and vicinity during Lee's 1865 surrender, including Union and Confederate troop positions, this period sketch map was found years later in a back closet of a construction company and donated to the Library of Congress.

FLEEING RICHMOND Fire rages in the Confederate capital on April 2, 1865, as cavalrymen escort carriages of government officials across the James River in hopes of escaping capture by the Union army. President Davis would be caught in Georgia in May.

The War of Railroads and Ironclads

Although the American Civil War of 1861–1865 would see the first use of ironclad warships, in 1859 the French launched the *Gloire*, the first sea-going armored steam battleship. The British soon followed with their own ironclad, the *Warrior*, but it was the Americans who first built and fought whole fleets of ironclad ships and riverboats. One of the most effective naval innovations was the rotating gun turret used on "monitor" class warships. Most ironclads belonged to the North, whose overwhelming industrial superiority led to victory in the Civil War.

This was the first "railroad war," with both sides using trains to shift troops and supplies from place to place. The South's awkward mixture of unconnected rail lines, various track gauges and engines caused transport difficulties, while the North built thousands of miles of new track to support military operations. Rapid troop movements were facilitated by the widespread use of the electric telegraph.

In 1862 the rapid-fire Gatling Gun was patented, but it was little used during the war. The Civil War saw the development of rifled cannon made of high-quality cast iron. One such, the Parrott Gun, was an accurate artillery piece favored by both sides for field and naval guns. A few imported breech-loading cannon saw service with the Confederacy.

The seven-shot Spencer repeating rifle using metallic cartridges was introduced in 1863 and found immediate favor, especially in the Federal cavalry. Late in the war some Union infantry were armed with these weapons. Their firepower astonished the enemy, who believed they faced a whole division rather than just one regiment.

WILLING PATIENTS A Zouave regiment's ambulance crew demonstrates removal of wounded soldiers from the field by stretcher and loading them onto an ambulance wagon; most wounds were in the extremities, almost 90 percent by bullet, most of the rest by artillery fire.

ARMSTRONG HEAVY CANNON This C.S.A. gun of British manufacture defends Fort Fisher, North Carolina, during the Union's January 1865 amphibious landing and assault. Similar Union heavy naval guns battered the fort before the attack, which succeeded after seven hours of hand-to-hand fighting.

HENRY REPEATING RIFLE This breechloading 16-shot repeating rifle, was issued to Union troops late in the war. Bullets inside a metal tube located in the butt were fed into the firing chamber from the "breech," or back end, of the gun barrel.

BALLOON ASCENSION After being inflated with hydrogen produced from the reaction of sulfuric acid on iron filings, this reconnaissance balloon will fly, on a tether, high above the battlefield, carrying Union observers to study Confederate positions.

STEAM MONITORS AND RAMS A line of Union ironclads of the Monitor class steam past C.S.A. Fort Morgan in August 1864, attacking Mobile Bay. The ironclads protected Admiral David G. Farragut's fleet of wooden vessels, entering the bay at right. The leading monitor, *Tecumseh*, heels over, having just struck a Confederate "torpedo," or underwater mine. In the foreground the Confederate ram *Tennessee* fires back at the Union ships.

SPRINGFIELD RIFLE
The 1861 Model of the Springfield Rifle Musket, which was carried by most Federal troops, fired a .58 caliber conical Minié bullet.

SABOTAGING WIRES
A Union soldier cuts an enemy telegraph wire, then splices the broken connection so it cannot be detected from the ground. Vital telegraph lines required constant maintenance.

COLT PISTOL This .36 caliber "cap and ball" revolver of the Civil War accepted powder and bullet in wrapped cartridges, and each cylinder needed a percussion cap. The Army and Navy each had its own model.

ARTILLERY A battery of 20-pounder Parrott rifles—some of the heaviest and most accurate artillery used in the field—sits ready to move into action. Artillery batteries contained four to six cannon, each gun pulled by six horses, plus numerous ammunition caissons and wagons.

REBUILT BRIDGE
Union military engineers were skilled at swiftly reconstructing damaged railroad bridges, as they did with this one in eastern Virginia. The United States Military Railroad was organized by the Union to build and maintain railroads in areas of active operations.

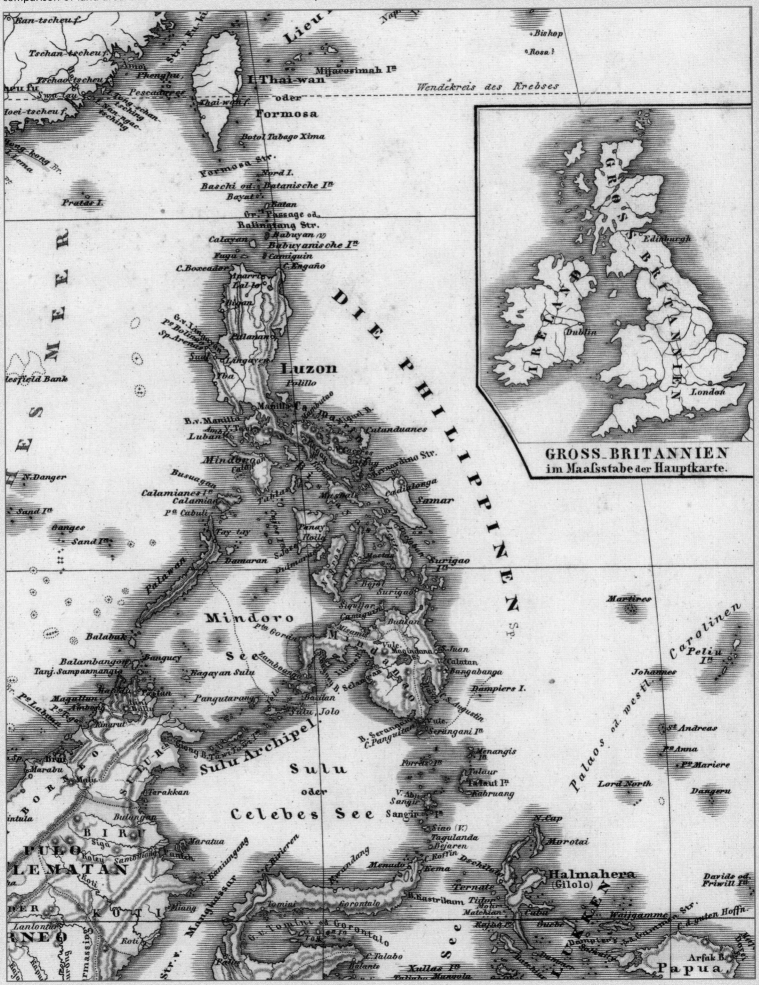

GROSS-BRITANNIEN
im Maassstabe der Hauptkarte.

DIE PHILIPPINEN

PART FOUR

An Emerging World Power

AFTER THE CIVIL WAR, THE UNITED STATES ARMY and navy were drastically reduced in size. The army policed native peoples in the trans-Mississippi West and enforced Reconstruction (1865–1877) policy in the former Confederate states. Troops were also used—as late as the 1900s—to suppress labor strikes and quell worker unrest.

Native peoples who had been forcibly removed west of the Mississippi were unable to live undisturbed in the second half of the 19th Century. Migrations to California, Oregon, and the Southwest sent thousands of people through Indian country and brought on conflict with the nations. Between 1860–1890, Indian wars involved more than 100,000 soldiers, a number comparable to the total populations of the nations that took up arms. By the late 1870s, the army had broken the power of the Plains Indians.

The military began to grow again in 1898, with the Spanish-American War that won the United States control of Cuba, Puerto Rico, and the Philippines, as well as other islands. Ruling the Philippines, which required the ruthless and bloody conquest of Filipino rebels, gave America a military and economic foothold in Asia. In 1900, the United States joined Britain, France, Germany, Russia, and Japan to crush the anti-foreign Boxer Uprising in China.

Military incursions in the Caribbean after 1900 established American supremacy over that region. The Pershing expedition of 1916 humbled Mexico yet again and helped prepare the American army for entering World War I in 1917.

U.S. cavalry in the West, ca. 1875

14: AMERICAN INDIAN CONFLICTS IN THE WEST

BUFFALO SOLDIERS Two African-American cavalry regiments (9th and 10th) and two infantry (24th and 25th) served on the western frontier after the Civil War. For 25 years, they fought hostile Indians, Mexican bandits, and frontier outlaws.

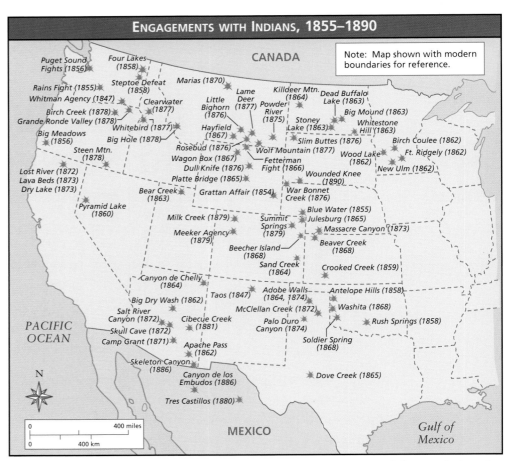

ENGAGEMENTS WITH INDIANS, 1855–1890

Note: Map shown with modern boundaries for reference.

CANADA

Puget Sound Fights (1856)
Four Lakes (1858)
Rains Fight (1855)
Steptoe Defeat (1858)
Marias (1870)
Whitman Agency (1847)
Clearwater (1877)
Lame Deer (1877)
Killdeer Mtn. (1864)
Dead Buffalo Lake (1863)
Birch Creek (1878)
Little Bighorn (1876)
Powder River (1875)
Big Mound (1863)
Grande Ronde Valley (1878)
Whitebird (1877)
Stoney Lake (1863)
Whitestone Hill (1863)
Big Meadows (1856)
Big Hole (1878)
Hayfield (1867)
Slim Buttes (1876)
Birch Coulee (1862)
Steen Mtn. (1878)
Rosebud (1876)
Wolf Mountain (1877)
Wood Lake (1862)
Ft. Ridgely (1862)
Wagon Box (1867)
Fetterman Fight (1866)
Lost River (1872)
Dull Knife (1876)
New Ulm (1862)
Lava Beds (1873)
Platte Bridge (1865)
Wounded Knee (1890)
Dry Lake (1873)
Bear Creek (1863)
Grattan Affair (1854)
War Bonnet Creek (1876)
Pyramid Lake (1860)
Blue Water (1855)
Milk Creek (1879)
Summit Springs (1879)
Julesburg (1865)
Massacre Canyon (1873)
Meeker Agency (1879)
Beaver Creek (1868)
Beecher Island (1868)
Sand Creek (1864)
Crooked Creek (1859)
Canyon de Chelly (1864)
Adobe Walls (1864, 1874)
Antelope Hills (1858)
Big Dry Wash (1862)
Taos (1847)
McClellan Creek (1872)
Washita (1868)
Salt River Canyon (1872)
Cibecue Creek (1881)
Palo Duro Canyon (1874)
Rush Springs (1858)
Skull Cave (1872)
Camp Grant (1871)
Apache Pass (1862)
Soldier Spring (1868)
PACIFIC OCEAN
N
Skeleton Canyon (1886)
Canyon de los Embudos (1886)
Dove Creek (1865)
Tres Castillos (1880)
MEXICO
Gulf of Mexico

0 — 400 miles
0 — 400 km

INDIAN WARS IN THE WEST There were few battles with Native Americans of the West before the Civil War; increased westward migration and railroad-building provoked uprisings from 1862-1878, especially among the peoples of the Northern and Southern Plains.

In 1828, the land the Choctaws called Oklahoma, meaning "red people," was established for the displaced native peoples of the East, South, and Midwest. Much of the remainder of the West was inhabited by tribes that remained free, although new treaties were moving them onto reservations. By the late 1850s, the Indians saw their country being taken over as wagon and stagecoach roads brought thousands of whites through the West. New army posts appeared, and railroad tracks were under construction—the workers feeding on buffalo from herds that were being rapidly reduced.

By now, Indian resistance in Oregon Territory and elsewhere in the Northwest had been forcibly put down. At Ash Hollow, Nebraska, in 1855 the Brulé Sioux had suffered 150 killed, many of them noncombatants, in a fight with 600 troops. In Colorado, prospectors were flooding into the Rockies, building mining towns in search of gold and silver. To the South in Texas the Comanches and Kiowas remained hostile for several years. In the Southwest, Chiricahua Apaches led by Cochise were on the verge of resuming guerrilla warfare.

Sioux uprising of 1862

The Santee Sioux of Minnesota and Iowa were being crowded out by thousands of settlers as farms sprang up where once

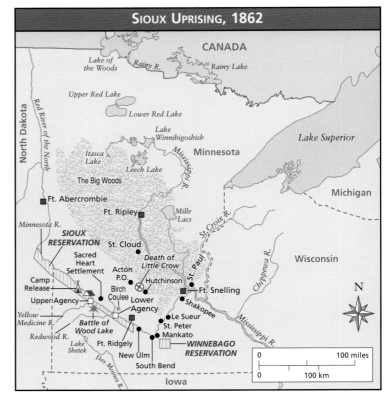

SIOUX UPRISING, 1862

CANADA

Lake of the Woods
Rainy R.
Rainy Lake
Upper Red Lake
Lower Red Lake
Lake Winnibigoshish
Lake Superior
North Dakota
Red River of the North
Itasca Lake
Leech Lake
Minnesota
Mississippi R.
The Big Woods
Michigan
Ft. Abercrombie
Ft. Ripley
Mille Lacs
St. Croix R.
Minnesota R.
SIOUX RESERVATION
St. Cloud
Sacred Heart Settlement
Death of Little Crow
Acton P.O.
St. Paul R.
Chippewa R.
Wisconsin
Camp Release
Birch Coulee
Hutchinson
Ft. Snelling
Upper Agency
Lower Agency
Shakopee
Yellow Medicine R.
Le Sueur
Mississippi R.
N
Battle of Wood Lake
St. Peter
Redwood R.
Lake Shetek
Ft. Ridgely
Mankato
New Ulm
WINNEBAGO RESERVATION
Des Moines R.
South Bend
Iowa

0 — 100 miles
0 — 100 km

SIOUX UPRISING A mid-1862 insurrection, led by Little Crow, was sparked by corrupt Indian agents, who caused starvation on Minnesota reservations. Troops from Fort Ridgley were defeated and New Ulm devastated before the revolt was quelled. Settlers killed Little Crow a year later.

there had been open prairie. In August 1862, with most soldiers shipped off to the East for the Civil War, the Sioux of Minnesota attacked farms and towns and besieged an army post. Led by Little Crow, they killed more than 800 settlers, beginning the Sioux Wars, which continued in several phases into the 1890s. The uprising was put down in September by a quickly organized army expedition, and a number of warriors were hanged.

Sioux in the Dakotas took the warpath in 1863, among them Sitting Bull, a Hunkpapa and leader of the Strong Heart warrior society. The Sioux joined with Cheyenne and Arapaho, their anger intensifying with the unprovoked massacre in November 1864 of peaceful Cheyenne at Sand Creek, Colorado. Volunteer Colorado cavalry, 700 strong, attacked the village of elderly Chief Black Kettle, taking no prisoners, killing and mutilating more than 300. Black Kettle escaped, but continued to advocate peace and moved onto a reservation. More warriors took up arms, shutting down wagon roads, such as the Bozeman Trail, and forcing army posts to be evacuated.

In December 1866, Sioux and Cheyenne led by Crazy Horse of the Oglala Sioux wiped out 81 cavalrymen near Fort Phil Kearny in Wyoming.

"There are not Indians enough in the country to whip the Seventh Cavalry."

— Lt. Colonel George A. Custer, on campaign, 1868

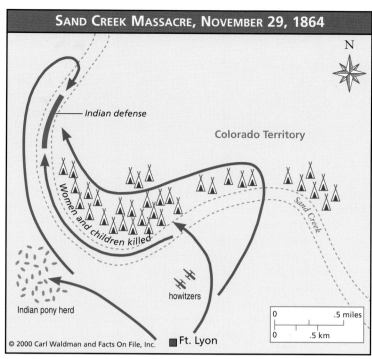

SAND CREEK MASSACRE, NOVEMBER 29, 1864

Indian defense

Colorado Territory

Women and children killed

Sand Creek

Indian pony herd

howitzers

Ft. Lyon

© 2000 Carl Waldman and Facts On File, Inc.

SAND CREEK MASSACRE The Third Colorado Volunteers, under Colonel John Chivington, galloped from three sides into this sleeping Cheyenne village on November 29, 1864. An investigation chastised Chivington, who had left the army and received no punishment.

The generals take charge in the West

Veteran Civil War generals William T. Sherman and Philip H. Sheridan took command of army departments in the West. Other high-ranking Civil War officers who also came West included George Crook, John Gibbon, Alfred H. Terry, and George A. Custer. The army's strategy was to campaign right through cold weather, when the tribes were gathered in large encampments and were least mobile. A treaty negotiated at Fort Laramie in April 1868 sent many Indians to reservations, but others—including Sitting Bull—continued to fight.

In September, 50 volunteers under Major George Forsyth were attacked at Beecher's Island in western Kansas. For seven days, armed with devastating repeating rifles, they held off assaults by 700 Cheyenne, Sioux, and Arapaho until saved by a charge from the 10th Cavalry Regiment of black troopers.

In November, an 800-strong force of 7th Cavalry led by Custer attacked a Cheyenne village on the Washita River, killing more than 100, many of them women and children. Among the dead was Black Kettle, who four years earlier had escaped the Sand Creek Massacre. Custer lost 22 killed.

BEECHER'S ISLAND Volunteers patrolling the Arikaree fork of the Republican River were pinned down by a force under Roman Nose on September 17, 1868. A distinguished Cheyenne war chief, Roman Nose was killed in the battle. His warriors were driven off by a charge of the 10th Cavalry.

RED RIVER WAR PACIFIES THE SOUTHERN PLAINS

n the years just after 1868, outbreaks of violence recurred across the West, but seldom developed into battles or campaigns. Grant, now president, insisted on making peace with the Indians rather than wantonly destroying them. His policies prevented hard-hearted commanders like Sheridan from launching destructive campaigns, but Grant could not control the corrupt Indian agents who managed the reservation system and made life miserable for the inhabitants. Hatred of reservations bred new hostiles among the young warriors.

At times, there was serious bloodshed. An incident revealing the military's worst side occurred in January 1870, when 170 Blackfoot villagers, most of them noncombatants, were massacred at Blood River, Montana.

The Salt Creek Raid

After Sherman became overall commander of the United States Army, he came West on an inspection tour in the spring of 1871. One of his tasks was to address Texan complaints about Comanches and Kiowas raiding ranches and settlements. Apparently, the raiders were immediately returning to Indian Territory and the Fort Sill Agency to take shelter from pursuit. While visiting the vicinity in May, Sherman heard Kiowa hostiles had just destroyed a supply wagon train at Salt Creek Prairie, torturing and killing several teamsters and stealing 40 mules.

The leader of the raiders was Satanta, who brazenly brought the mules back to the Fort Sill Agency and boasted openly about his exploits. Sherman immediately went to Fort Sill and called Satanta and other Kiowas into the fort commander's office. There, the Kiowas admitted the raid, and Sherman ordered them arrested. The Kiowa raised their guns, but Sherman coolly gave a signal that brought out a company of 10th Cavalry troopers, their own weapons presented. Satanta and the others were arrested and tried. He was sentenced to life in prison, where he committed suicide.

RED RIVER WAR Angry Southern Plains Indians retaliated for the bison slaughter by raiding white ranches, which brought retribution from the army. Ranald Mackenzie destroyed a Kiowa-Comanche camp at Palo Duro Canyon, helping break the power of the region's nations.

Red River War

After the Salt Creek Prairie Raid, the U.S. military became more aggressive in pursuing hostiles. In September 1871, Cochise of the Chiricahua Apaches gave up his struggle and soon moved onto a reservation. The Modoc War from 1872 to 1873 in northern California and Oregon involved few Indian fighters, but it cost the life of General Edward R.S. Canby, murdered by the leader of a band of Modocs during a peace conference. The few-score hostile Modocs were relentlessly chased down by hundreds of troops, the assassins tried and hanged, and the rest placed on reservations. Canby was the only general officer killed in the Indian wars.

On the Plains, the destruction of buffalo herds and the unceasing development of railroads and new towns caused profound bitterness and fury among the nations. Resultant conflicts brought about the Red River War, sparked in June 1874 by the Battle of Adobe Walls in

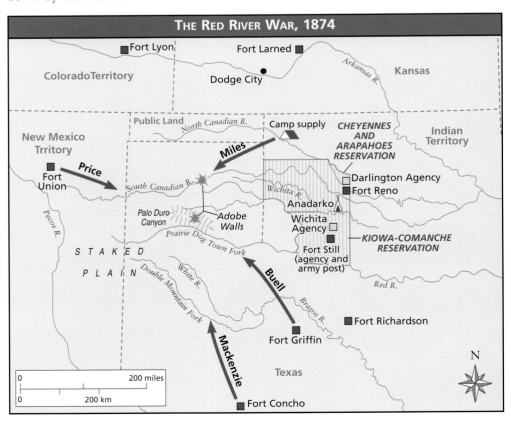

SLAUGHTER OF THE BUFFALO The Plains Indians depended on migrating herds of bison for food, clothing, and shelter. Professional hunters and sportsmen destroyed the herds, shown stopping a train. The slaughter enraged the native hunters, who killed only what they needed for daily sustenance.

"All you had to do was pick them off, one by one . . . until you wiped out the entire herd . . . I once took 269 hides with 270 cartridges."

—FRANK MAYER, BUFFALO HUNTER, ON THE EASE WITH WHICH BUFFALO WERE KILLED.

THE RED RIVER WAR, 1874

Fort Lyon • Fort Larned
Colorado Territory • Dodge City • Kansas
Arkansas R.

Public Land • Camp supply • CHEYENNES AND ARAPAHOES RESERVATION • Indian Territory
North Canadian R.
New Mexico Trritory • Miles
Fort Union • Price • South Canadian R. • Darlington Agency • Fort Reno
Pecos R. • Palo Duro Canyon • Adobe Walls • Wichita R. • Anadarko
Prairie Dog Town Fork • Wichita Agency
STAKED PLAIN • Double Mountain Fork • White R. • Fort Still (agency and army post) • KIOWA-COMANCHE RESERVATION
Red R.
Buell • Brazos R.
Mackenzie • Fort Griffin • Fort Richardson
Texas
Fort Concho

N

0 — 200 miles
0 — 200 km

THE MODOC WAR, 1872–1873

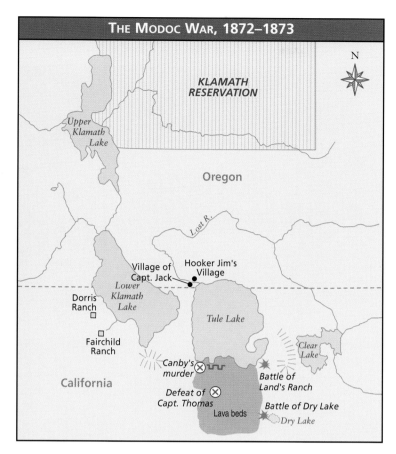

THE MODOC WAR A Modoc band under Captain Jack and Hooker Jim left the Klamath Reservation, and in 1872 the army defeated them at Dry Lake. Captain Jack was hanged for murdering General Edward Canby, a Civil War hero, under a flag of truce.

northern Texas. Defending a walled trading post, 28 buffalo hunters successfully stood off several hundred Cheyenne and Comanche attackers. Other serious Indian belligerence spurred Sherman to order Philip Sheridan into action. Sheridan sent five columns of cavalry, infantry, and Indian scouts, totaling 2,000 men, toward Indian encampments in northern Texas.

The army commanders were colonels Nelson Miles and Ranald Mackenzie, who led their forces through stifling August heat to confront the tribes. The Arapaho were not about to make war, but approximately 1,200 Comanche, Cheyenne, and Kiowa warriors took up arms, only to be defeated in several small, one-sided engagements that ended with them on the run. Winter closed in, and the troops continued for months to harry the fugitives, capturing their supplies and killing their pony herds. With each passing day, the Indians suffered more severely from hunger and exposure. Most surrendered by the following spring, ending the Red River War and finally breaking the power of these warlike nations.

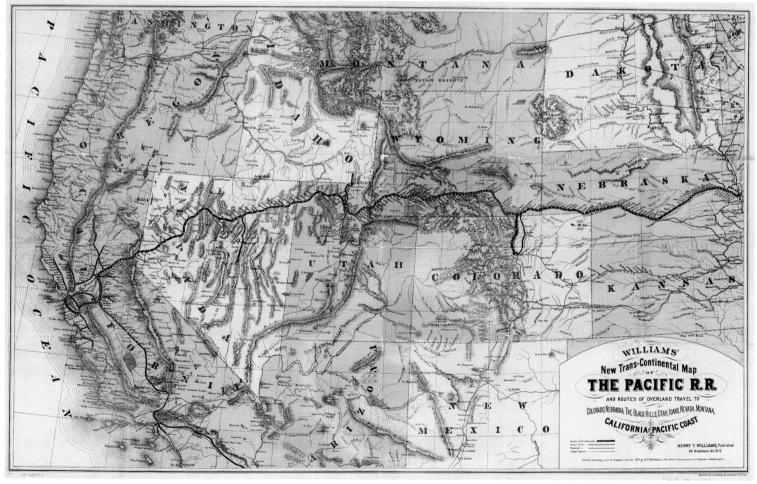

TRANSCONTINENTAL RAILROAD The main line on the central railroad route from the Mississippi, through the Rockies, to California and the Pacific Coast is shown on this contemporary map. The coming of the "Iron Horse" opened the West to rapid settlement and doomed the power of the tribes.

111

BATTLES OF THE ROSEBUD AND THE LITTLE BIG HORN

COLONEL CUSTER Victory in the Black Hills would have enhanced Custer's political reputation, perhaps making him a Democratic presidential candidate.

7th CAVALRY ON EXPEDITION Officers and scientific corps members of the 1874 "Custer Expedition" rest while exploring for mineral wealth in the Dakota Sioux's Black Hills. Many of these men died two years later at the Little Big Horn.

The American Indian struggle with the U.S. army and the reservation system won support from many white sympathizers, especially in the eastern cities. In 1870, Teton Sioux leader Red Cloud visited New York City to meet individuals and organizations opposing the government's Indian policies. Ruthless Indian agents and their cronies embezzled cash and stole supplies meant for the reservations, where living conditions were grim. After his well-publicized tour, Red Cloud returned to the West, settled on a reservation named after him, and kept his promise never again to take the warpath.

Custer enters Dakota's Black Hills

In 1873 the second phase of the Sioux Wars began. Though treaties had guaranteed the Sioux possession of the Black Hills of Dakota, which the nations considered sacred, an army expedition marched through the region that year, and skirmishes took place. The following year, Custer led a large military scouting expedition through the Dakotas, also bringing on clashes.

In 1875, sensational newspaper reports of Custer's expedition discovering gold in the region attracted thousands of prospectors. The government offered to buy the Black Hills, but the Sioux refused. In violation of past treaties, the Black Hills were opened to gold mining. Embittered, many Sioux left their reservations, with some bands attacking ranches and settlements. Leading the Sioux was Sitting Bull, now a wizened medicine man and a diplomat who made alliances with

Cheyenne and Arapaho. Crazy Horse of the Oglala Sioux was the war chief.

In the spring of 1876, the army pursued the Indians in force, determined to push them back to the reservation. Three military columns converged on the region, trying to find the Indian encampments, but unaware that as many as 15,000 people, including 4,000 warriors, had gathered near the Little Big Horn River in Montana's Yellowstone country. The largest column numbered 1,000

men—10 troops of cavalry and five companies of infantry, led by General George Crook, whose task was to drive the hostiles toward the other two columns, which totaled 1,400 men. On June 17th, Crazy Horse and 1,200 warriors surprised Crook's camp on the Rosebud River, and a pitched battle raged for six hours before the Indians were compelled to withdraw. Shaken at such unexpectedly strong resistance, Crook retreated to his main base.

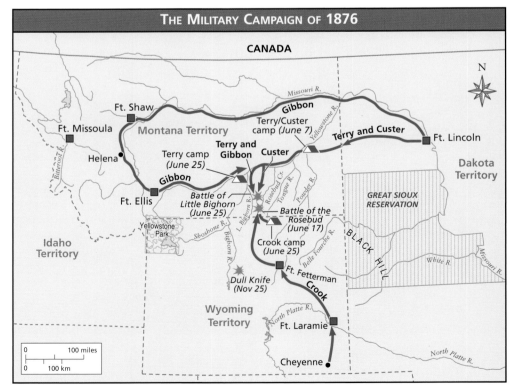

THE MILITARY CAMPAIGN OF 1876

MARCH TO LITTLE BIG HORN In 1876 three army columns set out to find encampments of Sioux and Cheyenne, who had left the reservation. Crook was driven back at the Rosebud, and Custer was wiped out at Little Big Horn. That fall the army took revenge, destroying the Cheyenne winter encampment of Chief Dull Knife on the Big Horn River.

Battle of the Little Big Horn

The other columns—under General Alfred Terry and General John Gibbon—continued marching, unaware Crook had been checked. Terry's advance troops were under Custer, who had the 7th Cavalry and Indian scouts, almost 650 men.

On June 25, Custer located the Little Big Horn encampment, but had no idea how large it was. He divided his force into three formations, himself taking 210 men and recklessly charging the village, expecting his other troops to approach from different directions. Too late, Custer saw the overwhelming enemy he had stirred up. His command dismounted and fought desperately from a hill above the river. Surrounded, Custer fought for two hours before being wiped out. The other two cavalry formations managed to reunite and dig in, besieged.

Two days later, as army reinforcements approached, the Indians abandoned their encampment, and the 7th Cavalry survivors were rescued. Custer's force lost 268 dead and 59 wounded, while the Sioux, Cheyenne, and Arapaho suffered an estimated 50 dead.

The United States was shocked by the massacre of Custer and the 7th Cavalry, and many people wanted revenge. Reinforcements hurried westward for another campaign, this time to destroy the renegades or force them once and for all onto the reservation.

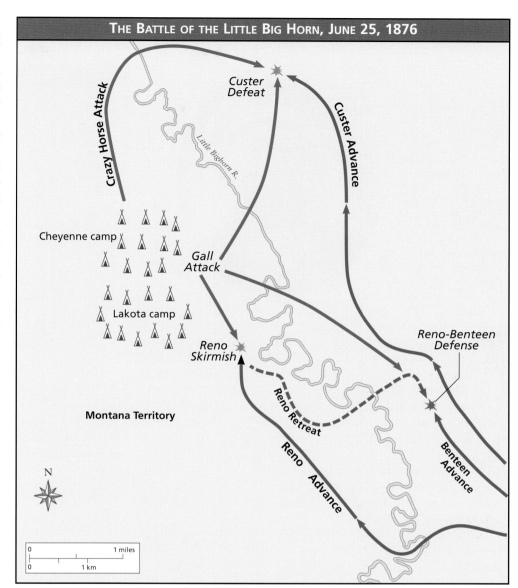

THE BATTLE OF THE LITTLE BIG HORN, JUNE 25, 1876

Custer Defeat

Crazy Horse Attack

Custer Advance

Little Bighorn R.

Cheyenne camp

Gall Attack

Lakota camp

Reno Skirmish

Reno-Benteen Defense

Reno Retreat

Reno Advance

Benteen Advance

Montana Territory

N

0   1 miles
0   1 km

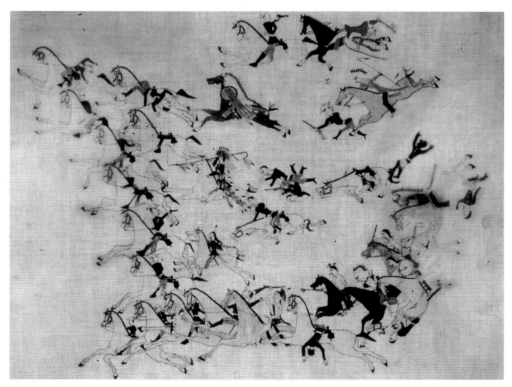

CUSTER'S AMBITIOUS PLAN Expecting to gallop into an unprepared village, Custer was met head-on by hundreds of warriors, who wiped out his detachment and drove back Major Marcus A. Reno's supporting attack. Reinforced by Captain Frederick W. Benteen's battalion, Reno dug in and fought until rescued the next day.

"Ho hechetu! *That was a fight, a hard fight. But it was a glorious fight, I enjoyed it . . .*"

—White Bull, a Lakota warrior, recalling the ferocity of the Little Big Horn battle.

INDIANS ROUT RENO Major Reno's battalion is pursued by Sioux and Cheyenne warriors in this painting by White Bird, a Northern Cheyenne, who fought at the Little Big Horn, where Custer was defeated on June 25, 1876.

NATIVE AMERICAN RESISTANCE: GALLANT AND DESPERATE

CHIEF JOSEPH
Thunder Rolling Over Mountains, as he was known to the Nez Percé, often spoke to white audiences, with the theme that all peoples should have equal rights.

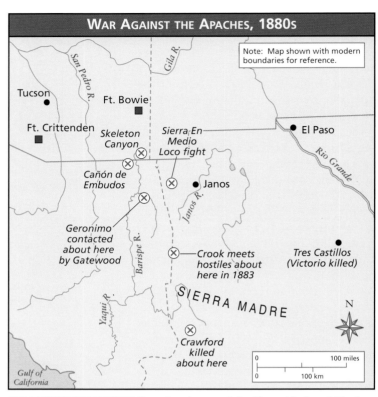

WAR AGAINST THE APACHES, 1880s

Note: Map shown with modern boundaries for reference.

GERONIMO'S TERRITORY Geronimo haunted the Sierra Madre of Mexico, where Crook persuaded him to return to the reservation in 1883. Geronimo again broke out, but in 1886 Lieutenant Charles B. Gatewood convinced him to surrender to General Nelson Miles at Skeleton Canyon.

At Cedar Creek, Montana, in October 1876, General Nelson Miles defeated Sitting Bull, who fled to Canada. In November, Ranald Mackenzie defeated a Cheyenne encampment at the Powder River, Montana. The second phase of the Sioux Wars ended in January 1877, at Wolf Mountain, Montana, when Miles defeated Crazy Horse, who surrendered in May. That September, Crazy Horse was killed while allegedly resisting his guards.

Defying confinement on reservations
Much of the continuing troubles from 1877–1889 arose from the unhappiness of "reservation Indians," some of whom tried to escape government control.

The traditionally peaceful Nez Percé of the Northwest defied orders to go to another reservation, and 800 followed Chief Joseph on a flight to Canada in June 1877. Several army detachments were sent to stop Chief Joseph, who inflicted heavy casualties on the soldiers. In October, after journeying 1,700 miles, Joseph and his exhausted people were trapped by Nelson Miles at Bear Paw Mountain, Montana, just 40 miles from the border.

The Paiutes, who had unsuccessfully fought resettlement in 1867–1868, joined with the Bannocks to flee their Idaho and Oregon reservations in 1878. They were captured six weeks later. In 1879, the Utes of Colorado objected to orders to move and took up arms, but before long they had no choice but to give up.

In mid-1881, Sitting Bull, too, came in peacefully to save his homeless followers from famine. In 1885, Buffalo Bill Cody featured him in his touring "Wild West Show," where he became internationally famous as "The Killer of Custer."

Geronimo fights on in the Southwest
Renegade Apaches kept raiding in the Southwest and along the Mexican border, with Geronimo of the Chiricahua their best leader. More than once, Geronimo returned to the reservation, but then fled, unwilling to live like a captive. In the early 1880s, General George Crook's cavalry and Apache scouts joined with thousands of Mexican soldiers in campaigns against Geronimo and his few hundred followers. Assuming this duty early in 1886, Nelson Miles persuaded Geronimo that autumn to surrender. The last Indian leader to give up, Geronimo was taken from his homeland and confined to a reservation, never allowed to return.

The Ghost Dance and Wounded Knee
By 1889, a religious inspiration known as the "Ghost Dance," had been sweeping through the reservations. Medicine men and shamans saw visions of an Indian savior who would destroy their enemies and restore freedom and happiness to the nations. The people joined in hypnotic dancing that caused trances and exalta-

GERONIMO AND COMRADES Armed and determined to fight, Chiricahua Apache renegade Geronimo, far right, and stalwart companions, pose for a photograph in 1886.

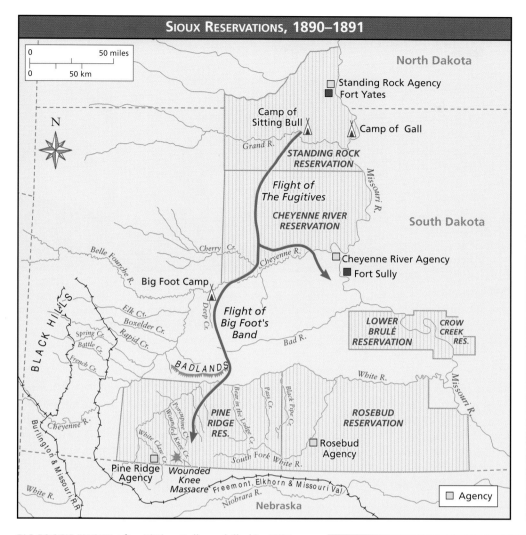

SIOUX RESERVATIONS, 1890–1891

THE GHOST DANCE

The first Ghost Dance cult appeared among the Paiutes in 1869, promising a glorious return of the dead, defeat of the whites, and restoration of traditional Indian life. This Ghost Dance inspired several tribes, but soon faded away. Another, much stronger Ghost Dance cult appeared among the Paiutes in January 1889, when their shaman Wovoka received a vision during an eclipse. Wovoka's teachings, and the stigmata that manifested on his hands and feet, caused many to believe he was the true Indian messiah.

With its rituals, music, and trances, the Ghost Dance spread like wildfire throughout the reservations. Ghost Dancers experienced visions and communed with the dead. Wovoka promised that magic "Ghost Shirts" worn into battle would protect the wearer from harm. Many of the Sioux at the Wounded Knee massacre wore their "Ghost Shirts" in anticipation of a battle.

BIG FOOT'S FLIGHT After Sitting Bull was killed in 1890, Chief Big Foot's band fled Standing Rock Reservation and went to Pine Ridge in South Dakota, where they were surrounded by soldiers at Wounded Knee.

tion, worrying the Indian agents, who feared many warriors would be persuaded to take up arms again.

Since Sitting Bull was the greatest living symbol of Indian prowess, the army decided to place him in close custody. On December 15, 1890, the attempt resulted in a fight with Sitting Bull's followers, and he was killed by Indian police. Expecting to be arrested next, Chief Big Foot of the Miniconjou Sioux fled with several hundred followers toward Red Cloud's Pine Ridge reservation. The army caught Big Foot and his band, then escorted them to a camp at Wounded Knee, South Dakota. On December 29, the captives were surrounded by 500 troops and four Hotchkiss guns, as soldiers began to search them for weapons. When a shot rang out, the troops indiscriminately opened fire, killing Big Foot and 150 men, women, and children. Army gunfire was mainly responsible for killing 25 soldiers and wounding 39 more.

There was a brief campaign against Minnesota's Ojibwas in 1898, but Wounded Knee was the last major clash of the American Indian Wars, which had continued since the 1600s.

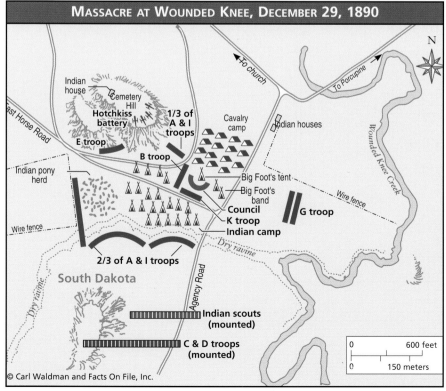

MASSACRE AT WOUNDED KNEE, DECEMBER 29, 1890

WOUNDED KNEE The army recorded the slaughter at Wounded Knee as a battle, but as shown on this map, the council site with Big Foot's people was hemmed in by soldiers and covered by Hotchkiss guns. Escape was blocked by mounted scouts and troopers.

15: THE SPANISH-AMERICAN WAR

Even before the Civil War, American business interests had eyed Spanish possessions in the Caribbean—Cuba and Puerto Rico. Rich in sugar, rice, and fruit, these colonies did a thriving trade with the United States. By 1897, American politicians and businessmen were also considering building a ship canal across the Isthmus of Panama, territory that belonged to Colombia. To control such a strategic canal, American arms must dominate the region, and Spain's colonies would make ideal military bases.

Since 1895, an insurrection had been raging in Cuba between the Spanish colonial government's forces and a determined Cuban independence movement. Despite facing 100,000 government troops and suffering from heavy-handed oppression, the 30,000 rebels kept up a guerrilla war that cost tens of thousands of lives. Taking the rebel side, the American press stirred up public opinion against Spain and called for Cuban independence.

Sinking of *Maine* sparks war with Spain

In January 1898, the battleship USS *Maine* was sent to Havana to protect United States interests there, but on February 15 she blew up and sank in the harbor, with the loss of 260 lives. Although later investigations pointed to an internal explosion as the cause, American politicians and the sensationalist press—blaring "Remember the *Maine*!"—blamed Spanish sabotage for the sinking. Congress declared war on April 25, with Cuba's independence as its stated objective, but Spain's colonies were ripe for the taking.

THE MAINE EXPLODES The battleship *Maine* entered the United States fleet in 1895. When she blew up in Havana harbor in 1898, 260 of her crew were lost. In 1976, a study by Admiral Hyman G. Rickover concluded the explosion was from spontaneous combustion in the coal bins, a hazard common to ships of the time.

The United States Army numbered approximately 30,000, with elderly Civil War generals as its top commanders. President William McKinley called for 200,000 volunteers, mostly drawn from the national guard system. The public rallied to the romance of waging what was portrayed as a righteous war against an oppressive European colonial power. There was a serious deficiency in the military, however: the army had no organization capable of training or supplying so large a force.

WAR WITH SPAIN IN THE CARIBBEAN This period map shows the 1898 Spanish-American War military movements among the islands of the Caribbean, many of which belonged to Spain. Insets show San Juan, Puerto Rico, Havana, and the Santiago campaign.

The navy was ready, however, with a modern "steel fleet" of five battleships, two cruisers, another 13 armored vessels, and six torpedo boats. Spain had a weak naval force, poorly maintained, and lacking convenient bases or coaling stations. While American troops mustered and trained in overcrowded camps at Tampa, New Orleans, and Mobile, the navy went into action.

Attack on Manila Bay

The main American squadron, led by Rear Admiral William T. Sampson, steamed toward Cuba to blockade her major port cities, Havana and Santiago. A second squadron, commanded by Commodore Winfield S. Schley, would soon join Sampson in operations against Cuba and the other Spanish islands. The American Asiatic Squadron, under Commodore George Dewey, proceeded to blockade the Philippines.

Hostilities began on the night of April 30, when Dewey's fleet of six armored warships steamed into Manila Bay, risking the danger of floating mines. At 7 a.m., Dewey engaged a squadron of seven Spanish warships, one of which was wooden-hulled. Dewey's 100 guns were heavier than the 37 carried by the Spaniards, and his gun crews better trained. By midday all the Spanish vessels were sunk or disabled. The Americans suffered only nine wounded, the Spanish 161 killed and 210 wounded.

Manila, itself, was already under siege by Filipino rebels, who had been waging a war of independence since 1896. The United States now arranged an alliance with the rebels and sent troops to help capture the city.

"You may fire when you are ready, Gridley."

—DEWEY, TO CAPTAIN CHARLES GRIDLEY OF THE FLAGSHIP OLYMPIA, BEGINNING THE BATTLE OF MANILA BAY IN APRIL 1898

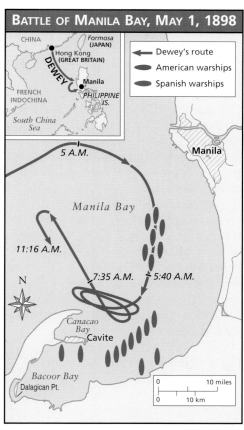

BATTLE OF MANILA BAY, MAY 1, 1898

Dewey's route
American warships
Spanish warships

BATTLE OF MANILA BAY The aging warships of Admiral Patricio Montojo y Parasón were outgunned by Admiral Dewey's modern squadron, which cruised elliptically for five hours, pounding the Spanish until they surrendered.

STEEL-ARMORED WARSHIPS "Our Victorious Fleet in Cuban Waters" is the title of this romanticized depiction of the American warships that defeated the Spanish fleet in the Caribbean in 1898.

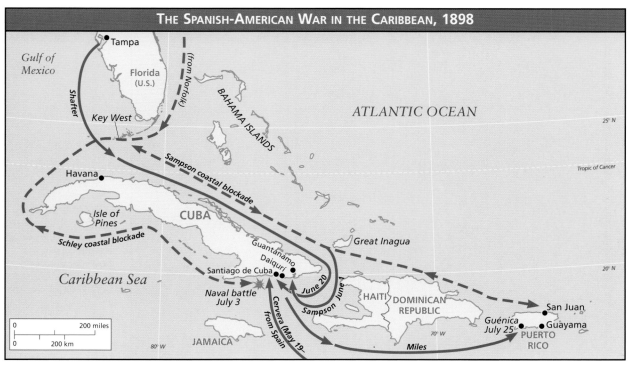

THE SPANISH-AMERICAN WAR IN THE CARIBBEAN, 1898

NAVAL BLOCKADE AND BATTLE The United States fleet blockaded Cuba, transported the main expeditionary force, and destroyed Cervera's squadron off Santiago; next it carried General Miles's 3,300 troops to take Puerto Rico.

117

AMERICA VICTORIOUS IN A "SPLENDID LITTLE WAR"

With Dewey's dramatic defeat of the Spanish Pacific squadron, American strategy changed, and 20,000 troops were shipped to San Francisco for transport to Manila as other expeditions set off to invade Cuba. Meanwhile, a handful of Spanish warships, commanded by Admiral Pascual Cervera y Topete, entered Santiago de Cuba harbor. Cervera was soon blockaded by vastly more powerful ships under Sampson and Schley.

Marines cooperating with Cuban rebels took over Guantanamo Bay on June 10, and on June 22 and 24 General William R. Shafter landed 17,000 men at Daiquiri and Siboney, southeast of Santiago. Like Nelson Miles, the commanding general of the army, Shafter was a Civil War and Indian wars veteran. Miles was at the head of his own invasion force, which had not yet arrived.

Though mainly regulars, Shafter's corps had several regiments of volunteers, one being the 1st United States Volunteer Cavalry, largely made up of Western cowboys and Eastern college boys. Calling itself the "Rocky Mountain Riders," the regiment later would be named the "Rough Riders." Logistical problems landed them in Cuba without their mounts, however, and only one officer found a horse—their second in command, Theodore Roosevelt, who had resigned as assistant secretary of the navy to serve in the war.

Rough Riders capture San Juan Hill

Other than minor skirmishing with American advance parties, the Spanish did not resist, but retreated toward Santiago. They numbered 12,000, many well-armed with modern Mauser rifles, but their artillery was deficient, and they lacked machine guns. On July 1, the Americans attacked Santiago's strongpoints at San Juan Hill and Kettle Hill and at El Caney to the north. The 6,600 American regulars attacking El Caney were held up by 520 dug-in Spanish defenders, who fought for more than 11

ROUGH RIDERS The 1st Volunteer Cavalry atop San Juan Hill with their commander, future president Theodore Roosevelt, center,

hours before retreating. Attacking San Juan Hill, Roosevelt's Rough Riders were joined by the 9th and 10th cavalry regiments, both African-American. Here, 500 Spaniards were entrenched around reinforced blockhouses, and they put up a fierce fight against the 8,000 American troops before them. San Juan Hill was taken after several hours, dooming Santiago, now under siege. The United States lost 205 killed and 1,180 wounded in the siege of Santiago, while the Spanish had 215 killed and 376 wounded.

The Battle of Santiago de Cuba

Admiral Cervera was given direct orders by the colonial government to break out and escape. Cervera knew he could never succeed, but he loyally obeyed, and on July 3, led his six ships on a

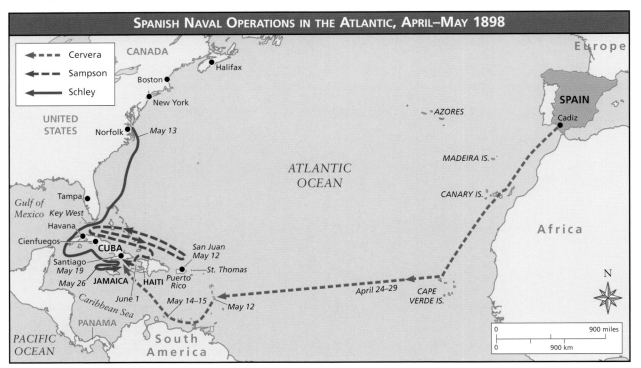

SPANISH NAVAL OPERATIONS IN THE ATLANTIC, APRIL–MAY 1898

- ◄--- Cervera
- ◄-- Sampson
- ◄— Schley

CANADA
Halifax
Boston
New York
UNITED STATES
Norfolk ● — May 13
Europe
SPAIN
Cadiz
AZORES
MADEIRA IS.
ATLANTIC OCEAN
CANARY IS.
Gulf of Mexico
Tampa
Key West
Havana
Cienfuegos
CUBA
Santiago May 19
May 26 JAMAICA
HAITI
Puerto Rico
San Juan May 12
St. Thomas
June 1
May 14–15
May 12
Caribbean Sea
PANAMA
PACIFIC OCEAN
South America
Africa
April 24–29
CAPE VERDE IS.
N

0 — 900 miles
0 — 900 km

CERVERA'S LONG JOURNEY Unprepared for war, Spain hastily assembled Admiral Cervera's fleet and rushed it more than 3,000 miles across the Atlantic to the Caribbean to help government forces oppose the American invasion of Cuba.

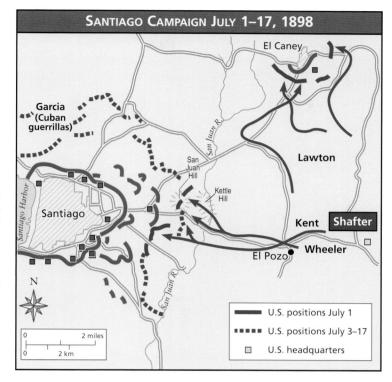

SANTIAGO CAMPAIGN JULY 1–17, 1898

El Caney

Garcia (Cuban guerrillas)

San Juan R.

Lawton

San Juan Hill

Kettle Hill

Santiago Harbor

Santiago

Kent

Shafter

N

El Pozo

Wheeler

San Juan R.

| 0 | 2 miles |
| 0 | 2 km |

▬▬▬ U.S. positions July 1
■■■■■ U.S. positions July 3–17
☐ U.S. headquarters

SANTIAGO CAMPAIGN Shafter's attack was led by generals Henry W. Lawton, Joseph Wheeler, and Jacob F. Kent. Spanish forces, under General Arsenio Linares y Pombo, numbered 28,000, and were scattered across the island, unable to concentrate at Santiago.

dash out of the bay. The American blockading fleet, under tactical command of Commodore Schley, utterly destroyed the outgunned Spanish warships within four hours. More than 300 Spanish were killed, and 1,700 taken prisoner, including Cervera.

Santiago surrendered on July 17. Except for a quick capture of Puerto Rico by Miles's expedition at the end of July, and the fall of Manila to American troops and Filipino rebels in August, the fighting was over. The United States lost fewer than 400 men in combat, but another 2,000 would die from tropical disease. A general armistice took hold on August 12, with a final peace treaty signed in Paris on December 10. Secretary of State John M. Hay told Roosevelt this was a "splendid little war."

Spain was required to leave Cuba and cede Puerto Rico and the Pacific island of Guam to the United States, which paid $10 million for the Philippines. Filipino rebels, however, were unwilling to trade one foreign occupier for another. The Americans would have to fight harder than ever to control the Philippines.

"We've got the damned Yankees on the run."

—U.S. CAVALRY COMMANDER IN CUBA AND FORMER CONFEDERATE GENERAL "FIGHTING JOE" WHEELER, FORGETTING WHICH WAR HE WAS IN AS HIS MEN FORCED SPANISH TROOPS TO RETREAT

ASSAULT ON SAN JUAN HILL Americans fall, shot down by Spanish defenders of San Juan Hill, as the crew of a rapid-fire Gatling gun prepares to support the attack.

SUDDEN MOBILIZATION FOR WAR AND EMPIRE

After the Civil War, the United States reduced its enormous field army of hundreds of thousands to 27,000 troops by 1876. The 700 vessels of the Civil War navy were decommissioned until the fleet was comparable to before the war.

As the military shrank, the United States burgeoned in size, with Secretary of State William H. Seward purchasing Alaska from Russia in 1867 and pushing for the acquisition or annexation of islands in the Caribbean and Pacific. At first, Congress opposed more acquisition, but American expansion would not be stopped for long. Hawaii was annexed in 1898, near the start of the Spanish-American War, which won America a colonial empire.

The beginning of the conflict was a logistical nightmare for the War Department as it attempted to train and equip a force that ballooned to 250,000 men. With only a handful of staff in the quartermaster corps, confusion reigned and supply systems virtually collapsed. This chaos resulted in troops being sent to war without gear and lacking proper supplies or hospital facilities. More than from battle-wounds, soldiers died from illness: malaria, yellow fever, and typhoid. Yellow fever was especially feared because of its high death rate, and typhoid affected a large number of troops.

TROOP TRAIN DEPARTING Soldiers of the 17th Infantry Regiment pile into railroad cars on their way to battle Filipino insurgents.

CONFLICT IN A COLONY: PHILIPPINE-AMERICAN WAR

EMILIO AGUINALDO (1869–1964) Filipino patriot leader and first president, Aguinaldo fought for independence against Spain, then against the United States.

Manila's surrender in August 1898 created a complicated situation, for a revolutionary army of 20,000 Filipinos had been besieging the city when the Americans arrived. In fact, Dewey had transported Filipino leader Emilio Aguinaldo to the Philippines from Hong Kong, where he had been living in exile. Aguinaldo at first was supported by the Americans, but now his forces were not permitted to enter Manila, nor were they given any credit for the defeat of the Spanish colonial army.

The Americans occupied Manila, while Aguinaldo's powerful force was on its outskirts, each side entrenched and patrolling a no-man's land between them. By January 1899, a Philippine republic had been established, and Aguinaldo named president. The United States, however, refused to recognize the government. The resentment of Filipino rebels and the imposition of American rule made for a volatile brew.

A short-lived peace

Taunts and insults were exchanged by the American Expeditionary Force and Filipino rebel troops, and they often got

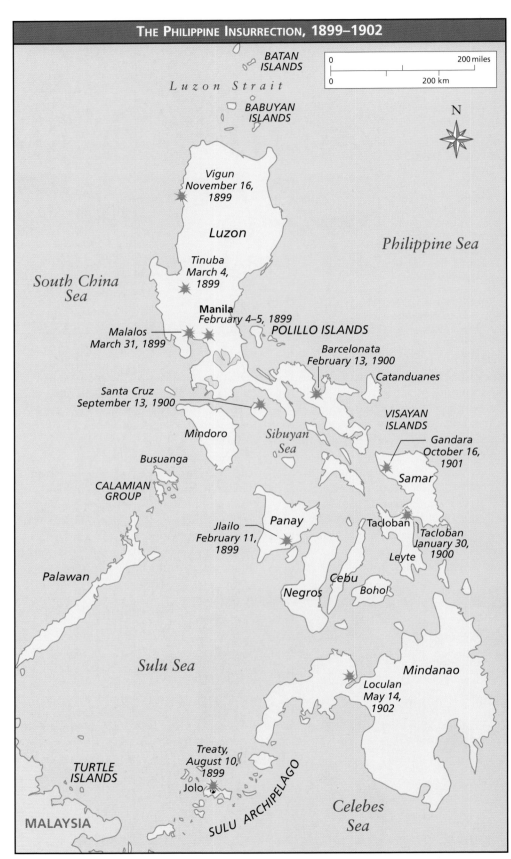

THE PHILIPPINE INSURRECTION, 1899–1902

PHILIPPINES CAMPAIGN Known in the United States as the "Philippine Insurrection," Filipino resistance against American colonialism brought about several engagements. Aguinaldo's capture in 1901 did not put an end to the hostilities. Hundreds of thousands of Filipino civilians died, most from starvation, many at the hands of American soldiers rooting out guerrilla fighters or destroying villages alleged to be supporting guerrillas.

into brawls. An uneasy few months exploded in February 1899 when an American patrol shot and killed Filipino sentries who challenged them. Full-scale combat erupted in and around the city, and 3,000 Filipinos died in just the first few days. The Philippine-American War, also known as the Philippine War for Independence, or the Philippine Insurgency, would rage for more than three years.

The major engagements took place on the island of Luzon, where Manila stood. General Ewell S. Otis led approximately 12,000 troops of the Eighth Corps, who were better-trained and armed than Aguinaldo's 40,000-strong army. American forces immediately pushed outward from Manila to split the Filipino forces and seize key towns and rivers. General Arthur MacArthur seized Caloocan in February and Malolos, the rebel capital, in March. Communications were cut between insurgent forces in north and south Luzon. American control was established over other important islands: Panay and Cebu in February, Negros in March, and Jolo in the Sulu Archipelago in May. In June, the American force numbered 47,500 men and would grow to 75,000 within a year.

Atrocity and starvation

By November 1899, the rebel field army was defeated, with heavy casualties, and its remnants began to wage a fierce guerrilla war. Otis was succeeded early in 1900 by MacArthur, who established

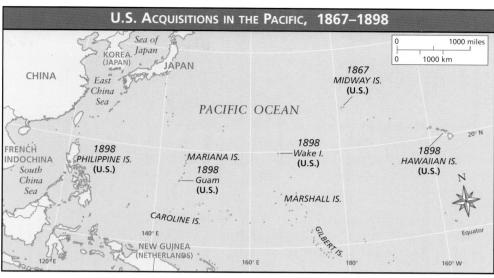

AMERICA'S PACIFIC ACQUISITIONS From Hawaii to the Philippines, the United States created a colonial empire in the Central Pacific during the 19th Century. The China trade was increasingly important, and the Philippines were ideal for American military bases and commerce.

martial law in certain military zones and filled concentration camps with civilians, separating them from the guerrillas. Both sides committed savage atrocities, and American troops often killed Filipinos without bothering to distinguish between combatant and civilian. Villages were wiped out or the population fled as their buildings were burned, livestock slaughtered, and crops ruined in order to starve out the insurgents.

In March 1901, General Frederick Funston and four American officers pretended to be prisoners of rebel troops—who actually were loyal Filipinos. They daringly entered the rebel camp, took Aguinaldo by surprise, and captured him.

The war continued until July 1902, with more than 125,000 American troops eventually committed to the conflict.

Estimates put Filipino deaths at between 200,000-600,000—some say far higher. Most died of starvation and disease caused by economic disruption and by the concentration camps; about 18,000 died in combat. More than 4,500 Americans died, many of disease, with 2,800 wounded.

Warfare was not yet over in the Philippine islands, however, because the Moros—Muslims of the southern islands—had never been defeated by the Spanish and did not consider the Americans their overlords.

"The slaughter at Manila was necessary. . . . We are the trustees of civilization and peace throughout the islands."

—CHICAGO TRIBUNE, REPORTING THE DEATHS OF 3,000 FILIPINOS IN MANILA IN 1899

INSURGENT LEADERS Filipino commanders pose for a group portrait during a gathering of veterans of the Philippine-American War, considered the Filipino war for independence.

121

BATTLING THE MOROS—A FIGHT TO THE DEATH

The warlike Muslim tribes of the islands of Sulu and Mindanao had fought the Catholic Spanish for 300 years by 1898, and all Spain had to show for it were a few garrison towns and plantations here and there. The long-bladed *kris* was the weapon of the fighting men of these people, called "Moros," Spanish for Muslims—Moors. Wielding the kris resolved disputes, and the law on these islands was the power of the warlord—a power the United States set out to break.

Moros strike at the Spanish

In the spring of 1899, while American troops defeated Aguinaldo, the Moros of Mindanao and Sulu attacked isolated Spanish garrisons. Cut off from supplies or rescue, these garrisons were wiped out to a man or abandoned.

"Moroland," as the region was known, entered a dangerous state of anarchy, with bandits roving the country and slaughtering the last of the Spanish colonials. The Moros were angry to hear Spain claimed to have sold their land to the Americans. Soon, American planters and soldiers were being attacked and murdered, and General Leonard Wood, governor of the Philippines, sent troops to quell Moro hostilities.

In 1902 and 1903, expeditions of 1,200 men or more campaigned on Mindanao, with considerable bloodshed. Although the Americans held the field in pitched battles, they were under almost continual attack and ambush on the narrow trails of dank, malarial swamps, and even in their camps at night. Yet, their artillery reduced the stone forts of leading warlords and killed warriors at long range. One officer, Captain John J. Pershing, found his small command being steadily increased in size because of his successes. He eventually had an army under him and was promoted to the rank of general by order of President Theodore Roosevelt—leaping over many senior officers.

THE PHILIPPINES At the end of the 19th Century, Filipinos were mostly a Malay people, some with Chinese and Spanish blood. Most practiced Roman Catholicism, while the Moros of the central and southern islands were Muslims who fiercely resisted attempts to convert them to Christianity.

"They say that they will never submit to America. They say that they will fight until they can no longer raise aloft the kris."

—DATU KALBI, A MORO ADVISING AMERICANS IN 1913

CAPTURE OF BUD BAGSAK American 8th Infantry and Philippine Scouts battle their way into the Moro stronghold, fighting hand-to-hand with tribesmen who are firing antiquated rifles or using shields and the traditional kris, a serpentine sword, seen lying at the feet of the officer with the pistol.

THE MORO WARS Savage and fearless in battle, the Moros had never been beaten by the Spaniards, and their mountainous, jungle islands seemed invulnerable until Pershing arrived. Starting out as a young captain, he campaigned for nine years in the Philippine wars, especially against the Moros on Mindanao and Luzon.

Battles of Bud Dajo and Bud Bagsak

By 1906, determined campaigns against bands of Moro rebels—known to the Americans as outlaws or bandits—finally had cleared Mindanao of organized resistance. On Sulu, several hundred Moro warriors and their families gathered around the volcano of Bud Dajo, where they built fortifications. From there, they raided ranches and settlements, murdering inhabitants and carrying some off.

In March, Wood sent 800 troops to Bud Dajo to dislodge the Moros—approximately 1,000 people in all. They would not surrender, and the subsequent assault cut them down with rifle fire or blasted them with artillery. Desperate warriors hurled stones down on the Americans and counterattacked with the kris. Some fighting was hand-to-hand, bayonet against sword. At nightfall, the surviving Moros retreated into the volcano's crater, which had been fortified. The Americans moved close with artillery and rapid-firing guns, and the next day poured destructive fire into the crater before attacking. Few Moros escaped. The Americans lost 21 killed and 75 wounded.

Moro resistance was sporadic after Bud Dajo, but banditry continued. In June 1913, Pershing himself led an assault on 500 Moros—warriors and their families—gathered at the mountain Bud Bagsak, on Sulu Island. This time, many were armed with rifles, and the American attack up steep slopes and cliff faces came under heavy fire. Once again, artillery did its lethal work, and bombardments slaughtered the Moros. Desperate counterattacks that invited death were all the warriors could do, and they were mowed down, kris in hand. Almost all the Moros were killed, while the Americans had only about two dozen casualties.

Moro resistance was broken, but it would flare up again in a few decades as part of the Huk insurgency.

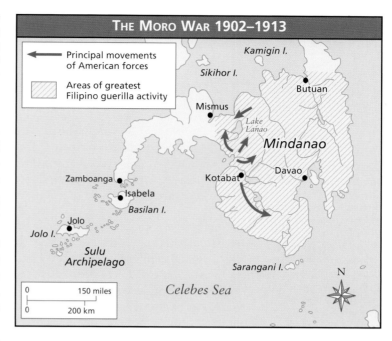

THE MORO WAR 1902–1913

- → Principal movements of American forces
- ▨ Areas of greatest Filipino guerilla activity

Kamigin I.
Sikihor I.
Butuan
Mismus
Lake Lanao
Mindanao
Zamboanga
Isabela
Kotabat
Davao
Basilan I.
Jolo
Jolo I.
Sulu Archipelago
Sarangani I.
Celebes Sea

0 — 150 miles
0 — 200 km

N

MORO WARRIORS Proudly independent, the Moros—Spanish for "Muslims"— fought fanatically and ruthlessly against the American forces, often battling to the death alongside their families.

IN QUEST OF A MORO STATE

Segregated by their Muslim faith and customs, the Moros were far different from the peaceful Filipinos of the north. Traditionally sea pirates and slave-traders, Moros recognized only the authority of their sultans. Moreover, there was intense hatred between them and Christian Filipinos.

At first, the American political approach seemed successful, as some Moro sultans accepted United States authority—as long as the foreigners did not interfere in local affairs. The Kiram-Bates Treaty of 1899 granted local rule and financial stipends to the warlords. Yet Moros continued to raid villages and attack soldiers. From 1902 to 1906, a series of military expeditions destroyed Moro strongholds. On March 2, 1904, President Theodore Roosevelt declared the Kiram-Bates Treaty null and void.

Moro resistance was suppressed, but it again erupted in the Huk Rebellion—mainly on Luzon—between 1946 and 1954. After the Huks were defeated, another insurgency arose: the Moro National Liberation Front called for a sovereign Moro Islamic state. Late in the 20th Century, this group took the name, "Moro Islamic Liberation Front" and claimed 120,000 armed fighters and another 300,000 militia volunteers.

16: EXPEDITIONS, INCURSIONS, AND PURSUIT

Throughout the second half of the 19th Century, the world's strongest nations carved up Chinese trade and forced the Manchu imperial court to yield land concessions and access to ports. These "Great Powers" demanded rights and privileges that humiliated the Chinese people and government, while Christian missionaries set up churches that won over thousands of converts. Then, in 1894–1895, Japan's modern army and navy smashed the obsolete Chinese forces in the Sino-Japanese War.

As the Western powers and Japan competed for influence in China, a groundswell of opposition developed among the younger Chinese, who formed secret societies to fight the foreigners. One of the largest of these societies was the "Boxers"—as Westerners interpreted their name, *I Ho Ch'uan:* the Society of Righteous Harmonious Fists.

The Boxer uprising begins, Peking invaded

Boxer hostility steadily increased until they attacked foreigners and Chinese Christians in 1899, killing a British missionary in September. The Boxers were armed with little more than knives and sticks, but the elderly Manchu empress dowager, Tz'u Hsi (Cixi), and elements in her government supported their effort to get foreigners out of China.

In mid-June 1900, Boxers gathered in great numbers and invaded Peking (Beijing), killing 300 Christian converts and a German government official, burning down churches, and destroying foreign property. Foreigners and converts fled into the Legation Quarter, which had been fortified in anticipation of trouble. Soon, all means of communication from Peking were cut off, isolating the legations, which came under gunfire and sporadic attack. Although the Boxers numbered 140,000, they made no concerted effort to wipe out the defenders: 3,000 Chinese civilians, 475 Europeans, and 450 soldiers, sailors, and marines of various nations.

The "China Relief Expedition"

The United States joined Great Britain, Japan, Russia, Germany, France, Austria, and Italy to immediately assemble a force to march on Peking and rescue the legations. An advance column of 2,200 under British admiral Edward Seymour captured Tientsin (Tienjin), 80 miles from Peking, but on June 17

SHANGHAI Meaning "on-the-sea," Shanghai is one of the world's great seaports, sited near the mouth of the Yang Tze River, which empties into the East China Sea. This late 19th-century Chinese map shows the "old city wharves," the heart of the nation's trade with the West.

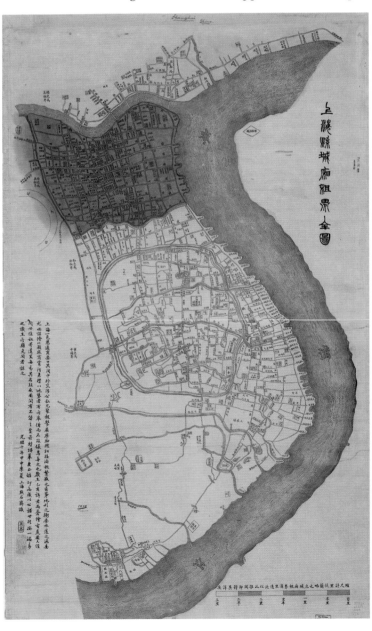

BOXERS ON THE MARCH Anti-western and anti-Christian members of the fanatical Society of Righteous Harmonious Fists pass through the streets of Tientsin in 1901, during the uprising known as the "Boxer Rebellion."

ADVANCES ON PEKING From June 10-26, Admiral Seymour led the first Allied attempt to rescue the foreign legations in Peking, but he was driven back. The Chinese coastal forts at Taku were captured. A second expedition, headed by General Chaffee, took Peking on August 14.

OPERATIONS IN CHINA, 1900

Peking (Forbidden City)
Tungchow
Allied troops relieve foreign legations, August 14
Hun-ho R.
Lang-fang
Matou
Hiang-ho
Pei-ho R.
Lung-ho R.
Tung-an
Lofa
①
②
Yung-tsing
①
Yang-tsun
N
Pa-chau
②
Tung Tien
Tientsin
Tientsin captured July 14
0   20 miles
0   30 km
Pei-ho R.   Taku
North Fort
South Fort
East China Sea
Surrender of Taku Forts June 17

① Route of first allied relief force
② Route of second allied relief force
✳ Battles and naval bombardments
⬅ Other allied movements

was driven back by Chinese troops. That same day, warships opened fire on Chinese forts at Taku on the Yellow Sea, destroying them and causing the imperial government to declare war and ally with the Boxers.

The "China Relief Expedition" was organized, with approximately 19,000 troops, but without a unified command. The largest contingent was the Japanese, with 10,000 men; the Russians were next with 4,000, and the British had 3,000. There were 2,500 Americans under General Adna R. Chaffee, fresh from fighting in the Philippines. The Americans formed two brigades: the 9th and 14th infantry regiments and the 1st Marine Regiment as well as cavalry, artillery, and elements of another infantry regiment.

The allies captured Tientsin in mid-July, after two days of fierce fighting. The victors wreaked vengeance indiscriminately on the Chinese population, looting shops, private homes, and government buildings. The campaign for Peking began on August 4. The expedition marched along dusty roads under blazing heat, breaking through Chinese defensive positions at Peitsang and Yangtsun. The

invaders were impressed by the unexpected ability of Chinese artillerymen and riflemen, who had been trained by Europeans and equipped with fairly modern weapons. The imperial army had learned much since its defeat by Japan, but it was not enough to stop the invasion.

The gates and walls of Peking were boldly assaulted on August 14. The best fighting force was the Japanese, distinguished by their courage and determination in battle. The American 14th Infantry performed the notable feat of scaling the face of a 30-foot undefended wall and breaching the fortifications.

Once the city walls were taken and several gates blasted down, the foreign troops rushed in and began ruthlessly slaughtering Chinese soldiers and civilians alike. Even after the city surrendered on August 16, the invading soldiers kept on killing as they looted everything they could carry, destroying the rest, including ancient Confucian temples.

Many thousands of Chinese died in the the Boxer Rebellion. Its defeat brought on more concessions, and $330 million in indemnities was demanded by the foreign powers. American casualties totaled 33 killed and 178 wounded.

"I do not remember a more satisfying musical performance than the bugles . . . playing 'There'll Be a Hot Time in the Old Town Tonight.'"

—PRESIDENT HERBERT HOOVER, RECALLING THE MARINES' ENTRY INTO TIENTSIN IN 1900, WHERE HE WAS A YOUNG MINING ENGINEER

SCALING THE PEKING WALL As companions provide covering fire, men of the American 14th Infantry scale the outcropping stones of Peking's city wall to raise the Stars and Stripes near Tung Pien Gate. Allied forces soon captured the city. Trumpeter Calvin P. Titus, who led in the ascent, was awarded the Congressional Medal of Honor.

INTERVENTIONS AND INVASIONS IN THE CARIBBEAN

A CENTURY OF INTERVENTIONS
The Caribbean and Central America saw considerable United States intervention in the 20th Century. American arms, influence, advice, and funds toppled and raised governments, supported and quelled revolutions, and established American domination over the region's economy and politics.

Political stability in Latin America was essential to the conduct of American business there, and in the first decades of the 20th Century Marines were often employed to enforce that stability. The United States was especially active in the Caribbean, backing governments or helping overthrow them, intervening in revolutions, and protecting American business interests in the face of nationalism and movements for workers' rights. American forces intervened most notably in the Dominican Republic, Cuba, Panama, Haiti, Mexico, and Nicaragua.

The "Roosevelt Corollary" and Panama

In 1904, President Theodore Roosevelt announced the United States would police Latin American nations that committed "chronic wrongdoing" or that suffered civil unrest. This policy was known as the "Roosevelt Corollary" to the Monroe Doctrine of 1823, which asserted American opposition to European nations expanding their influence in Latin America.

Already in 1903, Roosevelt had supported a rebellion in Colombia's province of Panama, where the United States wanted to build a canal across the isthmus. Failing to arrange a favorable treaty with Colombia, the United States had encouraged a Panamanian uprising and landed Marines to hold off Colombian government troops. A treaty was negotiated with the new Republic of Panama for the 100-year lease of a 10-mile wide "Canal Zone" across the isthmus, where military bases were built to strengthen America's presence in the Caribbean Basin. The Panama Canal opened in 1914. American forces had intervened in Panama four times by 1918.

Preventing wars, suppressing taxes

The Dominican Republic and Haiti, sharing the island of Hispaniola, were often invaded by American Marines between 1904–1915 because frequent uprisings overthrew governments and threatened American interests. The United States sent customs agents to the Dominican Republic in 1904 to make sure the country paid its foreign debt and thus

U.S. INTERVENTIONS IN THE CARIBBEAN, 1900–1933

Columbus
El Paso
U.S. forces
Parral

UNITED STATES

New Orleans

Tampa

ATLANTIC OCEAN

MEXICO
1916–17 U.S. punitive expedition in northern Mexico
1914 U.S. occupation in Veracruz

Gulf of Mexico

CUBA
1898–1902 U.S. occupation
1902–34 U.S. maintains right to intervene under Platt Amendment
1906–09 U.S. occupation
1917 U.S. occupation

Miami

BAHAMAS

Havana

HAITI
1915–34 U.S. occupation

Veracruz

Isle of Pines
1903–25 Formally claimed by U.S.

Guantánamo Bay

DOMINICAN REPUBLIC
1916–24 U.S. occupation

Virgin Islands
1917 Purchased from Denmark

Mexico City

JAMAICA

Port-au-Prince

Santo Domingo

Puerto Rico
1898 Annexed by U.S.

BELIZE

Caribbean Sea

GUATEMALA

EL SALVADOR

HONDURAS

NICARAGUA
1921–25 U.S. occupation; finances under U.S. control
1926–33 U.S. occupation

Managua

Panama Canal Zone

Colón

COSTA RICA

VENEZUELA

PANAMA
1903 U.S.-supported revolution against Colombia
1903 U.S. granted control of Canal Zone

Panama City

COLOMBIA

PACIFIC OCEAN

MARINES IN SANTO DOMINGO U.S. Marine Corps patrol boats are shown on the Ozoma River, Santo Domingo in 1919. In 1916, American Marines had captured Santo Domingo, capital of the Dominican Republic, in an amphibious assault. United States forces occupied the Caribbean nation from 1916–1924.

avoided threats from the European powers that held its loans. Marines landed in Haiti in 1915 to quell civil unrest. They trained a national police force and remained until 1934. Marines invaded the Dominican Republic in 1916, after the elected government was overthrown. An American counter-insurgency campaign established some stability, and the Marines withdrew in 1924.

Nicaragua was a persistent problem for American business, and three interventions had occurred there by 1912. When liberal president, José Santos Zelaya, proposed in 1909 that American mining and banana companies pay taxes, pressure

from the United States compelled him to resign. The next president was the former treasurer of an American mining company. The following year, and in 1912, Marines returned to Nicaragua to support this unpopular regime, staying until 1925. Civil conflict in 1926 brought back several hundred Marines to fight rebels led by Augusto Sandino, who resisted until the Americans departed in 1933.

In 1905, American troops landed in Honduras in one of half a dozen incursions over a 20-year period, including one in 1907 when Marines intervened to stop a war with Nicaragua. In 1911, Honduran president Miguel Dávila provoked the American State Department by establishing warm relations with Nicaragua's President Zelaya, and by doing business with Britain. Dávila was overthrown with the aid of United States fruit companies, and an American mercenary took command of the Honduran army.

The Cuban protectorate

After the Spanish-American War, the United States obliged the new Cuban government to accept the Platt Amendment to the Cuban constitution, permitting American military interventions. Cuba was a United States protectorate by the time American troops left in 1902. In 1906, Marines went back to put down an uprising by blacks who objected to election irregularities. The American "Army of Cuban Pacification," eventually numbering 5,600 troops, remained until 1909.

In 1912, Marines again intervened to put down a rebellion of Cuban sugar workers, returning in 1917 to prop up the government and at the same time to guarantee sugar exports during World War I.

THE GREAT WHITE FLEET

America's military prowess was exhibited on December 16, 1907, when 16 battleships and 14,000 sailors of the Atlantic Fleet set off from Hampton Roads, Virginia, on a voyage around the world. Although most contemporary warships were camouflage gray, the hulls of these battleships were painted white, earning the name "The Great White Fleet." It was said that white symbolized America's peaceful intentions, yet her strength was evident whenever this imposing fleet entered harbors from South America to Hawaii, Yokohama to Gibraltar. The Great White Fleet, at first commanded by Rear Admiral Robley D. Evans, made a 14-month circumnavigation of 45,000 nautical miles with 20 port calls. One objective was to test the war-readiness of the vessels and to train crews. President Theodore Roosevelt, a former assistant secretary of the navy, wanted a battle fleet that was second to none, but even the best American warships were being made obsolete by the heavily armed Dreadnought-class battleships under development by Britain, Germany, France, and Russia. After the Great White Fleet's cruise, new efforts to modernize the American navy got under way.

SAN FRANCISCO HARBOR The Great White Fleet was heartily cheered in 1908 when it put in at San Francisco Harbor while making a round-the-world voyage.

AMERICA'S CONFLICT WITH REVOLUTIONARY MEXICO

The Mexican Revolution, which started in 1910, was a civil war that cost one million Mexican lives over the next decade and complicated the country's relations with the United States. President Woodrow Wilson's government wanted peace in Mexico but was unsure which side to support. At first, Wilson leaned toward Francisco "Pancho" Villa, a leader of anti-government forces. Villa was the only important revolutionary who had not publicly objected to the American occupation of the port city of Veracruz in 1914.

The occupation of Veracruz

The Veracruz intervention occurred after Mexican authorities at Tampico mistakenly detained eight American sailors, who had come ashore from the USS *Dolphin*. Already opposed to Mexican dictator General Victorio Huerta, who had assassinated the previous president to gain power, Wilson demanded an apology for the detentions. He also wanted Huerta to raise an American flag and give it a 21-gun salute. The apology was accorded, but the salute was not.

Learning that a German ship was carrying military supplies to Veracruz, Wilson ordered the navy to seize the city's customs house and docks to prevent the shipment's arrival and so put pressure on Huerta. On April 21, almost 800 Marines and sailors came ashore, expecting no resistance. Instead, general fighting broke out, and by the next day the invasion force was rein-

FIGHTERS ON THE MOVE Rebels to some, revolutionaries to others, horsemen in traditional sombreros and with bandoliers across their chests make their way through the Mexican countryside.

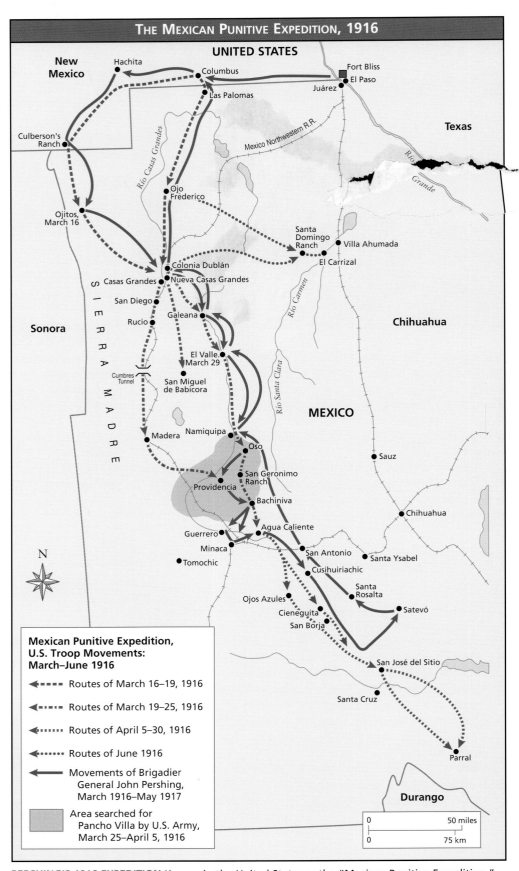

THE MEXICAN PUNITIVE EXPEDITION, 1916

UNITED STATES

New Mexico · Hachita · Columbus · Fort Bliss · El Paso · Juárez

Texas

Culberson's Ranch · Rio Casas Grandes · Mexico Northwestern R.R. · Rio Grande

Ojo Frederico

Ojitos, March 16 · Santa Domingo Ranch · Villa Ahumada · El Carrizal

Colonia Dublán · Casas Grandes · Nueva Casas Grandes

Sonora · San Diego · Galeana · Rio Carmen · Chihuahua

SIERRA MADRE · Rucio · El Valle, March 29 · Rio Santa Clara · MEXICO

Cumbres Tunnel · San Miguel de Babicora

Madera · Namiquipa · Oso · Sauz

San Geronimo Ranch · Providencia · Bachiniva

Guerrero · Agua Caliente · Chihuahua

Minaca · San Antonio · Santa Ysabel

Tomochic · Cusihuiriachic

Ojos Azules · Santa Rosalta · Satevó

Cieneguita · San Borja

San José del Sitio

Santa Cruz

Parral

Durango

N

Mexican Punitive Expedition, U.S. Troop Movements: March–June 1916

◀---- Routes of March 16–19, 1916

◀-·-·- Routes of March 19–25, 1916

◀······ Routes of April 5–30, 1916

◀······ Routes of June 1916

◀—— Movements of Brigadier General John Pershing, March 1916–May 1917

▢ Area searched for Pancho Villa by U.S. Army, March 25–April 5, 1916

0 ———— 50 miles
0 ———— 75 km

PERSHING'S 1916 EXPEDITION Known in the United States as the "Mexican Punitive Expedition," more than 5,000 troops under Pershing campaigned in Mexico in futile pursuit of Pancho Villa. The American military intervened whenever the long-running Mexican Revolution threatened Americans or their interests.

YANKEES ON THE SOUTHWEST BORDER The 2nd Connecticut National Guard Regiment patrols the Arizona border in 1916, against forays by Pancho Villa; the motorcycle, recently popularized, was a speedy means of travel for couriers and scouts.

forced to 6,000, mainly army troops. The two days of fighting saw the first American aircraft employed in military operations—and the first damaged in conflict. The Americans lost 19 men killed and 71 wounded, the Mexicans at least 200 killed and 300 wounded—mostly civilians caught in the middle.

Huerta gave up power that July, and American forces reached a settlement with Venustiano Carranza, who took power as president in Mexico City. This meant Wilson recognized Carranza over other revolutionaries. The Americans ended the Veracruz occupation that November.

In pursuit of Pancho Villa

The civil war continued between the various factions, and Carranza's forces decisively defeated Pancho Villa in 1915, forcing him to withdraw northward. Bitter that Wilson had recognized Carranza, Villa menaced the United States-Mexico border region, where American troops watched his movements cautiously.

In early March 1916, 500 of Villa's followers crossed into New Mexico and attacked the town of Columbus, where 350 troopers of the 13th Cavalry quickly counterattacked. Before Villa's men were driven out, however, they burned and looted extensively and killed 17 Americans, suffering 100 casualties. A cavalry detachment went across the border in hot pursuit, engaging the revolutionaries on Mexican soil several times and killing 100 more. By mid-March, more than 5,000 Americans under General John J. Pershing were in Mexico looking for

Villa, who became elusive, winning legendary status for defying and outwitting the Americans.

Carranza's government did not cooperate with Pershing, refusing the expedition the use of railroad lines. Necessity forced Pershing to develop America's first motorized military supply system, with more than 300 trucks. The Carranzista army began to clash with Pershing's expedition, with the sharpest skirmish taking place at Carrizal, Chihuahua, on June 21. There, an American reconnaissance patrol lost 12 killed, 10 wounded, and 24 captured, while the Mexicans had 74 casualties.

By now, it appeared a full-scale war might be approaching, although neither side wanted it. More than 100,000 American National Guard troops were being mobilized and sent to camps near the Mexican border. At the same time, American relations were deteriorating with Germany, whose U-boat war against merchant shipping threatened to bring the United States into World War I alongside the Allies. That summer, both the United States and Mexico agreed to negotiate a settlement before matters became worse. By February 1917, the last American troops had withdrawn from Mexico.

Although he had not caught Pancho Villa, Pershing's performance had made him a favorite of the War Department. He would lead the American Expeditionary Force to Europe in the summer of 1917.

"Am sure Villa's attacks are made in Germany."

—JAMES GERARD, UNITED STATES AMBASSADOR TO BERLIN, AS RELATIONS WITH GERMANY AND MEXICO DETERIORATED IN 1916

THE GENERAL ON CAMPAIGN Pershing fords a river in northern Mexico, where he failed to run down Pancho Villa, but instead embellished his own reputation for leadership and won command of American forces in World War I.

The 'Steel Navy' and Submarines

There were few major wars in the last half of the 19th Century, but military technology made steady progress, including the development of breechloading, magazine-fed, bolt-action rifles, smokeless powder, and improved artillery and ammunition. Also, the tremendous power of rapid-fire weapons such as the Gatling Gun and the Maxim machine gun became better understood.

Telegraphy became common for military communications, and the telephone, invented in 1876, also showed promise for use on static battlefronts.

The most dramatic advances were in the navies. In the 1890s, the United States reversed a post-Civil War policy of reducing its military and began building a first-class "steel navy" of heavily armored warships with speeds up to 30 knots and carrying a mix of powerful guns, some with a range of five miles or more. Swift torpedo boats built to attack armored warships evolved into the fast and maneuverable sea-going destroyers, and practical submarines appeared. The French were the most advanced in submarine technology, but their experimental vessels operated solely by battery power and so were very limited in range. In the mid-1890s, Irish-American inventor John P. Holland developed a submarine with electric engines for operating under water and internal combustion engines for surface cruising and recharging. The U.S. Navy bought its first Holland submarine in 1900.

The horse remained an integral part of all land forces, pulling field artillery and supply wagons, and regiments of cavalry still formed the mobile striking and scouting force in all armies.

HOLLAND SUBMARINE Preserved for posterity in a Paterson, New Jersey, display, one of John Holland's innovative submarines was memorialized in this 1930s photograph.

NAVAL REVIEW Continuous advances in naval and weapons technology throughout the late 19th Century resulted in navies with a mixture of warship types, many being experimental hybrids of varying success. Steam-powered steel warships with a full array of masts and sails were common in the 1870s and 1880s. By 1900 such ships were obsolete.

TELEPHONE The Signal Corps had portable field telephones available, requiring wire and an array of heavy batteries. Their use was limited to fixed positions, such as camps, headquarters, and fortifications.

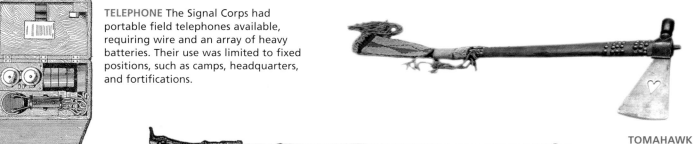

TOMAHAWK Although the Plains Indians used modern rifles and pistols, traditional weapons were still a part of every warrior's outfit. Indians relied on the bow and arrow and acts of personal bravery; "counting coup" required a warrior to touch an enemy with a lance or other hand weapon.

BREECHLOADER After the Civil War, the army converted the percussion rifle musket into a single-shot breechloader. Developed by Springfield Armory master armorer E.S. Allen, the "trapdoor" modification used an ingenious system to manually eject the metallic cartridge.

TRAPDOOR Allen's system equipped American infantrymen until the adoption of the Krag rifle in the mid-1890s. Many United States soldiers in the Spanish American War carried obsolete firearms.

KRAG RIFLE The .30-caliber five-shot M1892 Krag-Jörgensen rifle was adopted by the Army after extensive trials in the 1890s, the first magazine firearm to become general-issue. The modified M1896 was carried by United States troops in the Spanish-American War.

HOTCHKISS GUN Warships of the 1890s mounted numerous "quick-fire" Hotchkiss guns, firing a two-pound shell. Guns mounted outside the hull were shielded, but the crews were still vulnerable to explosions and shell fragments in combat.

MANILA BAY Led by the cruiser USS *Olympia*, Admiral Dewey's powerful and modern battle fleet destroys the weaker Spanish ships defending Manila Bay in 1898. Within 10 years, most of these ships were rendered obsolete by the British battleship *Dreadnought,* but some were refitted and saw service during the First World War.

COLT REVOLVER The use of metallic cartridges led rapidly to the improvement of revolvers capable of firing five or six shots in quick succession. Colt's revolvers, especially the 1873 models, became the standard sidearm for soldier and civilian alike.

GATLING GUN By the 1880s Gatling Guns were reliable but remained large and unwieldy. Experiments with more advanced mechanical methods of rapid fire, especially by Sir Hiram Maxim, led to the modern, belt-fed machine gun. Gatling guns quickly fell out of favor, but returned in the 1960s and 1970s as multiple-barrel electrically-driven machine guns for aircraft and warships.

PART FIVE

The War to End All Wars

T HE MAJORITY OF AMERICANS wanted to keep out of World War I when Europe called it down upon herself in 1914. Europeans were driven by long memories of conflicts won and lost—memories that mingled with bright new ambitions as each nation was sure it would prevail, certain that divine justice was on its side. War approached, not like a storm cloud and calamity, but like a coming glory manifested in the glittering armies that paraded for emperors, prime ministers, and generals.

President Woodrow Wilson won reelection in 1916 with the motto, he "kept us out of war." Wilson genuinely tried to mediate a peace then, but failed, for Europe was too deep in the abyss, with each nation fighting grimly just to keep from losing. In early 1917, Germany embarked on an unrestricted U-boat war that attacked American merchant shipping—shipping laden with supplies and munitions purchased by the Allies. Now, the United States declared war on Germany and joined the international fray.

When the "War to End All Wars" was done in 1918, having consumed a generation, the United States was a world power whose future course would determine the fate of all the nations.

W.W.I ace Eddie Rickenbacker.

17: WORLD WAR I IN EUROPE AND AT SEA

"We come from a nation that for one hundred and fifty years has stood before the world as the champion of the sacred principles of human liberty. We now return to Europe, the home of our ancestors, to help defend the same principles upon European soil."

— GENERAL JOHN J. PERSHING 1918

GENERAL JOHN J. PERSHING (1860–1948)
Commander in chief of the AEF, Pershing is pictured at his Chaumont, France, headquarters. His service included the Indian, Spanish-American, and Philippine wars, and the 1916 Mexican Intervention. Pershing was Army Chief of Staff from 1921–1924.

President Wilson did not fully agree with the military goals of Britain, France, and Russia, the leading Entente Powers (or Allies), who wanted total victory over the Central Powers—Germany, Austria-Hungary, Turkey, and Bulgaria. Further, Wilson called for world disarmament after hostilities, and for addressing the claims of colonial peoples. The Allies did not support these and other such positions. Wilson declared the official status of the United States to be an "associate" of the Allies.

An unprepared military

Still, the United States entered the war with the full intention of mobilizing, training, and equipping millions of men, building a first-class navy, and getting into action. Wilson believed that the sooner Americans reached the front in force, the sooner Germany would be compelled to sue for peace.

Taking up positions on the Western Front would require months of training, however, since the U.S. Army's 200,000 troops in 1917 were largely National Guardsmen and draftees inducted by the new Selective Service Act. Further, the quartermaster corps was incapable of supplying and equipping the military fast enough, as it grew by hundreds of thousands every month.

American industry had to gear up to produce armaments, so tanks, field guns, and aircraft were acquired from the Allies. The American army and navy each had its own air arm, but these were weak and inexperienced. When hostilities began, the army had only 55 available aircraft.

One strength of the American military was its officer corps, especially the general staff, which for the first time was completely professional. No citizen soldiers or political appointees took command of large units. Career officers supervised training and prepared the way for the arrival of American troops in France. One of the most experienced generals, John J. Pershing, was advanced over a number of more senior officers when

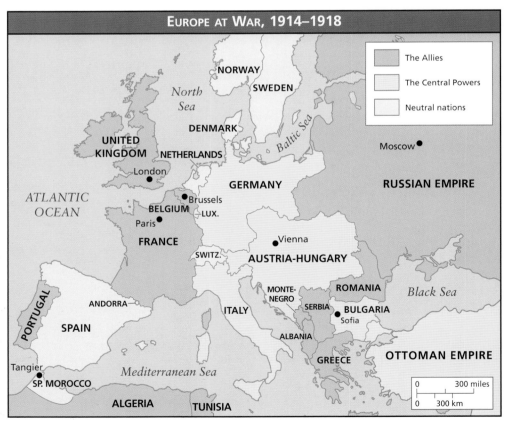

EUROPE AT WAR, 1914–1918

The Allies
The Central Powers
Neutral nations

ALLIANCES OF 1914 The Triple Entente (Allies) included Britain, France, and Russia, joined by Belgium, Japan, Montenegro, and Serbia. Before the war, the Triple Alliance (Central Powers) was Germany, Austria-Hungary, and Italy, later joined by the Ottoman Empire and Bulgaria. In 1915, Italy entered the war on the side of the Allies.

he took command of the American Expeditionary Force (AEF) in May 1917.

The regular army's 1st Division, with approximately 28,000 officers and men—a unit double the size of the typical Allied or German division—landed in France on June 26, in time to parade in Paris on July 4. They would have a long wait before going into battle, because extensive training in trench warfare was first required by the Allied high command.

Reinforcing the front

Pershing established AEF headquarters at Tours, in central France, and developed supply lines from the seaports to his units. He wanted to keep his troops together in their own army, responsible for a section of battlefront. This was not yet possible, however, since they had not gained enough experience or training. Moreover, the Allied high command requested that American regiments be dispersed to provide needed reinforcements to the French and British lines. Pershing was promised his own front-line sector as soon as practical, and he reluctantly agreed to the dispersal, aware the Germans were bringing hundreds of thousands of troops from the eastern front, where Russia was dropping out of the war.

In late October, the 1st Division entered the front lines in Lorraine, and that November some American units saw action in the Cambrai offensive launched by the Allies—notable for its use of massed tanks in the attack. This two-week campaign, despite initial success, was driven back by the Germans, and the front resumed its former shape.

On December 7, the United States officially declared war on Germany's main ally, Austria-Hungary. There would, however, be little conflict between Americans and Austro-Hungarians other than some minor actions in northern Italy and naval operations in the Adriatic Sea.

By the end of 1917, five American divisions were in France, totaling more than 180,000 troops, a tiny force compared with the millions of Allied and German soldiers already in action. Fewer than 170 Americans had been killed in battle by then. The following autumn, 1.4 million Americans would have seen action, and every available American soldier would be needed on the Western Front.

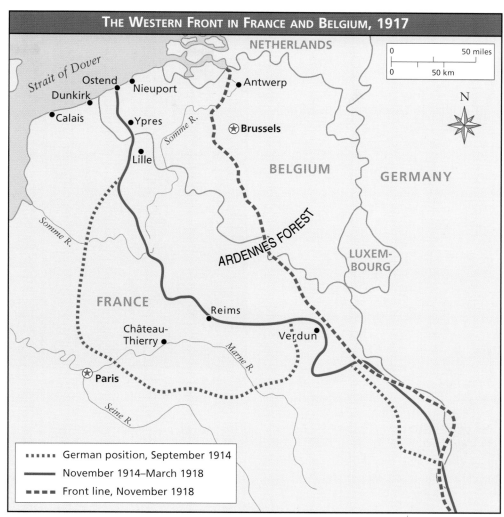

THE WESTERN FRONT The 1914 German offensive almost reached Paris before being forced back by the French and British. Until mid-1918, the Western Front remained relatively static, as even the largest offensives against fixed positions gained little ground.

YOUNG MEN OFF TO WAR High-spirited American soldiers embark for France in 1917; more than 4.7 million Americans served in the war, which cost 320,629 United States casualties, including 53,513 battle deaths.

135

THE UNITED STATES NAVY IN WORLD WAR I

With the 1916 Naval Act, Congress authorized the creation of a fleet that was to include 60 new battleships. When the United States declared war on Germany in April 1917 the navy had 361 vessels, including 151 warships, and was second in size only to the Royal Navy. Now, however, the battleship-building plans came to a virtual stop.

The most pressing need was for fast and agile destroyers to defend against German submarines that were torpedoing merchant ships carrying armaments, munitions, and foodstuffs to the Allies—and soon would carry American troops. As the U-boats began a major offensive to stem the flow of American men and matériel to Europe, destroyers, armed yachts, and cruisers were required more than ever for anti-submarine patrols.

That April, U-boats sank 860,000 tons of Allied and neutral shipping, the war's greatest monthly loss, which seriously threatened the Allied war effort, especially that of the British, who depended on imported food.

The destroyer flotillas

In May 1917, United States Destroyer Division Eight arrived at Queenstown, Ireland, to participate in anti-submarine operations. American admiral William S. Sims, coordinating American and British naval operations, was a staunch proponent of establishing a "convoy system."

GERMAN SUBMARINE ATTACKS U-boats usually surfaced to sink defenseless merchant ships with cannon fire, saving their torpedoes for enemy warships or armed merchantmen.

This involved merchant vessels rendezvousing at a predetermined meeting point on the ocean to be escorted in a convoy by destroyers and other warships. Eastbound convoys assembled west of Ireland, just before entering the danger zone, where U-boats lurked in wait.

By July, 35 American destroyers under the command of a British admiral were stationed at Queenstown, representing one third of all Allied destroyers on escort duty. When American troop transports began sailing to French ports, a destroyer flotilla took station at Brest to escort them. By mid-1918, more than 300,000 troops were arriving in France each month, and the remarkable success of the convoy system was proven by the fact that only six transports were sunk by U-boats in European waters. Four of these were empty, returning westward.

Battleships and naval "firsts"

In November 1917, five battleships of the United States Navy's Battleship Division Nine joined the British fleet at Scapa Flow, off northern Scotland. There, the Allies watched for another breakout

> *"Starting with almost nothing at the beginning of the war, a United States naval transport service has been built up which has carried [more than] a million soldiers to Europe."*
>
> —COMMANDER CHARLES C. GILL, POSTWAR REPORT ON USN TRANSPORT DEPARTMENT

UNITED STATES DESTROYERS Fast and maneuverable, destroyers were essential for the protection of merchant convoys; the arrival of American destroyers turned the Atlantic contest in favor of the Allies.

attempt by the German High Seas Fleet, which in 1916 had been turned back at Jutland. These American battleships, however, saw no action in World War I.

During 1917, the navy had a number of notable firsts. May: First operational oil-refueling while underway, which was between a destroyer and an oil tanker. June: First naval aviation unit, the First Aeronautical Detachment, arrived in France. October: First American submarines, four of them, arrived in the European theater, putting in at the Azores. November: First American warships sank a German submarine, and the first American naval aviation coastal patrol was carried out in the European theater. One first in November was a loss, as the USS *Alcedo* was the first American warship sunk by a German submarine.

"The Battle of the Atlantic"

An unglamorous but extremely effective operation in which the American navy participated was the expansion of the North Sea Mine Barrage, a massive field of underwater mines. In little over a year, the navy laid more than 56,500 mines to prevent enemy submarines from slipping out into the Atlantic. Until then, the British had laid 13,600 mines.

Few German U-boats ever went all the way across the Atlantic to operate in American waters, although half a dozen did so in mid-1918, with minimal success in interdicting merchant shipping. With the convoy system, Allied merchant losses in the Atlantic dropped steadily until it was below 300,000 tons a month in the spring of 1918. Thus did the Allies win what was known as the "Battle of the Atlantic."

UNTERSEE BOOT
A crewman checks equipment in the engine room of a German U-boat; "undersea boats" ran on oil while most surface vessels burned coal.

IN EUROPEAN WATERS, 1917-1918 American battleships based at Scapa Flow remained out of the action, but destroyer and subchaser bases provided harbors and repair facilities for busy warships fighting the U-boats.

U.S. NAVAL OPERATIONS, 1917–1918

HQ	Naval headquarters	Sub-chaser base	Air force
Main base, destroyers	Battleships	Mine barrage
Minor base	Submarines	Mine base

AMERICAN DREADNOUGHT The heavily armored hull of the battleship USS *New Jersey* was painted with camouflage colors to make her less visible from a distance.

AMERICANS IN BATTLE: CANTIGNY AND CHÂTEAU-THIERRY

German commander General Erich Ludendorff faced severe adversity in the spring of 1918, even though he had been reinforced by divisions from the Eastern Front. The naval blockade threatened Germans with starvation, giving rise to civilian and military unrest. Convoys were bringing division after division of Americans to France, compelling Ludendorff to strike before they were on the front in strength.

The German offensives of 1918

In late March, Ludendorff launched a massive assault, with 71 divisions attacking along a 50-mile front south of Arras. Opening with a bombardment by 6,000 guns, this Second Battle of the Somme River lasted until early April. It gained Ludendorff 40 miles, captured 70,000 prisoners and inflicted 160,000 Allied casualties. German losses were comparable, but the Allies were now becoming anxious, for they had barely prevented a breakthrough. French general Ferdinand Foch, who now took command of Allied forces, wanted American reinforcements to bolster the front line. Pershing insisted his men be committed in units no smaller than divisions.

Ludendorff followed with a second major offensive in early April. The Lys River campaign in Flanders gained another 10 miles before stalling at the end of the month in the face of fierce British defensive fighting. The Germans suffered 350,000 casualties, the Allies 305,000, mostly British.

At Cantigny, a little village in the Picardy region, the Americans soon would have a chance to prove themselves.

The Men of Cantigny

Near the end of April, the 1st Division had just taken up positions at Cantigny, when the Germans commenced a steady bombardment, inflicting 60 casualties a day. On one night in early May, a bom-

FIRST AMERICAN VICTORY The Battle of Cantigny on May 28, 1918, earned French praise for the green American soldiers, who gained half a mile and captured the town after bitter fighting.

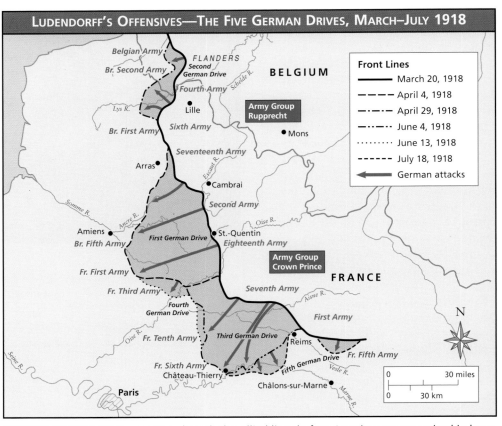

GERMAN OFFENSIVES Desperate to breach the Allied lines before American troops arrived in large numbers at the battlefront, Ludendorff launched repeated offensives from March through July 1918, but did not make a decisive breakthrough.

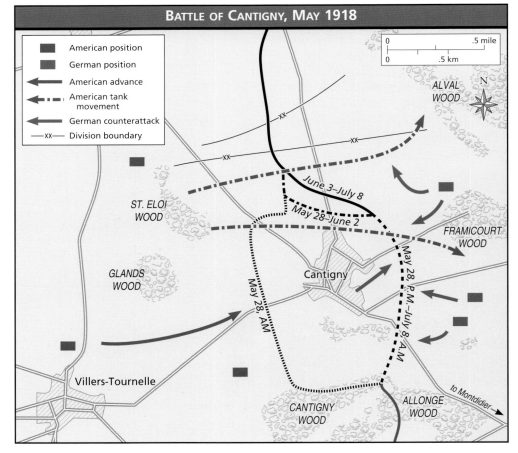

bardment of mustard gas and high-explosives put the 8th Regiment out of action, with 900 casualties.

On May 27, Ludendorff attacked the French lines at the Aisne River. The defenders were swept away by a bombardment of 4,600 guns followed by the assault of 41 divisions. With Paris less than 40 miles distant, the Germans saw great opportunity in this attack, and they hurled their reserves into the breach. Now the Americans were called upon.

Spearheaded by the 28th Regiment, the 1st Division, with a vanguard of borrowed French tanks, attacked the German 82nd Reserve Division occupying Cantigny and quickly drove them out. This was the sort of fighting Pershing wanted—in the open rather than in trenches. The eager Americans immediately found themselves under determined and repeated counterattacks and artillery bombardment. For three days, the Germans relentlessly battled to regain Cantigny, but the Americans held, and the enemy finally gave up.

Although the Americans had more than 1,800 casualties, this was a relatively minor battle in the midst of the great German offensive. Yet, as the first American victory of the war, Cantigny began to build the American reputation for courage and determination. The French corps commander in charge of the battle zone proudly offered "the men of Cantigny" his congratulations.

German offensive continues

Meanwhile, the Germans were on the Marne River at Château-Thierry, driving back three French armies to achieve their deepest advances since 1914. To contest the river crossings, Foch rushed reserves forward, including the American 3rd Division commanded by General Joseph Dickman.

On May 31, an American machine gun battalion joined the French to hold off the enemy attacking the town of Château-Thierry on the main road to Paris. The rest of the division soon arrived by rail and relieved the exhausted French troops defending the town. Fierce fighting raged until June 4, when the German push at Château-Thierry was finally blunted, preventing an enemy breakout toward Paris. The 3rd Division still had to fight day after day through the month of June around Château-Thierry, where it earned the nickname, "Rock of the Marne."

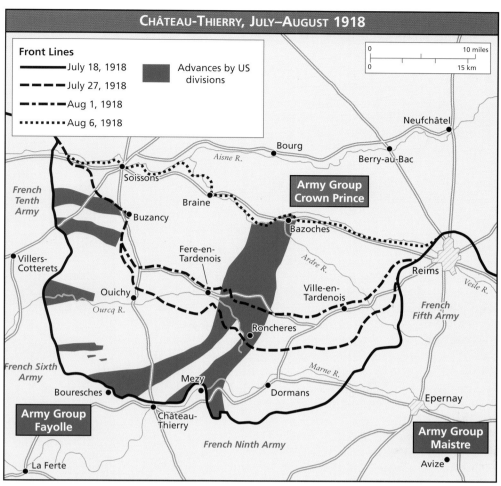

CHÂTEAU-THIERRY, JULY–AUGUST 1918

Front Lines
— July 18, 1918
– – – July 27, 1918
–·–·– Aug 1, 1918
······· Aug 6, 1918

▮ Advances by US divisions

0 ____ 10 miles
0 ____ 15 km

Neufchâtel
Bourg
Aisne R.
Berry-au-Bac
Soissons
French Tenth Army
Braine
Army Group Crown Prince
Buzancy
Bazoches
Fere-en-Tardenois
Villers-Cotterets
Ardre R.
Reims
Vesle R.
Ouichy
Ville-en-Tardenois
French Fifth Army
Ourcq R.
Roncheres
French Sixth Army
Marne R.
Mezy
Bouresches
Dormans
Epernay
Army Group Fayolle
Château-Thierry
Army Group Maistre
French Ninth Army
La Ferte
Avize

STOPPING A BREAKTHROUGH As Ludendorff's offensive, known as Aisne River III, reached Château Thierry, just 37 miles from Paris, Pershing rushed in his 2nd and 3rd Divisions to contest the Marne crossings and retake Belleau Wood.

"Don't let them get you down, Colonel. These tanks of yours will dominate the character of war for the next hundred years."

—GENERAL DOUGLAS MACARTHUR TO GEORGE S. PATTON, JR.,
BEING TEASED BY INFANTRY OFFICERS WHEN HIS TANKS STUCK IN MUD

MACHINE GUN POSITION United States troops of the 9th Machine Gun Battalion set up their gun in an empty railroad repair shop at Château Thierry in 1918.

THE WINDS OF WAR CHANGE ON THE WESTERN FRONT

In early June 1918, the deepest penetration of the German Aisne Offensive pushed into the western Marne Valley to capture Belleau Wood, threatening to cut the road between Metz and Paris. Pershing resolved to drive the enemy out of this mile-square forest, which he mistakenly thought was lightly defended.

The Battle of Belleau Wood

On June 6, General Omar Bundy's 2nd Division and its attached 4th Marine Brigade and 3rd Infantry Brigade went on the attack through these dense woods, discovering strong enemy forces in entrenched positions. The Marines and the 3rd Brigade did much of the fighting, which required bayonet attacks and bitter hand-to-hand struggles. In the first day alone, the Marines had more than 1,000 casualties. They were relieved on June 17, then returned to the fray on the 22nd.

The bloody Battle of Belleau Wood lasted three weeks until the last Germans were forced by heavy artillery fire to withdraw. The Americans suffered almost 8,800 casualties in this, their first major engagement of the war.

The battles at Château-Thierry and Belleau Wood were the high-water mark of Ludendorff's offensives and the beginning of the end for German arms. The Americans were becoming significant factors on the Western Front. Their 25 divisions were being prepared for Foch's own counteroffensive, but in mid-June Ludendorff attempted to maintain the initiative by launching a fourth drive against Paris.

The Noyon-Montdidier campaign aimed to capture the city of Compiègne, but it soon failed, stopped by the French Army, which inflicted heavy German losses.

BAYONETS AND FISTS American Marines struggle hand-to-hand with Germans in the tangle of mile-square Belleau Wood. This grim conflict began on June 6 and by July 1 the Americans had completely cleared the wood.

"There is no romance in modern war. It is a matter of machinery and blood; a concentration of all the destructive forces of the world."

—CAPTAIN JESSE W. WOOLDRIDGE, 38TH INFANTRY REGIMENT, JULY 1918

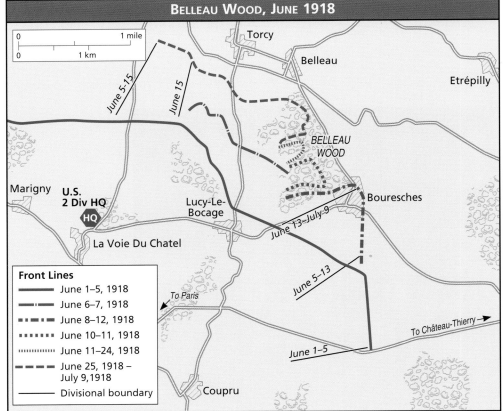

BELLEAU WOOD, JUNE 1918

Torcy
Belleau
Etrépilly
June 5–15
June 15
BELLEAU WOOD
Marigny
U.S. 2 Div HQ
HQ
Lucy-Le-Bocage
Bouresches
June 13–July 9
La Voie Du Chatel
June 5–13
To Paris
June 1–5
Coupru
To Château-Thierry

Front Lines
— June 1–5, 1918
—·—· June 6–7, 1918
—■—■ June 8–12, 1918
······· June 10–11, 1918
·········· June 11–24, 1918
– – – June 25, 1918 – July 9, 1918
—— Divisional boundary

BATTLE OF BELLEAU WOOD General Omar Bundy's 2nd Division, along with the 4th Marine and 3rd Infantry brigades, attacked the nose of the German advance and, after fierce fighting, substantially controlled Belleau Wood by June 26.

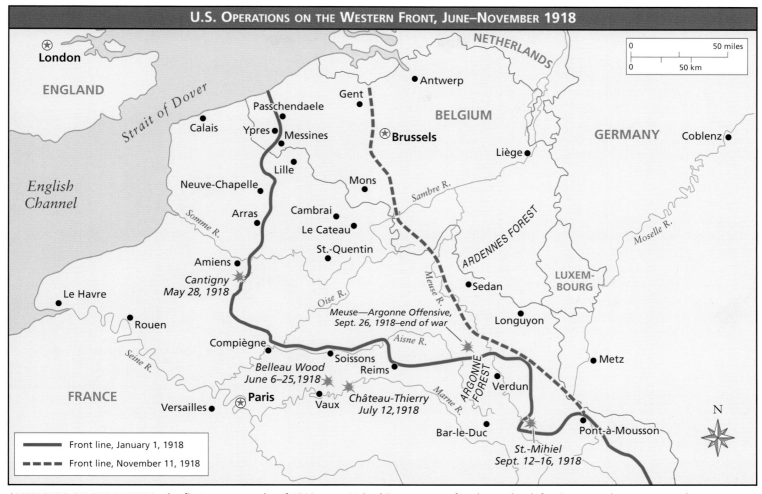

U.S. OPERATIONS ON THE WESTERN FRONT, JUNE–NOVEMBER 1918

Legend:
— Front line, January 1, 1918
- - - Front line, November 11, 1918

AMERICANS ON THE FRONT In the first seven months of 1918, most United States troops fought on the defensive or made counterattacks. Then they went on the offensive in a broad Allied push that drove the Germans back 100 miles.

The Aisne-Marne campaign

Ludendorff was not finished yet, and on July 15 began a fifth campaign, known as the Champagne-Marne offensive, which included the Second Battle of the Marne River. The Marne near Château-Thierry was an initial objective as 52 German divisions attacked 36 Allied divisions, including nine American. Four of the American divisions were west of the city of Reims, in the front lines alongside the French. Together, these defenders endured the preliminary German artillery bombardment, then held off a major enemy thrust that tried to cross the Marne in their front.

After two days of fighting, it was apparent Ludendorff's offensive had failed, and he called it off. Ludendorff was to begin yet another attack in the north, against the British, but Foch had plans for his own counteroffensive which would decisively wrest the initiative from the Germans. When Ludendorff attacked, Foch had held 20 divisions in reserve, intending to eliminate the enemy Soissons salient, which aimed at Paris. This was one of several such salients the Allies would attack in several limited offensives.

On July 18, the 50,000 men of two American divisions (1st and 2nd) joined the French assault on Soissons. Another three American divisions supported the action, and four were held in reserve. The 1st and 2nd, along with a Moroccan division, spearheaded the attack, meeting heavy fire and poison gas as German resistance stiffened. After four days of heavy fighting, in which more than 310,000 Americans participated, the salient was

pushed back. This success cost the Americans 67,000 casualties.

To the north, a campaign near Amiens began in August. Two American divisions joined the British in a successful counteroffensive that drove back the German lines.

Now, Pershing wanted to bring his divisions together, with part of the front designated as the United States sector. The Americans had proven they could fight, so Foch could not refuse.

SNIPING AT THE ENEMY Ohio National Guardsmen of the 166th Infantry Regiment fire on Germans at the edge of Villers sur Fère in July 1918. Americans were nicknamed "Doughboys," after the floured dumplings of army fare.

141

OFFENSIVE VICTORY IN THE ST.-MIHIEL SALIENT

On July 24, 1918, Foch approved the establishment of the American First Army under Pershing. By mid-August a headquarters staff was organized, and Pershing made plans for an offensive in the American sector at St.-Mihiel. Foch had assigned the task of destroying the powerful German salient there, south of the city of Verdun, and Pershing gathered his forces. Meanwhile, the Allies kept up the pressure on the Germans on the Western Front, launching the Oise-Aisne Offensive east of Paris.

The Oise-Aisne Offensive wins territory

Two United States National Guard divisions and one of conscripts took part in this campaign. Instead of being under foreign generals as in the past, they composed the American III Corps, commanded by General Robert Bullard. The offensive took control of the region north of the Vesle River up to the Aisne River.

Meanwhile, other Americans were also in action, including three divisions with the British in Belgium, taking part in the renewed Ypres-Lys Offensive. In September, the Germans were forced eastward, giving up territory they had occupied since early in the war. Even the German-held Belgian capital, Brussels, now seemed in the reach of Allied forthcoming attacks. Most of the Allied offensives would be ongoing, keeping the Germans on the defensive, until the Armistice in November.

FIELD ARTILLERY IN ACTION A spent shell casing flies clear as Battery C of the 6th Field Artillery fires a French "75" cannon at enemy positions on the Lorraine front in mid-1918. American forces used foreign arms to quickly equip units sent to the front.

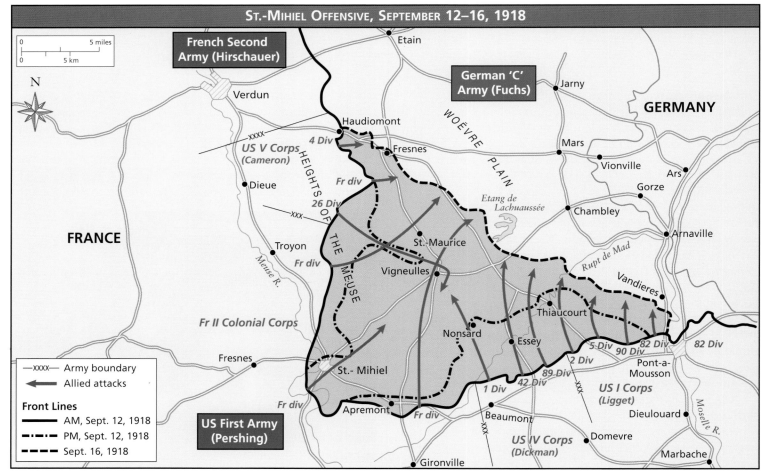

ST.-MIHIEL CAMPAIGN The Germans were attacked while withdrawing from the St.-Mihiel salient, but they gave ground grudgingly and reestablished a flat defensive front. The Americans had no time to celebrate success at St.-Mihiel, for the Meuse-Argonne Offensive was imminent.

"The tremendous . . . energy which America's fresh troops brought into the fray more than balanced the weakness of their allies, who were exhausted."

—LUDENDORFF, GERMANY'S COMMANDER ON THE WESTERN FRONT

Pershing's St.-Mihiel campaign

Defending the St.-Mihiel salient were 500,000 German troops, strongly dug in, with concrete shelters and barbed wire. This was a formidable objective that was likened to a triangular fortress 25 miles wide at the base, its apex extending 16 miles into Allied-held territory.

The plan was for American attacks to converge in a pincers at the base of the salient, with the V Corps striking from the northwest and the I and IV corps coming from the south—500,000 men. The French would support the attacks with 110,000 men, mainly the II Colonial Corps, attacking the western German positions to hold them in place, thereby preventing their reinforcing other parts of the salient. The American assaults would be led by 400 tanks, mostly French-made, 144 of which would be manned by American crews of the United States Tank Corps. This was the first battlefield appearance of American tank units.

One of the most remarkable aspects of the St.-Mihiel offensive would be the cooperation of 1,500 aircraft, the largest concentration of the war until then. Led

THE MUD OF WAR The glamour of fine uniforms and marching in parades had long faded for these Doughboys hauling an ammunition wagon stuck on a slimy, rutted road east of St.-Mihiel in the early fall of 1918.

by American colonel Billy Mitchell, the aircraft were to attack German airfields and support the ground attack.

The Germans anticipated the offensive, however, and decided to withdraw from the salient. They began to transfer equipment, but their troops were still there when Pershing struck on the 12th, sooner than the Germans had expected. In just four hours, more than 2,900 Allied artillery pieces fired 1.1 million shells to prepare for the assault. The Americans moved fast, but the withdrawing Germans fought stubbornly, keeping the pincers from closing on the main body, which was retreating. Most escaped

before the American attacks converged near Vigneulles. By September 16, the German front line had been reestablished across the base of the salient, now in American hands.

The First Army suffered 10,000 casualties in the St.-Mihiel offensive, which captured 16,000 prisoners, large amounts of armaments and munitions, and 200 square miles of French territory that had been occupied since the start of the war. Pershing wanted to continue attacking toward the city of Metz, but Foch would not permit it. Plans for the coming Meuse-Argonne Offensive required the First Army's participation.

AMID THE RUINS A column of 18th Infantry Regiment machine gunners halts as it passes through destroyed St. Baussant during the St.-Mihiel Offensive of 1918.

AMERICAN AIR POWER DEVELOPS AT THE FRONT

The United States Army had only 250 aircraft when entering World War I in 1917, and military aeronautics was carried out by the Aviation Section of the Signal Corps. There were 65 officers involved in aviation, only 35 of whom could fly. The Americans learned swiftly, however, learning combat tactics from the French and British.

In May 1918, the Army Air Service became a military arm separate from the Signal Corps. This was when American army pilots began to see extensive action, flying mainly French and British aircraft because American manufacturing had not yet produced enough planes. When the United States entered the war, Congress ordered 27,000 aircraft to be built, and by the end of hostilities 11,000 had been delivered—of which almost 4,000 were combat planes. Yet, fewer than 200 reached the front before the war was over.

American pilots trained on American-built planes, however, the best being the Curtis JN-4 Jenny. One American-manufactured aircraft won special distinction: the H-12 Large America "flying boat" was the first American model to shoot down an enemy aircraft, and also the first to sink a submarine.

Volunteers serve in the Lafayette Escadrille

A year before the United States entered the war, several American volunteer pilots served in the French combat air squadron known as the Lafayette Escadrille, named in honor of the Marquis de Lafayette, a French general in the American revolutionary army. Established in April 1916 as the *Escadrille Americaine*, the squadron had seven American pilots and two French commanders. Its name was soon changed to Lafayette Escadrille because the original name compromised United States neutrality.

On February 18, 1918, all but one of the Lafayette Escadrille pilots transferred to AEF command and became the 103rd Pursuit Squadron. They were instrumental in training and leading new American pilots and formed the nucleus of the new American Air Service. By the time the squadron was disbanded, its 38 American and four French pilots had flown thousands of sorties, with 39 confirmed kills and more than 100 unconfirmed. Six of the squadron's pilots, including four of the original Americans, were killed in the war, and two others died in air accidents. Three Lafayette Escadrille pilots became aces—downing at

BOMBERS OVER THE ENGLISH CHANNEL Germany set the standard for aerial bombardment with her long-range Gotha bombers, which flew at 15,000 feet and carried 660 pounds of bombs. The British established an air force, distinct from the army, to shoot down these bombers, but the United States air force remained part of the army.

TOP AMERICAN ACE
EDDIE RICKENBACKER (1890–1973)

The most famous American ace was Edward V. Rickenbacker, a former auto racer who had been a driver for Pershing's general staff. General Billy Mitchell arranged for Rickenbacker to transfer to the Army Air Service, and in March 1918 he joined the 94th Aero Pursuit Squadron, whose "hat-in-the-ring" insignia gave the unit its nickname. A month later, Rickenbacker tallied his first kill, and, by the end of May had five, qualifying as an ace.

Rickenbacker's exploits were legendary as he participated in 134 aerial combats, once attacking seven enemy planes, shooting down two of them. He downed at least 24 enemy planes and was the top American ace of the war. Rickenbacker, who became commander of the 94th Squadron, was awarded the Medal of Honor and the Croix de Guerre.

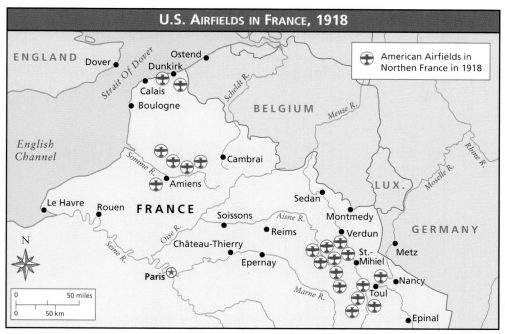

U.S. AIRFIELDS IN FRANCE, 1918

American Airfields in
Northen France in 1918

AIRFIELDS IN FRANCE United States "aero" squadrons usually shared French and British airfields, which were strategically placed to reach the battlefront rapidly.

least five enemy planes—and six became aerial unit commanders for the AEF.

Firsts in U.S. military aeronautics

American combat aviation came into its own in 1918, achieving a number of firsts. In January, the 1st Marine Aeronautical Company arrived at Ponta Delgada, Azores Islands, to undertake anti-submarine operations. In March, Stephen Potter won the first naval air victory. In April, the first American air victories over France were won by Alan F. Winslow and Douglas Campbell, and the first submarine was sunk by United States aircraft. In May, the AEF received its first American-built plane, a DH-4 Liberty. Also in May, the United States had its first air ace, as Douglas Campbell qualified by shooting down his fifth enemy plane.

In June, the first naval aviation unit arrived in France, and the first American daylight-bombing raid was conducted, followed in August by the first night-bombing raid.

Also in August, Congress officially created the United States Air Service as a distinct arm of the military.

"General Pershing told me that if I kept insisting that the organization of the Air Service be changed, he would send me home. I answered that if he did, he would soon come after me."

—"BILLY" MITCHELL, PRESSING THE CASE
FOR AN INDEPENDENT AIR CORPS

PIONEER OF AMERICAN AIR POWER
BILLY MITCHELL (1879–1936)

Before the war, Colonel William "Billy" Mitchell was a member of the army general staff with Signal Corps responsibilities, and in that capacity learned aeronautics. In 1916, Mitchell became director of army aviation. and he was an observer on the Western Front before the United States entered the war. When the American Expeditionary Force came to France, Mitchell was put in charge of American air units. He pushed for the expansion of air power, and by 1918 commanded a force of 1,500 American and French aircraft, which he employed in innovative large-scale bombing raids and in close air-support of ground troops.

Mitchell's squadrons gave valuable assistance in the American offensives of St.-Mihiel and the Meuse-Argonne. After the war, he became a controversial, fiery proponent of establishing an independent air force led by officers who fully understood its potential. Mitchell met so much resistance in the high command that his public protests earned him a court martial for insubordination, and he resigned. His ideas proved to be right, however, and in 1946 Congress vindicated Mitchell, posthumously awarding him the Medal of Honor.

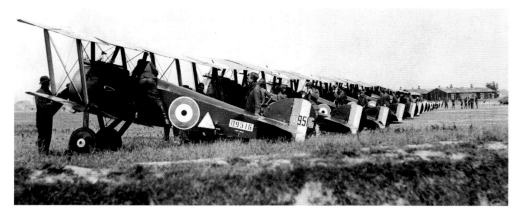

FRENCH FIGHTER PLANES American pilots flew mostly French-built aircraft, such as these Spad XIII pursuit fighters of the United States Army's 148th Aero Squadron, preparing to take off from an airfield at Petite Sythe, France.

William L. Mitchell

FINAL PUSH: THE MEUSE-ARGONNE OFFENSIVE

The Meuse River-Argonne Forest Offensive was the lower arm of a giant pincers movement, with the British and French attacking from the west and north. The aim was to seize strategic railroad lines and cut off supplies to the German front lines. The Americans, however, had just 10 days to move into position to meet Foch's timetable.

Before the St.-Mihiel campaign, Pershing had promised to be ready for Foch's next offensive, but now the logistical difficulties of transport and organization seemed insurmountable. Into the breach stepped Colonel George C. Marshall, destined to become one of the century's most important military leaders. As the First Army's operations officer, Marshall brilliantly organized the movement of troops, equipment, and matériel over miserable roads, through rainy weather, transferring 400,000 men and 900,000 tons of matériel 60 miles in six days.

Marshall would rise to chief of staff during World War II, and later serve as secretary of state and secretary of defense, winning the Nobel Prize for rebuilding Europe.

Assailing the Hindenburg Line

Pershing's most battle-tested divisions—the 1st, 2nd, and 3rd—were not yet prepared to leave St.-Mihiel, so he had to use less-experienced troops, some only partly trained. The rugged, overgrown ravines of the Argonne Forest, where machine gun nests were everywhere in years-old fortifications, promised to be a hell on earth for any troops. Barbed wire was

entangled with underbrush and wrapped around trees. Concrete walls were placed to stop tanks, and tank-traps—pits camouflaged with branches—were ready to swallow them up.

German defenses, from the Argonne to the hills above the rivers Aire and Meuse, were four lines deep and manned by seasoned troops. Pershing planned to attack along a 20-mile front with eight divisions in three corps—the I, III, and V. The first objective was the *Kreimhilde*

Stellung, part of a formidable defensive works nicknamed the Hindenburg Line, which ran along the Western Front.

The Americans jumped off before dawn on September 26, taking the enemy by surprise, but still running into murderous machine gun fire that burst out of the morning fog. For four brutal days in pouring rain, the Americans battled ever forward as the Germans defended every foot of ground. The attack on the right moved rapidly, but it was slow going in the Argonne, where adversaries were often just yards apart. Conditions were so obscure that men could only see where to fire by observing the flash of enemy guns. Pershing's troops had gained eight miles by September 30, but had to dig in before the *Kreimhilde Stellung*, unable to take it.

The three veteran American divisions arrived to relieve the exhausted troops in the front lines. Along with five more divi-

---

FIRST PHASE, MEUSE-ARGONNE OFFENSIVE, SEPTEMBER 26–OCTOBER 3, 1918

0 — 5 miles
0 — 5 km

N

Grand Pré · Saint-Juvin · Romagne · Brieulles · Cunel · Chevières · Sommerance · Marcq · Fléville · Nantillois · Montfaucon · Béthincourt · Consenvoye · Châtel-Chéhéry · Apremont · Baulny · Binarville · Cheppy · Varennes · Vauquois · Samogneux · Vacherauville · Boureuilles

Meuse R.
To Damvilliers
To Verdun

Line of September 26, A.M. ---- Line of October 3 --XXXX-- Army boundary
Line of September 26 —— Hindenburg Line ◄— Route

THE LAST OFFENSIVE In the first week of the 1918 Meuse-Argonne Campaign, the American First Army pushed back the enemy in its sector only a few miles, but these hard-won gains led to more spectacular advances and ultimate German defeat.

TANKS IN THE ARGONNE American crews drive French Renault tanks along a road in the Argonne Forest during the Meuse-Argonne Campaign of September-November 1918.

THE FINAL WEEKS ON THE WESTERN FRONT, OCTOBER–NOVEMBER, 1918

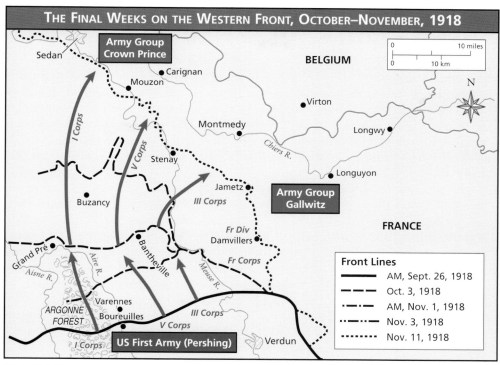

Front Lines

———	AM, Sept. 26, 1918
– – –	Oct. 3, 1918
–·–·–	AM, Nov. 1, 1918
··–··–	Nov. 3, 1918
·········	Nov. 11, 1918

THE ARMISTICE LINE The Western Front retreated toward Germany in mid-1918, pushed back by the great Allied offensive made possible by the battle-readiness of more than a million American troops.

sions, these three began a second offensive phase that lasted from October 4 until the 14th, without breaking through. As new divisions arrived at the front, the American Second Army was created, commanded by General Bullard, and the First was placed under General Hunter Liggett. A third attack was launched, and on October 16 the Americans finally captured the *Kreimhilde Stellung,* forcing their way into open terrain.

The Americans inflicted more than 100,000 enemy casualties in the Meuse-Argonne Offensive and took 25,000 prisoners. Their own loss was 26,000 dead and 95,000 wounded. The Germans had been pushed out of their strong positions, while the Allied offensive in the north also triumphed. Ludendorff resigned, and Germany asked for peace terms.

Armistice Day: November 11, 1918

American forces had been crucial to the final Allied victory. The United States military had grown to almost 3.7 million men by mid-1918, with 1.39 million serving in France. American losses in the war were 50,475 killed and 205,600 wounded.

At 11 a.m. on the 11th day of the 11th month, the Armistice took hold, and the guns fell silent, ending what became known as the Great War. Germany was defeated, but in just one generation there would be yet another, and greater, world war.

LOADING A HEAVY GUN American gunners of the 35th Coast Artillery ram home a shell in a mobile railroad cannon near the Argonne front in September 1918.

THE "LOST BATTALION" AND SERGEANT YORK

Two of the war's most celebrated incidents occurred during the Meuse-Argonne Offensive. In one, 550 men from the 77th Division (conscripts) battled ahead in the Argonne only to be surrounded, cut off from reinforcement or supply. The battalion's commander, Major Charles Whittlesey, refused German offers to surrender. The grim predicament of this "Lost Battalion" became sensational news, as radio communication flashed the latest developments around the world.

The detachment held on from October 3rd to the 7th, without food, unable to communicate with headquarters, and pinned down by machine guns and mortars. When American troops finally broke through to rescue them, only 194 walked out; 190 were seriously wounded, the rest dead or missing.

The other famous incident was the performance of Corporal Alvin C. York of the 82nd Division (conscripts). On October 8, York led 17 men into action and was surrounded, half his men killed or wounded. Almost on his own, he knocked out machine gun nests, killed 20 of the enemy, and captured 132, including officers. Promoted to sergeant and awarded the Medal of Honor and the Croix de Guerre, York was described by Supreme Allied Commander, Marshal Ferdinand Foch, as having achieved the "greatest accomplishment by any private soldier of all the armies of Europe."

Alvin C. York

18: ALLIED INTERVENTION IN RUSSIA'S CIVIL WAR

"[White Army detachments] inspected trains, and when they found someone who in their opinion was party to Bolshevism, or suspected of it, they arrested that person [and] dealt with [them] entirely as they pleased."

—AMERICAN MILITARY REPORT ON THE CHAOTIC RUSSIAN CIVIL WAR

The Russian Empire suffered from growing civil unrest in early 1917, as the army reeled from defeat after defeat against the Central Powers. In March, soldiers were brought into the capital, Petrograd (St. Petersburg), to quell strikers and rioters protesting food shortages and government inadequacy. The troops took the side of the civilians, however, destabilizing the army and bringing its loyalty into question.

A provisional government headed by Alexander Kerensky was formed, and Tsar Nicholas was compelled to abdicate. In November, Bolshevik Communist revolutionaries mounted a coup, led by Vladimir Ilyich Lenin, and established a Soviet (Committee) of People's Commissars. A cease-fire was agreed to with the Central Powers, and Russia demobilized. Soon, Russian counter-revolutionary forces struck back, bringing on a civil war between the Bolshevik "Reds" and the opposition "Whites."

Allies intervene in civil war

The Allies favored the Whites, hoping to get Russia back in the war. Moreover, Lenin was calling for all workers everywhere to oppose the war and for all soldiers to stop fighting. After thousands in the French army had mutinied in 1917, Allied commanders feared any impulse that would again inspire mutiny.

Allied troops were dispatched to northern Russia to support the Whites. A small number of American troops landed in May 1918 at the seaport of Murmansk, where Allied forces were gathering. At first, President Wilson protested that Russia should have the right to self-determination without foreign intervention, but by July he was persuaded to send in more troops. Ostensibly, the purpose was to aid the extrication of the 60,000-strong Czech Legion, a pro-Allied force of Czechs and Slovaks who after the Russian collapse had been trying to escape eastward over the Trans-Siberian Railway.

On September 4, almost 4,500 Americans landed at Murmansk, under the command of Colonel George E. Stewart. Conscripts for the most part, they immediately were rushed into action under British leadership, moving against the Bolsheviks. This was a prolonged and indecisive conflict that shed some American blood in a fight the troops little understood or cared about. The Allies and Whites each had about 20,000 troops at Murmansk.

Guarding the railway in East Asia

Also that September, 10,000 American troops arrived in Russia's East Asia port city of Vladivostok, Siberia. Led by General William S. Graves, their duty was to police the city along with British, French, and Italian troops, and keep open the Trans-Siberian Railway, the only usable railroad Russia had to the outside world. The Americans were ordered not to become caught up in Russian factional

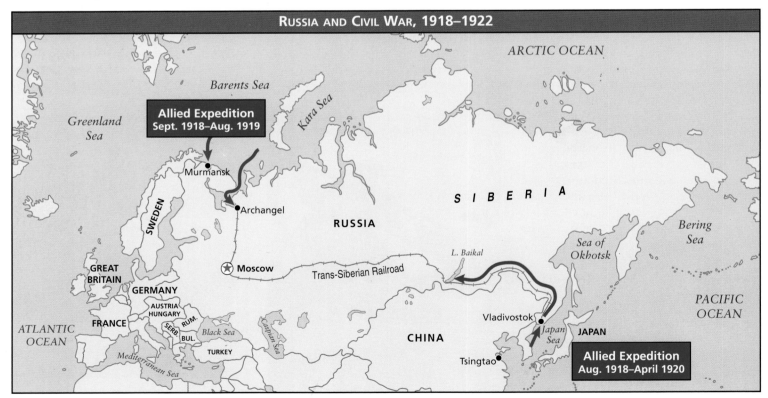

RUSSIA AND CIVIL WAR, 1918–1922

Allied Expedition
Sept. 1918–Aug. 1919

Allied Expedition
Aug. 1918–April 1920

ARCTIC OCEAN
Barents Sea
Greenland Sea
Kara Sea
SIBERIA
Murmansk
Archangel
SWEDEN
RUSSIA
Bering Sea
Sea of Okhotsk
L. Baikal
GREAT BRITAIN
Moscow
Trans-Siberian Railroad
GERMANY
AUSTRIA HUNGARY
FRANCE
Vladivostok
Japan Sea
JAPAN
PACIFIC OCEAN
ATLANTIC OCEAN
SERB. RUM.
BUL.
Black Sea
Caspian Sea
CHINA
Mediterranean Sea
TURKEY
Tsingtao

REDS VS. WHITES After World War I, American troops landed at Murmansk and Vladivostok, extreme ends of the expiring Russian Empire that was ablaze with civil war between revolutionary Reds and anti-revolutionary Whites. The Reds triumphed by 1922.

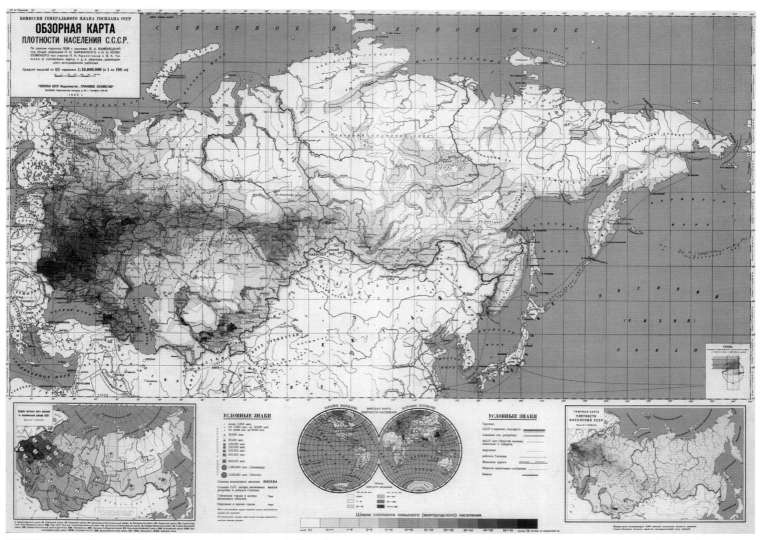

SOVIET UNION IN THE 1920S Under the iron rule of the Bolsheviks, who ruthlessly eradicated political opponents among the population of 147 million, the Union of Soviet Socialist Republics took shape as the world's largest country—8.1 million square miles.

fighting, but their very presence antagonized the Bolsheviks.

The Allies formed a commission to manage the railroad, thwarting the Bolsheviks, who wanted access to vast stores of munitions and supplies that had been stored in Vladivostok during the war. The Americans eventually found themselves guarding 1,000 miles of railway. They suffered casualties fighting off partisan raiders—mostly Cossacks of the Whites faction—who often attacked and looted trains. In one engagement, the Americans lost 25 killed and as many wounded.

Meanwhile, the Japanese also resented the American presence, which prevented outright conquest of Russian territory by Japanese forces. Japan had the strongest army in East Asia, and she was looking for the opportunity to expand her empire, as she had done in the Russo-Japanese War in 1905. Her resentment would lead to deeper animosity against the Americans in the following decades.

Allied withdrawal from Russia

At Murmansk, the onset of fierce winter intensified the difficulties of the operation, in which 5,000 Americans took part. The troops became so disgruntled with their involvement in the civil war that they openly protested to their officers. Wilson withdrew them by mid-1919, but those in Siberia remained until the spring of 1920.

By 1922, the Bolshevik Reds had decisively defeated the Whites, and the Japanese withdrew from Siberia, ending the Russian Civil War.

MARINES ENTER VLADIVOSTOK A detachment of Marines arrives in Siberia in June 1918 to guard the American consulate; eventually, 9,000 Americans were stationed in the region.

149

Air Power, Machine Guns, and Armor

American promoters of a big-battleship navy pushed for the construction of magnificent "Dreadnoughts" (named for the British big-gun battleship built in 1905), but even the mightiest surface ship could be targeted by the newest weapon of war at sea: the submarine. Improved range and speed, more torpedo tubes, and the periscope made the submarine increasingly lethal to surface ships during World War I.

In 1900, flight was limited to lighter-than-air dirigibles and balloons. That changed rapidly with the invention of the powered, fixed-wing aircraft. In the years just before World War I, airplanes swiftly became faster and more dependable. The United States Army conducted tests on Wright aircraft in 1909. The early warplanes were used for reconnaissance and were not very maneuverable. When air combat began, designers made planes speedier and more nimble. The German-built Fokker set the technology standard as the first to have its machine guns synchronized with its propeller, allowing the pilot to fire straight ahead. Planes improved from rickety crates to speedy combat aircraft flying at hundreds of miles an hour over the battlefield.

Among World War I's many firsts, anti-aircraft guns were introduced, as were aircraft carriers, depth charges, trench mortars, flame throwers, and poison gas. Like the ruthlessly effective machine guns of trench warfare, the first tanks proved they had the capability of changing military tactics forever. The role of the horse began to diminish, especially as motor vehicles became commonplace in military operations.

The Dreadnought battleships, however, had lesser roles to play. Air power and submarines would soon diminish their military importance.

SOPWITH CAMEL FIGHTER This capable British fighter saw much front-line service. The fledgling Army Air Force was often equipped with British or French aircraft.

BOMBING BY HAND A German aviator demonstrates World War I bombing techniques, which were inaccurate and ineffective. Aircraft speed and maneuverability rapidly improved during the war, as did the capacity for strafing troops, vehicles, and vessels.

DREADNOUGHT The 27,000-ton USS *Arkansas,* built in 1911, was 562 feet in length, with a top speed of 21 knots and a crew of 1,053. Her armament consisted of 12 12-inch guns, 21 five-inch guns, and two torpedo tubes. *Arkansas* and several other USN battleships operated as the 6th Battle Squadron, part of the Allied Grand Fleet blockading the North Sea.

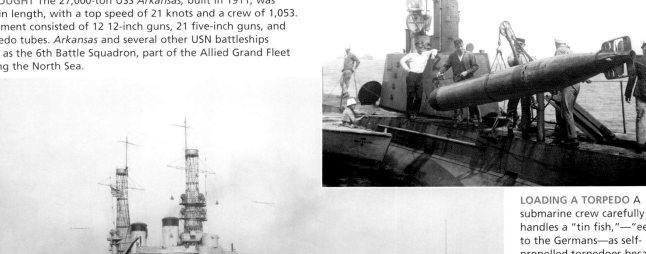

LOADING A TORPEDO A submarine crew carefully handles a "tin fish,"—"eel" to the Germans—as self-propelled torpedoes became known. Gyroscopic directional and depth control with either compressed air or electric propulsion sent early torpedoes on their deadly course to sink more ships than did mines or gunfire.

ENEMY TELEPHONE A signal officer of the American 42nd Division tries out a captured German field telephone at St. Mihiel in September 1918. Battlefield command and control were enhanced by phones, but bombardments and machine gun fire regularly destroyed the wires.

SPRINGFIELD RIFLE The infantryman's principal weapon in World War I was much like this Springfield 1903 Model breechloading, bolt-action rifle, with cartridges that employed smokeless propellant. Many experts consider this the finest military rifle ever produced.

GAS ATTACK Members of the army engineers demonstrate the effects of a phosgene gas attack on an unprepared soldier who does not wear a gas mask.

SURGICAL KIT This army medical field kit was for emergency battlefield treatment. About eight per cent of American World War I wounded died, compared with 15 per cent in the Civil War.

ARTILLERY ON THE MOVE French horse artillery haul 75mm field cannon into action on the Somme River; Americans often used French 75s. The failure of even heavy guns to destroy enemy bunkers in pre-assault bombardments cost the infantry dearly.

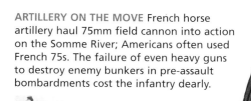

TIN HAT Americans used a British-style steel helmet that could protect the wearer from indirect shrapnel bursts.

FORD TANK Most American tankers used French-made Renault light tanks as well as Renault copies that were produced Stateside. American industry also designed tanks, such as this 1918 two-man model by Ford Motor Company—a tank that came too late to see service in France.

MACHINE GUN CREW American machine gunners of the 23rd Infantry duck under heavy fire. The machine gun changed the face of war, giving dug-in defenders devastating firepower that could wipe out the most determined attackers crossing open land.

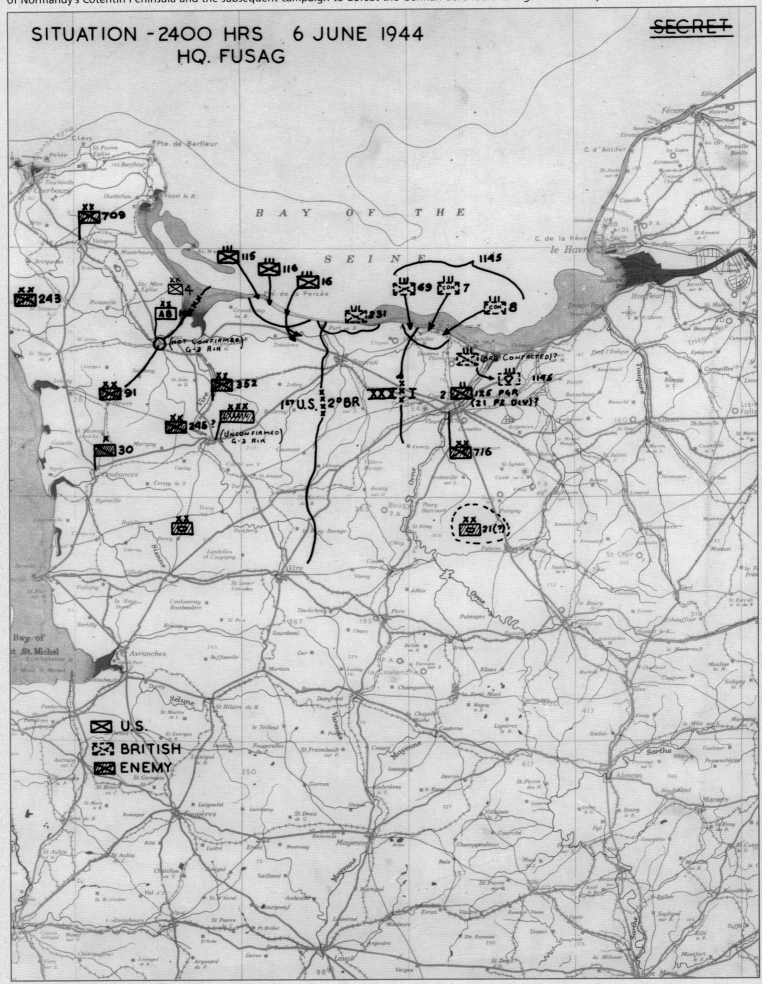

D-DAY AND THE BATTLE FOR NORMANDY 12th Army Group's engineers created this situation map of the June 6, 1944, invasion of Normandy's Cotentin Peninsula and the subsequent campaign to defeat the German defenders who gathered to repulse the Allies.

PART SIX

Global
War

IN 1919, THE LEAGUE OF NATIONS WAS FORMED for international cooperation to prevent another "Great War." The United States Senate, reluctant to become embroiled in world affairs, refused to join. Without American backing, the League could not curb the militaristic expansionism of Nazi Germany and Fascist Italy, who seized territory in the 1930s. Militarists also gained power in Imperial Japan, which occupied Manchuria and attacked China. There was hope the Soviet Union under Josef Stalin would stop Nazi expansion in Europe, but Hitler and Stalin signed a non-aggression pact in August 1939. Germany invaded Poland that September.

Pledged to protect Polish sovereignty, Great Britain and France immediately declared war on Germany. World War II had begun. The United States tried to keep out of it while supplying the embattled British with war matériel, but neutrality became increasingly difficult to maintain. At the same time, relations with Japan rapidly deteriorated.

On December 7, 1941, World War II came to America in a Japanese surprise attack on the naval base at Pearl Harbor, Hawaii. After four more years of hostilities, the war was brought to a sudden, shocking end in August 1945, when atomic bombs were dropped on the cities of Hiroshima and Nagasaki, compelling Japan's surrender.

The United Nations was formed in 1944 to mediate future conflicts, and America played a leading role in its creation. In the coming Nuclear Age, isolation from the world's affairs would no longer be possible for the United States.

Flag-raising on Iwo Jima, 1945

19: SURPRISE ATTACK HURLS AMERICA INTO WAR

*"A day that will live
in infamy."*

—PRESIDENT ROOSEVELT, ABOUT
JAPAN'S DECEMBER 7, 1941, ATTACK ON
PEARL HARBOR

In 1941, the United States was moving toward open hostility with the Axis powers. In July, President Franklin D. Roosevelt declared that America would help Great Britain in any way possible, short of war.

Japanese industry was in crisis because America had instituted a steel and oil embargo in response to Japanese military aggression. Japan needed raw materials to continue its war of conquest in China and Southeast Asia. When the United States refused to end the embargo, Japanese leaders planned a surprise attack to destroy American naval power in the Pacific. If the American Pacific Fleet based at Pearl Harbor on Hawaii's Oahu Island could be defeated, there would be no stopping Japanese conquest of Southeast Asia and the oil-rich Dutch East Indies. By the time the United States rebuilt her navy, a powerful Japanese empire would stretch across Asia's Pacific edge.

A Day of Infamy

The surprise attack came on Sunday morning, December 7. The base at Pearl Harbor was unprepared, and 3,861 American servicemen were killed as Japanese bombers sank two battleships and damaged six others. Almost 200 American planes were destroyed on the ground. As the Japanese had hoped, the Pacific Fleet was crippled, but the American carriers, which were not at port when the attack was made, remained ready for battle.

Within hours of the Pearl Harbor assault, Japanese planes hit American and British positions throughout the Pacific. In the Philippines, American planes were once again caught on the ground and destroyed. Without air power, the Philip-

pines lay open to Japanese invasion, which would soon come.

President Roosevelt called December 7 a "day of infamy," and the next day the United States declared war on Japan. On December 11, Germany declared war on the United States, with Italy soon to follow suit. America now joined in the 20th Century's second world-wide conflict.

Allied leaders look to Europe first

In 1940, Roosevelt had said America must be the "Arsenal of Democracy." Now at war, the full power of American industry was brought to bear against the Axis. Even before American troops could be trained and sent to fight, American light and medium tanks arrived in North Africa, giving British forces in Egypt the ability to stop the advance of the victorious German general Erwin Rommel.

British and American leaders made the strategic decision to defeat Germany and Italy before turning to Japan. The first American forces arrived in Britain on January 26, 1942. Roosevelt and Army Chief of Staff George C. Marshall wanted to break into German-occupied Europe with a landing on the coast of France as soon as possible. The British convinced them that Rommel must be defeated first, however, and the war in North Africa won.

F.D.R. SIGNS DECLARATION With members of Congress looking on, President Franklin D. Roosevelt signs the declaration of war against Japan after the surprise attack by more than 360 aircraft on Pearl Harbor on December 7, 1941.

When the Allies invaded North Africa late in 1942, the operation was backed by the growing military might of a fully mobilized United States.

A DYING BATTLESHIP The USS *Arizona* lists and settles on the bottom after Japanese dive bombers set her ablaze during the attack on Pearl Harbor. One of eight battleships put out of action that day, *Arizona* became a permanent memorial to Americans who died in on December 7.

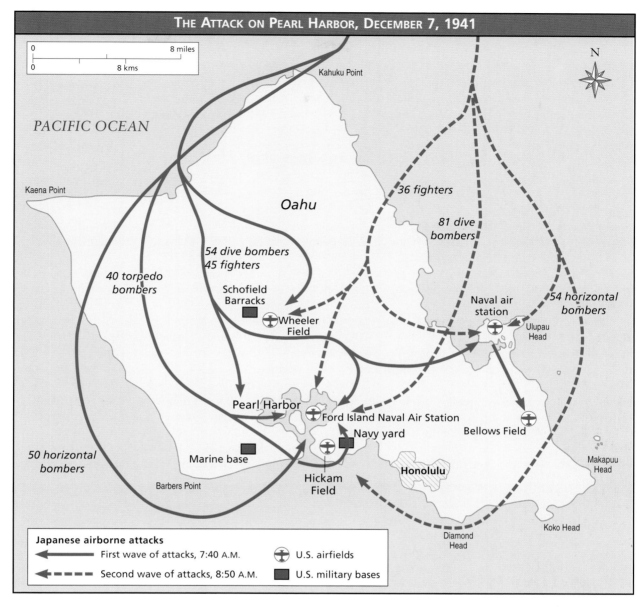

THE ATTACK ON PEARL HARBOR, DECEMBER 7, 1941

0   8 miles
0   8 kms

N

PACIFIC OCEAN

Kahuku Point

Kaena Point

Oahu

AIR ASSAULT ON PEARL HARBOR
Japanese warplanes struck from several approaches to do the most damage to vessels in the harbor and aircraft on the ground. Few American fighters got airborne—enemy warplanes destroyed them, most being lost at Hickam Field.

36 fighters

81 dive bombers

54 dive bombers
45 fighters

40 torpedo bombers

Schofield Barracks

Naval air station

54 horizontal bombers

Wheeler Field

Ulupau Head

Pearl Harbor

Ford Island Naval Air Station

Navy yard

Bellows Field

50 horizontal bombers

Marine base

Hickam Field

Honolulu

Makapuu Head

Barbers Point

Koko Head

Diamond Head

Japanese airborne attacks

⟵   First wave of attacks, 7:40 A.M.   ✛ U.S. airfields

⟵- - -   Second wave of attacks, 8:50 A.M.   ■ U.S. military bases

Internment of the Nisei

American outrage at the Pearl Harbor attack, and fear of sabotage at home, caused the internment of 112,000 Japanese-Americans in "relocation centers"—prison camps with barbed wire and armed guards. Most internees were "nisei," the Japanese term for American-born citizens. Though charged with no crime, the nisei were stripped of their rights. None would be allowed to return home until after the war, although large numbers were released and allowed to live elsewhere. Meanwhile, many of their young men volunteered, and Japanese-American units were formed, mostly campaigning in Europe. The army's 442nd Regimental Combat Team, composed of nisei, fought from Italy to France, becoming the most highly decorated American unit of the war. In 1946, this unit was specially honored at a White House ceremony.

FORBIDDING LANDSCAPE The Manzanar Relocation Center in California's arid Sierra Nevadas became the grim home for thousands of Japanese-Americans, rounded up and interned as enemy aliens after the United States entered World War II in December 1941.

UNITED STATES SUFFERS DEFEATS IN THE PACIFIC

From December 1941 to early 1942 the United States and Britain were dealt a series of defeats throughout the Pacific and Southeast Asia. The armed forces of Imperial Japan conducted a series of swift and successful operations that overwhelmed Allied resistance at every turn.

Empire of the rising sun

United States Marines on Guam surrendered on December 10. A small garrison of Marines defending Wake Island fought Japanese forces to a standstill, but were finally bombed into surrender on December 23.

Japanese imperial forces began an invasion of Malaya on December 8, capturing British-held Singapore by February 1942. British crown colony Hong Kong fell on December 25, and Burma was conquered by May 1942. An invasion of the Dutch East Indies was launched in January.

In Burma, American general Joseph Stilwell was sent to serve under Chiang Kai-shek and given command of two Chinese armies. As the Japanese drove through Burma in early 1942, defeating Chinese and British forces, Stilwell had to escape, leading a small group of refugees in a 140-mile march to India.

Fall of the Philippines

The Philippines had the largest concentration of United States troops and planes in the Pacific. General Douglas MacArthur, in charge of American and Filipino forces, saw Japanese bombers destroy his air force on the ground on December 8, 1941. MacArthur had a force of 31,000 United States troops and 100,000 Filipino fighters, but without air power he could not stop an invasion.

Japanese General Masaharu Homma's Fourteenth Army landed on the island of Luzon on December 22, with 43,000 men. MacArthur was rapidly driven back, declaring Manila an open city before Japanese tanks rolled in on January 2. Retreating to the Bataan Peninsula, he began a last-ditch defense. Homma sustained 7,000 casualties in attempts to

"There's no such thing as a glorious retreat. All retreats are ignominious as hell. I claim we got a hell of a licking."

—GENERAL JOSEPH STILWELL, ON THE EARLY JAPANESE OFFENSIVES

break the American-Filipino lines. By March, MacArthur's forces were weak from lack of supplies and exhausted from constant fighting. There was no hope of immediate reinforcement. Roosevelt ordered MacArthur to escape to Australia, leaving Lieutenant General Jonathan Wainwright in charge.

The final Japanese offensive began on April 3, forcing the surrender of the American-Filipino army on Bataan. Troops on the island fortress of Corregidor continued to hold out until May 6, when Wainwright finally ordered all his forces in the Philippines to lay down their arms. Homma captured 84,000 American and Filipino troops. In what became known as the "Bataan

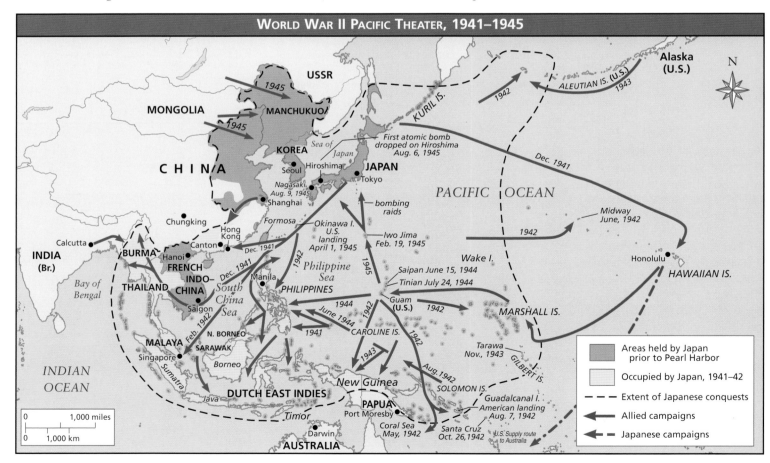

WORLD WAR II PACIFIC THEATER, 1941–1945

WAR IN THE PACIFIC Japanese advances reached their furthest limits by mid-1942. Their naval repulse at Midway that year was followed by Allied counteroffensives that wrested island after island in the Central and Southwestern Pacific, converging on the Philippines.

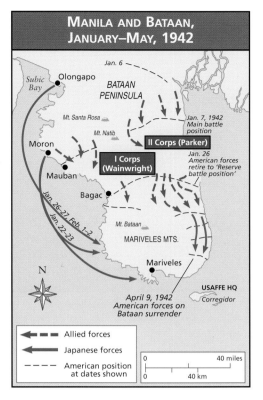

MANILA AND BATAAN, JANUARY–MAY, 1942

Subic Bay
Olongapo
Jan. 6
BATAAN PENINSULA
Mt. Santa Rosa
Jan. 7, 1942 Main battle position
Mt. Natib
Moron
II Corps (Parker)
I Corps (Wainwright)
Jan. 26 American forces retire to 'Reserve battle position'
Mauban
Bagac
Jan. 26-27 Feb 1-2
Jan. 22-23
Mt. Bataan
MARIVELES MTS.
Mariveles
N
USAFFE HQ
Corregidor
April 9, 1942 American forces on Bataan surrender

◄- - - Allied forces
◄─── Japanese forces
- - - - American position at dates shown

0   40 miles
0   40 km

BATAAN AND MANILA Outnumbered and outgunned American and Filipino troops under MacArthur fought a losing battle against Japanese invaders. Withdrawing to the Bataan Peninsula and Corregidor, they battled stubbornly despite knowing the United States was unprepared to rescue them.

and central areas of the Pacific. General MacArthur took command of Allied forces in the southwest Pacific, including Australia, the Solomon Islands, Bismarck Archipelago, New Guinea, the Philippines, Borneo, and much of the Dutch East Indies. These commanders were given instructions to act on the defensive, but to threaten the enemy whenever possible.

In early 1942, the United States had little strength with which to attack the Japanese, but Nimitz ordered carrier raids on the Marshall Islands, Wake, and New Guinea. On April 18, American forces struck Tokyo itself in a daring bombing attack.

The Doolittle Raid on Tokyo

Colonel James H. Doolittle's strike force of 16 B-25 bombers flew from the deck of the carrier USS *Hornet* to make a surprise bombing raid on Tokyo. Land-based B-25s had never before taken off from carriers, and the *Hornet's* runway, at 750 feet, was a bit too short. Doolittle, a former World War I ace and a test pilot and air racer, got his planes off the carrier and bombed Tokyo. Though the attack did little serious damage, it embarrassed Japan's military leaders, who had promised the home islands would never be bombed. The Doolittle Raid lifted American confidence after so many early defeats.

Death March," they were forced to tramp 60 miles under a blazing sun to a prison camp. Many were sick from disease and poor rations. Those who collapsed were often killed by their guards. Some 21,000 died on the march.

Japan had lost 12,000 troops in the Philippines campaign. United States-Filipino forces lost 16,000 in addition to those taken prisoner. This was the largest United States army in history ever to surrender.

Allied leadership restructured

In early 1942 the Pacific leadership was reorganized. Admiral Chester W. Nimitz became commander-in-chief of the Pacific Fleet, responsible for the Pacific Ocean Area, and in direct control of the northern

GENERAL JOSEPH W. STILWELL A scholar and soldier, Stilwell was a China expert as well as a skilled infantry officer.

General Joseph W. Stilwell had a 10-year career as an American officer serving in China in the 1920s and 1930s. Stilwell was fluent in Chinese, but was also an infantry battalion commander and an instructor at Fort Benning's Infantry School. A general by 1940, Stilwell was named commander of the China-Burma-India Theater, where he became chief of staff to Nationalist Chinese generalissimo Chiang Kai-shek.

At war with the Japanese since the mid-1930s, the Nationalist Chinese gave Stilwell command of two field armies. He led a prolonged campaign in northern Burma and was supported by the United States air unit based in southern China, the China Air Task Force, or "Flying Tigers," commanded by General Claire L. Chennault. Stilwell had considerable success against the Japanese, but did not get enough cooperation from Chiang Kai-shek, whose ambitions to rule China often overrode the need to fight the Japanese.

Also with Stilwell were two battalions of "Merrill's Marauders," American raiders commanded by General Frank Merrill. In mid-1945 Stilwell left the theater to take command of the U.S. Tenth Army in Okinawa, where he accepted the Japanese surrender on September 2.

LUMBERING B-25 TAKES OFF The 16 B-25s of the daring Doolittle Raid dismayed the Japanese by bombing Tokyo, Kobe, Nagoya, Yokohama, and Yokusuka. The raid earned Doolittle promotion to brigadier general, and he was awarded the Congressional Medal of Honor.

157

VICTORY AT MIDWAY AS THE TIDE OF WAR TURNS

In spring of 1942 the Empire of the Rising Sun stretched from Burma in the West to Wake Island in the East, and as far south as New Guinea. Imperial forces planned their next conquest—Australia. First the Solomon Islands and New Guinea must be secured. A powerful fleet was sent to capture Port Moresby, MacArthur's base of operations in southern New Guinea. Strategic Port Moresby controlled the sea-lanes for United States supplies to Australia.

Battle of the Coral Sea

In May 1942, imperial troop transports with a naval covering group left the Japanese stronghold of Rabaul, New Britain. The fleet steamed south in the Coral Sea toward Port Moresby. At the same time, a powerful carrier strike group under Vice-Admiral Takeo Takagi entered the Coral Sea from the east to destroy any Allied warships in the area.

American code-breakers had informed Admiral Nimitz of the planned invasion, and he ordered a force led by the carriers *Lexington* and *Yorktown* into the Coral Sea. So began the first naval battle in which the opposing ships never came in sight of one another. Carrier planes searched out then attacked the enemy fleet. The battle ended with the *Yorktown* damaged, and the *Lexington* so badly ablaze that she had

to be abandoned. One Japanese carrier was sunk, many planes shot down, and the invasion fleet turned back. The Japanese still had five large aircraft carriers ready for action against three large carriers for the United States.

Japan's Admiral Isoroku Yamamoto decided to force an engagement that would crush the Pacific Fleet. He would attack Midway Island with five separate groups totaling more than 200 vessels, including four large carriers. The United States Navy would have no choice but to fight for Midway, which could serve as a base for a Japanese invasion of Hawaii.

The turning point

Again code-breakers warned Nimitz of the impending attack. Late in May all his available carriers were concentrated at Midway. Also ready for action was the carrier *Yorktown*, which had been hurriedly repaired.

JAPANESE ATTACKERS Aichi D3A "Val" dive bombers hit American warships in the Battle of the Coral Sea, which put two United States carriers and one Japanese out of action.

"We were unable to avoid the dive bombers because we were so occupied in avoiding the torpedoes."

—CAPTAIN OF THE *AKAGI*, CARRIER SUNK AT THE BATTLE OF MIDWAY

CODE-BREAKING MAGIC

Before the Pacific war began, American code-breakers had already cracked the most secret Japanese diplomatic code, nicknamed "Purple." Code-breakers of the United States Army Signal Intelligence Service—led by William F. Friedman, the foremost American cryptologist—so impressed authorities that they were called "magicians," and the code word for their deciphered communications became "Magic." Friedman and his colleagues began work to break the code in 1939, requiring 18 months to do so. Once they had succeeded in their "decryption," the cryptologists constructed a machine that worked like "Purple" encoding equipment. This machine was used for the rest of the war to decipher intercepted messages quickly, giving Allied leaders a great strategic advantage against the Japanese.

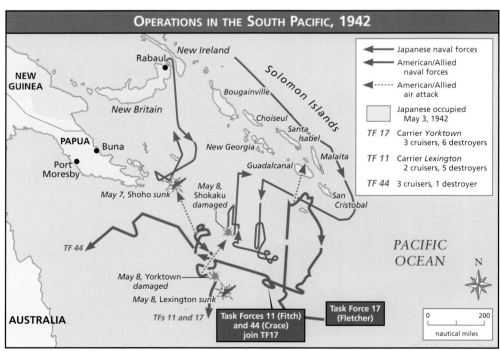

OPERATIONS IN THE SOUTH PACIFIC, 1942

Rabaul · New Ireland · New Britain · Bougainville · Choiseul · Santa Isabel · New Georgia · Guadalcanal · Malaita · San Cristobal

NEW GUINEA · PAPUA · Buna · Port Moresby · Solomon Islands

May 7, Shoho sunk
May 8, Shokaku damaged
May 8, Yorktown damaged
May 8, Lexington sunk
TF 44
TFs 11 and 17

PACIFIC OCEAN · N

AUSTRALIA

Task Forces 11 (Fitch) and 44 (Crace) join TF17
Task Force 17 (Fletcher)

→	Japanese naval forces	
→	American/Allied naval forces	
◄······	American/Allied air attack	
	Japanese occupied May 3, 1942	
TF 17	Carrier *Yorktown* 3 cruisers, 6 destroyers	
TF 11	Carrier *Lexington* 2 cruisers, 5 destroyers	
TF 44	3 cruisers, 1 destroyer	

0 ———— 200
nautical miles

AUSTRALIA'S DOORSTEP The Japanese attempt to cut off Australia by controlling New Guinea and the Solomons brought on the Battle of the Coral Sea in May 1942.

On June 4, 108 bombers from the Japanese invasion fleet attacked Midway. Few of the American land-based torpedo bombers survived the strike, but those that did went for the Japanese carriers. As the carriers directed their guns against the low-flying torpedo planes, shooting down every one, dive-bombers from the carriers *Yorktown* and *Enterprise* struck from above in a devastating surprise attack. The American dive-bombers sank three carriers, the *Akagi*, *Kaga*, and *Soryu*. The carrier *Hiryu* launched its own planes in a counter-attack that heavily damaged the *Yorktown*—later sunk by a Japanese submarine. *Enterprise* dive-bombers then sank the *Hiryu*. Stunned by the loss of his four carriers, Yamamoto ordered an immediate retreat.

This dramatic American victory made the balance of naval power in the Pacific more even, but the United States was becoming superior in large carriers. American war industry churned out more planes and warships, and after Midway the tide began to turn against Japan.

On American soil

In a feint to draw away part of the Pacific Fleet before the drive against Midway, Yamamoto ordered the invasion of the United States islands of Attu and Kiska in the Aleutians. Japan wanted to control the Aleutians, which could be a base for an American invasion against Japan. Nimitz conserved his forces for the main strike on Midway and did not attempt to stop the Japanese from capturing the islands.

Japanese bases in the Aleutians were a threat to Alaska and the Pacific Northwest. In 1943 American forces invaded to retake Attu and Kiska, attacking Attu on May 11. A fierce battle raged for 11 days in dense, icy fog. The last Japanese defenders were killed in a suicide charge on May 29.

On Kiska, a Canadian and American force landed to discover the garrison had just evacuated.

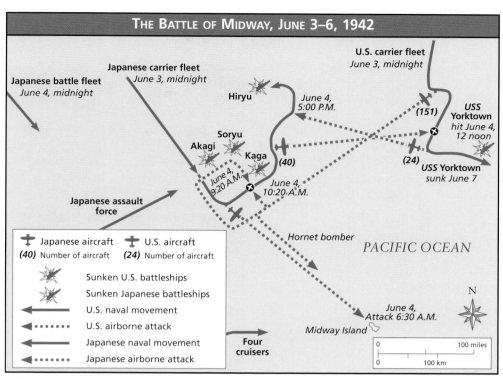

THE BATTLE OF MIDWAY, JUNE 3–6, 1942

AMERICAN TRIUMPH AT MIDWAY The Japanese navy suffered a devastating defeat attempting to capture Midway Island in June 1942. USN dive bombers from Admiral Raymond A. Spruance's carriers blasted Japanese carriers when their decks were crowded with aircraft being refueled, causing massive explosions. Japanese losses leveled the balance of naval power in the Pacific.

ALEUTIANS DIVERSION The Japanese captured United States territory by landing on Attu and Kiska in early 1942. This was an effort to draw American naval forces away from Midway, but Nimitz kept his carriers and major ships in the Central Pacific.

NAVY FIGHTERS A burning Japanese warship far below shows the way for Grumman TBF-1 Avenger torpedo bombers going into action at the Battle of Midway, June 4-6, 1942.

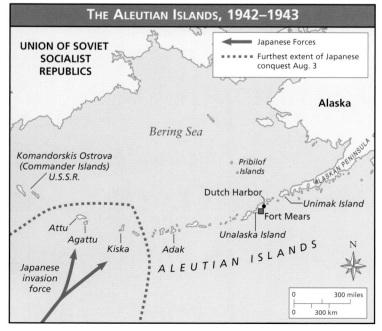

THE ALEUTIAN ISLANDS, 1942–1943

SECURING THE SOLOMON ISLANDS AND NEW GUINEA

From the stronghold of Rabaul, on the island of New Britain, the Japanese continued a campaign to isolate Australia. In the summer of 1942 imperial forces landed on Guadalcanal in the Solomon Islands and built an airfield. Bombers from Guadalcanal could attack American convoys supplying Australia. In New Guinea, Japanese jungle fighters were driving on Port Moresby, but a counteroffensive earned the Allies their first land victories in the Pacific.

Battle for Guadalcanal

At dawn on August 7, the 1st Marine Division under General Alexander Vandegrift landed unopposed on Guadalcanal in "Operation Cactus." Within 48 hours, Vandegrift's 16,000 Marines gained control of a partially completed airfield, naming it Henderson Field. The Marines dug in and fought off counterattacks. During the day, warships and planes of the United States Navy controlled the sea and skies, but at night Japanese convoys from Rabaul were landing troops, bringing in 20,000 men by the end of September. Enemy convoys, which the Marines called "The Tokyo Express," kept coming until November,

when the Navy finally managed to block them. The 2nd Marine Division and the Army's Americal Division reinforced the Guadalcanal garrison to almost 50,000 men, and a jungle battle raged through February 1943, when the last Japanese troops were evacuated. The Japanese had 24,000 men killed, the United States lost 1,752 men killed.

A GUADALCANAL BEACH In mid-1942, the Japanese fortified key islands of the Southwest Pacific and built air bases. These islands were successively captured by the Allied counteroffensive that began with the Guadalcanal landing, shown here as the 160th Infantry Regiment comes ashore.

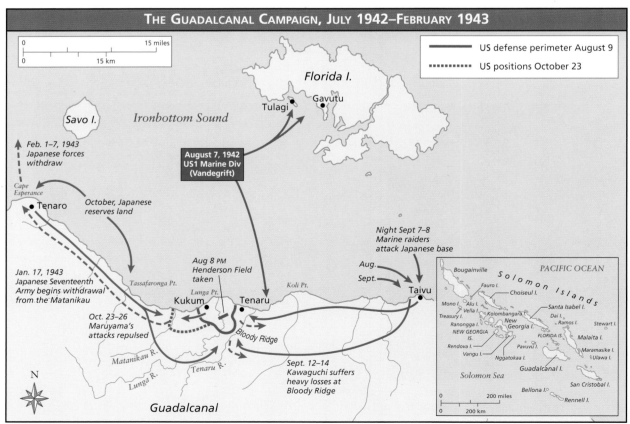

THE GUADALCANAL CAMPAIGN, JULY 1942–FEBRUARY 1943

— US defense perimeter August 9
······· US positions October 23

Florida I.

Gavutu
Tulagi

Savo I.   Ironbottom Sound

Feb. 1–7, 1943
Japanese forces
withdraw

August 7, 1942
US1 Marine Div
(Vandegrift)

Cape
Esperance

Tenaro

October, Japanese
reserves land

Night Sept 7–8
Marine raiders
attack Japanese base

Jan. 17, 1943
Japanese Seventeenth
Army begins withdrawal
from the Matanikau

Aug 8 PM
Henderson Field
taken

Tassafaronga Pt.

Lunga Pt.

Koli Pt.

Aug.

Sept.

Taivu

Kukum   Tenaru

Oct. 23–26
Maruyama's
attacks repulsed

Bloody Ridge

Matanikau R.

Tenaru R.

Lunga R.

Sept. 12–14
Kawaguchi suffers
heavy losses at
Bloody Ridge

N

Guadalcanal

PACIFIC OCEAN

Bougainville   Solomon Islands
Fauro I.
Alu I.   Choiseul I.
Mono I.   Vella I.
Treasury I.   Kolombangara I.   Santa Isabel I.
Ranongga I.   New   Dai I.
NEW GEORGIA   Georgia I.   Ramos I.   Stewart I.
IS.   FLORIDA IS.   Malaita I.
Rendova I.   Pavuvu I.
Vangu I.   Nggatokaa I.   Maramasike I.
Ulawa I.
Guadalcanal I.
Solomon Sea
San Cristobal I.
Bellona I.
Rennell I.

0   200 miles
0   200 km

ARENA OF ACTION
The Guadalcanal invasion of August 1942 was part of a larger campaign for the eastern Solomons, in which both sides lost heavily in ships and aircraft. Naval clashes, air strikes, and amphibious landings chopped away at Japanese strength.

In 1943, the Allies began to close in on Rabaul. As MacArthur fought for control of New Guinea, American forces under Admiral William F. Halsey, Jr., moved up the Solomons. One island after another fell to the Marines and Army: in February the Russel Islands; June, New Georgia; August, Vella Lavella; October, the Treasury Islands; and in November, Bougainville. Meanwhile, around the Solomon Islands, there were a series of naval engagements.

Winning the war at sea

With the opposing fleets fighting to support their troops, naval battles went on from August 1942 well into 1943.

Most engagements took place in "the Slot," the route taken by Japanese convoys through the Solomons to Guadalcanal. The waters off Guadalcanal became known as "Iron Bottom Sound," because of the great number of ships sunk there. In the Battle of Savo Island, August 8–9, 1942, a Japanese night attack surprised Allied warships off Guadalcanal, sinking four cruisers and a destroyer. A naval war of attrition followed, with both sides losing heavily. These engagements, from August through November, included the Battle of the Eastern Solomons, August 23–25, the Battle of the Santa Cruz Islands, October 26, and the massive Naval Battle of Guadalcanal, November 12–15. American military production was going at full speed, but Japan could not afford the high cost in planes and warships.

Campaign for New Guinea

The Allies had thought New Guinea's Owen Stanley Mountains impassable, but Japanese jungle fighters made it across from Buna, coming within 32 miles of Port Moresby. MacArthur rushed in Australian and American troops for a hard-fought 10-month counteroffensive that drove the Japanese back.

Allied forces stalled before Buna, and in December MacArthur sent General Robert L. Eichelberger to take command. Eichelberger restored the morale of an Allied force shaken by disease and failure. By the end of January he had captured Buna, but it took two more years to finally liberate all of New Guinea.

In March 1943 Japanese hopes for victory in New Guinea were shattered in the Battle of the Bismarck Sea, when General George C. Kenney's Fifth Air Force, based in Papua, New Guinea, sank

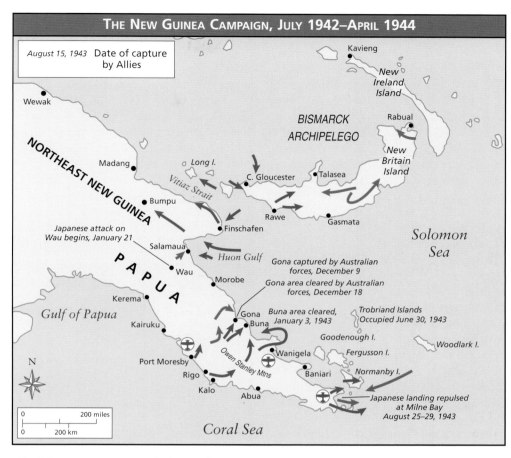

THE NEW GUINEA CAMPAIGN, JULY 1942–APRIL 1944

August 15, 1943 Date of capture by Allies

Wewak
NORTHEAST NEW GUINEA
Madang
Bumpu
Long I.
C. Gloucester
Talasea
Rawe
Gasmata
Finschafen
Japanese attack on Wau begins, January 21
Salamaua
Huon Gulf
Wau
PAPUA
Morobe
Kerema
Gulf of Papua
Kairuku
Gona
Buna
Port Moresby
Rigo
Owen Stanley Mtns
Kalo
Abua
N
0   200 miles
0   200 km
Coral Sea

Kavieng
New Ireland Island
Rabual
BISMARCK ARCHIPELEGO
New Britain Island
Solomon Sea
Gona captured by Australian forces, December 9
Gona area cleared by Australian forces, December 18
Buna area cleared, January 3, 1943
Trobriand Islands Occupied June 30, 1943
Goodenough I.
Woodlark I.
Wanigela
Fergusson I.
Baniari
Normanby I.
Japanese landing repulsed at Milne Bay August 25–29, 1943

all eight transports and four of seven destroyers in an imperial troop convoy.

Instead of attacking Rabaul in 1943, which would have resulted in heavy casualties, the Allies began a strategy of "island-hopping," which they would continue through the Pacific War. Rabaul had been isolated by occupying the Solomons and New Guinea. Now it was bypassed, as MacArthur moved against the Philippines. Rabaul would remain under heavy Allied bombardment for the rest of the war, finally surrendering in August, 1945.

NEW GUINEA CAMPAIGN Determined ground and air attacks combined with naval operations to push the Japanese from New Guinea and adjacent islands; "island-hopping" cut off many enemy positions.

"Fortitude is admirable under any flag and those Japanese soldiers had it."

—GENERAL ROBERT L. EICHELBERGER, COMMANDER, I CORPS, WHO CAPTURED BUNA, NEW GUINEA

FLAK PEPPERS THE SKY American ships fight off dive bombers during the October 1942 Battle of Santa Cruz, a Japanese tactical victory, but she lost 100 irreplaceable airmen.

W.W.II'S LONGEST STRUGGLE: THE BATTLE OF THE ATLANTIC

The struggle for supremacy over the Atlantic and Mediterranean was well under way when the United States became a belligerent in World War II. Winning the Battle of the Atlantic was especially crucial to supplying Britain, shipping American troops and matériel to the European and North African theaters, and providing the Soviet Union's war effort with essential equipment.

At the start of 1942, German U-boats (*Unterseeboot*) were waging a fairly even contest with Allied warships and aircraft, with heavy losses on both sides. The British convoy system had escort vessels such as sub-chasing corvettes and destroyers protecting fleets of merchant ships. The Germans had convenient and well-defended submarine pens on the French coast from which to sally forth, unseen, and attack.

America loses heavily

At first, the United States declined to organize its merchant shipping into convoys, which offered U-boat commanders a fruitful harvest. German admiral Karl Dönitz, head of the U-boat fleet, organized "*Paukenschlag*"—"Operation Drumroll"—attacks on shipping along the American Atlantic seaboard and in the Gulf of Mexico and Caribbean. In first three months of 1942, 60 American tankers were sunk in the Caribbean alone, The U-boats had little opposition to their attacks on American shipping.

Later in 1942, the United States adopted the convoy system. Also protecting convoys were patrolling shore-based warplanes that looked for German submarines, which usually traveled on the surface when not in action, using their diesel engines. Surface operation was necessary for recharging the vessel's batteries, which even when fully-charged allowed only for limited mobility and endurance while submerged.

The Battle of the Atlantic began to favor the Allies thanks to the convoy system, better air cover from land and from small "escort" carriers, enhanced radio communications, and the improvement of the depth charge that pounded U-boats with underwater explosions. The German secret code was broken by a program named "Ultra," so the Allies could read

radio instructions transmitted to the underwater fleet.

By the fall of 1942, U-boats were losing the battle, but the "Torch" invasion of North Africa diverted many escort vessels and planes to that campaign, leaving convoys far less protected.

Outfighting the U-boats

"Wolf packs" of as many as 20 U-boats working together sank ships faster than the Allies could build them. In March 1943, the more than 300 U-boats in the Atlantic sank 500,000 tons of shipping. In the first five months of 1943, 95 U-boats were sunk, three-fourths with no survivors. Many were supply submarines termed "milch cows."

After Torch was completed in mid-1943, Allied naval escorts and aircraft patrols were increased in the Atlantic. Improved anti-submarine aircraft now had the range to patrol the mid-Atlantic area formerly known as the "mid-Atlantic

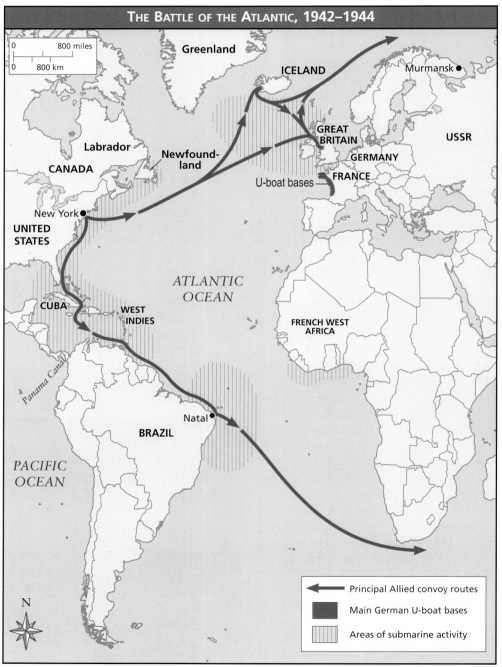

THE BATTLE OF THE ATLANTIC, 1942–1944

0   800 miles
0   800 km

Greenland

ICELAND

Murmansk

Labrador

Newfound-
land

GREAT
BRITAIN

USSR

CANADA

GERMANY

U-boat bases

FRANCE

New York

UNITED
STATES

ATLANTIC
OCEAN

CUBA

WEST
INDIES

FRENCH WEST
AFRICA

Panama Canal

PACIFIC
OCEAN

Natal

BRAZIL

N

→ Principal Allied convoy routes

■ Main German U-boat bases

▦ Areas of submarine activity

SUPPLY ROUTES AND DANGER ZONES Matériel and troops crossed the Atlantic on merchant ships and transports vulnerable to U-boat attack. Many ships went on to Murmansk, supplying the Soviets, and others around Africa to the Pacific and the Middle East.

"[An] ear-shattering roar, and the deck bucked and heaved [and] a huge tower of black smoke, tons of water, and debris was flung into the air . . . ."

—OFFICER ABOARD MERCHANTMAN *NARVIA* AS SHE WAS TORPEDOED

"TYPE VII" U-BOAT This workhorse of the German submarine fleet fires its 88mm deck gun at a fleeing merchant ship. As Allied anti-submarine and air patrol capabilities improved, such surface attacks by U-boats became too dangerous.

air gap," or the "black pit," which aircraft previously could not reach. This was where the most ships had been sunk by U-boat attacks. In addition, U-boats had to cope with converted merchant ships carrying anti-submarine planes. New radar developments permitted Allied aircraft to home in on a U-boat before the vessel's own equipment detected them coming. Furthermore, prodigious Allied shipbuilding was now turning out merchant ships much faster than U-boats could sink them.

Severe U-boat losses forced Dönitz to withdraw most of his fleet out of reach of shore-based planes in Labrador, Northern Ireland, and Iceland, but the Battle of the Atlantic remained a hard-fought contest. German U-boats had improved torpedo technology to take on fast-moving escort vessels. Other improvements such as the snorkel—a tube that drew in air and eliminated exhaust from the diesel engines while submerged—permitted U-boats to stay underwater longer. Toward the end of the war, new German submarines appeared, with vastly longer range, improved underwater endurance and more speed. These vessels were formidable, but they appeared too late to change the course of the conflict.

The Allied capture of U-boat pens along the European coast by late 1944 finally shut off Germany's ability to wage effective submarine warfare in the Atlantic.

A TANKER BURNS Torpedoed in the Atlantic, an oil tanker crumbles amidships as it rapidly sinks. Vital to the Allied war effort, tankers were prime targets of prowling U-boats.

DEPTH CHARGES EXPLODE Crewmen of a Coast Guard destroyer look astern to see the effects of their depth charge. Antisubmarine operations —sonar, radar, and tactics—improved over the course of the Battle of the Atlantic. Relentless pursuit of German submarines by "hunter-killer" groups of convoy escorts led to crippling U-boat losses.

20: FROM TORCH TO KASSERINE: FORGING VETERANS

"Our valiant and courageous troops are now storming the beaches of North Africa."

—F.D.R., HEARD ON THE BBC BY TORCH SOLDIERS HOURS BEFORE THEY BOARDED ASSAULT CRAFT FOR THE LANDING

DESERT FOX General Rommel earned this nickname for brilliant handling of armor and mechanized infantry in the North African desert. He is seen with the 15th Panzer Division in late 1941.

n mid-1942, the hard-pressed Soviet Union was eager for a second front to be opened in Western Europe. At first, the U.S. Joint Chiefs of Staff favored an immediate cross-Channel invasion, but further strategic planning led to a campaign to capture French North Africa, controlled by France's Vichy government.

Operation Torch

An Allied victory in Morocco, Algeria, and Tunisia would clear Axis forces from North Africa and lay the groundwork to invade Italy and Greece. The 10,000 Vichy forces in North Africa might put up a fight, but it was likely they would instead join the Allies.

American general Dwight D. Eisenhower was given overall command of "Operation Torch," planned to cooperate with General Bernard L. Montgomery's British Eighth Army in Libya. That October, the Eighth Army repulsed Field Marshal Erwin Rommel's formidable Afrika Korps at El Alamein in Egypt. Rommel's spectacular early successes were now reversed. His army withdrew across Libya to a strong defensive position—the

GENERAL OF THE ARMY General Eisenhower commanded the invasions of North Africa, Sicily, and Italy prior to becoming Supreme Allied Commander in the European theater.

"Mareth Line"—in southern Tunisia, awaiting reinforcement and an attack.

On November 8, 1942, more than 130,000 troops simultaneously invaded North Africa across a thousand-mile front, from French Morocco in the west to Algeria in the east. The main landings

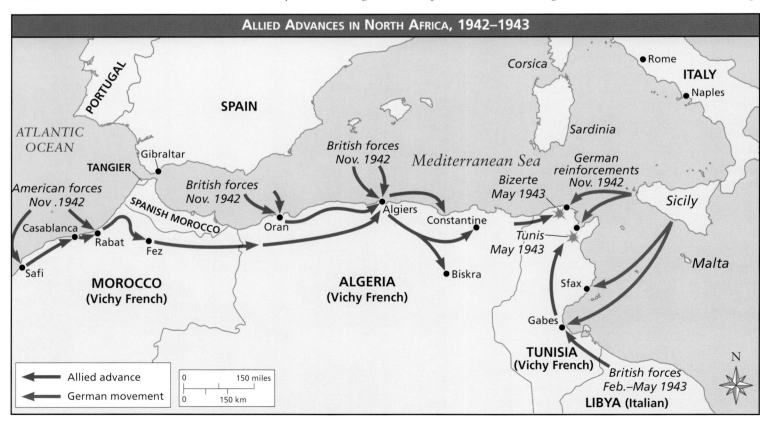

ALLIED ADVANCES IN NORTH AFRICA, 1942–1943

ATLANTIC OCEAN

PORTUGAL

SPAIN

Gibraltar

TANGIER

American forces Nov. 1942

SPANISH MOROCCO

Casablanca

Rabat

Fez

Safi

MOROCCO (Vichy French)

British forces Nov. 1942

Oran

British forces Nov. 1942

Algiers

Constantine

Biskra

ALGERIA (Vichy French)

Mediterranean Sea

Corsica

Sardinia

German reinforcements Nov. 1942

Bizerte May 1943

Tunis— May 1943

Sfax

Gabes

TUNISIA (Vichy French)

British forces Feb.–May 1943

LIBYA (Italian)

Rome

ITALY

Naples

Sicily

Malta

N

Allied advance

German movement

0   150 miles

0   150 km

ROMMEL CAUGHT IN AN ALLIED VISE Eisenhower's force pushes east as Montgomery's Eighth Army drives westward from the Libyan Desert, pressing the Axis in Tunisia. Hitler sent reinforcements, but German troops in North Africa surrendered in May 1943.

NORTH AFRICA INVASION American troops storm ashore from a Coast Guard "Sea Horse" landing craft during the November 1942 Operation Torch, which captured French North Africa, led to Rommel's defeat, and set the stage for invading Sicily and Italy.

were at Casablanca, Oran, and Algiers, all of which had valuable French naval bases and airfields. The Casablanca invasion force of 38,000 Americans led by General George S. Patton, sailed all the way from Norfolk, Virginia. The other two forces, totaling almost 50,000 British and 47,000 Americans, came from Britain. Most British landed at Algiers and most Americans landed at Oran.

Some French defenders did fight at first, but a ceasefire was soon arranged. Many French came over to the Allies to fight for

liberation of their homeland. Hitler now ordered the military occupation of all France, which until then had been only partly under Nazi control. He also sent reinforcements to Rommel in Tunisia, where Vichy French installations were taken over by German and Italian troops. In November, Allied forces advancing eastward into Tunisia were thrown back by German counterattacks led by General Jürgen von Arnim.

By early winter, a stalemate existed between the Allies and Axis in Tunisia. The American II Corps, in an advanced position to the south, was commanded by General Lloyd R. Fredendall. To Fredendall's north was a Free French corps, and beyond was the British First Army.

American defeat at Kasserine Pass

With the seasoned Eighth Army to his east, Rommel was outnumbered and apparently without any hope of resuming the offensive, but he did just that in mid-February 1943.

Rommel's veteran Panzer divisions, augmented with powerful new Mark VI Tiger tanks, were eager to attack. On February 14, the Panzers hurled back the unsuspecting French and Americans, smashing the green II Corps at Kasserine Pass and driving them 21 miles in nine days. American resistance stiffened, supported by heavy air strikes and by a British armored counterattack from the north. By February 22, Rommel had resumed his original positions and fighting continued. Patton now took command of II Corps.

In late March, Montgomery broke through from the east, and on April 6 joined up with forces from the Torch invasion. General Omar N. Bradley assumed command of II Corps while Patton left to organize the Seventh Army for a forthcoming invasion of Italy. Rommel steadily retreated, but by early May his troops were surrendering wholesale. The battle for Tunisia was over by May 13. There were 250,000 German and Italian prisoners, 40,000 dead and wounded—although Rommel had been ordered back to Germany before the surrender of the Axis armies in Tunisia. The British had 33,000 casualties, the Americans 18,500.

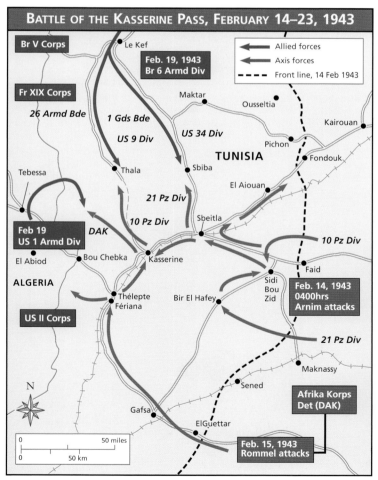

BATTLE OF THE KASSERINE PASS, FEBRUARY 14–23, 1943

THE FOX STRIKES AGAIN The American commanders were new to desert fighting, when the Afrika Korps, led by Rommel's subordinate, General Hans-Jürgen von Arnim, dealt them a defeat at Kasserine Pass.

PANZERS RACE TO BATTLE German armored formations had a mixture of tanks, some the best in the world, but almost always too few. The United States produced more than 49,000 Sherman tanks, whose sheer numbers gave the Allies an advantage in the North African campaign.

AIR POWER AND THE IMPACT OF STRATEGIC BOMBING

Even before the United States entered World War II, Americans volunteered as pilots in the Royal Air Force (RAF). Between September 1940 and late 1942, 240 Americans were in the RAF. Once America became an ally, however, she needed every pilot for her own military, and the fast-growing Army Air Force (AAF) needed the best of them.

The AAF had 2.4 million personnel by late in the war, and American industrial production poured 25 per cent of its output into the development of air power.

The Pacific Theater

While Roosevelt and British Prime Minister Winston S. Churchill decided that Germany must be defeated first, the war effort in the Pacific, which was mainly American, had to stop Japanese expansion and prepare to counterattack. The American battleship fleet had been badly damaged by the Japanese air attack on Pearl Harbor, but the aircraft carriers took up the burden.

Doolittle's raid on Japan in April of 1942 boosted American spirits, but it was the Battle of the Coral Sea, April 28-May 4, that set the standard for war in the Pacific. The first naval battle fought with aircraft as the main weaponry, Coral Sea was equally costly for both sides, but it prevented the Japanese from taking New Guinea. Within weeks, on June 4, the Battle of Midway pitted Admiral Chester Nimitz's three carriers with 180 aircraft against Admiral Chuichi Nagumo's strike force of four carriers with 272 planes. One American advantage was that the Japanese secret code had been broken, and Yamamoto's approach to Midway was anticipated. At first, American attack aircraft suffered heavy losses while inflicting little damage on the Japanese fleet. Then dive bombers from the carriers *Hornet, Enterprise,* and *Yorktown* found their targets. When the battle was over, four Japanese carriers were sunk, as was the *Yorktown.*

From now on, carrier-based air power dominated the war in the Pacific, which at the Battle of Midway decisively turned in favor of the United States and her allies.

The European Theater

Strategic bombing campaigns involved a series of massive raids by heavy bombers on enemy military, industrial, and civilian

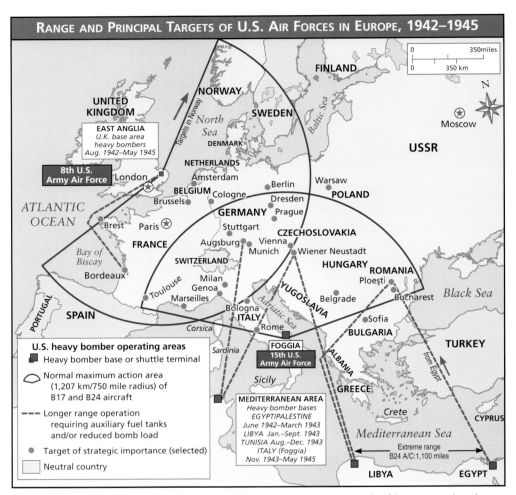

RANGE AND PRINCIPAL TARGETS OF U.S. AIR FORCES IN EUROPE, 1942–1945

U.S. heavy bomber operating areas
- Heavy bomber base or shuttle terminal
- Normal maximum action area (1,207 km/750 mile radius) of B17 and B24 aircraft
- - - Longer range operation requiring auxiliary fuel tanks and/or reduced bomb load
- Target of strategic importance (selected)
- Neutral country

AIR WAR OVER EUROPE Western Europe and Germany were within reach of long-range bombers from England, and flights from North Africa could hit Southern Europe. By 1943 Italian air bases put eastern European targets well within the 750-mile bombing range.

AMERICAN AIR POWER A formation of B-17 "Flying Fortress" bombers heads for its target over Germany. P-38 "Lightning" long-range interceptor fighters, called "fork-tailed devils" by the German airmen, provide an escort for the bombers.

"If you see fighting aircraft over you, they will be ours."

—EISENHOWER, TO HIS TROOPS INVADING EUROPE

targets. By early 1941, the British had stopped daylight strategic bombing because of the immense losses from anti-aircraft fire and pursuit fighters. The British favored "area bombing" at night, but American military strategists believed in "precision daylight bombing," where targets could be seen.

The United States Eighth Air Force, led by General Ira C. Eaker, began strategic bombing in the summer of 1942. Eaker's planes took off from bases in Britain to attack Germany, and by early 1943 American bombers from bases in North Africa struck Italy. The AAF developed heavily armed, high-flying B-17 "Flying Fortresses" and B-24 "Liberators" in hopes of repelling fighter attacks, but many of these bombers were shot down. Only fighter escorts could fend off German fighters, but no fighter plane had the range of the bombers, which flew unescorted for much of their missions. After the escorts had to turn back, German fighters relentlessly attacked the bomber formations.

Through 1943, American daylight bombing suffered devastating losses. In one October week, 148 Eighth Air Force bombers were downed. It appeared that daylight precision bombing was a failure, but the P-51 Mustang fighter appeared late that year. The P-51 had the range of a bomber and was excellent in combat.

Bombing populations

By mid-1944, the Allies had air superiority over Europe. German industrial and military facilities were mercilessly bombed as were the hearts of towns. Controversial incendiary raids such as the one that devastated Dresden in February 1945, killing 100,000 people, caused fire storms that turned whole cities to ashes overnight.

In the Pacific, two long-range American B-29 "Superfortress" bombers flying more than five miles high brought a sudden end to World War II. Each dropped an atomic bomb—one on the city of Hiroshima on August 6, and the other on Nagasaki on August 9—compelling Japan's unconditional surrender.

LONG-RANGE BOMBING AND THE P-51 "MUSTANG"

Long-range strategic bombing was instrumental in slowing Axis military-industrial production and was crucial to amphibious invasions such as Normandy. The might of the American Eighth Air Force was indicated by its need for 75 airfields in Britain.

In 1943, recently captured North African air bases offered "shuttle bombing," with bombers flying from Britain, dropping bombs on Europe, and continuing on to North Africa. There, they were refueled for the return mission. Still, their fighter escorts had to turn back when short of fuel. Unescorted "Flying Fortresses" kept in tight formation to repel enemy fighters, but this was insufficient protection.

AAF commander General Henry H. "Hap" Arnold wanted a long-range fighter, and in December 1943 got his wish when the P-51 Mustang arrived. The P-51 could fly at 35,000 feet with enough fuel to escort bombers from London to Warsaw and back (1,200 miles) while also engaging enemy aircraft in dog-fights at 455 mph. More than 14,000 P-51s were produced during the war.

By early 1945, 7,000 well-escorted American bombers were operating over Germany, and the outnumbered, overwhelmed *Luftwaffe* (German air force) was defeated. American air crews paid a heavy price for victory, however, with 29,000 airmen lost over Europe alone.

COMPLETING ITS MISSION B-17 bombers such as this one over Marienburg, Germany, had a crew of 6–10, a dozen .50 caliber machine guns for defense, and carried up to 12,000 pounds of bombs. Nearly 13,000 B-17s were built during the war.

P-51 MUSTANGS Before D-Day, all Allied planes had broad black and white "invasion stripes" painted on their wings for easy identification from the ground.

"OPERATION HUSKY" AND THE ITALIAN CAMPAIGN

After capturing Tunisia in May 1943, completing the conquest of North Africa, the Allies wasted no time in taking the offensive against Italy. Anglo-American forces invaded the island of Sicily on the night of July 9 in "Operation Husky," the first major incursion onto Axis home territory. The "Husky" amphibious invasion involved 3,000 ships carrying 160,000 troops with 14,000 vehicles, including 600 tanks.

The destructive strategic bombing of Italy and the successful Sicily landing persuaded the Italian Fascist governing council to demand dictator Benito Mussolini's resignation on July 24. After the fall of Sicily in mid-August, the British Eighth Army crossed the Strait of Messina on September 3, capturing the toe of the Italian boot. On September 7, the Italian government agreed to an armistice.

Immediately, German troops swarmed over Italy, seizing key positions and installations and preparing to hold the peninsula.

The Battle of Salerno, Naples falls to Allies

The next Allied thrust was at Salerno, 150 miles north of the Eighth Army's bridgehead. On September 9, American general Mark Clark's Allied Fifth Army—mainly British and American troops—made another amphibious invasion, "Operation Avalanche," taking Salerno and threatening the strategic port of Naples.

German commander Field Marshal Albert Kesselring launched a counterattack on September 12, attempting to dislodge the Salerno bridgehead, but his forces came under ferocious bombardment from heavy naval guns and aircraft. Allied planes made

"He ordered his men to withdraw . . . while he drew the enemy fire to himself."

—MEDAL OF HONOR CITATION FOR ARMY 2ND LIEUTENANT ROBERT CRAIG, KIA SICILY

MOVING UP Americans of the 370th Infantry Regiment trudge through mountainous Prato, Italy, in April 1945, just before "Victory in Europe."

THE CAMPAIGN IN SICILY, JULY–AUGUST 1943

Tyrrhenian Sea

US landings outflank German rearguards

Cape S. Vito
Palermo
Castellammare
Termini Imerese
Cefalu
Patti
Messina
1015 hrs, 7 August
US 3 Div enters Messina
Reggio
Trapani
Sant' Agata
Strait of Messina
Marsala
HQ
Ital Sixth Army
Nicosia
Bronte
Mt. Etna
Menfi
Ribera
Enna
Catania
Sciacca
Calanissetta
Piazza Armerina
Agrigento
Porto Empedocle
Caltagirone
Augusta
Priolo
Palma di Montechiaro
Licata
Syracuse

N

Ragusa
Modica

0   40 miles
0   40 km

Gulf of Gela

Br XIII Corps (Dempsey)

← Allied forces
- - - Front line, 18 July
········· Front line, 3 August

US II Corps (Bradley)
'HUSKY', 10 July 1943
15 Army Group (Alexander)
Br XXX Corps (Leese)

US Seventh Army (Patton)
Br Eighth Army (Montgomery)

OPERATION HUSKY After a heavy bombardment, American and British paratroopers led the July 9, 1943, Sicily assault, which was covered by the incessant attacks of 3,680 Allied bombers, dive bombers, and fighters. Next came the invasion of the mainland in September, compelling the Italian government to withdraw from the war.

"OPERATION HUSKY" TAKES SICILY

The largest amphibious operation of the war to date, "Operation Husky" was also a test for new landing craft that would be used in the 1944 D-Day landings at Normandy. The invasion was carried out by eight divisions of the Allied Fifteenth Army Group, commanded by British general Sir Harold Alexander. The army group included the British Eighth Army and the four divisions of Patton's Seventh Army. American 82nd Airborne paratroopers joined British paratroopers in a drop behind enemy defenses. Commandos and Rangers also participated in the invasion.

The Allies faced 350,000 defenders in three German and four Italian field divisions and six Italian coastal defense divisions. The battle for Sicily lasted 38 days, ending with the fall of Messina to General Omar Bradley's II Corps on August 17. A key to victory was Patton's force making several amphibious landings on the north coast to outflank the enemy.

The Axis evacuated 40,000 German troops and 60,000 Italians, along with many of their vehicles, suffering 167,000 casualties and captured. The Allies had more than 31,000 casualties, including almost 12,000 Americans.

A ROCK-RIBBED PENINSULA Italy's rugged central mountains offered the tenacious Germans good defensive positions, which they strengthened with deep rows of fortifications, such as the Gothic, Winter, Hitler, and Gustav lines.

LONG TOM Shielded by camouflage netting, an American 155mm gun—they were nicknamed "Long Toms"—opens fire at enemy troops near Nettuno, Italy, in February 1944.

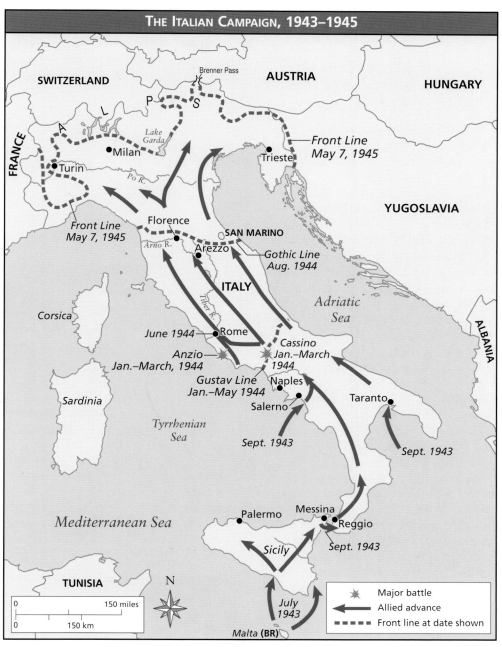

THE ITALIAN CAMPAIGN, 1943–1945

more than 2,000 strikes to support their ground troops, helping to stop Kesselring's counteroffensive. A series of smaller amphibious landings captured harbors and airfields in southern Italy, and on September 16, the British Eighth Army joined up with the Fifth Army. Naples fell on October 1, giving the Allies a major port capable of handling the men and matériel for the Italian campaign.

The Nazis reinstalled Mussolini as their puppet, prompting a groundswell of Italian resistance to continuing the war. The dictator would be assassinated by anti-Fascist partisans in April 1945.

Slow going up the boot of Italy

The Germans were dug-in, unwilling to be dislodged, especially on the defensive front known as the Gustav Line protecting Rome, the next Allied objective. The British were on the right, pushing up the Adriatic coast, and Clark's Fifth Army—with a Free French Corps—was on the left. Their flanks met on Italy's rugged central spine of mountains, which bristled with German armaments. By mid-November, the Allied advance had ground to a halt in the face of a stout defensive belt comprised of nine enemy divisions on the front line and nine more in reserve.

While the Allies had air superiority, the Axis positions were extremely strong, especially in harsh winter conditions. Added to Allied difficulties was the withdrawal to Britain of seven veteran divisions for the forthcoming invasion of France. Eisenhower, Montgomery, and Patton also departed the Mediterranean theater to plan the invasion.

Five Allied offensives between October 1943 and January 1944 failed to break through the Gustav Line. In an effort to turn the Axis flank, the American VI Corps landed on January 22 at Anzio, 30 miles south of Rome. The Germans recovered from their surprise and pinned down the invasion force, at the same time holding firm at the Gustav Line. One of the most famous Gustav

Line strongpoints was 1,100-foot-high Monte Cassino, where a monastery stood. The Cassino defenders held out against repeated assaults, even after savage air bombardments turned the monastery to rubble. Monte Cassino fell to Polish troops on May 17, during an all-out Allied offensive across a 20-mile front that pushed the Germans back. The Gustav Line was breached, as was a second fortified belt known as the Adolf Hitler Line.

On June 4, the American 88th Infantry Division rolled into Rome, which had been declared an open city and left undefended. The Germans withdrew 250 miles to yet another prepared defense, the Gothic Line, which they would hold for much of the rest of the war.

169

"OPERATION OVERLORD"—THE BATTLE OF NORMANDY

"The Tricolor flying from the Arc de Triomphe looked pretty good as we went through.""

—AMERICAN TANK CREWMAN DURING LIBERATION OF PARIS

In June 1944, a map of Europe showed Axis domination from the coasts of France eastward to the Soviet border. That was soon to change, as the Soviet Red Army prepared for a massive assault on the German center and for a charge into Romania and Bulgaria.

Moreover, the 800,000 American and British combat troops assembled in Great Britain were about to launch "Operation Overlord," the invasion of Europe.

D-Day breaches "Fortress Europe"

German field marshals Erwin Rommel, tactical commander, and Gerd von Rundstedt, theater commander, had been trying to anticipate the invasion they knew was coming, but not when or where. Eisenhower now directed Supreme Headquarters, Allied Expeditionary Force (SHAEF) for the approaching campaign. Montgomery was his tactical commander, in charge of the 21st Army Group, which would make the invasion.

Success hinged on keeping Rommel and Von Rundstedt in the dark as long as possible. Elaborate deceptions were foisted on the Germans, including the creation in England of false assembly camps that seemed like staging areas for attacking beaches farther north. By the time the invasion was ready, on June 5, 1944, the Germans were, indeed, expecting it at Pas-de-Calais, the region of France across the narrow Straits of Dover. Eisenhower's invasion plans were confounded by stormy weather, however, and he postponed it one day.

The weather remained foul as June 6 approached, but Eisenhower gambled, ordering Overlord to proceed, and more than 4,000 vessels sailed for Normandy. As the weather briefly relented, 5,800 heavy bombers and 4,900 fighters bombarded the German "Atlantic Wall" coastal defenses. These consisted of hundreds of artillery pieces in thick concrete bunkers and thousands of machines guns in well-protected

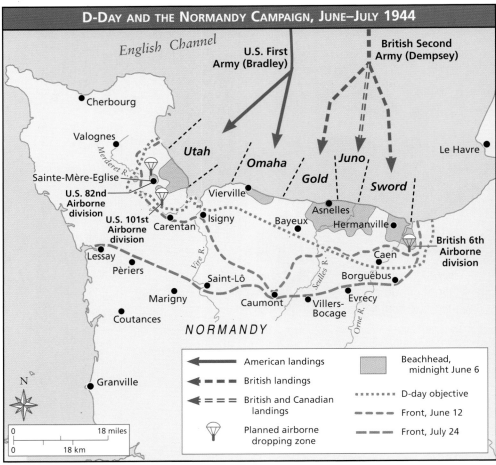

D-DAY AND THE NORMANDY CAMPAIGN, JUNE–JULY 1944

English Channel

U.S. First Army (Bradley)
British Second Army (Dempsey)

Cherbourg
Valognes
Le Havre
Sainte-Mère-Eglise
Utah
Omaha
Juno
U.S. 82nd Airborne division
Gold
Sword
Vierville
Asnelles
Hermanville
U.S. 101st Airborne division
Isigny
Bayeux
British 6th Airborne division
Carentan
Lessay
Caen
Périers
Vire R.
Borguébus
Saint-Lô
Seulles R.
Marigny
Caumont
Villers-Bocage
Evrecy
Coutances
Orne R.
Granville

NORMANDY

Merderet R.

⬅ American landings
⬅ - - - British landings
⬅ = = = British and Canadian landings
🪂 Planned airborne dropping zone

Beachhead, midnight June 6
⋯⋯ D-day objective
— — — Front, June 12
— — Front, July 24

N

0   18 miles
0   18 km

NORMANDY INVASION The Battle of Normandy was grueling, as German defenders held their ground. It was not until late July that the German high command committed its reserves, but by then it was too late to defeat the invasion of Hitler's *Festung Europa*: "Fortress Europe."

HITTING THE BEACH This most-famous image of D-Day, June 6, 1944, shows American soldiers disembarking from a Coast Guard landing craft to make the long journey under heavy enemy fire onto the Normandy shore.

pill boxes. Beaches and tidal waters were festooned with barriers, mantraps, and landing craft traps, which were blasted apart by advance demolitions experts.

Before dawn on June 6, 23,000 American and British paratroopers dropped inland on villages, fields, and hedgerows. Five assault divisions hit code-named beaches along a 50-mile stretch: the American 4th Infantry on Utah, the American 1st Infantry on Omaha, the British 50th on Gold, the Canadian 3rd on Juno, and the British 3rd on Sword. The heaviest casualties were at Omaha, where troops were pinned down for four hours, and where Rangers scaled nearby cliffs

under fire to engage the enemy. The Allies fought their way off the beaches with a loss of 11,000 men, including 2,500 dead. More than 156,000 troops landed in the first hours after D-Day.

The struggle to break out
The nearest Panzer units counterattacked, but the German high command—expecting the main invasion to come on the Channel front—waited a full six weeks before committing its main Panzer reserve, held near Paris. This gave the Allies in Normandy precious time to build up and strengthen their positions, although fighting was still fierce, from hedgerow to

AMERICANS AT THE ARC DE TRIOMPHE In August 1944, an armored scout car drives past Paris's famous Champs-Élysées monument that celebrates the victories of Napoleon Bonaparte. Hitler had ordered Paris burned, but his subordinates did not obey.

"OPERATION COBRA"

Normandy's dense hedgerow country restricted the use of armor and gave German defenders places to hide from air attack. By July 25, after seven weeks, Normandy was filled with almost a million men and their equipment hemmed in by the Germans.

Montgomery now launched "Operation Cobra" with a devastating 4,200 tons of bombs dropped west of Saint Lô in less than a square mile. Two mobile columns from the American First Army fought through, with one column holding off German counterattacks as the other battled forward. More columns followed, penetrating German defenses. On August 1, Patton's Third Army burst through a gap at Avranches, turned east to take LeMans, and swung northward. This maneuver threatened to cut off 21 German divisions in the "Falaise-Argentan Pocket." Most Germans escaped, but their losses were heavy, with 10,000 dead, 50,000 prisoners, and the loss of thousands of vehicles.

German opposition was temporarily in disarray, and the Allies raced toward Paris, 100 miles to the east.

hedgerow and down tree-shrouded lanes. The invaders attacked across the entire front, but even small advances were hard-won. The Germans fought furiously, though there was little to be heard from the Luftwaffe's remaining 1,000 combat aircraft. On June 27 the Americans captured Cherbourg, which became the supply base for the campaign. Now the object was to break through the German perimeter before the invasion was stalemated.

In early July, Hitler replaced Von Rundstedt with Field Marshal Gunther von Kluge, and the German reserves began to move in. Soon afterwards, Rommel's car was machine-gunned from the air, and he was wounded, never to return to command.

Montgomery pivoted his force on the coastal city of Caen and attempted to turn the German left. In mid-July, Americans from five divisions assaulted Saint-Lô for 12 days, losing 11,000 men without breaching the enemy defenses. The first 48 days of fighting cost the Allies 122,000 casualties, the Germans 117,000.

At the end of July, "Operation Cobra" wedged an opening near St. Lô, and by August 10 Patton's Third Army had captured Nantes. The breakthrough was under way. Patton crossed the Seine on August 20. Free French forces attached to Patton's Third Army joined with the French Resistance to liberate Paris on August 25.

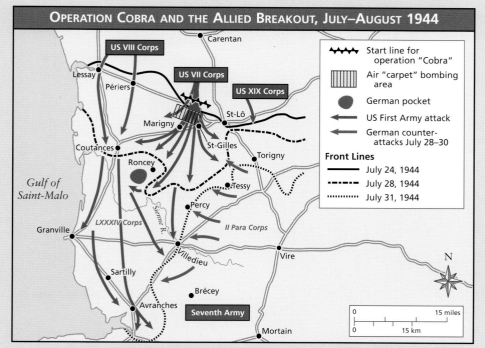

OPERATION COBRA AND THE ALLIED BREAKOUT, JULY–AUGUST 1944

US VIII Corps
US VII Corps
US XIX Corps

Carentan
Lessay
Périers
Marigny
St-Lô
Coutances
St-Gilles
Roncey
Torigny
Gulf of Saint-Malo
Tessy
Percy
Sienne R.
Granville
LXXXIV Corps
II Para Corps
Villedieu
Vire
Sartilly
Brécey
Avranches
Seventh Army
Mortain

N

Start line for operation "Cobra"
Air "carpet" bombing area
German pocket
US First Army attack
German counter-attacks July 28–30
Front Lines
July 24, 1944
July 28, 1944
July 31, 1944

0   15 miles
0   15 km

BREAKOUT FROM NORMANDY Allied attacks to the south drove through German defenses, fending off counterattacks, then turned northward, nearly trapping the retreating Germans.

SEA, AIR, AND LAND VICTORIES IN THE CENTRAL PACIFIC

Air superiority in East Asia and the Pacific was a key factor in the American campaigns to regain lost islands and inflict crushing blows on the Japanese navy. Admiral Nimitz's Central Pacific campaign of November 1943 to February 1944 capitalized on air superiority to defeat the Japanese fleet again and again.

Conquering the Central Pacific

Nimitz followed the broad strategy of taking key islands that offered bases for attacking the Japanese mainland. Many occupied islands would be "hopped," their defenders left behind or neutralized by air attacks.

The Fifth Fleet, under Vice Admiral Raymond A. Spruance, led off the campaign by attacking the Gilbert Islands, 2,400 miles southwest of Hawaii. The Fifth Fleet had 19 aircraft carriers and 12 battleships and was protected by a screen of submarines. On November 20, the 27th Infantry and 2nd Marine divisions made amphibious landings on the heavily fortified Makin and Tarawa atolls. The Marines battled four days for "Bloody

Tarawa," which cost 3,200 American casualties and 4,700 Japanese killed.

The assault on the Marshall Islands began on February 1, 1944, and was completed by February 17. The outer ring of Japanese defenses now was broken, and Nimitz pushed through the breach. He bypassed the fortresslike naval and air base complex on Truk, in the Caroline Islands, which was battered by two destructive air and naval strikes from the Fifth Fleet.

Nimitz moved on to the Marianas—Guam, Saipan, Tinian—which could not be hopped, because their airfields were needed for B-29 bombing of Japan. The assault was carried out by Vice Admiral Mark Mitscher's Fast Carrier Force, with 15 carriers, seven battleships, 21 cruisers, 69 destroyers, and a thousand aircraft. Mitscher carried 127,000 Marines and Army troops for the campaign. Landing on Saipan on June 15, two Marine divisions and one Army division battled 30,000 Japanese troops, many of whom died in *banzai* suicide attacks. Saipan fell on July 9, with all but 1,000 Japanese dead. The Americans had approximately

14,000 casualties, with 3,426 dead.

Next, Guam was invaded on July 21, falling on August 10. Tinian was attacked on July 24 and fell by July 31. These invasions cost almost 10,000 American casualties and almost 30,000 Japanese. While the troops fought, the navies met in the Battle of the Philippine Sea, June 19-21.

Return to the Philippines

American commanders, headed by MacArthur, debated the next move after the Marianas, the capture of which cut Japan's sea lanes to the East Indies. The Navy preferred to attack Formosa. Invading the Philippines would be costly, but it was decided upon as a way to force

SAIPAN BOMBARDMENT
Big guns of the United States Navy fire salvo after salvo to support amphibious landings on Saipan in June 1944.

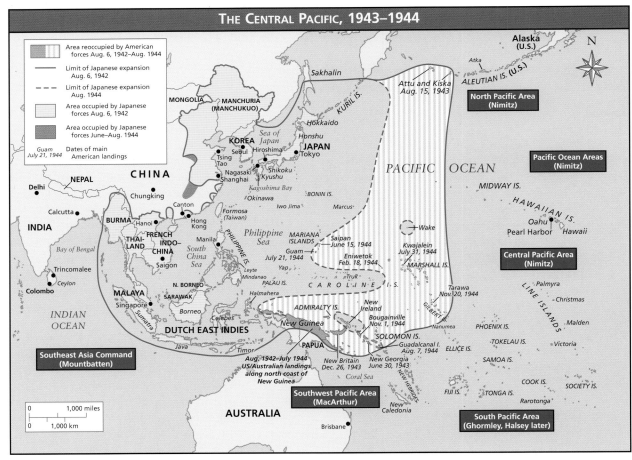

THE CENTRAL PACIFIC, 1943–1944

Area reoccupied by American forces Aug. 6, 1942–Aug. 1944

Limit of Japanese expansion Aug. 6, 1942

Limit of Japanese expansion Aug. 1944

Area occupied by Japanese forces Aug. 6, 1942

Area occupied by Japanese forces June–Aug. 1944

Guam
July 21, 1944
Dates of main American landings

ISLAND WAR
Japanese-held islands fell in the "Central Pacific Drive" of November 1943–February 1944. The Gilberts saw some of the fiercest fighting of the Pacific War, which opened the way to the Marianas and Philippines.

the Japanese to commit their army to defending the islands. The southern Philippines was bypassed to strike at central Leyte Island.

On October 20, after a two-day bombardment, the Seventh Fleet landed more than 132,000 men of the Sixth Army on Leyte's east coast. At noon that day, MacArthur himself waded ashore, fulfilling his public promise to return to the Philippines. American gains were swift at first, but the Japanese rallied for a campaign that would last until the end of the war. When the Leyte landings were under way, the Japanese navy attacked from three directions, hoping to draw the American navy away and destroy the invasion fleet.

The Battle of Leyte Gulf, October 23-26, involved the American Third and Seventh fleets in a series of engagements east and west of the Philippines. One powerful Japanese force almost slipped past the Seventh Fleet to attack the amphibious landing, but an outnumbered escort carrier group under Admiral Clifton Sprague intercepted the attack and narrowly fought it off.

American aircraft and submarines inflicted catastrophic losses on the Japanese navy at Leyte. This time the Japanese launched hundreds of aircraft in deadly *kamikaze* (divine wind) suicide dive-bombing attacks that sank one light and two escort carriers. The Americans also lost three destroyers. The Japanese lost three battleships, four carriers, 10 cruisers, and nine destroyers.

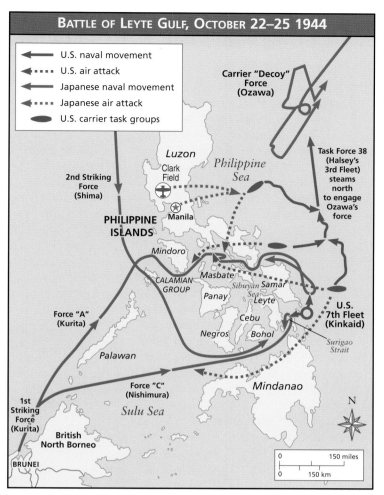

BATTLE OF LEYTE GULF, OCTOBER 22–25 1944

- ← U.S. naval movement
- ◄···· U.S. air attack
- ← Japanese naval movement
- ◄···· Japanese air attack
- ⬭ U.S. carrier task groups

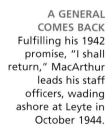

A GENERAL COMES BACK Fulfilling his 1942 promise, "I shall return," MacArthur leads his staff officers, wading ashore at Leyte in October 1944.

VICTORY AT LEYTE As Admiral William F. Halsey was drawn northward, a battlegroup from Admiral Thomas C. Kinkaid's Seventh Fleet turned back an enemy task force at Surigao Strait. Led by Admiral Jesse Oldendorf, the group had six old American battleships, five of which had been damaged at Pearl Harbor.

"Our Jungle Road to Tokyo"

—Postwar Memoir of General Eichelberger, jungle fighter, key to Philippines' liberation

BATTLE OF THE PHILIPPINE SEA

Fought between June 19-21, this engagement was brought on by the Japanese Mobile Fleet, which desperately tried to support the forces defending Saipan. Hopelessly outnumbered, Vice Admiral Jisaburo Ozawa had nine carriers to take on Mitscher's Fast Carrier Force with 15 carriers. Even before the main engagement, Ozawa's flagship, the carrier *Taiho*, was hit by a single torpedo from a submarine and blew up.

The Japanese sent a wave of 320 land-based aircraft into action, but 240 were quickly shot down without damage to the American fleet. A second air battle involved 430 Japanese carrier planes against 450 American aircraft. Only 100 Japanese planes returned, while 30 American planes were lost. A submarine sank another Japanese carrier, and Ozawa retreated northward. Mitscher's aircraft pursued and destroyed a third carrier. Six Japanese carriers escaped, but Japan had lost almost all her carrier pilots.

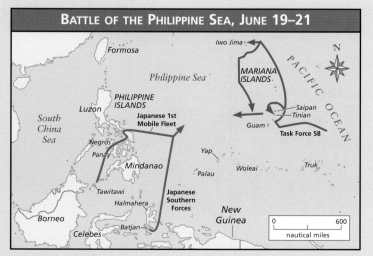

BATTLE OF THE PHILIPPINE SEA, JUNE 19–21

TOYODA'S DISASTER Admiral Soemu Toyoda sent Ozawa's fleet to destroy the Saipan landings, but Ozawa was decisively repulsed in the Philippine Sea.

21: BRINGING WAR TO THE AXIS HEARTLAND

Ten days before Paris fell, the Allies landed on the coast of southern France in "Operation Dragoon." The American Seventh Army came ashore between Toulon and Nice on August 15, aiming to move northward against the left and rear of German forces opposing Eisenhower. The Seventh Army was led by General Alexander M. Patch, who had captured Guadalcanal in 1942.

Gliders and paratrooper drops landed 8,000 men in an advance strike, followed by almost 250,000 troops in 10 American and Free French divisions. More than 4,000 aircraft covered the assault, which met only light resistance from nine under-manned divisions of the German Nineteenth Army. Many Americans were battle-hardened veterans of the Italian campaign.

The American VI Corps led the way, charging up the Rhone Valley, cutting off the retreating enemy. In the first 31 days, "Dragoon" advanced 270 miles and captured almost 80,000 prisoners. On September 11, VI Corps met up with the right flank of Patton's Third Army near Dijon, as planned.

"We are now required to undergo . . . physical hardening, mental readjustment, and the building of morale that will fortify individual soldiers. . . ."

—GENERAL PATCH, ON LEADERSHIP

FIGHTING FOR THE LOWLANDS United States troops of the 60th Infantry Regiment move into a Belgian town on September 9, 1944.

The Germans regroup

Retreating German divisions joined with reinforcements to establish strong fixed positions from the Vosges Mountains to the Dutch coast. For all the bitter fighting of the past three months, and Allied domination of the air, the German army showed no sign of breaking. Its most powerful defense was the fortified zone known as the Siegfried Line, or West Wall, which covered the German border with France and the Lowlands.

Finding his forces outrunning supply capabilities, Eisenhower ordered fast-moving units, such as Patton's, to slow down and cooperate with the main army. Early in September, the Allies took Brussels and the great port city of Antwerp, where supplies and reinforcements for the push into Germany could be landed and quickly reach the battlefront.

German "flying bombs" or "pilotless aircraft," as V-1 and V-2 rockets were termed, were launched at Antwerp, London, and Paris. More than 10,000 of these rockets were fired before the launching sites were silenced by Allied bombing or captured by ground troops in 1945. V-missiles or *Vergeltungswaffen*—vengeance weapons—killed almost 9,000

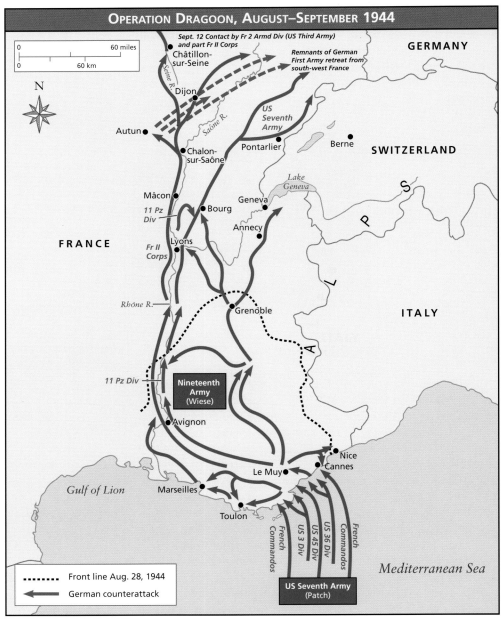

THE GREAT OFFENSIVE General Eisenhower's broad-front advance, attacking everywhere at once, wore down the Germans and "used up" their reserves.

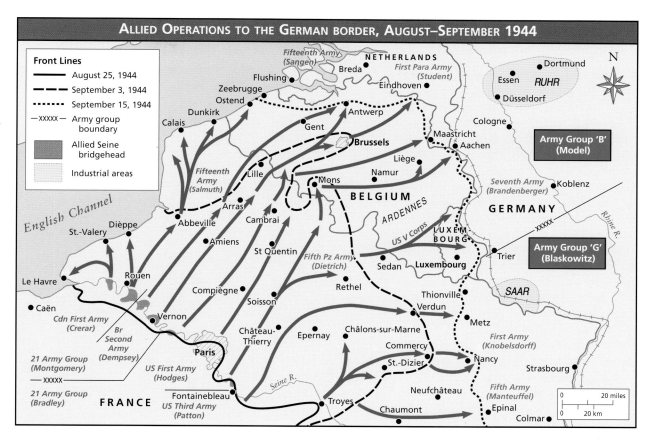

ALLIED OPERATIONS TO THE GERMAN BORDER, AUGUST–SEPTEMBER 1944

Front Lines
- August 25, 1944
- September 3, 1944
- September 15, 1944
- XXXXX Army group boundary
- Allied Seine bridgehead
- Industrial areas

AFTER NORMANDY The Allies advanced swiftly as the Germans pulled back to prepared positions, such as the West Wall fortifications on Germany's western border. Late in 1944, the Allies cleared Alsace-Lorraine and the Hürtgen and Ardennes forests of enemy forces and liberated much of Belgium and The Netherlands.

persons, mostly civilians, but had negligible impact on the course of the war.

Now, Montgomery conceived a daring plan to force a surprise crossing of the lower Rhine. Eisenhower approved "Operation Market Garden," which aimed to outflank the Siegfried Line. In mid-September, American and British para-

OPERATION MARKET GARDEN Some said the American and British paratroopers dropped behind German lines in The Netherlands had overly ambitious objectives—trying for "a bridge too far."

troopers dropped into the southeast Netherlands to capture key bridges, but the Germans powerfully counterattacked, and the effort was defeated with heavy loss.

Assaulting the Siegfried Line

Still the Allies advanced. The American First Army broke through the center of the Siegfried Line on September 12, and a month later fought its way into Aachen. After more than a week of house-to-house battle, the Americans took Aachen, the first German city to fall to the Allies.

The American Ninth Army joined the First Army for a continued offensive, much of it a savage, close struggle in the dense Hürtgen Forest. To the southeast, the Seventh Army battled through the Vosges Mountains, making considerable progress and joining the Third Army to push against the Siegfried Line. A Free French armored unit captured Strasbourg in late November. During the autumn of 1944, more than 75,000 Germans surrendered, but the approach of winter and the Siegfried Line's stout defensive positions slowed the Allied advance almost to a stop.

Hitler prepares to gamble all

Hitler narrowly escaped an assassination attempt in July 1944, and several top officers, including Rommel, were condemned to death as conspirators. Rommel committed suicide to save the lives of his family.

Other generals were advising Hitler to surrender, but he refused. With the Russians pressing in from the East, he chose to bring on a decisive battle in the West, believing the British and Americans could be derailed by a massive counterattack through the Ardennes forest, with a swing north to recapture Antwerp. In 1940, the Ardennes had been the site of the German breakthrough that led to Hitler's spectacular victory over France.

HITLER'S LAST GAMBLE: ARDENNES II, BATTLE OF THE BULGE

With the onset of winter in 1944, Eisenhower did not expect an enemy offensive. Instead, he was preparing for the next Allied push across the Rhine and onto the North German Plain, which favored fast-moving Allied armor and air attacks. He did not know that Hitler had been rebuilding Panzer divisions, equipped with powerful new-model tanks and manned by veterans of the Normandy defeat. Hitler's planned offensive through the Ardennes Forest aimed to decisively halt American and British momentum and give him time to turn and rally against the Soviets.

Field Marshal Walter Model's Army Group B of three armies would carry out the offensive, which was to capture Antwerp and stop the flow of Allied supplies. The secondary objective was the destruction of four Allied armies in the immediate vicinity.

Operation "Wacht am Rhein"

Germany's Second Ardennes Offensive was code-named after a patriotic German war song from 1870, translated as "Watch on the Rhine." It soon earned another name: "Battle of the Bulge," after the large salient created when Allied defenses bent under this mighty German assault.

Model massed Army Group B's 200,000 men along a front of 60 miles. In advance were 13 infantry and seven Panzer divisions with nearly 1,000 tanks and 2,000 guns. Five more divisions were in a second wave, and others, equipped with 450 tanks, were in reserve. The initial target was the American First Army, commanded by General Courtney H. Hodges, who had four divisions stretched thinly across 40 miles of the Ardennes front. First Army veterans were among the most battle-scarred of Allied troops, having taken Aachen and fought in the bloody Hürtgen Forest. Hodges had many raw replace-

OBJECT ANTWERP German plans to dash through the Ardennes were foiled by stubborn American resistance, especially at the vital Bastogne crossroads, which blocked enemy supplies and reinforcements. Thus, a near-breakthrough by the Germans remained only a bulge in the front line, a position the Germans could not defend.

ments, however, and one division was green, just arrived from training camp.

The German attack jumped off on December 16, sending three American divisions into retreat and capturing thousands of men. Model dropped 1,000 paratroopers to block one of the few roads through the Ardennes, and sent a unit disguised as Americans into action, causing further confusion. The weather was overcast, as Model had hoped, limiting Allied aircraft sorties.

The Americans struggled to recover, fighting a series of desperate delaying actions to give Eisenhower time to send reinforcements and mount a counterattack. The crossroads towns of Bastogne and Saint-Vith were stubbornly held, deflecting the Panzers around them. Bastogne was surrounded, and the Germans demanded its surrender, but commanding general Anthony McAuliffe refused and held on. This foiled Model's

WINTER CAMPAIGN Weary troops of the 347th Infantry Regiment line up for chow near LaRoche, Belgium, in January 1945. Part of the 87th Infantry Division of Patton's Third Army, this regiment was in the thick of the Ardennes fighting at Bastogne.

plans for a quick breakthrough and rapid movement along the Ardennes roads to open country beyond.

When the weather cleared on December 23, Allied air operations intensified, taking on the Luftwaffe, which suffered irreplaceable losses. Model's offensive had reached its deepest penetration, forming a 60-mile-deep salient, now under attack on three sides. The full-scale Allied counteroffensive began on Christmas Day, as Eisenhower threw everything he had into the fight, launching simultaneous assaults, air attacks, and a bombardment by 1,000 guns. Bastogne was relieved by Patton on December 26. Patton's skillful disengagement of his Third Army from its original front, followed by his swift attack on the salient's southern perimeter, is considered one of the outstanding exploits of the war.

The Germans dug in, refusing to give up until, on January 8, 1945, Hitler at last ordered a withdrawal, and Model conducted a fighting retreat to save what he could. The original front was restored by January 16. Secondary conflicts erupted in nearby Alsace-Lorraine, and the Battle of the Bulge was considered part of the Ardennes-Alsace Campaign, which ran from December 16, 1944 to January 25, 1945.

Of the 610,000 Americans at the Battle of the Bulge, approximately 19,000 died, 50,000 were wounded, and more than 21,000 captured. Germany suffered more than 120,000 casualties, losing 600 tanks and more than 1,500 aircraft. Nazi Germany's reserves had been severely depleted by this defeat, which helped speed her demise.

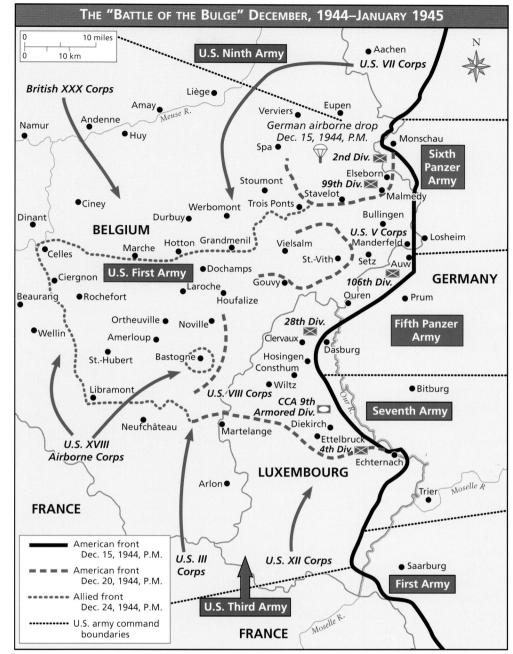

THE "BATTLE OF THE BULGE" DECEMBER, 1944–JANUARY 1945

BATTLE OF THE BULGE Eisenhower rushed both his most experienced and his greenest troops into the month-long battle in the Ardennes. With besieged Bastogne as a goal, the Allies hammered at the Germans, driving them back to the original front line by January 16, 1945.

"Their casualties [were] exorbitantly high; all of them new to combat, they had to fight in the severest cold. . . ."

—ROBERT E. MERRIAM, ARMY HISTORIAN, ON THE 87TH DIVISION IN THE ARDENNES

SNOWBOUND ROADS Moving columns of tanks and other vehicles along the narrow roads of the densely forested Ardennes was difficult. Both Allied and German columns found themselves snarled in traffic jams that hampered operations. Once the skies cleared, German formations on the roads were easy prey for Allied fighters and bombers.

THE FINAL ALLIED OFFENSIVE IN WESTERN EUROPE

"Conquest . . . is not enough; we must . . . do all in our power to conquer the doubts and the fears, the ignorance and the greed, which made this horror possible."

—F.D.R. ADDRESS PLANNED FOR APRIL 13, 1945,
THE DAY AFTER HE DIED

In the spring of 1945, Eisenhower had 37 divisions in the northern European theater—half a million combat troops—and his air superiority was 30 to 1. In northern Italy, Germany's Gothic Line had held out since mid-1944 against the Allied Fifth and the British Eighth armies. To the East, the Red Army was pushing toward Berlin, and Hitler's forces in the West readied for Eisenhower's next move.

The Allies on the Rhine were organized into the British 21st Army Group under Montgomery and the American 12th Army Group under Bradley. Eisenhower planned for Bradley to encircle the Ruhr Valley, at the center, while Montgomery led the main assault across the Rhine and onto the North German Plain. The problem was how to cross the broad Rhine, with its swift current and enemy defenses.

Crossing the Rhine

On March 7, before Montgomery jumped off, the American 9th Armored Division discovered a railway bridge still standing at Remagen. The Ludendorff Bridge, inadvertently not destroyed, was the only Rhine bridge left. The Americans boldly seized it, and 8,000 troops crossed over in one day to fight off German counterattacks.

The Germans bombarded the Ludendorff Bridge from the air, fired on it with artillery, and even launched V-2 rockets, but it stood for 10 days as more soldiers crossed and expanded the bridgehead. Soon after, Patton's Third Army to the south of Remagen battled across the Rhine in assault boats, following up with a pontoon bridge. At the same time, Montgomery's 21st Army Group fighting in the north crossed the Rhine in "Operation Plunder," which dropped a 14,000-man airborne assault—almost as large as "Operation Market Garden." Winston Churchill, himself, was on the scene with Montgomery to watch the crossing. During the last week of March, both the American Seventh and First French armies also crossed the Rhine, and the stage was set for the final offensive in Germany.

Meanwhile, the stalemate in northern Italy was broken when Mark Clark led the newly formed Fifteenth Army Group in a

GIs TAKE COVER Huddled in a crowded barge, troops make a Rhine crossing under enemy fire to establish a bridgehead. Army engineers quickly followed up with pontoon bridges capable of carrying tanks and trucks.

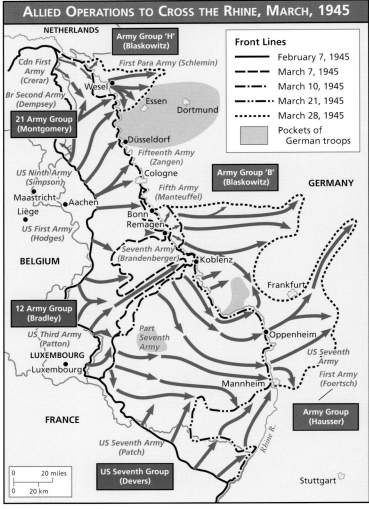

ALLIED OPERATIONS TO CROSS THE RHINE, MARCH, 1945

Front Lines
- ——— February 7, 1945
- – – – March 7, 1945
- –·–·– March 10, 1945
- –··–··– March 21, 1945
- ·········· March 28, 1945
- Pockets of German troops

NETHERLANDS
Army Group 'H' (Blaskowitz)
First Para Army (Schlemin)
Cdn First Army (Crerar)
Wesel
Essen
Dortmund
Br Second Army (Dempsey)
21 Army Group (Montgomery)
Düsseldorf
Fifteenth Army (Zangen)
US Ninth Army (Simpson)
Cologne
Fifth Army (Manteuffel)
Army Group 'B' (Blaskowitz)
GERMANY
Maastricht · Aachen
Liège
Bonn
Remagen
US First Army (Hodges)
BELGIUM
Seventh Army (Brandenberger)
Koblenz
Frankfurt
12 Army Group (Bradley)
US Third Army (Patton)
Part Seventh Army
Oppenheim
LUXEMBOURG
US Seventh Army
· Luxembourg
First Army (Foertsch)
Mannheim
Army Group (Hausser)
FRANCE
US Seventh Army (Patch)
Rhine R.
0   20 miles
0   20 km
US Seventh Group (Devers)
Stuttgart

INTO THE FATHERLAND Allied attempts to cross the broad Rhine River succeeded in several places, with the most dramatic being the American capture of the Ludendorff Bridge at Remagen. Allied troops soon swept onto the German plain and raced eastward.

mid-April offensive that soon caused a million German troops to capitulate. The 20-month Italian campaign had cost 350,000 Allied casualties.

The Americans and British were dismayed on April 12, when Roosevelt died suddenly. Vice President Harry S. Truman took office with the daunting task of reorganizing the map of postwar Europe while also overseeing the campaign to defeat Japan.

The last act in Europe

Eisenhower sent massive columns of armor and motorized infantry on fast-moving advances across northern Germany, where any resistance was quickly overwhelmed. The American Ninth, First, and Fifteenth armies captured the Ruhr, taking more than 325,000 prisoners.

The German military was falling apart, and endless columns of prisoners trudged westward along the Autobahn as Allied trucks and armor in another endless column hurried eastward. To the north, thousands of Germans were cut off in Denmark and Norway. To the south, Allied columns entered Czechoslovakia and Austria. By mid-April the Allies in the West had reached the rivers Elbe and Mulde, where they waited to meet the approaching Soviet Army.

The Soviets had completely encircled Berlin by April 25, the day their advance elements came in contact with Americans at Torgau on the Elbe. As Berlin erupted with fierce street fighting, Hitler committed suicide in his bunker on April 30—two days

FIGHTING HOUSE TO HOUSE American infantry, supported by a Sherman tank, advance relentlessly against German opposition. The American preference for massive firepower to suppress enemy resistance before sending in troops left many German towns and villages in ruins.

after Mussolini was killed by Italian partisans, who caught him trying to flee.

The surviving German troops in Berlin surrendered on May 2. Germany and Italy were defeated. Japan was next.

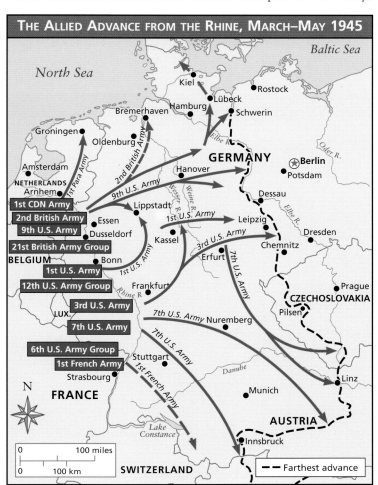

THE ALLIED ADVANCE FROM THE RHINE, MARCH–MAY 1945

GERMANY OVERRUN Soviet armies advance from the east all through the winter and spring of 1945, as Allies in western Europe fight through the West Wall and Siegfried Line, crossing the Rhine, and cutting off hundreds of thousands of German troops.

NEW PERILS FOR WAR-WEARY EUROPE

By May 1945, the communists of the East and the democracies of the West stood astride defeated Germany, facing each other, armed to the teeth. The United States, Great Britain, and the Soviet Union had agreed in February to the postwar structure of Europe and the right of nations to free elections. The Soviets, however, quickly installed communist puppet governments in the countries they occupied.

Prime Minister Churchill, who did not trust Stalin, wrote: "New perils, perhaps as terrible as those we had surmounted, loomed and glared upon the torn and harassed world."

Churchill and Truman toured the ruins of Berlin on July 16. The following day, they received the momentous news that the first Anglo-American atomic bomb had been tested in the New Mexico desert. This awesome weapon promised a quick end to the war with Japan, without the need for Soviet armies to come in. This meant Europe's future now could be resolved without making concessions to the Soviets in exchange for help against Japan.

After the war in Europe, the Americans and British withdrew from 20,000 square miles of territory in Germany and Czechoslovakia, leaving the latter country in Soviet hands. Germany and Austria were divided into American, British, French, and Soviet zones of control, as was the "international zone" that encompassed Berlin. Millions of refugees immediately fled westward to escape the Soviets, who now were firmly established in the center of Europe.

RESISTANCE IN THE PHILIPPINES, BUT IWO JIMA FALLS

As 1944 drew to a close, the Japanese in the Philippines fought hard against MacArthur, though their defeat was inevitable. Five Japanese divisions were wiped out defending Leyte alone. Without aircraft or sea power to back them up, they could do little more than buy time for the empire to strengthen other islands, which like New Guinea, the Moluccas, and the Palau Islands, were under attack or had fallen. Where islands were invaded by the Allies, losses were heavy on both sides, but American strategy continued to call for leapfrogging Japanese garrisons if possible, while moving ever closer to Japan. One of the toughest battles was for Peleliu, where Japanese occupiers fought for two and a half months, at a cost of 10,500 American and 11,000 Japanese casualties, in some of the most savage fighting of the war.

MacArthur made an amphibious landing on Luzon on January 9, 1945, and other landings near Manila at the end of the month. The city was defended by 16,000 men, mostly naval personnel. Manila fell early in February, after a fierce struggle that cost the lives of thousands of civilians, many wantonly killed by the Japanese. Bataan and Corregidor also fell, and the surviving Japanese went into the mountains of Luzon and Mindanao, where they resorted to guerrilla warfare. More than 50,000 Japanese would lay down their arms in the Philippines when they finally surrendered in mid-August.

The Marines at Iwo Jima

In February, Admiral Nimitz shifted the campaign northward against Iwo Jima in the Bonin Islands, planning to attack Okinawa and other islands in the Ryukyus early in the spring. Though only eight square miles in area, Iwo Jima had two valuable military airfields, with a third under construction, and was just 660 miles from Tokyo. The island's radar was part of the Japanese air-warning system, and fighters from its airfields attacked Allied shipping, aircraft, and troops. Iwo was a worthy objective in the campaign to wear down Japan's military capabilities.

After a massive air and naval bombardment, the 4th and 5th Marine divisions made the main amphibious assault on February 19 and at first were not opposed, but not for long. The 3rd Marine Division reinforced the assault, which soon met fanatic resistance from 21,000 Japanese in more than 2,000 bunkers, pill boxes, and fortified caves with miles of interconnecting tunnels. Japanese machine guns and artillery took a heavy toll that first day, inflicting more than 2,400 Marine casualties, with approximately 600 killed.

Mount Suribachi, 550 feet high, was key to Iwo's defensive system, considered the strongest fortifications American forces encountered during the entire Pacific War. Flamethrowers came into wide use by the Americans, who incinerated dug-in defensive positions and fortified caves. Suribachi was cut off from the rest of the island, as the Marines methodically fought their way from one side to the other. Men of the 5th

> *"Among the Americans who served on Iwo Jima Island, uncommon valor was a common virtue."*
>
> —ADMIRAL NIMITZ, COMMANDER-IN-CHIEF, PACIFIC FLEET, 1945

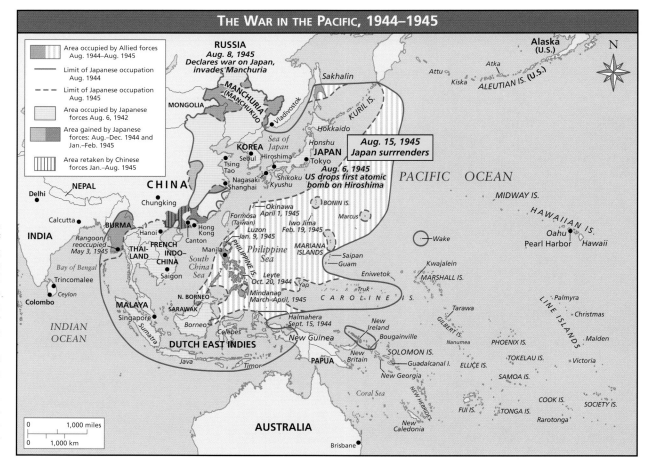

THE WAR IN THE PACIFIC, 1944–1945

PACIFIC WAR The Allied retaking of Pacific islands cut off crucial oil to Japan and forced her commanders to commit dwindling naval and air resources to desperate counteroffensives, such as the battles of the Philippine Sea and Leyte Gulf. Defeated at sea and in the air, the Japanese could only fight defensively in 1945.

AIRFIELD AT SEA
Carriers dominated the Pacific War, at the start of which the USS *Lexington* and *Saratoga,* at 38,500 tons, were the world's largest. The USN's primary offensive weapon was the 27,100-ton attack carrier, with its 90-plane air group.

BATTLE FOR IWO
After two weeks of bombardment, Americans landed and aimed for the airfields and Mount Suribachi. All fell by February 24.

Marine Division scaled Suribachi under deadly fire, finally capturing it on February 23. A photographer recorded the raising of an American flag on the summit, perhaps the most famous photograph of United States military history.

Bloody fighting continued for a month before Iwo was secured on March 26. The defenders were wiped out, virtually to a man. The United States suffered more than 6,800 dead and 18,000 wounded. The Congressional Medal of Honor for valor on Iwo Jima was awarded to 26 Americans, 12 of them posthumously.

One of Iwo's airfields was immediately of value on March 4, when a B-29 running out of fuel made an emergency landing. More than 2,200 heavy bombers would use the island for emergency landings in the following months. By the end of March an airstrip on Iwo was fully operational for fighter planes, and before long engineers built an airfield for heavy bombers.

The battle for Okinawa was already under way.

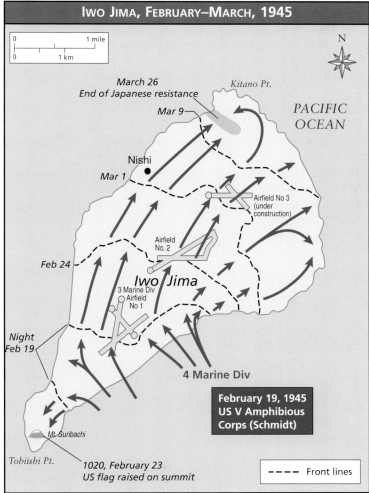

IWO JIMA, FEBRUARY–MARCH, 1945

March 26
End of Japanese resistance

Kitano Pt.

Mar 9

PACIFIC OCEAN

Nishi

Mar 1

Airfield No 3 (under construction)

Airfield No. 2

Feb 24

Iwo Jima

3 Marine Div
Airfield No 1

Night Feb 19

4 Marine Div

**February 19, 1945
US V Amphibious
Corps (Schmidt)**

Mt. Suribachi

Tobiishi Pt.

1020, February 23
US flag raised on summit

- - - - Front lines

"How could I feel like a hero when only five men in my platoon of 45 survived, and only 27 in my company of 250 escaped death or injury?"

—MARINE IRA HAYES (1923–1954), WHO HELPED RAISE THE FLAG AT IWO JIMA, ON HEARING TRUMAN HAD CALLED HIM A HERO

MOMENT OF VICTORY Members of the 28th Marine Regiment raise the flag atop Suribachi on Feb. 23, 1945, as news photographer Joe Rosenthal took one of the war's most famous pictures.

THE ATOMIC BOMB AND JAPAN'S SURRENDER

Admiral Chester Nimitz, commander-in-chief of the Pacific Fleet, organized a task force of 290,000 troops and 1,500 vessels for the invasion of Okinawa, which was only 350 miles from Japan. On April 1, 50,000 troops of the army's XXIV Corps and the III Marine Amphibious Corps landed on Okinawa. Two more army divisions and a Marine regiment reinforced the Okinawa assault, carried out by the American Tenth Army under General Simon B. Buckner, Jr.

Land, sea, and air battles

Defending prepared positions in the natural caves and tunnels of 800-square-mile Okinawa, the 100,000 Japanese defenders were determined to keep fighting and so give their kamikaze pilots time to inflict damage on Admiral Raymond Spruance's Fifth Fleet, which covered the invasion. Suicide planes sank some 36 American ships during the campaign and damaged many more, but the Japanese also suffered heavy naval losses. On April 7, American carrier planes sank the *Yamato*, the world's largest battleship.

On Okinawa, savage ground fighting raged at close quarters, with attack and counterattack, often in torrential spring rains. Heavy concentrations of naval, air, and artillery bombardment were needed to blast the Japanese from their fortifications, as were satchel charges thrown by hand into cave mouths and bunkers. General Buckner, who often went dangerously close to the fighting, was killed on June 18. Buckner was the highest-ranking American officer to die from hostile fire.

A few days later, Okinawa fell, although fighting continued until July 2. Only 10,000 Japanese survived, all taken prisoner. United States casualties were close to 40,000, including 4,675 army and 2,938 Marine dead. The United States Navy suffered more casualties at Okinawa—5,000 dead and 4,600 wounded—than it had lost in all its wars combined until then. General Joseph Stilwell took over the Tenth Army for the next phase of the Pacific War, the invasion of Japan, planned for November 1945.

The Japanese surrender, World War II ends

Germany's unconditional capitulation on May 8 released 1 million Allied troops to the Pacific for World War II's final act, which surely would be bloody. The Japanese had proven their tenacity even in the face of certain defeat, so the Allies expected a prolonged and bitter battle to the end.

Japan still had 5 million men under arms, 2 million of them in the home islands. She had 3,000 warplanes available, but her navy was destroyed, and her cities were being devastated by heavy bombing. Japanese shipping throughout the Pacific, the Indies, and Southeast Asia was under relentless attack by war-

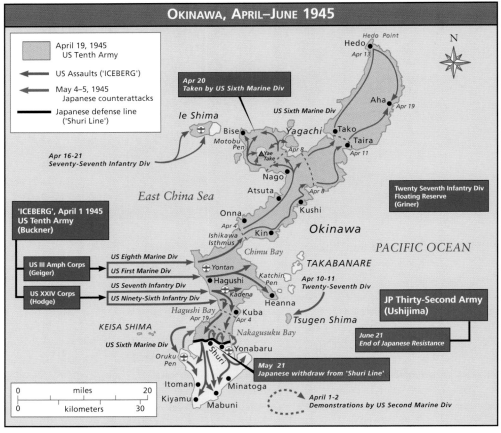

OKINAWA, APRIL–JUNE 1945

▢	April 19, 1945 US Tenth Army
←	US Assaults ('ICEBERG')
←	May 4–5, 1945 Japanese counterattacks
—	Japanese defense line ('Shuri Line')

Apr 20 Taken by US Sixth Marine Div

Hedo Point — Hedo *Apr 13*

Aha *Apr 19*

US Sixth Marine Div

Ie Shima — Bise, Motobu Pen, Yagachi, Tako, Taira *Apr 11*

Apr 16-21 Seventy-Seventh Infantry Div

Yae Take △ *Apr 8*

Nago

East China Sea — Atsuta *Apr 8*

Twenty Seventh Infantry Div Floating Reserve (Griner)

'ICEBERG', April 1 1945 US Tenth Army (Buckner)

Onna *Apr 4*, Kushi, Kin

Ishikawa Isthmus

Okinawa

US III Amph Corps (Geiger) — US Eighth Marine Div

US First Marine Div — Yontan

Chimu Bay

PACIFIC OCEAN

TAKABANARE

US XXIV Corps (Hodge) — US Seventh Infantry Div, Hagushi

Katchin Pen

Apr 10-11 Twenty-Seventh Div

US Ninety-Sixth Infantry Div — Kadena, Heanna

Hagushi Bay *Apr 19* — Kuba *Apr 4*

JP Thirty-Second Army (Ushijima)

KEISA SHIMA

Tsugen Shima

Nakagusuku Bay

June 21 End of Japanese Resistance

US Sixth Marine Div — Oruku Pen, Shuri, Yonabaru

May 21 Japanese withdraw from 'Shuri Line'

Itoman, Minatoga

Kiyamu, Mabuni

April 1-2 Demonstrations by US Second Marine Div

| 0 | miles | 20 |
| 0 | kilometers | 30 |

A FUTURE BASE Okinawa was to be the jumping-off point for invading Japan. To capture the island, the Americans feinted a landing in the East then came ashore from the West.

"Our flag will be recognized throughout the world as a symbol of freedom . . . and of overwhelming power."

— GEORGE C. MARSHALL, ARMY CHIEF OF STAFF

COMBAT ON OKINAWA A member of the 1st Marine Division, on a ridge near the town of Shuri, fires his submachine gun to cover his companion who moves into position.

AMERICAN NAVAL MIGHT A massive flotilla crowds Okinawa's waters in April 1945 as vast supply dumps build up on the shoreline. This last great campaign of the war positioned the Allies to invade Japan.

planes and submarines. Since the start of the Pacific War, American submarines had drastically curtailed Japan's ability to wage war, and now they increased their efforts.

By June, Japanese diplomats had secretly asked Stalin—with whom they had a nonaggression pact—to be an intermediary for making peace. Stalin had not agreed by July 17, when he, Truman, and Churchill met for a conference at Potsdam, Germany. By now, the Americans and British wanted to end the war before the Soviets attacked Japan and grabbed territory. At the close of the conference on August 2, the "Big Three" Allies issued the Potsdam Declaration, which called upon Japan to surrender immediately.

On August 6, Japan was waiting for Stalin's response to her peace overtures when an American B-29 dropped an atomic bomb on Hiroshima, killing an estimated 78,000 persons and wounding more than 51,000. On August 9, the Soviet Union declared war on Japan. That day a second nuclear bomb was dropped, this time on Nagasaki, killing and wounding 66,000. Immediately, Emperor Hirohito asked the Japanese military to sue for peace.

Surrender terms were signed aboard the USS *Missouri* in Tokyo Bay on September 2, 1945, ending World War II, which cost 15 million military dead, and as many civilian dead. The Pacific War took the lives of 90,000 American and 1.14 million Japanese servicemen. The United States had approximately 16.1 million in uniform during World War II (1941-1945); her casualties numbered 1,076,245, with battle deaths of 291,567, and total deaths of 405,399. Only the Civil War took more American lives.

THE ATOMIC BOMB
"EFFECTIVE SHOCK"

The final decision to use the atomic bomb belonged to President Harry Truman, who closely consulted with Secretary of War Henry L. Stimson, overseer of the "Manhattan Project," code name for the bomb's development.

The principal justification for dropping the bomb on Japan was the desire to shorten the war by shocking the Japanese into surrender. Another justification was that the bomb would make Stalin less aggressive. Yet another was that $2 billion had been spent from 1941–1945 on the Manhattan Project, and if the bomb were not used, then after the war the administration would be accused of unparalleled wastefulness.

A more idealistic justification was that exhibiting the terrible destructive power of this doomsday weapon would make an end to all war for all time.

Many of the Manhattan Project's atomic scientists objected to the bomb's use. They proposed a demonstration explosion on some remote site, with United Nations observers on hand, followed by a clear warning to the Japanese before the bomb was dropped on them. This was turned down because top brass feared the bomb might not work—might not go off—and the Allies would be humiliated.

Stimson later wrote: "Nothing would have been more damaging to our effort than a warning or demonstration followed by a dud—and this was a real possibility."

Stimson and a special presidential advisory committee recommended using the nuclear bomb. He said, "Such an effective shock would save many times the number of lives, both American and Japanese, than it would cost."

UTTER DESTRUCTION Much of Hiroshima was built of wood, which incinerated completely when a nuclear bomb was dropped on the city on August 6, 1945.

World War II: Total War

America's immense industrial capacity was critical to victory in World War II, and a prime factor was the ability to repair and replace warships rapidly. Specifically, building new aircraft carriers gave the United States a military advantage in the Pacific. In 1941, the USN had only seven large carriers and one escort carrier. By the end of the war 33 large and 78 small "escort carriers" had been put into service.

Before World War II, the navy modernized its fleet, converting from coal to oil, which improved ship speed and efficiency. New plastics and aluminum allowed for lighter construction, and advances in radar and radio communications benefited every branch of the service. New or improved military equipment and weapons included long-range heavy bombers, fighters, submarines, tanks, portable anti-tank weapons like bazookas or the German *Panzerfaust*, anti-tank guns, sophisticated mines for land and sea, landing craft, parachutes, and the M1 Garand semiautomatic rifle. Motorized vehicles, from battle tanks to jeeps, came into their own, as each side strove for speed on the battlefield.

Allied air power took the war to the enemy, massively bombing cities and military-industrial facilities. By the close of the war, American air power dominated land and sea, but as destructive as strategic bombing campaigns were, World War II's most remarkable and ominous technological feat was the atomic bomb. The world entered the Atomic Age in August 1945.

Germany, in the face of overwhelming odds, managed to develop and use combat jet aircraft, advanced submarines, and V-2 ballistic missiles—all too late to influence the outcome of World War II. These weapons systems were quickly adopted and expanded for use in the coming "Cold War."

LONG-RANGE BOMBER Armed with a dozen heavy machine guns, the B-17 "Flying Fortress" was designed for precision bombing in daytime raids. More than 12,700 B-17s were built; each carried 17,600 lbs. of bombs and flew at 325mph.

DESTROYER ESCORT The escorts were designed to protect Allied convoys against U-boats. Smaller and with less fire-power than a destroyer, they were more maneuverable and equipped with the latest anti-submarine equipment.

USN SUBMARINE American submarines sank half the 9.5 million gross tons of shipping lost by the Japanese during the war—a crucial factor in the Allied victory. Here the USS *Robalo* is launched on May 9, 1943.

CARRIERS SUPREME The queen of the Pacific War was the large aircraft carrier, and USN triumphs in the carrier battles of the Coral Sea and Midway Island turned the tide in favor of the Allies. These two carriers, with full flight decks, are escorted by several battleships.

GRUMMAN AVENGER These torpedo bombers became part of the USN air arm by 1942; they supported Marine ground action and operated effectively against submarines. Almost 10,000 were built.

BOLT-ACTION TO TOMMY GUN British Lee-Enfield bolt-action rifles are at top, one with a grenade-launcher cup. The M1 Garand, bottom, was the firearm of most U.S. infantrymen. Others had submachine guns, below: the Thompson M1, top, known as the Tommy Gun, and M3, a favorite of paratroopers, nicknamed "Grease Gun."

G.P. VEHICLE More than 640,000 command and reconnaissance cars were built by Willys for the American army during World War II. The four-wheel-drive "Jeep" got its nickname from the initials G.P. in General Purpose Vehicle.

SHERMAN TANK This medium American tank, introduced in 1942, was the Allies' principal armored vehicle, with more than 49,000 built. Weighing 33 tons, the Sherman tank—pictured rumbling through St. Lô, France—was armed with a 75mm cannon

HALFTRACK An armored personnel carrier with tractor tracks is shown during training at Fort Knox, Kentucky, in 1942. Halftracks came into use in the effort to "motorize" infantry and could carry a machine gun or an anti-aircraft gun.

ANTI-AIRCRAFT ARTILLERY Ringed by sandbags and steel drums, this 90mm anti-aircraft gun defends American positions on Okinawa. Air defenses included radar detection and also proximity fuses that exploded shells close to enemy aircraft.

185

KOREA DMZ This detail from a 1969 CIA map shows the Demilitarized Zone (DMZ) in yellow. Since the 1953 armistice that ended the Korean War, cross-border tensions have remained high on this, the world's most heavily fortified border.

PART SEVEN

The Hot Wars Of The Cold War

Victory in World War II in 1945 left the United States and Soviet Union as the world's greatest powers. With American democratic capitalism in direct opposition to Soviet Communist authoritarianism, these two adversaries established rival alliances. Hostility and mistrust between the American-led "West" and the Soviet-led "East" generated a "Cold War" standoff, with massive military buildups of potential destructive power that dwarfed World War II militaries.

The Korean War (1950–1953), the first "hot war" of the Cold War, was overshadowed by the danger of nuclear conflagration. That risk had diminished, thanks to arms-control treaties, when the United States fought the Vietnam War (1962–1975). Attempting to prevent Communism's spread in Southeast Asia, America underestimated the power of nationalist movements fighting on their own soil. The result was defeat for the United States, though its military never lost a major battle in Vietnam.

From 1945–1990, the United States engaged in many secret interventions and subversions—involving few American troops, but effective in supporting or destroying governments. United States backing of Afghan guerrillas in the Afghan-Soviet War (1979–1989) was crucial to the Soviet defeat, which contributed to the collapse of the Soviet Union and the end of the Cold War.

Planes and carrier, Korean War.

22: WARFARE ENTERS THE JET AGE IN KOREA

Since the spring of 1948, open clashes had occurred on the 38th parallel demarcation line between troops of the Republic of Korea (ROK) in the south and the Democratic People's Republic of Korea (DPRK) in the north. President Syngman Rhee, the strongman ruling South Korea, was suspected of trying to spark a war that would draw in the United States, with the objective of conquering Communist North Korea. At the same time, North Korea's dictator, Kim Il Sung, was conspiring with Communist China and the Soviet Union. They planned a campaign that would sweep down the Korean peninsula so rapidly that neither the United States nor the United Nations would be able to bring soldiers in soon enough to stop it.

Rhee's ROK forces were extremely weak compared to Kim's. The United States, in the process of reducing its own military from World War II, had done little to arm South Korea other than providing defensive weapons. The Soviets, however, supplied North Korea with modern equipment, including heavy artillery, 180 aircraft, and 120 powerful T-34 tanks. The 10 divisions of the North Korean People's Army (KPA) had 135,000 men, while the ROK's eight understrength divisions numbered 95,000. The ROK had no heavy artillery or tanks, and only a few training aircraft for an air force.

America unprepared for combat

Both the United States and the Communists underestimated each other's willingness to fight in Korea. Americans thought the threat of nuclear retaliation would deter the Communists from attacking South Korea. Neither Truman nor Stalin wanted to

AMERICAN TROOPS IN KOREA GIs of the 24th Infantry Regiment ride to the Pusan Perimeter battlefront in July 1950; they countered determined North Korean attacks until UNC forces under Walton Walker began to counterattack.

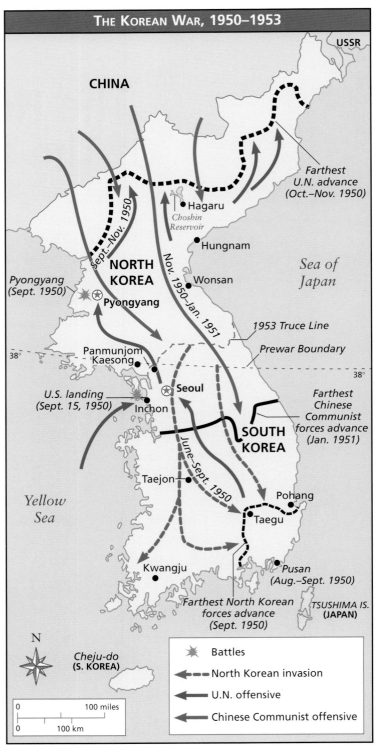

THE KOREAN WAR, 1950–1953

KOREAN WAR PHASES The North Korean invasion in June 1950 was stopped by the UNC at the Pusan Perimeter. Next, UNC forces drove almost to the Chinese border, and the Chinese offensive in November pushed the UNC south of Seoul. The UNC then drove the enemy back once more. A truce was made in 1953.

"It is fatal to enter any war without the will to win it."

—MACARTHUR, WHO WANTED TO INVADE CHINA

start a conventional war that might lead to nuclear strikes. At the same time, the Americans were confident a Communist Chinese incursion would be easily defeated. Meanwhile, Mao Zedong's government was sure the Americans were too soft to defend South Korea.

American military strength had been drastically reduced, from just under 9 million men in 1945 to 591,000 in 1950. In the Far East, there were only the four divisions of the Eighth Army, stationed in Japan. Mainly undertrained and poorly armed conscripts, these divisions were not at full-strength, lacking rifles and other essential equipment. Kim Il Sung weighed these factors and added to the equation the 30-40,000 veteran Korean volunteers of two divisions that had fought for the Chinese Communists. These troops were released by China to join the North Korean forces.

Invasion surprises South Korea

On June 25, 1950, the KPA attacked across the 38th parallel and quickly pushed back the surprised, outgunned South Koreans. The United Nations immediately demanded that the North Koreans withdraw, to no effect. Truman ordered General of the Army Douglas MacArthur to support the South Koreans with air and naval forces in an effort to slow the North Korean advance. When Seoul, the South Korean capital, fell on the 27th, Truman authorized ground troops to be sent in. The UN followed suit, calling on member states to provide military support. The Soviet Union, at this time, was boycotting the UN and did not participate in the decision-making.

MacArthur hastily pulled a force together and rushed men to Korea, throwing them into the path of the advancing KPA. In early July, the first Americans reached the battlefront near Osan, south of Seoul. Task Force Smith, as it was known, after its commander Colonel Charles B. Smith, numbered just 540 men, mostly draftees from the 24th Division. With only five 105mm guns as its main firepower, the task force took the full brunt of a 12,000-man North Korean division led by T-34 tanks. The Battle of Osan began on July 5 with American guns taking out two tanks, but that effort expended their only anti-tank rounds. Task Force Smith narrowly fought its way out of encirclement, losing 150 men killed or captured. More Americans and some UN troops rushed into the breach alongside the ROK divisions, forming a new force known as United Nations Command (UNC).

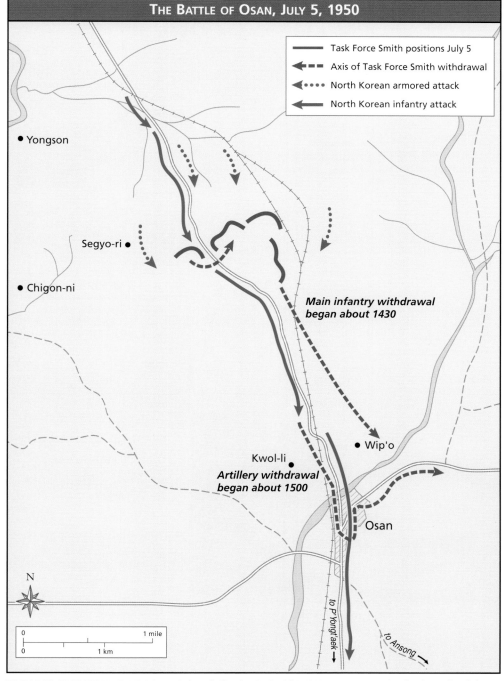

THE BATTLE OF OSAN, JULY 5, 1950

— Task Force Smith positions July 5
◄ - - - Axis of Task Force Smith withdrawal
◄ • • • • North Korean armored attack
◄——— North Korean infantry attack

• Yongson

Segyo-ri •

• Chigon-ni

Main infantry withdrawal began about 1430

• Wip'o

Kwol-li •
Artillery withdrawal began about 1500

Osan

N

0 — 1 mile
0 — 1 km

to P'yongt'aek
to Ansong

TASK FORCE SMITH HIT AT OSAN Colonel Charles B. Smith's 540 men were attacked north of the city of Osan by 12,000 North Korean troops with heavy T-34 tanks. The American force was nearly surrounded and destroyed, but held off the attack before beginning a fighting retreat southward.

ROCKET BARRAGE American Marines fire rocket launchers at enemy positions in Korea in 1951. The United States military had firepower far beyond the enemy's, but the Communists' superior numbers and fanatical frontal attacks took a heavy toll on the UNC.

THE PUSAN PERIMETER AND THE LANDING AT INCHON

General Walton H. Walker, commander of the United States Eighth Army, took charge of UNC troops and made a skillful fighting withdrawal southward. Joining ROK divisions to the understrength 24th and 25th Infantry divisions, and the 1st Cavalry Division—an infantry unit—Walker established a defensive pocket to protect the key southeast port of Pusan. The "Pusan Perimeter" was a hastily formed defensive line anchored on several strongpoints. The KPA might be able to drive past these strongpoints, but could not easily take them. Walker assembled reserves in a system of "mobile defense" designed for counterattacking and plugging near-breaches in the perimeter.

Although Walker had 92,000 men to the KPA's 70,000, the enemy held the initiative and chose the points of attack. One decisive UNC advantage was unchallenged air power that gave close support to the ground troops. The battle for the Pusan Perimeter continued into September, with Walker brilliantly blunting each KPA attack.

MacArthur and his staff planned to outflank the North Koreans by making an amphibious attack at Inchon, west of Seoul. While Walker launched an offensive from the Pusan Perimeter, MacArthur would recapture Seoul and cut off KPA supply and communications lines. Port facilities and an airport in the Inchon-Seoul region would offer the UNC a base for a major counteroffensive.

The Inchon landing, KPA driven back

MacArthur's invasion force included the 1st Marine Division and Army 7th Division as well as attached ROK troops. Designated as X Corps, the force was commanded by General

COUNTEROFFENSIVE "Operation Chromite," on July 23, 1950, landed two American divisions and ROK Marines to cut NKPA supply lines and recapture Seoul. General Edward M. Almond, MacArthur's chief of staff and a veteran of the Italian Campaign, was in charge of the invasion, carried out by X Corps.

INCHON CAMPAIGN, SEPTEMBER 15–30, 1950

"I regard all of Korea open for our military operations unless and until the enemy capitulates."

—MACARTHUR, TO SECRETARY OF DEFENSE GEORGE C. MARSHALL, JUST BEFORE THE INCHON LANDINGS

THE INCHON INVASION A daring UNC amphibious landing at Inchon in September 1950 outflanked the NKPA. The North Korean offensive was forced back under heavy pressure from the Pusan Perimeter and Inchon.

Edward M. Almond. By deciding to invade at Inchon, MacArthur overrode the opinions of the American Joint Chiefs of Staff, which considered the extremely high tides, tall sea walls, and readily defensible ship channel as too risky a gamble. That gamble succeeded, however, as the UNC landing on September 15 met little resistance. Air superiority and barrages from naval guns were key factors in the swift conquest. The landing cost fewer than 200 American casualties, including 20 dead. The KPA lost more than 3,300 killed and captured. Almond took Seoul on September 26, and on that same day advance elements of Walker's army, driving out of the Pusan Perimeter, met up with the Inchon force. The KPA struggled to escape being trapped in the south, but only one-third got through to the north.

Now at issue was whether MacArthur should push on into North Korea and destroy the remnants of the KPA, risking intervention by the the Chinese, or must he stop at the 38th parallel and reestablish the pre-invasion frontier.

Truman tells MacArthur to advance

Although President Truman was concerned about sparking a war with the Soviets, MacArthur assured him not to worry about the warmaking abilities of the Communist Chinese People's Liberation Army (PLA). The Republicans applied political pressure, blaming the Democrat Truman for "losing" China to the Communists in 1949. Truman wanted a decisive victory in Korea and agreed that MacArthur should continue the offensive.

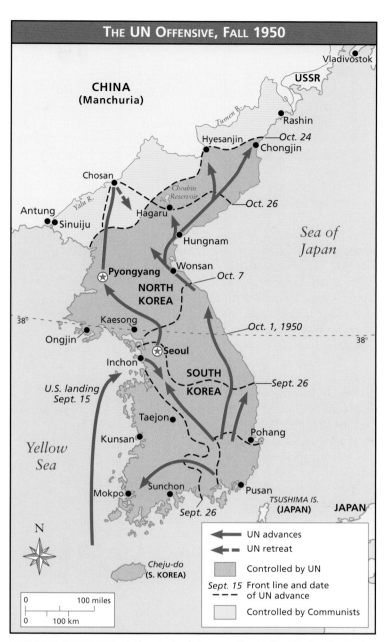

THE UN OFFENSIVE, FALL 1950

UN advances
UN retreat
Controlled by UN
Sept. 15 Front line and date of UN advance
Controlled by Communists

UNC 1950 OFFENSIVE At the start of the war, the United States Far East Command's 108,500 troops were short of everything—men, artillery, and tanks. The 135,000-man KPA was in worse shape, however, lacking equipment, training, and even rations. The UNC's Pusan breakout and Inchon invasion in September rolled back the overextended KPA.

2ND INFANTRY IN ACTION This division was badly mauled by Chinese forces in November 1950. Reinforced by Dutch, Belgian, and French battalions, the 2nd stopped a major Chinese attack in February 1951.

On October 1, an ROK division crossed the 38th parallel into North Korea, and within a week, the UN General Assembly authorized the UNC to do the same and continue to pursue the KPA. The advance dashed up both sides of the Korean peninsula. The X Corps made another amphibious landing, this time at Wonsan on the east coast. The North Koreans could not counter UNC sea or air power. To the west, the Eighth Army captured the North Korean capital, Pyongyang, on October 19. By now, Communist Chinese units were crossing the Yalu River into North Korea, preparing to challenge the UNC offensive.

The Joint Chiefs of Staff warned MacArthur that no non-Korean forces should approach the Chinese border. MacArthur paid little attention, however, and urged his commanders to keep driving forward. The Joint Chiefs reluctantly permitted him to continue pursuing the shattered KPA before it could regroup.

ADVANCE TO THE YALU BRINGS CHINA INTO WAR

The UNC offensive was split in two by a mountain range that ran north-south, creating in effect two separate campaigns, uncoordinated and lacking good communication with each other. To the east, Almond's X Corps and the ROK I Corps moved up the coast and inland toward the Yalu. West of the mountains, Walker's Eighth Army reached the Yalu by the end of October. The Communist Chinese had publicly warned that their forces would not stand idly by if North Korea were invaded. MacArthur, however, assured Truman that any Chinese offensive would be quickly destroyed before it reached Pyongyang.

The KPA had been virtually wiped out, with more than 100,000 men taken prisoner, but now there came heavy clashes in the northwest between Chinese PLA troops and ROK forces backed up by the 1st Cavalry. At Unsan on November 1–3, the ROK and Americans were driven back with severe casualties.

By now, MiG jet fighter planes piloted by Soviet airmen were patrolling the border area to keep American aircraft out of China. On November 8, the world's first-ever air combat between jets took place, with an American F-80 shooting down a MiG-15 over North Korea.

China joins the battle

The Chinese 9th and 13th Army Groups, massed on the border under the command of Marshal Peng Du-hai, worried General Walker, who prudently withdrew his extended forces to stronger positions. MacArthur wanted the offensive to resume even though the Chinese were

covertly transporting men and matériel into North Korea. By mid-November, 300,000 Chinese troops in 30 divisions were taking up positions.

MacArthur was convinced UNC air power would blunt any Chinese aggression. To stop Chinese troops from invading, he called for the bombing of key river bridges across the Yalu. Washington opposed this provocative step, but MacArthur won the day. The bridges were blasted by 400 aircraft, but it was too late to stop the Chinese field army, which by now was south of the river.

"A president cannot always be popular."

—President Truman, who fired MacArthur, hero of World War II

CHINESE INTERVENTION By November 10, the Chinese had paused to regroup, and the American 7th Division had occupied Hyesanjin on the Yalu, the most northerly point reached by UNC forces. When MacArthur again attacked on November 24, the Chinese counterattacked; many UNC troops were evacuated by sea to Pusan.

FRIGID OBSERVATION POST Marines on the forward line at the Yalu River endure harsh winter conditions as they watch for movement by Chinese Communist troops assembling across the river. The Chinese attacked on November 3.

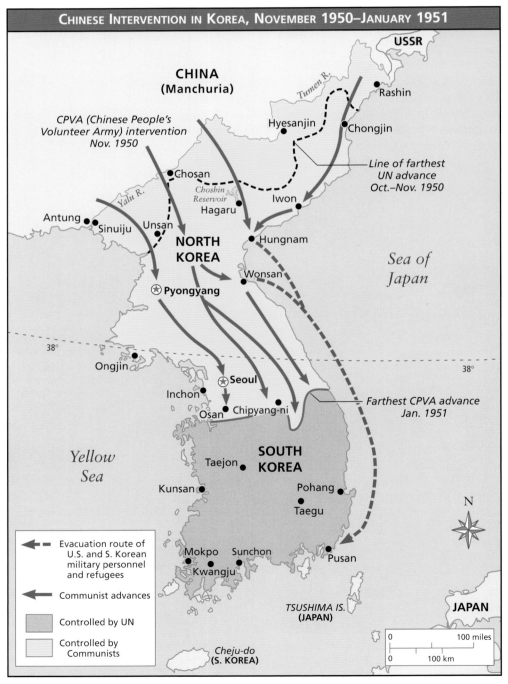

CHINESE INTERVENTION IN KOREA, NOVEMBER 1950–JANUARY 1951

- USSR
- CHINA (Manchuria)
- Tumen R.
- Rashin
- CPVA (Chinese People's Volunteer Army) intervention Nov. 1950
- Hyesanjin
- Chongjin
- Line of farthest UN advance Oct.–Nov. 1950
- Chosan
- Choshin Reservoir
- Iwon
- Yalu R.
- Hagaru
- Antung
- Sinuiju
- Unsan
- NORTH KOREA
- Hungnam
- Wonsan
- Pyongyang
- Sea of Japan
- 38°
- Ongjin
- Seoul
- Inchon
- Chipyang-ni
- Osan
- Farthest CPVA advance Jan. 1951
- Yellow Sea
- SOUTH KOREA
- Taejon
- Pohang
- Kunsan
- Taegu
- N
- Evacuation route of U.S. and S. Korean military personnel and refugees
- Communist advances
- Controlled by UN
- Controlled by Communists
- Mokpo
- Sunchon
- Kwangju
- Pusan
- TSUSHIMA IS. (JAPAN)
- JAPAN
- Cheju-do (S. KOREA)
- 0   100 miles
- 0   100 km

FIGHTING RETREAT With enemy on all sides, the 1st Marine division battled back from the Chosin Reservoir in the mountainous north. Carrying their wounded throughout a 13-day ordeal, the Marines conducted one of history's finest withdrawals under fire.

Now that winter had set in, UNC forces were running short of supplies, especially gasoline. Walker and Eighth Army commanders were troubled by MacArthur's call for a resumption of attacks without having reliable supply lines. Stationed just 60 miles from the Yalu River, Marine general Oliver P. Smith of Almond's X Corps mistrusted MacArthur's strategy. Smith cautiously slowed his advance and set up a main base. To the west, General Walker obeyed and attacked on November 24, but the Chinese immediately counterattacked in overwhelming force, destroying three ROK divisions on Walker's right flank. The Chinese sent 18 divisions smashing through the breach, threatening to envelop the entire Eighth Army.

The American 2nd Infantry Division met the Chinese attack at Kunu-ri and held out for two days while the rest of the Eighth Army and ROK troops retreated across the Chongchon River. By November 30, the Chinese offensive was in full swing, and MacArthur ordered the Eighth Army's withdrawal to below the 38th parallel.

Defeat in the Northeast

Meanwhile, X Corps and the ROK I Corps east of the central mountain range were under fierce attack. They were ordered to withdraw to the Hamhung-Hungnam region, but the enemy were rushing in to cut them off. Most at risk were General Smith's 22,000 troops— Marines, 7th Division, and UNC elements. Caught scattered around the hilly Chosin Reservoir area, Smith's command was attacked by 12 enemy divisions totaling 120,000 troops. The UNC force fought in bitter cold and snow to regroup and withdraw. Their only advantage was artillery support and dominant air power, which kept the balance from tipping completely against them.

Isolated units fought off attack after attack and launched their own strikes, while trying to break out and reach the road junction of Hagaru-ri, a main supply base. From there, Smith hoped to reach the port of Hungnam, where UNC forces were to be evacuated.

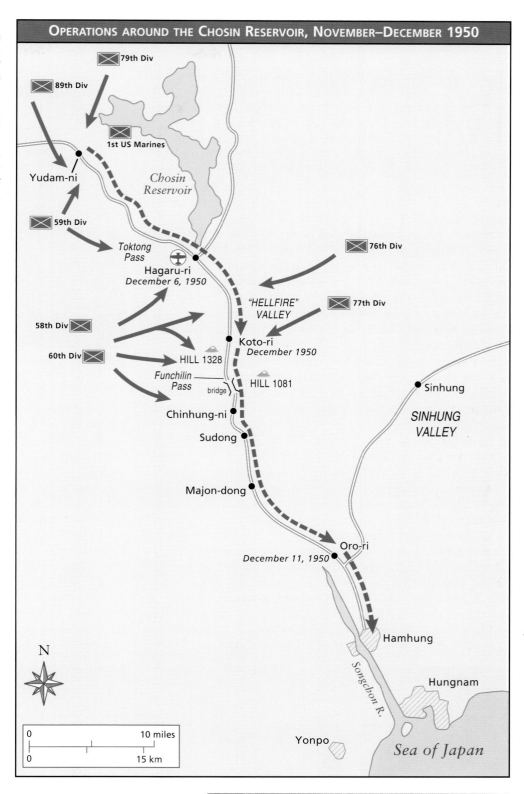

OPERATIONS AROUND THE CHOSIN RESERVOIR, NOVEMBER–DECEMBER 1950

79th Div

89th Div

1st US Marines

Yudam-ni

Chosin Reservoir

59th Div

76th Div

Toktong Pass

Hagaru-ri
December 6, 1950

"HELLFIRE" VALLEY

77th Div

58th Div

Koto-ri
December 1950

60th Div

HILL 1328

Funchilin Pass

bridge

HILL 1081

Sinhung

Chinhung-ni

SINHUNG VALLEY

Sudong

Majon-dong

Oro-ri

December 11, 1950

Hamhung

Hungnam

N

Songchon R.

| 0 | | 10 miles |
| 0 | | 15 km |

Yonpo

Sea of Japan

MOVING TO THE FRONT In January 1951, men of the 19th Infantry Regiment plod over rugged hilly terrain 10 miles north of Seoul.

A BLOODY ROAD TO STALEMATE AND TO ARMISTICE

Most of the UNC troops on the west side of the Chosin Reservoir had escaped to Hagaru-ri by December 4, but a force of 2,500 on the eastern side, mostly Marines, was almost wiped out. About 1,000 survivors finally escaped across the reservoir ice, with hundreds wounded or suffering frostbite. Surrounded at Hagaru-ri, Smith's 10,000 troops began to fight their way southward to Koto-ri, over 11 miles of road that earned the name "Hellfire Valley," where dug-in Chinese poured gunfire into retreating UNC columns.

Smith picked up another 4,000 men at Koto-ri and pushed on for Hungnam, more than 30 miles distant. In one remarkable operation, the air force dropped bridge sections to span a gorge that blocked the UNC escape. Between December 6-8 Smith's 14,000 troops—almost all Americans—managed to fight their way to the coast. His casualties numbered more than 5,000, with another 7,000 suffering frostbite. Chinese combat losses are estimated at 25,000.

Next came the evacuation from Hungnam of X Corps and ROK troops, totaling 105,000 men. Also evacuated were 91,000 Korean refugees. The process was completed on Christmas Eve, when the port facilities were blown up by UNC engineers.

Ridgway takes command of UNC forces

UNC difficulties were compounded by the loss of the Eighth Army's brilliant General Walker, who died in a jeep accident on December 22. Walker was replaced by the army's deputy chief of staff, General Matthew B. Ridgway.

Ridgway stemmed the UNC retreat, but early in January another Chinese offensive forced the abandonment of Seoul. At the end of the month, when Chinese supply lines became overextended and their offensive halted, Ridgway took the initiative. He engaged the enemy in limited battles intended mainly to inflict heavy Chinese losses rather than win territory. American artillery and air-power advantages caused far more Chinese casualties than the UNC suffered. By springtime 1951, Seoul

SUPPORTING INFANTRY A 31st Regimental Combat Team gun crew fires a 75mm recoilless rifle across a South Korean Valley to lend firepower to UNC infantry units in June 1951.

was retaken and the 38th parallel again crossed by UNC forces.

MacArthur still wanted to widen the war and strike at China, to bomb Manchuria and land Chinese Nationalist troops on the Chinese mainland. Truman had heard enough. In April, MacArthur was removed and replaced by Ridgway. Although MacArthur came home as a hero at first, his dangerous plans soon were recognized as reckless.

Late that month, Ridgway defended against another Chinese offensive across the 38th parallel. Again, the Chinese were shattered by artillery and air support, and in May were driven back by a UNC counteroffensive. Ridgway was not permitted to push on, and a "fighting stalemate" set in, with fierce limited attacks and counterattacks that took many lives but gained or lost little ground. Ceasefire talks began that summer, broke down, and began again as fighting continued.

The conflict was so savage that almost half the casualties suffered in the war fell during the armistice negotiations that dragged on into 1952. Each month saw approximately 2,500 American casualties.

"I shall make that trip. I shall go to Korea . . . and concentrate on the job of ending the Korean War."

—DWIGHT D. EISENHOWER'S 1952 CAMPAIGN PROMISE

TOURING KOREA President-elect Eisenhower fulfills a 1952 campaign promise to visit Korea. Eisenhower inspects troops of the ROK Capital Division near the combat zone in December 1952.

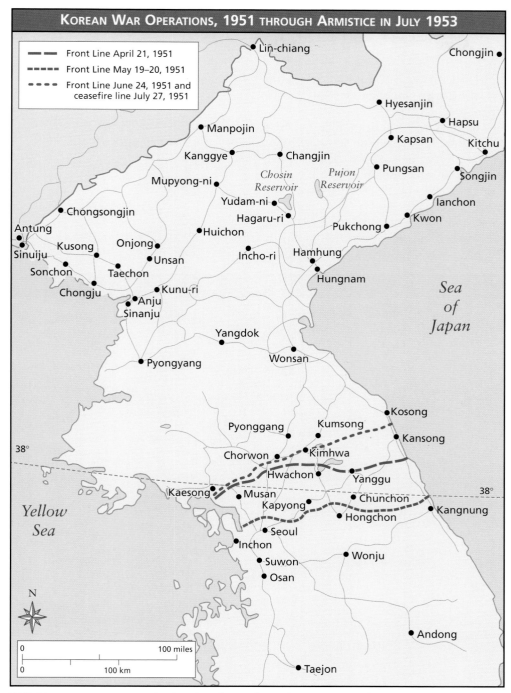

KOREAN WAR OPERATIONS, 1951 THROUGH ARMISTICE IN JULY 1953

– – – Front Line April 21, 1951
- - - - Front Line May 19–20, 1951
- - - - Front Line June 24, 1951 and
ceasefire line July 27, 1951

Lin-chiang
Chongjin
Hyesanjin
Manpojin
Hapsu
Kapsan
Kitchu
Kanggye
Changjin
Pungsan
Songjin
Chosin
Reservoir
Pujon
Reservoir
Mupyong-ni
Yudam-ni
Ianchon
Hagaru-ri
Kwon
Chongsongjin
Huichon
Pukchong
Antung
Onjong
Incho-ri
Hamhung
Kusong
Unsan
Sinuiju
Taechon
Sonchon
Hungnam
Chongju
Kunu-ri
Anju
Sinanju
Yangdok
Sea
of
Japan
Pyongyang
Wonsan
Kosong
Pyonggang
Kumsong
38°
Kansong
Chorwon
Kimhwa
Hwachon
Yanggu
Kaesong
Musan
Chunchon
38°
Kapyong
Hongchon
Kangnung
Yellow
Sea
Seoul
Inchon
Wonju
Suwon
Osan
N
Andong
0   100 miles
0   100 km
Taejon

UNC COUNTEROFFENSIVE United Nations forces drove the Communists back from Seoul in a 1951 offensive, January 25 to April 22. A subsequent advance from late June to July 27 gained more ground; then the war became a stalemate, leading to the 1953 armistice.

HELICOPTERS AND JET-AGE AIR WAR

One of the most significant innovations of the Korean War was the military's use of helicopters. At first, Air Force helicopters were used—mainly for rescue missions, airlifting casualties from the front. Many lives were saved that previously would have been lost. Later, the Army acquired its own fleet of helicopters for evacuating injured and also for limited reconnaissance and observation. Early military helicopters were meant for only light work, but their effectiveness led to development of better engines and designs that in future would bring them into battle as attack helicopters.

Jet aircraft came to the fore in the Korean War, with the swept-back American F-86 Sabre as the main UNC fighter. The F-86s dominated air combat, with their pilots shooting down 792 MiGs while losing 110 planes.

During 1952, the UNC air war intensified. Jet fighters, B-26 medium bombers, and B-29 heavy bombers struck Chinese troop positions in Korea, and UNC fighter pilots often crossed the Yalu River to attack Soviet-piloted MiG-15s over Manchuria. Bombing hydroelectric facilities on the Yalu was instrumental in persuading the Chinese to finally agree to a truce.

JET FIGHTERS F-86 fighters dominated Korean War air combat with Soviet-built MiGs.

Eisenhower becomes president

In November, Dwight D. Eisenhower was elected president—Truman had chosen not to run for a second full term. During his campaign, Eisenhower had made it clear to the war-weary American public that he intended to resolve the Korean crisis. Stalin's death in March 1953 caused uneasiness in the Communist world and contributed to the Chinese desire to make peace. An armistice was achieved at Panmunjom on July 27, 1953, but final peace terms were never officially signed.

The United States had lost more than 33,600 killed or missing in action, with more than 103,000 wounded. South Korea had 257,000 killed or missing and 429,000 wounded, while the allied nations suffered more than 15,000 casualties. North Korea had 295,000 military dead, the Chinese up to 1 million. More than 1 million Korean civilians died.

The first great conflict of the Cold War era, the Korean War has been neglected by the public memory and is sometimes termed the "Forgotten War."

23: INDOCHINA CAULDRON: THE VIETNAM WAR

In May 1954, France lost the Battle of Dien Bien Phu, in the mountains of northern Vietnam, defeated by the Vietminh—Vietnamese communists and nationalists commanded by Communist Ho Chi Minh (Nguyen That Thanh). This battle, which effectively ended the nine-year-old Indochina War, cost France 11,000 killed and wounded. In July, France and the Vietminh signed an agreement at Geneva, which recognized Vietnam as an independent state, temporarily dividing the country at the 17th parallel. The Vietminh would control the North and France the South until elections for a national government were held throughout Vietnam in 1956.

In World War II, the United States had helped organize the Vietminh resisting Japanese occupation of Indochina. At the end of the war, Ho Chi Minh's Communists established the Democratic Republic of Vietnam (DRV), but the French tried to hold on to Vietnam, and war began. Fearing Communist expansion in the region, the United States backed the French, whose defeat at Dien Bien Phu seemed one more step in Communism's march to take over the world. The prevalent "domino theory" purported that if Indochina became Communist—even by a fair election—adjacent regions would fall, one by one. When Ngo Dinh Diem declared the south to be the Republic of Vietnam in 1955, the United States fully backed him, though he was a Catholic in a mainly Buddhist nation. Diem and the Eisenhower Administration defied the Geneva agreement and opposed a national election. Open rebellion by the Vietminh in South Vietnam was soon under way.

The Ho Chi Minh Trail

The North Vietnamese established a supply route to rebel forces in the South, following the Vietnamese borders with Laos and Cambodia and branching off to areas of resistance against Diem's government. This route became known as the Ho Chi Minh Trail. Anti-government guerrilla fighters in the South became known by the pejorative, "Vietcong" or Vietnamese Communists, although many were nationalists, not Communists. In 1960, the insurgency called itself the National Liberation Front, or NLF, and claimed to be politically independent of North Vietnam.

By then, the American military had a few hundred "advisors" in South Vietnam in a training and supply capacity. The Army of South Vietnam (ARVN) learned from these Americans how to operate the modern weapons, armored personnel carriers, and helicopters they received from the United States. Soon after John F. Kennedy became president, he increased

"I don't agree with those who say we should withdraw."

—PRESIDENT KENNEDY, ON SOUTH VIETNAM, TO INTERVIEWER WALTER CRONKITE, SEPTEMBER 1963

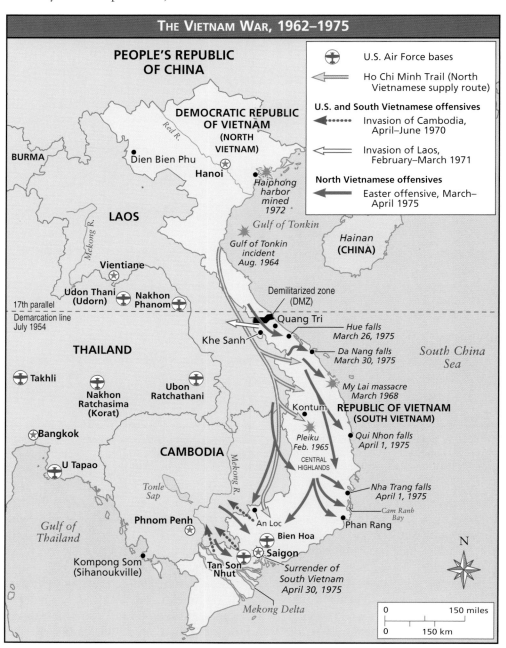

THE VIETNAM WAR, 1962–1975

Legend:
- U.S. Air Force bases
- Ho Chi Minh Trail (North Vietnamese supply route)
- **U.S. and South Vietnamese offensives**
- Invasion of Cambodia, April–June 1970
- Invasion of Laos, February–March 1971
- **North Vietnamese offensives**
- Easter offensive, March–April 1975

SOUTHEAST ASIA The region was a turmoil of insurrection and conflict in the 1960s, when the United States propped up South Vietnam's government against NLF insurgency and North Vietnamese incursions. Neighboring Laos and Cambodia, with North Vietnamese supply lines and bases, were drawn into the conflict.

THE HO CHI MINH TRAIL, 1965–1973

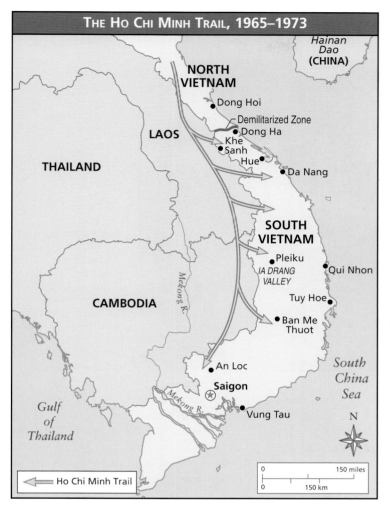

Hainan Dao (CHINA)

NORTH VIETNAM

Dong Hoi
Demilitarized Zone
Dong Ha
Khe Sanh
Hue
Da Nang

LAOS

THAILAND

SOUTH VIETNAM

Pleiku
IA DRANG VALLEY
Qui Nhon
Tuy Hoe

CAMBODIA

Ban Me Thuot

Mekong R.

An Loc

Saigon

South China Sea

Gulf of Thailand

Mekong R.

Vung Tau

N

0   150 miles
0   150 km

← Ho Chi Minh Trail

COMMUNIST LIFELINE Named for Ho Chi Minh, this supply route was established in the First Indochina War against the French. Steadily expanded, it became a 9,375-mile network of trails and paths.

ON THE MOVE South Vietnamese soldiers advance across the marshlands of the Mekong Delta in 1961 while on patrol in search of NLF guerrillas.

THE FIRST INDOCHINA WAR A French Foreign Legionnaire, followed by a tank, walks alongside a rice paddy near Hanoi in 1954 during the First Indochina War, which France lost to the Vietminh.

military assistance to South Vietnam, which then had about 1,300 American military advisors. Kennedy's government, guided by Secretary of Defense Robert McNamara, increased the advisors to more than 3,000.

In January 1962, helicopters flown by American pilots brought 1,000 ARVN troops into battle against an NLF stronghold near Saigon in "Operation Chopper," the first large-scale American combat mission in Vietnam.

Agent Orange and Battle of Ap Bac

Early that same year, "Operation Ranchhand" began in an effort to clear away vegetation from NLF bases, trails, and highways to prevent guerrillas from moving freely or setting ambushes. This "defoliation" policy continued for years, destroying thousands of acres of jungle sprayed with the herbicide "Agent Orange," which contained the dangerous chemical dioxin. Civilians and soldiers alike who were contaminated by dioxin often became severely ill.

In January 1963, a major NLF attack at the hamlet of Ap Bac killed or wounded almost 400 ARVN and killed three American advisors. More Americans were steadily sent in until there were 16,000 military advisors, led by General Maxwell Taylor, head of the Military Assistance Command, Vietnam (MACV).

Diem's government was proving unpopular, however, especially with Buddhists and students, who protested its harsh repression and corruption. By the fall of 1963, the United States, too, was disenchanted by Diem's inability to defeat the insurrection, which was winning militarily. On November 1, a group of ARVN generals overthrew Diem and killed him. The coup had American approval. Three weeks later, on November 22, President Kennedy was assassinated, and was succeeded by Vice-president Lyndon B. Johnson.

JOHNSON WIDENS THE WAR IN SOUTH VIETNAM

President Johnson did not want to get deeper into the war, but he was determined not to appear soft on Communism, and he committed the nation ever more deeply in Vietnam. In June 1964, General William C. Westmoreland took over MACV. For the next four years he would be in charge of the American war in Vietnam.

On August 4, the destroyer USS *Maddox* reported being fired on by North Vietnamese vessels, claiming it was under attack. No attack took place, but within six hours of the initial report, President Johnson ordered an air strike against North Vietnam, bombing naval bases and a major oil facility.

On August 7, Congress passed the Gulf of Tonkin Resolution, giving Johnson the power to do whatever was necessary "to defend" Southeast Asia.

SEARCH AND DESTROY American GIs watch the burning of an NLF shelter in 1965, as the war becomes "Americanized" with an influx of United States troops, who increasingly took part in ground action.

Americans enter the fray

In the first two months of 1965, NLF forces launched a series of attacks across South Vietnam. An American helicopter base in the Central Highlands was attacked by NLF commandos, who killed nine Americans and wounded more than 70.

In mid-February, Johnson authorized "Operation Rolling Thunder," a bombing offensive to force North Vietnam to stop supporting NLF insurgents. That April, a bombing campaign against North Vietnam's transport system hit bridges, roads, rail junctions, truck parks, and supply depots. That same month, the United States offered North Vietnam economic aid in exchange for peace, but the offer was rejected. Two weeks later, American com-

bat strength was at more than 60,000 troops, and allied forces from Korea, the Philippines, and Australia would be added.

NLF offensives increased through the rest of 1965, with American bases often as prime targets. In June, an ARVN district headquarters and American Special Forces camp at Dong Xai was overrun. That same month, the first offensive operation by American ground forces in Vietnam was launched, just northwest of Saigon. In August, the American army embarked on "Operation Starlite," the first major battle of the Vietnam War.

Assaulting an NLF regimental base and tunnel network, Starlite was a resounding victory, destroying an NLF regiment. American forces sustained 45 dead and approximately 200 wounded.

Search and destroy

The United States won another major engagement that fall, as the 1st Air Cavalry Division attacked the enemy in the Battle of the Ia Drang Valley. The battle raged for 35 days, often in hand-to-hand combat. The Americans suffered 305 killed, while the People's Army of North Vietnam (PAVN) had approximately 1,600 dead. Westmoreland believed such aggressive "search-and-destroy" missions could win a "war of attrition." For their part, NLF and PAVN commanders believed American resolve would be shaken if the United States suffered heavy losses.

In February 1966, four search-and-destroy missions were launched, but no major engagements were brought on, for the NLF melted away. In March, the initia-

THE GULF OF TONKIN INCIDENT

On the night of July 30, 1964, South Vietnamese commandos attacked two small North Vietnamese islands in the Gulf of Tonkin, between North Vietnam and China. An American electronic spy ship, the destroyer *Maddox*, was 123 miles south attempting to electronically simulate an air attack to draw North Vietnamese warships away from the commandos. On August 4, the captain of the *Maddox* reported that his vessel had been fired on, adding that he expected to be attacked. That attack never came, but President Johnson immediately decided to retaliate by ordering an air bombardment against North Vietnam.

On August 7, the United States Congress passed the Gulf of Tonkin Resolution, which authorized the president to do whatever was necessary to meet this alleged North Vietnamese aggression. The resolution was the basis for the United States build-up and war in South Vietnam. It was repealed by Congress in 1970.

USS *MADDOX* At the center of the so-called Tonkin Gulf Incident, this 3,200-ton warship was built in World War II. *Maddox* was decommissioned in 1972 and sold to Taiwan.

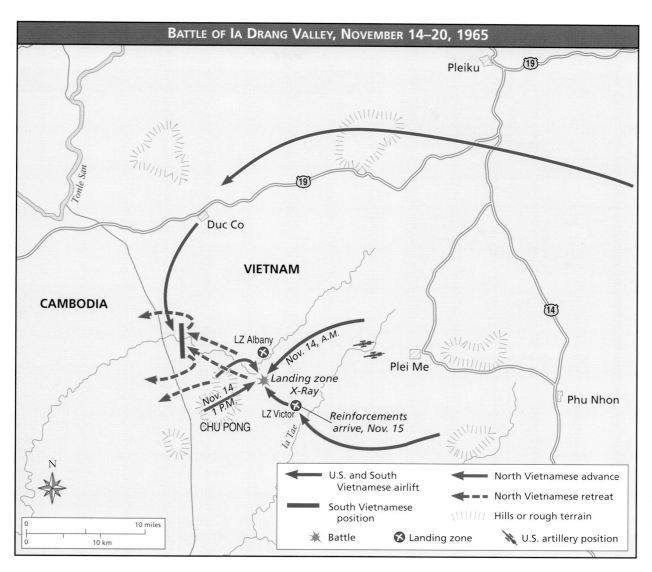

BATTLE OF IA DRANG VALLEY, NOVEMBER 14–20, 1965

Pleiku

19

19

Tonle San

Duc Co

VIETNAM

CAMBODIA

LZ Albany

Nov. 14, A.M.

Plei Me

Landing zone X-Ray

Nov. 14 1 P.M.

LZ Victor

Reinforcements arrive, Nov. 15

Phu Nhon

CHU PONG

Ia Tae

14

N

←	U.S. and South Vietnamese airlift	← North Vietnamese advance
▬	South Vietnamese position	◄--- North Vietnamese retreat
✳	Battle	||||| Hills or rough terrain
⊗	Landing zone	U.S. artillery position

0   10 miles
0   10 km

BATTLE OF IA DRANG VALLEY After the repulse of a PAVN attack on American special forces at Plei Me, the 1st Cavalry pursued the enemy and drove them off between November 14-18. This was an early employment of "airmobile tactics," extensively using helicopters.

"Our 'bear hug,' our 'grab-them-by-the-belt' tactics."

—NORTH VIETNAMESE GENERAL ON KEEPING TROOPS CLOSE TO AMERICAN POSITIONS AT IA DRANG TO DETER BOMBING

tive belonged to the NLF, which attacked the American base at Lo Ke. United States air support bombed the attackers into retreat, but two days later an NLF force launched another attack on American positions. This time, artillery fire drove the attackers away.

In late May, a PAVN division crossed the Demilitarized Zone (DMZ) separating North and South Vietnam and engaged a Marine battalion. The largest battle of the war to date now erupted near Dong Ha, drawing in 5,000 men of the 3rd Marine Division. After a battle lasting three weeks, the Marines, backed by ARVN troops and artillery and air power, drove the PAVN back across the DMZ.

By the end of 1966, Americans in Vietnam numbered 385,000, with an additional 60,000 sailors on ships offshore. In this year, more than 6,000 Americans were killed and 30,000 wounded. An estimated 61,000 NLF and PAVN died.

MID-AIR REFUELING Air. force F-105 fighter bombers on their way to attack North Vietnam in January 1966 take on fuel from a KC-135 Stratotanker.

AMERICAN MIGHT MEETS NLF AND PAVN DETERMINATION

RIVER GUNBOATS Nicknamed the "Brownwater Navy," USN gunboats patrolled the twisting, shallow rivers of South Vietnam, often surrounded by jungle where snipers lay in ambush. Gunboats cooperated with ground forces but often were on their own, plying remote, muddy waters in enemy territory.

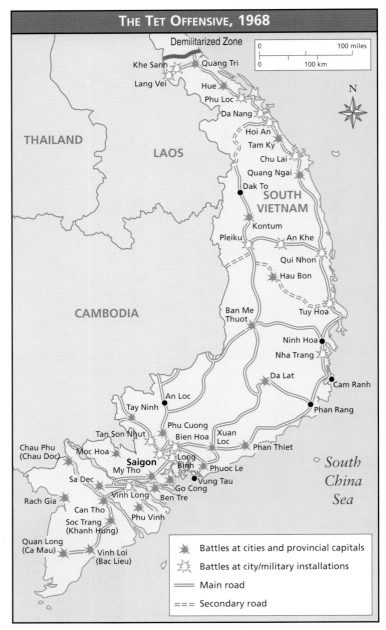

TET OFFENSIVE When the NLF and PAVN launched a coordinated offensive early in 1968, South Vietnam erupted in battle, from inner-city Saigon to American bases near the DMZ. The Communists lost heavily, but proved the war was far from over.

Between January and May 1967 North Vietnamese forces launched relentless bombardments on American bases south of the Demilitarized Zone. Especially hard hit was Khe Sanh, a strategic base six miles east of Laos and 14 miles south of the DMZ.

Also in January, "Operation Cedar Falls" began, aiming to drive NLF forces from the "Iron Triangle," a 60-square-mile zone about 40 miles north of Saigon. Nearly 16,000 American troops and 14,000 ARVN soldiers—many swiftly landing from UH-1 "Huey" helicopters—stormed the Iron Triangle. The enemy withdrew, however, offering little resistance. Great quantities of arms and supplies were captured, and a vast network of NLF tunnels was uncovered. In about three weeks, 72 Americans were killed, mostly by snipers and booby traps. An estimated 750 NLF fighters died.

Assault from the sky: air cavalry

"Operation Junction City" began in February, one of the war's largest assaults from the air. Thousands of soldiers were brought into Tay Ninh province north of Saigon by 240 helicopters on a 72-day search-and-destroy mission to wipe out the NLF headquarters there. Approximately 30,000 American troops and 5,000 ARVN took part, capturing stores, equipment, and weapons, but failing to bring on a major battle.

This strategy of avoiding full-scale battle on American terms was evolved by North Vietnamese general Vo Nguyen Giap, victor over the French in the First Indochina War.

That April, major air attacks on North Vietnam's airfields began. The North Vietnamese had few fighter pilots to oppose the Americans, who shot down 26 planes and half the North's available pilots. There was heavy fighting in South Vietnam's Central Highlands, where PAVN forces infiltrating from the Ho Chi Minh Trail in Cambodia came under frequent attack.

At the end of 1967, there were 500,000 United States troops in Vietnam.

1968: Communists launch the Tet Offensive

At dawn on the morning of January 21, 1968, the Marine base at Khe Sanh came under devastating bombardment from artillery shells, mortars, and rockets. This heavy bombardment, which went on for two days, was partly intended to distract American attention from a countrywide offensive that exploded across South Vietnam on January 30, the Vietnamese new year, known as Tet.

The "Tet Offensive" caught the Americans and ARVN by surprise. Intelligence had reported strong PAVN forces massing near Khe Sanh, but no one was prepared for a simultaneous assault on more than 100 cities and towns. NLF commandos and saboteurs sprang from concealment even in the center of

ARVN GUNNERS As the Tet offensive threatened to overwhelm the defenders of Saigon, these ARVN soldiers man their machine gun on a balcony overlooking the city.

Saigon, where the American Embassy itself came under assault. Thousands of NLF and North Vietnamese struck American and ARVN bases. Some of the heaviest fighting was in the north of the country, at the ancient city of Hue, lasting 25 days. Although the NLF and PAVN suffered 58,000 killed, the impact of the Tet Offensive's coordinated assaults shook the confidence of the Johnson government and Congress.

General Westmoreland had recently testified that the enemy was "on the ropes," and Americans believed there was "light at the end of the tunnel." The American public was deeply troubled now, realizing the Vietnam War was far from over. The United States lost 2,500 men in the Tet fighting. That spring, secret negotiations began in Paris in an effort to make peace. Those negotiations would drag on for more than four years.

Johnson refuses more troops

That spring, Khe Sanh continued to be bombarded daily. In the region around Saigon, including the swampy Mekong River delta, the Americans and ARVN launched large search-and-destroy missions.

By March, Westmoreland was asking for an additional 200,000 troops to be sent to Vietnam, but Johnson and his military advisors were against further escalation. McNamara had by now resigned as secretary of defense, replaced by Clark Clifford. Other Johnson advisors included the highly respected retired General Omar N. Bradley.

Antiwar feelings were running high in the United States, blaming Johnson for escalating the war. Later that same month, the disappointed Johnson announced that he would not run for another term as president.

"We have reached an important point when the end begins to come into view."

—GENERAL WESTMORELAND, MACV COMMANDER

THE TUNNEL WAR

A key to the success of the Vietnamese National Liberation Front was their well-hidden underground network of tunnels that laced South Vietnam. With American spotter planes constantly overhead, this complex system of tunnels offered supplies and concealment for NLF troops, even when American or ARVN soldiers were patrolling on the ground above. A village might be in enemy hands, but the fighters in the tunnels below could come out, attack unexpectedly, then quickly disappear again. The largest systems, some with nearly 200 miles of tunnels, were within 20 miles of Saigon.

Tunnels were meticulously designed and constructed. They linked with above-ground NLF facilities, which had underground access by hidden trapdoors. Tunnels had chambers for arms factories and store rooms for weapons and food. Rooms with ventilation to the surface served as hospitals, sleeping chambers, and kitchens. Long communications tunnels connected headquarters with other complexes that wound their way under villages and fields. Many tunnels were found and destroyed, but many others were operative throughout the Vietnam War and were essential to a Communist victory.

WAITING FOR BATTLE An NLF soldier concealed in a tunnel complex is ready for orders to surface and fight.

UNDER SIEGE The American Marine base at Khe Sanh had been under siege for a year when it was battered by enemy attacks during the Tet Offensive of early 1968. The defenders held out under artillery bombardments and ground assaults over 77 days.

MY LAI MASSACRE AND AN END TO "ROLLING THUNDER"

Heavy combat continued in Vietnam through 1968, as the anti-war movement in the United States and around the world grew in strength. Republican Richard M. Nixon campaigned for the presidency promising he had a secret plan for ending the war with honor. He would win the national election that fall.

On March 16, Lieutenant William L. Calley, Jr., led Charlie Company of the 1st Battalion, 20th Infantry Regiment, 23rd Infantry Division, into the hamlet of My Lai in northern South Vietnam. No enemy fighters were there, only women, children, and elderly men. Calley's company massacred everyone they found, as many as 500 people. Some were saved only by an American helicopter crew dropping between them and Charlie Company and training their machine guns on the marauding soldiers.

The massacre would not become public until one year later. In the meantime, it was covered up by at least 30 officers, including the division commander. Future United States secretary of state Colin L. Powell was the 23rd Division's assistant operations officer. Powell arrived in Vietnam shortly after the My Lai killings took place. He wrote the division's first response to rumors of the massacre, stating it did not happen. He said he knew nothing about the facts until years later.

Calley, who claimed to have been following direct orders, was the only officer found guilty of any war crimes. He received a life sentence, later reduced to 10 years, but Nixon pardoned him in 1974.

"Our purpose in Vietnam is . . . just to prevent the forceful conquest of South Vietnam by North Vietnam."

—President Lyndon B. Johnson in 1968

"AIR CAVALRY" American troops leap from a helicopter and go into action as "airmobile" or "air cavalry," a new tactical system made possible by improved helicopter technology that developed after the Korean War.

Abrams replaces Westmoreland

In April, the long-running siege of the base at Khe Sanh was finally lifted, but by June General Westmoreland had ordered its abandonment and demolition. Khe Sanh was no longer needed now that American forces in the region had been strongly reinforced and were highly mobile, operating with attack helicopters. That July, Westmoreland was replaced by his deputy, General Creighton Abrams, who assumed leadership of MACV. Westmoreland was promoted to army chief of staff.

Abrams focused on improving the mobility of his forces and strengthening the ARVN. He also changed the overall policy from "search-and-destroy" attrition warfare to one of securing and defending hamlets and villages. Small-unit patrols replaced massive combat operations, and Abrams ordered a reduction of artillery and air bombardments that destroyed villages and injured civilians.

Abrams also permitted the continuation of "Operation Phoenix," a clandestine, Central Intelligence Agency campaign to assassinate or imprison alleged NLF figures or supporters. From 1968 until its end in the spring of 1972, Operation Phoenix killed as many as 20,000 persons and imprisoned 34,000 more.

"Rolling Thunder" bombing campaign ends

In November 1968, just before leaving office, Johnson called a halt to the bombing campaign "Operation Rolling Thunder." Over the past three-and-a-half years, this campaign cost more than 900 American aircraft, with more than 800 airmen dead or missing, and many others in captivity. More than 182,000 North Vietnamese civilians were killed by the bombing, as were 20,000 Chinese support personnel.

Approximately 14,000 Americans died in Vietnam in 1968.

MEDEVAC Helicopters in Vietnam continued in the role that began in the Korean War—evacuating wounded from the battlefield, as shown here: soldiers and medics load the injured into a chopper.

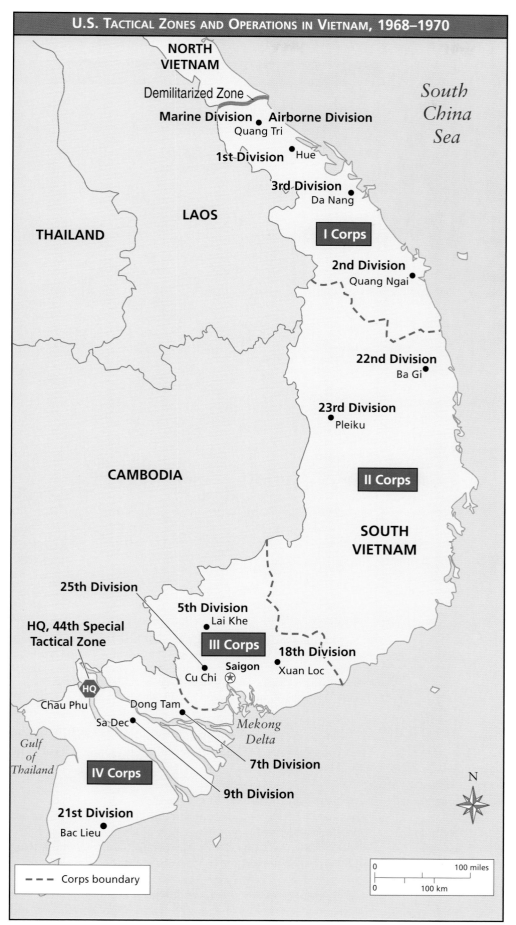

U.S. TACTICAL ZONES AND OPERATIONS IN VIETNAM, 1968–1970

NORTH VIETNAM

Demilitarized Zone

Marine Division Airborne Division
Quang Tri

1st Division Hue

3rd Division
Da Nang

LAOS

THAILAND

I Corps

2nd Division
Quang Ngai

22nd Division
Ba Gi

23rd Division
Pleiku

CAMBODIA

II Corps

SOUTH VIETNAM

South China Sea

25th Division

5th Division
Lai Khe

HQ, 44th Special
Tactical Zone

III Corps

18th Division
Xuan Loc

Saigon
Cu Chi

Chau Phu

Dong Tam

Sa Dec

Gulf
of
Thailand

IV Corps

Mekong
Delta

7th Division

9th Division

21st Division
Bac Lieu

N

– – – Corps boundary

0   100 miles
0   100 km

TACTICAL AREAS South Vietnam was divided up into "tactical zones" that were the responsibility of army corps. The most militarily active regions were near the DMZ and around Saigon and the swampy Mekong Delta.

OFFICERS IN THE FIELD Three officers are shown in battle dress: an army aviator, left, armed with a .45 pistol, carries his flier's helmet; center, a major of the 7th Cavalry, who is a Ranger, has mosquito repellent fixed to his helmet and carries an M2 carbine; right, a Special Forces lieutenant wears a distinctive beret.

Vietnam: Now Nixon's war

Taking office in January 1969, President Nixon wanted to negotiate a settlement while gradually withdrawing the half million Americans in Vietnam. At the same time, he wanted South Vietnam to survive as an independent republic. To pressure the North Vietnamese and NLF into making peace, Nixon approved the bombing of enemy bases in Cambodia. This "Operation Menu" defied Congressional restrictions on widening the war, but in the next four years more than a half million tons of bombs would be dropped on Cambodia.

A major PAVN and NLF offensive began in February, attacking American and ARVN bases and towns and cities in every part of South Vietnam. In May, a 10-day assault by American paratroopers and ARVN soldiers succeeded in driving PAVN units from Ap Bia Mountain. The Americans named it the "Battle of Hamburger Hill" because the bloody fighting was like sending men into a meat grinder. The enemy soon returned to their positions after the Americans and ARVN left. Now the United States public learned that the Vietnam War's American combat deaths exceeded the approximately 33,600 killed in the Korean War.

WITHDRAWAL, BOMBING, AND PEACE NEGOTIATIONS

DEATH OF STUDENTS
A Kent State student lies dead as others mourn after Ohio National Guardsmen opened fire on an anti-war demonstration in 1970.

In order to support the South Vietnamese government and ease enemy military pressure, Nixon intensified bombing campaigns that inflicted damage on the NLF and PAVN. Also, the ARVN was strengthened and trained to take on a greater burden of the fighting. This part of the war was known as the "Vietnamization" phase.

At the end of April 1970, Nixon mounted a secret, illegal invasion of Cambodia in which ARVN and American troops attacked NLF bases there in a two-month operation that captured vast enemy supply depots. The NLF and PAVN suffered more than 10,000 casualties, but most escaped and later regrouped to reestablish their Cambodian sanctuaries and supply routes.

Antiwar protests turn fatal

The bombing campaign and the Cambodian intervention at a time when Americans thought the war had been winding down brought about massive antiwar demonstrations in the United States. Ohio national guardsmen shot and killed four students during demonstrations at Kent State University, and students at Jackson State in Mississippi were also killed during antiwar protests.

By now, there were 400,000 American and allied forces fighting in South Vietnam, and the war dragged on.

As 1970 ended, morale suffered in American units. Many troops believed further combat was pointless since the United States military was obviously determined to leave Vietnam.

ARVN forces invade Laos

In February 1971, "Operation Lam Son" sent three ARVN divisions into Laos to attack enemy bases, but the result was a defeat, with more than 9,000 ARVN troops killed or wounded in a month of fighting.

That summer saw the end of "Operation Ranchhand," which had sprayed 11 million gallons of Agent Orange, defoliating and poisoning more than one-seventh of South Vietnam.

By early 1972, the number of American troops in Vietnam had fallen to 133,000. That March, a PAVN offensive captured key positions near the DMZ. By April, PAVN forces were trying for a major victory, attacking American and ARVN forces defending the city of Hue. There, determined fighting and counterattacks by South Vietnamese troops supported by American

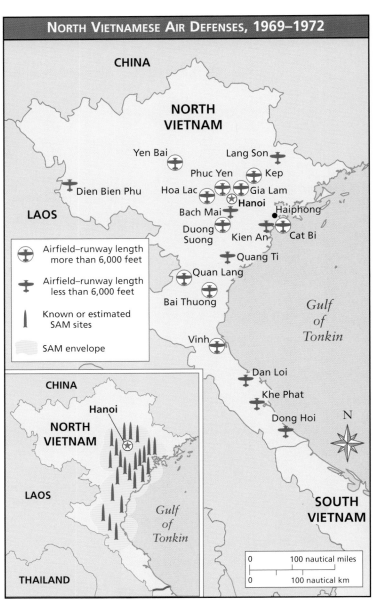

NORTH VIETNAMESE AIR DEFENSES, 1969–1972

Airfield–runway length more than 6,000 feet

Airfield–runway length less than 6,000 feet

Known or estimated SAM sites

SAM envelope

AIR DEFENSES North Vietnamese anti-aircraft sites took a heavy toll of American aircraft, with surface-to-air missiles (SAM) their deadliest weapon. Air force losses alone totaled 2,254 aircraft, with a final total of 3,322, including Army, Navy, and Marine aircraft.

B-52 bombings blunted the assault, but did not stop the offensive. In the following weeks the PAVN took Quang Tri City and Dong Ha.

New bombing: "Operation Linebacker"

Nixon ordered more heavy bombings of North Vietnam to prove the United States would not permit wholesale defeat of the ARVN. Known as "Operation Linebacker," this bombing campaign lasted from May to October and included mining Haiphong Harbor, North Vietnam's main port.

The number of Americans in Vietnam fell to 50,000.

Meanwhile, the Paris Peace Talks continued, but without results, breaking down in mid-December. To put pressure on the North Vietnamese, Nixon ordered a new bombing campaign, called "Operation Linebacker Two." For 12 days, the United

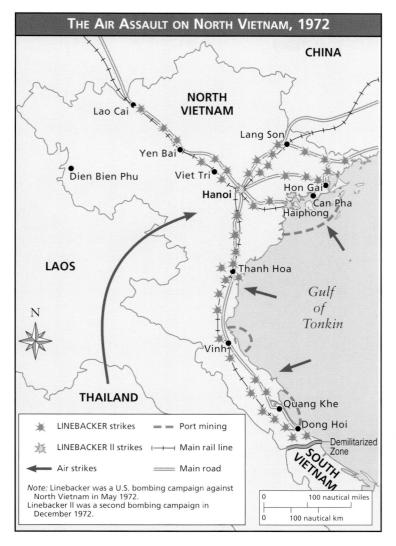

THE AIR ASSAULT ON NORTH VIETNAM, 1972

LINEBACKER strikes — Port mining
LINEBACKER II strikes — Main rail line
Air strikes — Main road

Note: Linebacker was a U.S. bombing campaign against North Vietnam in May 1972. Linebacker II was a second bombing campaign in December 1972.

0 — 100 nautical miles
0 — 100 nautical km

MAJOR AIR CAMPAIGNS The two heaviest United States bombing campaigns of North Vietnam were Linebacker I and II, launched in 1972, as the war wound down. The most severe American aircraft losses were during these air campaigns, which struck at military installations the length and breadth of North Vietnam.

WAR MEMORIAL The names of more than 58,000 Americans killed in the Vietnam War are engraved on the war memorial, a polished granite wall in Washington, D.C.

States unleashed the most massive bombing campaign since World War II, dropping more than 20,000 tons of bombs. Known as the "Christmas Bombing," this devastating assault shattered North Vietnam's air defenses and fighter force. The campaign cost 26 American aircraft and 93 airmen killed, captured or missing. North Vietnam estimated its losses as high as 1,600 dead. Now, Hanoi was persuaded to accept the Paris Peace Agreement. Signed on January 27, 1973, the agreement ended hostilities between the United States and the Democratic Republic of Vietnam.

Communists win Vietnamese Civil War

Warfare between the ARVN and the NLF and PAVN continued for two more years, ending on April 30, 1975, with the fall of Saigon and the South Vietnamese government—which had expected American assistance against North Vietnamese aggression but did not get it. This closed the Second Indochina War, known in the United States as the Vietnam War.

The conflict cost more than 58,000 American lives, with another 153,329 seriously wounded. ARVN forces lost 110,300 killed and 400,000 wounded. Hanoi estimated 1.1 million PAVN and NLF fighters killed and 600,000 wounded from 1954-1975. Civilian deaths were approximately 2 million.

The American defeat in Southeast Asia shook the nation's self-confidence. For decades to come, the role of the United States as policeman of the world would remain under a cloud of uncertainty and self-doubt.

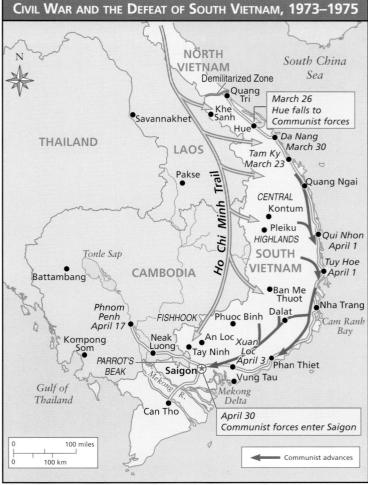

CIVIL WAR AND THE DEFEAT OF SOUTH VIETNAM, 1973–1975

March 26
Hue falls to Communist forces

April 30
Communist forces enter Saigon

Communist advances

0 — 100 miles
0 — 100 km

VIETNAM CIVIL WAR Saigon had more than a million men under arms, facing 230,000 Communists, but the ARVN had to defend territory while their enemy attacked at will. Without American air support, the Saigon government collapsed on April 30, 1975.

24: THE DANGEROUS WORLD OF THE COLD WAR

After World War II, antagonism developed between the democracies of the "Free World"—led by the United States, the British Commonwealth, and France—and the Communist nations behind the "Iron Curtain"—led by the Soviet Union and the People's Republic of China. Their opposing ideologies and competing national self-interests brought about the Cold War, which threatened to collapse into nuclear conflagration if it turned into a "hot war" like World War II.

The Berlin Airlift

The Soviet Union established Communist-led puppet governments in the Eastern European countries it occupied after the war. This included East Germany, where Berlin itself was partitioned into zones of control for the Soviets, Americans, French, and British. In June 1948 the Soviets established a land blockade of the three Western zones in order to force the others to withdraw and leave Berlin to East Germany. In response, President Truman set an airlift in motion, and the United States and its allies flew in supplies for the military as well as for civilians in defiance of the blockade. This "Berlin Airlift," as it was termed, continued until the land blockade was ended in May 1949.

In this year, a dozen nations of the West, led by the United States, founded the North Atlantic Treaty Organization (NATO) for mutual defense. In 1955, a similar alliance, known as the Warsaw Treaty Organization, or Warsaw Pact, was formed by the Communist nations of Europe. The balance of power between East and West

COLD WAR CRISIS West Berliners watch the flight of an American DC-3 transport during the Berlin Airlift that kept the city supplied.

A WORLD DIVIDED The two military antagonists of the Cold War were the NATO alliance and the Communist Warsaw Pact, each with the nuclear ability to annihilate the other.

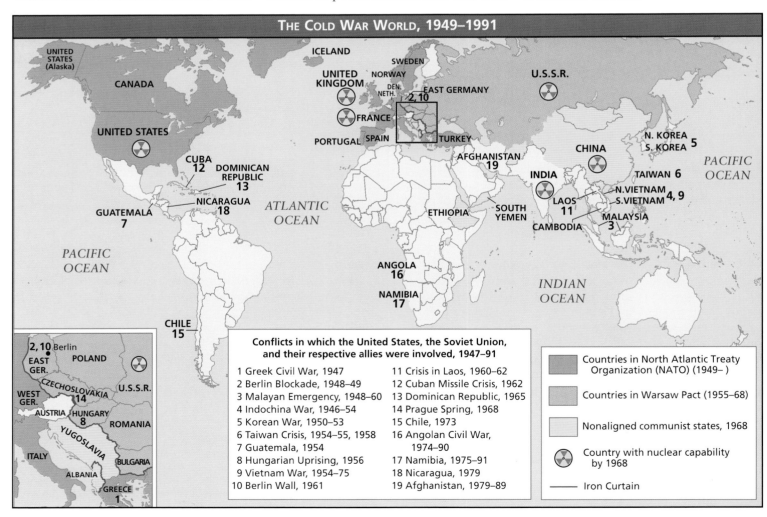

THE COLD WAR WORLD, 1949–1991

Conflicts in which the United States, the Soviet Union, and their respective allies were involved, 1947–91

1 Greek Civil War, 1947
2 Berlin Blockade, 1948–49
3 Malayan Emergency, 1948–60
4 Indochina War, 1946–54
5 Korean War, 1950–53
6 Taiwan Crisis, 1954–55, 1958
7 Guatemala, 1954
8 Hungarian Uprising, 1956
9 Vietnam War, 1954–75
10 Berlin Wall, 1961
11 Crisis in Laos, 1960–62
12 Cuban Missile Crisis, 1962
13 Dominican Republic, 1965
14 Prague Spring, 1968
15 Chile, 1973
16 Angolan Civil War, 1974–90
17 Namibia, 1975–91
18 Nicaragua, 1979
19 Afghanistan, 1979–89

Countries in North Atlantic Treaty Organization (NATO) (1949–)

Countries in Warsaw Pact (1955–68)

Nonaligned communist states, 1968

Country with nuclear capability by 1968

Iron Curtain

"We must guard against the acquisition of unwarranted influence . . . by the military-industrial complex. . . . We must never let the weight of this combination endanger our liberties. . . ."

— PRESIDENT EISENHOWER, IN HIS 1961 FAREWELL ADDRESS

hinged on the fact that each possessed nuclear weapons, which were a deterrent to waging all-out war. The ensuing Cold War struggle was for domination of the emerging and developing nations that were rich in natural resources and hungry for modernization and self-determination.

Communist China's victory

The Chinese Civil War between Mao Zedong's Communists and Chiang Kai Shek's Nationalists ended with Communist victory in 1949, creating the People's Republic of China. The United States had aided the defeated Nationalists, who evacuated to the island of Formosa, establishing the Republic of China. President Truman ordered the American military, specifically the Seventh Fleet, to prevent the Communists from attacking Formosa, which later became known as Taiwan. At the same time, the Americans opposed any actions by the Nationalists against the mainland that might result in a Communist attack on Taiwan.

The Middle East

By 1948, the state of Israel was founded after a fierce Jewish guerrilla insurgency against the British managing the protectorate of Palestine, from which Israel sprang. With the developed world's growing need for the Middle East's vast oil reserves, this region became a tinder box, its peoples manipulated by the Cold War adversaries. Each side armed and financed its own favored leaders and governments. For example, the United States backed Israel against its Arab neighbors, and the Soviets aided Egypt, an early opponent of Israel.

DIVIDED GERMANY Defeat in World War II reduced German territory even further than did the outcome of World War I. Germany was divided into occupation zones, with the Soviet zone becoming East Germany, a separate country from the three zones of West Germany.

One Middle Eastern arena of contention was Iran, where British and American oil interests appeared likely to be nationalized early in the 1950s. The American Central Intelligence Agency (CIA) helped overthrow the elected Iranian government in 1953, supporting Reza Shah Pahlevi, who established a repressive regime that was propped up for 25 years by United States military and financial aid. Support of the shah and Israel intensified anti-American feelings in the Middle East.

The Suez Crisis and Lebanon

The United States won praise from the Arab world in 1956 when President Eisenhower intervened diplomatically to compel Britain, France, and Israel to withdraw from Egypt, which they had invaded to prevent nationalization of the strategic Suez Canal.

Then in 1958, Marines landed in Lebanon to help protect against a coup. The United States and President Eisenhower helped bring about a truce between warring Lebanese Christians and Muslims, which made America appear to many as the world's peace keeper.

In that same year, Iraqi general Abdul Karim Kassem led a military revolt that assassinated the king, overthrew the monarchy, and killed the prime minister. In 1963, the CIA helped a subsequent coup overthrow Kassem, after an unsuccessful attempt to assassinate him. This coup led to the Ba'ath Party coming to power, establishing a brutal, repressive government to rule fractious Iraq, a nation composed of various national and religious factions, each seeking self-determination. A stable Iraq was essential for the country's oil to flow dependably to the developed countries.

STAGE OF CONFRONTATION Europe's division between NATO and Warsaw Pact nations established the front line of the Cold War in the continent's heart, from the Arctic to the Black Sea.

COUPS, INTERVENTIONS, AND SECRET SUBVERSION

CUBA'S RULER Since the 1959 revolution, President Fidel Castro stubbornly resisted United States influence in the Caribbean. At first closely aligned with the Soviets, Castro's government lost crucial economic and military support with the fall of Communism and the end of the Cold War.

Most American interventions in Latin America since the 19th Century had supported American business interests. In the 1930s, President Franklin D. Roosevelt proclaimed a "Good Neighbor Policy" toward Latin America and the Caribbean, meaning the United States would not forcibly intervene against governments in the region. With the advent of the Cold War, however, the "Good Neighbor Policy" ended. American interests stimulated a new era of interventions, although these were carried out in the name of fighting Communism.

U.S. interests in Latin America

In 1950, United States troops landed in Puerto Rico to crush a rebellion that sought independence from American rule. By 1954, the Central American country of Guatemala had seen its share of subversion and interventions when the CIA sponsored an invasion by exiles to prevent the nationalization of property belonging to American firms. United States bombers based in Nicaragua supported the insurrection, which destabilized the elected Guatemalan government and cleared the way for an authoritarian regime that favored American interests.

Crisis with Castro's Cuba

The 1959 Cuban Revolution, led by Fidel Castro, turned out to be Communist, and Cuba established close ties with the Soviet Union. Thousands of anti-Castro Cubans fled the country, most migrating to the United States as refugees. President John F. Kennedy decided to help Cuban exiles remove Castro from power, and in April 1961 a CIA-trained force of 1,300 exiles landed at the Bay of Pigs on Cuba's southern coast. Backed by an American naval task force, the rebels sought to cause an uprising against Castro, but they were overwhelmed by 20,000 militia, who defeated them on the shore.

This persuaded Castro to strengthen his Soviet alliance. Within a year, 40,000 Soviet troops and advisors were on the island. Soviet premier Nikita Krushchev and President Kennedy went head-to-head in mid-1962 over the Soviet installation of nuclear missiles on Cuba. The United States Navy stopped Soviet vessels from reaching Cuban ports, sparking Krushchev's outrage. After delicate negotiations, Krushchev and Kennedy came to terms: the Soviets withdrew their missiles, and the Americans promised not to invade Cuba. The "Cuban Missile Crisis" was the closest the world has ever come to nuclear war.

Assassination in Zaire

In 1960, the Eisenhower government opposed Patrice Lumumba, the elected prime minister of the newly independent former Belgian Congo. Considered a Communist, Lumumba was forced from office by Congo army chief of staff, Mobutu Sese Seko, and later assassinated. For more than 30 years, dictator Mobutu ruled the country, which he renamed Zaire. A declared anti-Communist, Mobutu had close connections with the CIA and profited from American military and financial aid.

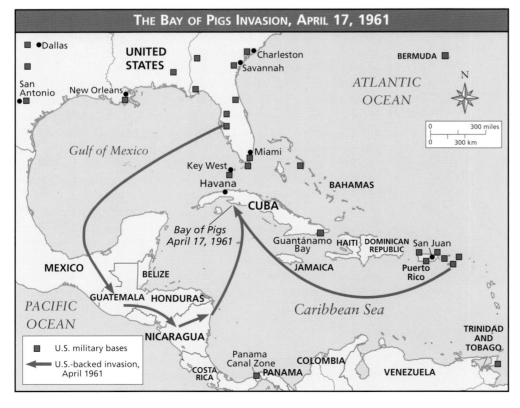

THE BAY OF PIGS INVASION, APRIL 17, 1961

Dallas
UNITED STATES
San Antonio
New Orleans
Charleston
Savannah
BERMUDA
ATLANTIC OCEAN
N
Gulf of Mexico
Miami
Key West
Havana
CUBA
BAHAMAS
Bay of Pigs April 17, 1961
Guantánamo Bay
HAITI
DOMINICAN REPUBLIC
San Juan
MEXICO
BELIZE
JAMAICA
Puerto Rico
GUATEMALA HONDURAS
PACIFIC OCEAN
Caribbean Sea
NICARAGUA
TRINIDAD AND TOBAGO
Panama Canal Zone
COSTA RICA
PANAMA
COLOMBIA
VENEZUELA

0   300 miles
0   300 km

■ U.S. military bases
◄— U.S.-backed invasion, April 1961

BAY OF PIGS INVASION This abortive assault opened with bombing by anti-Castro Cuban pilots flying American planes. Castro's air force was key to victory, which cost 3,650 Cuban casualties and 1,300 exile casualties, including 1,100 captured.

HIGH-FLYING SURVEILLANCE American U-2 "spy planes" conducted photographic reconnaissance from high altitudes, in violation of Communist air space. One was shot down over Russia in May 1960 and its pilot put on public trial. He was later exchanged for a Soviet spy.

Southeast Asia: Philippines, Thailand, and Indonesia

In the mid-Fifties, the United States military helped the Philippines defeat the Huk insurgency, which rose from among its Muslims. The Huks were alleged to have Communist leanings, but their anti-government stance harked back to the Moro wars of the early 20th Century.

The Sixties saw other American interventions in this region, which was wracked by troubles often related to the Vietnam War. Opposing a Communist threat, a Marine expeditionary force landed in Thailand in May 1962. More than 5,000 Marines remained in the country for two months before being withdrawn.

The CIA helped the Indonesian government prevent a potential coup in 1965. Subsequently, a civil war broke out, killing at least a million people. Among the leading anti-Communist fighters were conservative Muslim militias, who slaughtered people by the hundreds of thousands. The United States embassy provided the names of 5,000 alleged Communists, who were summarily killed.

Indonesian military atrocities continued for years under the rule of President Suharto. In 1975, Indonesia invaded the independent island of East Timor, using American-supplied arms for this aggression and thereby breaking American laws. As a key American ally in the region, Indonesia was supported in its annexation of East Timor. Over the next 10 years, Suharto's forces killed 200,000 of the 600-700,000 population of East Timor.

"We've been eyeball to eyeball, and the other fellow just blinked."

—SECRETARY OF STATE DEAN RUSK, OCTOBER 24, 1961, LEARNING THAT SOVIET SHIPS WOULD NOT CHALLENGE THE BLOCKADE OF CUBA

CARRIER ON BLOCKADE DUTY With President Kennedy demanding immediate removal of Soviet missiles from Cuba, the USN stationed a powerful fleet throughout the Caribbean and western Atlantic to "quarantine" Cuba and force Soviet vessels to turn back.

THE CUBAN MISSILE CRISIS, OCTOBER 1962

- ■ U.S. military bases
- ●●●● U.S. naval blockade, October 1962
- ▲ Soviet missile sites, 1962
- ← Cuba-bound Soviet ships, 1962

BLOCKADE OF CUBA In October 1962, U-2 photographs revealed intermediate-range Soviet missiles in Cuba. The USN blockaded the island to keep additional missiles out, and after a tense standoff a compromise was reached.

MAKING AND BREAKING LATIN AMERICAN GOVERNMENTS

A number of strongmen rose to power in Latin America during the Cold War. In the Fifties, dictators took over Panama (1951), Colombia (1953), Guatemala and Paraguay (1954), and Cuba (1959). Through the Sixties, military coups deposed presidents of El Salvador (1960), Ecuador (1961), Honduras (1963), Brazil and Bolivia (1964), and Peru (1968).

Strife and turmoil in Hispaniola

A military coup deposed the Dominican Republic's elected president, Juan Bosch, in 1963. When an insurrection to restore Bosch was accused of being under Communist influence, more than 21,000 American troops arrived in 1965 to support the government. Elections in 1966 brought Joaquin Balaguer in as president, ending the troubles.

In Haiti, which shares the island of Hispaniola with the Dominican Republic, the Duvalier family ruled despotically for 30 years with close American support. Haiti suffered a long-running reign of terror by the Duvalier secret police, but the government's anti-Communist stance was enough to warrant American backing.

CIA overthrows Chile's Allende

In 1973, America collaborated in the overthrow of Chile's elected president, Salvador Allende, a Marxist. The CIA had tried unsuccessfully to sabotage Allende's election in 1970, and for the next three years worked to destabilize his government. In September 1973, a junta made up of top Chilean generals overthrew Allende in a violent coup that ended with his death. American Secretary of State Henry Kissinger was a key player in the plot to remove Allende and install junta leader, General Augusto Pinochet, as president. The junta-led government executed at least 3,000 persons, and many others disappeared.

Nicaragua: Sandinistas and Contras

Nicaragua had its own family dictatorship, the Somozas, who were opposed by revolutionaries calling themselves "Sandinistas," after a hero killed decades earlier by the military. In 1978, the Sandinistas drove out the Somoza regime.

From 1981 to 1990, the CIA directed and financed anti-Sandinista forces called Contras, mainly former military men from the Somoza regime. CIA aircraft even dropped mines in Nicaraguan harbors to endanger shipping and thereby damage the

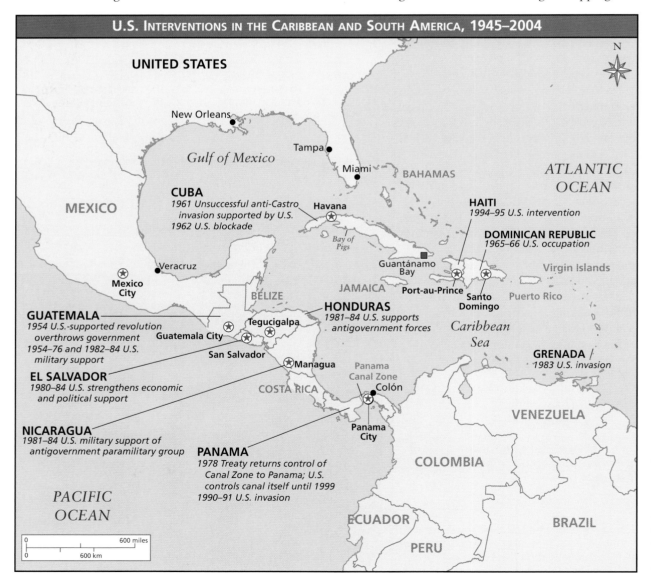

U.S. INTERVENTIONS IN THE CARIBBEAN AND SOUTH AMERICA, 1945–2004

N

UNITED STATES

New Orleans

Gulf of Mexico

Tampa

Miami

BAHAMAS

ATLANTIC OCEAN

CUBA
1961 Unsuccessful anti-Castro invasion supported by U.S.
1962 U.S. blockade

Havana

MEXICO

Veracruz

Bay of Pigs

HAITI
1994–95 U.S. intervention

DOMINICAN REPUBLIC
1965–66 U.S. occupation

Guantánamo Bay

Virgin Islands

Mexico City

BELIZE

JAMAICA

Port-au-Prince

Santo Domingo

Puerto Rico

GUATEMALA
1954 U.S.-supported revolution overthrows government
1954–76 and 1982–84 U.S. military support

Guatemala City

Tegucigalpa

HONDURAS
1981–84 U.S. supports antigovernment forces

Caribbean Sea

San Salvador

GRENADA
1983 U.S. invasion

EL SALVADOR
1980–84 U.S. strengthens economic and political support

Managua

Panama Canal Zone

COSTA RICA

Colón

VENEZUELA

NICARAGUA
1981–84 U.S. military support of antigovernment paramilitary group

Panama City

PANAMA
1978 Treaty returns control of Canal Zone to Panama; U.S. controls canal itself until 1999
1990–91 U.S. invasion

COLOMBIA

PACIFIC OCEAN

ECUADOR

BRAZIL

PERU

0   600 miles
0   600 km

"The United States has both the right, and . . . duty to protect and defend the canal under Article 4 of the Panama Canal Treaty."

—SECRETARY OF STATE JAMES A. BAKER, DECEMBER 20, 1989, JUSTIFYING THE INVASION OF PANAMA

SPHERE OF INFLUENCE
United States economic and political interests in the Caribbean and Central America in the second half of the 20th Century were backed up by military interventions. In some cases, secret CIA operations affected events but went unpublicized for years.

ATTACK BY AIR, SEA, AND LAND
On December 20, 1989, a coordinated assault by every branch of the American military attacked 27 targets in Panama, taking control of the country in four days. Strongman Noriega surrendered a few days later.

Sandinista government. During the Ronald Reagan presidency, the Contras were supported with secret United States programs that raised funds by illegal methods, including selling arms to Iran. In 1988, an accord reached by the presidents of Honduras, Costa Rica, El Salvador, and Guatemala brokered an end to the Nicaraguan war and dissolved the Contras.

El Salvador's civil war
In 1981, unrest and guerrilla offensives in El Salvador resulted in United States military advisors training government forces in counterinsurgency. The American military and the CIA played an active, though secret, role in the conflict, with about 20 Americans killed or wounded in helicopter and plane crashes while flying missions over combat areas. This civil war raged until a cease-fire was negotiated in 1992. More than 75,000 civilians died.

Invading tiny Grenada
In October 1983, Reagan sent troops to the tiny Caribbean island of Grenada. Four years earlier, this country of 110,000 had undergone a revolution led by Prime Minister Maurice Bishop. Grenada eventually invited Cuban workers and technicians to help build an airfield and so promote tourism. The United States considered Bishop's government to be Communist.

In mid-October 1983, a coup overthrew and killed Bishop, and civil conflict developed. The United States invaded to keep the peace and establish a stable government. The cost was 135 Americans killed and wounded, some 400 Grenadian

casualties, and 84 Cubans, mainly construction workers.

The arrest of Panama's Noriega
Although the United States had previously supported Panamanian military dictator General Manuel Noriega, that all changed in May 1989, when Noriega disregarded the results of an election. President George H.W. Bush sent more than 22,000 troops against him, backed by the air force. After several days of fighting, more than 500 Panamanian soldiers had been killed, 3,000 or more wounded. Twenty-three Americans died, and 324 were wounded. Noriega was arrested, accused of drug trafficking, and brought to the United States, where he was tried and sentenced to 40 years in prison.

U.S. INVASION OF PANAMA, 1989–1990

Caribbean Sea
Coco Solo Naval Station
Ft. Espinar
Colón
Madden Lake
Gatun Locks
Madden Dam
Miraflores Locks
Pacora R.
El Renacer Prison
Tocumen
Cerro Tigre
Gamboa
Pacora River Bridge
Gatun Lake
Pedro Miguel Locks
Torrijos
Panamá Viejo
Pantilla
Panama City
Arraijan Tank Farm
Balboa
Rio Hato 42 miles
PACIFIC OCEAN

Legend:
- ✳ Major point of attack
- **U.S. Task Forces**
- Airborne invasion
- ← Infantry invasion route
- ⇐ Airborne invasion route
- ■ U.S. military bases
- --- Panama Canal Zone
- = Panama Canal

0 — 10 miles
0 — 10 km

N

One of the important United States military efforts after the Cold War ended was the so-called "War on Drugs," which saw billions of American dollars and hundreds of military advisors sent to South American countries where drug traffickers, revolutionaries, and governments fought for supremacy.

The United States aided the governments against the revolutionaries and drug lords. One major push was the 1989 "Andean Initiative" of President George H.W. Bush, who offered military and law-enforcement assistance to the Andes Mountain nations of Colombia, Bolivia, and Peru. The main goal was to combat drug production and distribution, and soon there were up to 100 American military advisers in Colombia. Also, at least seven Special Forces teams trained troops in the three countries in counterinsurgency tactics.

The War on Drugs continued, with marginal success at drug interdiction, into the 21st Century.

INTO ACTION
American Marines rush from a fighting vehicle and deploy for battle during the 1989 invasion of Panama.

AFTER THE VIETNAM WAR: NEW CRISES IN THE MIDEAST

The Vietnamese Civil War closed with the fall of Saigon in April 1975, and the American embassy was hurriedly evacuated. The image of diplomats, Marines, and Vietnamese staff fleeing in helicopters was yet another embarrassment to the United States. Communist triumphs continued, as the Khmer Rouge took power in Cambodia, and the Pathet Lao guerrillas in Laos were defeating that government.

In May, the merchant ship SS *Mayaguez,* which had an American crew, was in international waters en route from Hong Kong to Thailand when a Cambodian patrol boat captured it. President Gerald R. Ford sent Marines to retake the ship in a battle that cost the lives of 15 American servicemen, with 50 wounded, and three missing. The engagement occurred just as the Cambodians were releasing the crewmen.

The Iran Hostage Crisis

After the shah took charge in 1951, Iran was a staunch American ally in the Middle East, but a revolutionary movement opposed this repressive regime. In January 1979, nationalists and Muslim fundamentalists overthrew the shah, who fled and later entered the United States for medical treatment.

Anti-American feelings ran high in Teheran, Iran's capital, where radicals demanded the return of the shah but were refused. In November, the United States embassy there was taken over, with 52 Americans made hostages. Although President Jimmy Carter attempted to reach a nonviolent settlement and prevent harm to the hostages, the crisis dragged on for months. In April 1980, Carter ordered a rescue attempt, known as "Operation Eagle Claw," involving Army Rangers and the antiterrorist strike unit Delta Force. The operation was complicated. Depending on H-53 heavy helicopters, it required the landing and takeoff of large transport aircraft, and there was a tricky rendezvous and refueling in mid-desert at a site code-named "Desert One." From Desert One, Delta Force was to rescue the hostages while Rangers captured an airfield, where a C-141 would land to evacuate the Americans. The plan hinged on sound machines.

On April 24, the strike force met at the desert rendezvous, but by then three helicopters had failed mechanically, and the operation was called off. During the withdrawal, a helicopter collided with a transport plane, killing eight men. The mission's failure dented American prestige and led to Carter's losing the presidential election later that year. The hostages were finally released, after 444 days of confinement, on the day Ronald Reagan was inaugurated.

By then, Iran was under attack from Iraq, beginning the decade-long Iran-Iraq War, also known then as the Gulf War. This conflict cost one million lives. The United States supported the aggressor, Iraq, led by Ba'ath Party dictator Saddam Hussein. America helped Iraq acquire weaponry of all kinds, including the ingredients for poison gas, and offered aerial reconnaissance assistance. The war ended in 1988, after United Nations mediation, with little change in Iran-Iraq borders.

Lebanese civil war

Bloodshed between Christians and Muslims left Lebanon in disarray by June 1982, when Israel invaded to attack

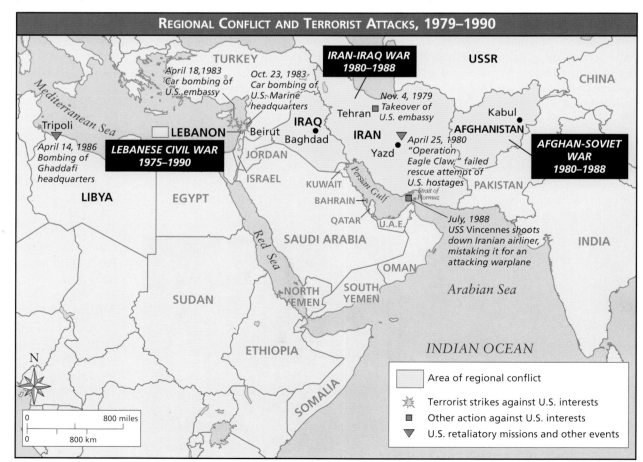

THE VOLATILE MIDDLE EAST
As conflict escalated in the Middle East, the United States increased its involvement, either through direct action or by lending aid to its allies in the region.

A REGION IN UPHEAVAL, 1973–1989

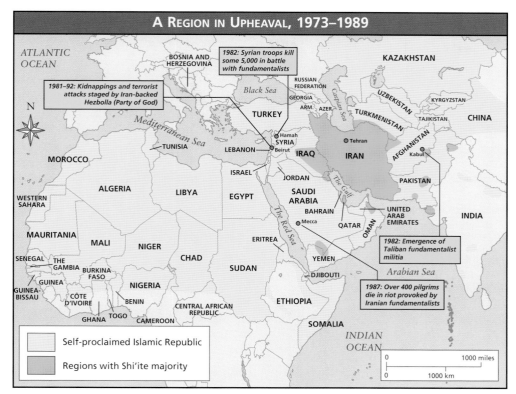

1981–92: Kidnappings and terrorist attacks staged by Iran-backed Hezbolla (Party of God)

1982: Syrian troops kill some 5,000 in battle with fundamentalists

1982: Emergence of Taliban fundamentalist militia

1987: Over 400 pilgrims die in riot provoked by Iranian fundamentalists

Self-proclaimed Islamic Republic

Regions with Shi'ite majority

0   1000 miles

0   1000 km

MIDDLE EAST HOT SPOTS The Persian Gulf is at the heart of a region that has seen much turmoil. With the developed nations hungry for its oil reserves—the world's largest—the Middle East has been the object of various international efforts to win its control.

Palestinian refugee camps that housed anti-Israel guerrillas. Israel also engaged Syrian military positions in Lebanon.

The United States sent 1,200 Marines in September to join an international peacekeeping force. That October, a suicide bomber blew up a truck full of explosives at the Marine barracks in Beirut, killing 241 men. Reagan soon withdrew the troops from Lebanon.

Air combat and tragedy at sea

The United States was at odds for decades with Libyan dictator Muammar Ghaddafi, who sponsored anti-American terrorism, especially in Europe, where American troops were based. On several occasions during the 1980s, Libyan jets were shot down after challenging American warplanes flying near the Libyan coast. In April 1986, the United States bombed Libya, targeting Ghaddafi, who escaped injury, although members of his family were killed. In 1988, a Libyan-planted bomb blew up an American airliner over Scotland, killing all on board.

In July that year, an Iranian airliner was shot down over the Strait of Hormuz by the USS *Vincennes*, which mistook it for an attacking warplane. All aboard died.

"We have vital interests in Lebanon, and our actions in Lebanon are in the cause of world peace."

—PRESIDENT REAGAN, OCTOBER 23, 1983, ADDRESSING THE NATION AFTER THE MARINE BARRACKS IN BEIRUT WAS BLOWN UP

OBSERVATION POST Overlooking the countryside, United States Marines guard against resumption of civil war between Christians and Muslims in Lebanon.

THE AFGHAN-SOVIET WAR

Throughout the 1970s and 1980s, the United States trained, armed, and financed Afghani Mujahedin—guerrillas fighting the Soviet-sponsored national government. This government was trying to modernize its backward people, improve education and social conditions, and give women equal rights. Such efforts were opposed by the Mujahedin, who were mostly conservative, fundamentalist Muslims. The United States opposed the government because it was Communist.

CIA subversion helped undermine the Afghan government, which was losing the conflict by 1979, when the Soviets invaded to fight the Mujahedin. This began the Afghan-Soviet War, in which the Soviets lost heavily and then withdrew in 1989, defeated. By then, Afghanistan had lost more than a million dead and three million wounded, and five million were refugees.

In the early 1990s, victorious Mujahedin warlords started a civil war for control of the country. The conflict virtually ended when the Taliban party came to power in the mid-Nineties, governing Afghanistan with the harsh rule of extreme fundamentalist Muslim doctrine.

ARTILLERY ATTACK An Afghan Mujahedin fighter prepares to fire artillery against government forces in the city of Jalalabad in 1986.

Cold War in the Nuclear Age

Developments in nuclear warheads and guided missiles proceeded rapidly in the 1950s. The Soviet Union acquired its own atomic weapons, and in the nuclear arms race both sides brought forth ever more powerful devices.

Jet aircraft made their first major wartime appearance during the Korean War, in which helicopters were first used extensively. Artillery continued to improve, with radar and electronics spurring advances in targeting.

In 1954, the United States successfully tested a hydrogen bomb. The advent of intercontinental ballistic missiles made nowhere in the world safe from nuclear attack. Soon, nuclear-powered submarines and surface warships also carried guided missiles. In 1963 the North American early warning radar system and the North American Air Defense Command (NORAD) employed satellite communications and the most advanced aircraft and weaponry. The Vietnam War saw the advent of surface-to-air anti-aircraft missiles. Helicopters, jet aircraft, rocketry, and computer technology came into their own in these decades.

The digital revolution of the 1980s produced Precision Guided Munitions (PGM)—cruise missiles and "smart" bombs—offering unprecedented accuracy. PGM could be delivered from aircraft, from launchers on land or from surface warships and submarines.

Deadly shoulder-fired missiles made the infantryman a threat to armor and helicopters, and rocket-propelled grenades and wire-guided antitank missiles further enhanced the firepower of ground forces. In response, new composite armor systems were developed. Using this armor, the M1 Abrams main battle tank became nearly invulnerable on the battlefield.

Infantry—now often "mounted" in armored fighting vehicles—benefitted from fully-automatic assault rifles, more effective field communications, and dramatically improved personal equipment and battlefield medical care.

B-52 BOMBING VIETNAM Introduced in the mid-1950s, the B-52 long-range heavy bomber can devastate wide areas of troop concentrations, fixed installations, and fortified bunkers. After redesigns and refits, many of the 744 B-52s that were built—the last delivered in 1962—continued in service into the 21st Century. This aircraft carries cruise missiles as well as conventional or nuclear bombs.

BALLISTIC-MISSILE SUBMARINE In the 1960s, the USN launched 41 nuclear-powered submarines, nicknamed "boomers" and armed with 16 nuclear-tipped Polaris missiles that could be launched from under water. By 1972, boomers carried more accurate Poseidon missiles. In the late 1970s, the first of 18 Ohio-class submarines was built, shown here, armed with up to 24 Trident I, and later Trident II, missiles.

NAVAL FORCES IN THE CUBAN MISSILE CRISIS In fall of 1962 President John F. Kennedy ordered a naval blockade of Cuba to prevent Soviet nuclear missiles from being installed there. The USN painting below shows an American destroyer, naval helicopter, and patrol plane taking part in the sea blockade of Cuba.

ICBM TEST LAUNCH A Minuteman III Intercontinental Ballistic Missile (ICBM) takes off from a launching pad at Vandenberg Air Force Base in California in the mid-1980s.

STANDARD-ISSUE RIFLE The M16 assault rifle was the basic firearm for United States forces in Vietnam. Designed in 1953, the M16 was not as accurate as earlier military rifles, but its rapid rate of fire and lightness made it an excellent infantry weapon.

"TOW" MISSILE Marines fire a Tube-launched, Optically tracked, Wire-guided (TOW) anti-armor missile during training exercises at Fort Pickett, Virginia. The TOW missile is guided by wires that transmit in-flight corrections from the launcher to the missile.

GATLING GUN Designed on the 1860 model, with six revolving barrels driven electrically or hydraulically, this "mini-gun" fired 2,000 rounds a minute. In Vietnam, where it was carried by helicopters and fixed-wing aircraft, the Gatling's withering barrage earned the AC-130 armed gunship the name "Puff the Magic Dragon."

AIR ASSAULT CHOPPERS Troops of the 1st Air Cavalry Division (Airmobile) are carried on UH-1 "Huey" helicopters into Vietnam's Bong Song District during operations in early 1966.

DOMINICAN CIVIL WAR Paratroopers of the 82nd Airborne search a suspect during the 1965 insurrection against the Dominican Republic's military government. These paratroopers, one carrying a grenade launcher, were among 21,000 Americans who landed to back the Dominican military.

LAND OF OIL AND CONFLICT Iraq's oil distribution infrastructure is seen on a CIA map of this mostly desert region, showing pipelines and major oil fields. Especially productive oil deposits lie in the Kurdish-populated North and the Shia-Arab Southeast.

216

PART EIGHT

A Lone Superpower

THE SOVIET UNION BEGAN TO BREAK UP in the late 1980s, its demise hurried along by defeat in the Afghan-Soviet War (1979–1989). The Cold War was ending, leaving the United States as the world's only superpower, but in the 1990s it took conventional armies, not nuclear weapons, to safeguard the world. When Saddam Hussein's Iraq invaded Kuwait in 1990, the United States led a United Nations coalition to defeat Iraq in a matter of months. There were other conflicts, however, such as strife in Somalia, which cost American lives and revealed the need for clearly defined objectives in an intervention. Yet another civil war broke out in crumbling Yugoslavia, where a fierce struggle involved ethnic cleansing and genocide. American-led air strikes and ground troops stopped the killing and prepared the way for peace talks.

America became a target on February 26, 1993, when Islamist terrorists exploded a bomb under New York's World Trade Center, attempting to bring it down. Several persons died and 1,000 were injured, but the building still stood.

Then came September 11, 2001, when four domestic airliners were hijacked, and two slammed into the World Trade Center's Twin Towers, which collapsed. The third plane hit the Pentagon, and the fourth crashed in a Pennsylvania field. Approximately 3,000 persons died.

President George W. Bush called for a worldwide "War on Terror," and immediately attacked Afghanistan, which harbored Islamist terrorists. Then in March 2003, the United States and Great Britain led an invasion of Iraq, accusing Saddam of collaborating with terrorists and of possessing weapons of mass destruction. This Third Gulf War was over quickly, but it left the United States occupying a shattered Iraq that was in danger of erupting in civil war.

M1A1 tank crossing pontoon bridge.

25: POST COLD WAR AND ANTI-TERRORISM

n the spring of 1991, the Warsaw Pact nations decided to dissolve, ending the Cold War alliance that counterbalanced the West's NATO. The collapse of the Soviet Union and its satellite states by the early 1990s seemed to offer a new world order of peace and stability, without the ever-present danger of nuclear war.

Neither peace nor stability were to reign, however, as new tensions developed from a coalescing of forces with anti-Western, anti-modern ideas. These forces ranged from anti-Soviet Muslims in Afghanistan and Chechnya to brutal Somali war lords and to the Kurds seeking autonomy in Iraq and Turkey. Terrorism grew, appearing in the eyes of developed countries to be almost monolithic. Kashmir separatists bombing targets in India were lumped with Basque assassins fighting Spanish rule and with Palestinian suicide bombers terrorizing Israel. Instead of the enemy being capitalism or communism, it became terrorism.

Attack on the World Trade Center

America saw its first major terror attack in 1993, when explosives were set in a failed attempt by Islamist terrorists to destroy New York City's World Trade Center. Six died and 1,000 more were wounded. Several Islamist extremists were convicted for the bombing. They had committed this act of terror to force the United States to change its policies in the Middle East, including compelling Israel to accept Palestinian rights.

In 1995 and 1996, two bombings in Saudi Arabia killed 26 Americans. In 1998, Islamic extremists bombed the United States embassies in Kenya and Tanzania, killing 12 Americans

"Americans will likely die on American soil, possibly in large numbers [as the result of terrorist attacks]."

—SENATORS GARY HART AND WARREN RUDMAN, IN A SEPTEMBER 1999 REPORT FROM THE UNITED STATES COMMISSION ON NATIONAL SECURITY

NEW YORK'S SKYLINE Lower Manhattan is dominated by the Twin Towers of the World Trade Center, heart of international finance and a terrorist target in 1993. A bomb in a van parked in the WTC was intended, but failed, to blow up structural members and cause a collapse.

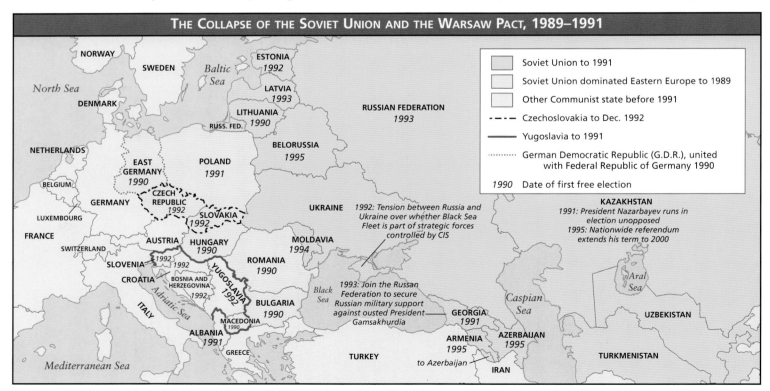

THE COLLAPSE OF THE SOVIET UNION AND THE WARSAW PACT, 1989–1991

Legend:
- Soviet Union to 1991
- Soviet Union dominated Eastern Europe to 1989
- Other Communist state before 1991
- - - - Czechoslovakia to Dec. 1992
- ——— Yugoslavia to 1991
- ·········· German Democratic Republic (G.D.R.), united with Federal Republic of Germany 1990
- 1990 Date of first free election

COMMUNISM CRUMBLES In 1989, East Berliners pulled down the Berlin Wall, defying Communist leaders. Nationalist and anti-Russian feelings brought about calls for greater independence in the Soviet Union's 15 republics, and by early 1990, many were establishing their own laws. On December 31, 1991, the Soviet government officially dissolved.

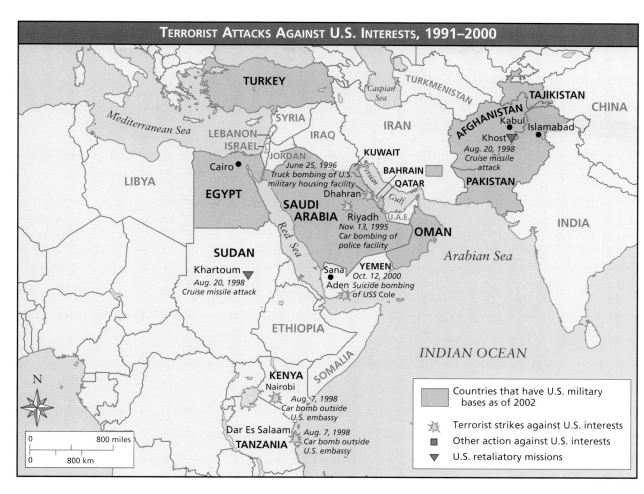

TERRORIST ATTACKS AGAINST U.S. INTERESTS, 1991–2000

Map labels:
TURKEY — Mediterranean Sea — SYRIA — LEBANON — ISRAEL — JORDAN — IRAQ — IRAN — Caspian Sea — TURKMENISTAN — TAJIKISTAN — CHINA — AFGHANISTAN — Kabul — Islamabad — Khost — Aug. 20, 1998 Cruise missile attack — PAKISTAN — LIBYA — EGYPT — Cairo — KUWAIT — BAHRAIN — QATAR — U.A.E. — Persian Gulf — INDIA — June 25, 1996 Truck bombing of U.S. military housing facility — Dhahran — SAUDI ARABIA — Riyadh — Nov. 13, 1995 Car bombing of police facility — OMAN — Red Sea — SUDAN — Khartoum — Aug. 20, 1998 Cruise missile attack — Sana — YEMEN — Aden — Oct. 12, 2000 Suicide bombing of USS Cole — Arabian Sea — ETHIOPIA — INDIAN OCEAN — SOMALIA — KENYA — Nairobi — Aug. 7, 1998 Car bomb outside U.S. embassy — Dar Es Salaam — Aug. 7, 1998 Car bomb outside U.S. embassy — TANZANIA

N

0   800 miles
0   800 km

Legend:
■ Countries that have U.S. military bases as of 2002
✳ Terrorist strikes against U.S. interests
■ Other action against U.S. interests
▼ U.S. retaliatory missions

ANTI-AMERICAN TERRORISM Africa and the Middle East saw a steady rise in major violence against United States interests in these regions; terrorist attacks brought American counterstrikes.

and 224 civilians, and wounding up to 5,000 more. These attacks opened a new phase of international conflict. It was believed that the Saudi extremist Osama bin Laden, whom the United States had supported when he was a guerrilla in the Afghan-Soviet War, was behind the anti-American terrorism. Bin Laden's organization, known as al-Qaida, or "The Base," was a world-wide association of terrorists determined to destabilize the developed countries and the governments allied with them.

Strike and counterstrike

Within three weeks of the embassy bombings, President Bill Clinton authorized firing long-range missiles at bin Laden's training bases in Afghanistan. This country was under control of the Taliban, an Islamist group that had won supremacy after the Afghan-Soviet War.

In "Operation Infinite Reach," American warships fired 70 Tomahawk missiles at terrorist bases in Afghanistan and also at targets in Sudan. The missiles killed an estimated 100 persons in Afghanistan, including key leaders. In Sudan, they destroyed a pharmaceutical factory that the United States asserted was developing biological or chemical weapons.

The terrorists struck again on October 12, 2000: a boat laden with explosives blew a hole in the side of the guided missile destroyer USS Cole, which was in Yemeni waters. The warship did not sink, but 17 sailors were killed and 31 wounded.

For the most part, the United States had not judged military responses to be the most effective way of dealing with terrorism that was not obviously state-sponsored. Instead, anti-terrorism efforts called for covert action, and international police work and arrests. Using massive military force too often caused

"collateral damage"—wounding and killing civilians, which created new hatreds that, in turn, spawned the next group of anti-American terrorists. After the 1983 bombing of the Marine barracks in Lebanon, for example, the battleship USS *New Jersey* fired salvos targeting suspected terrorist positions and causing hundreds of civilian casualties. Such indiscriminate bombardment helped recruit more terrorists.

UNDER TOW The bomb-damaged USS *Cole* is towed from the port of Aden, Yemen, by the ocean-going tug USNS *Catawba* of the Military Sealift Command. The destroyer was later carried to the United States by a heavy transport ship and laid up in dry dock for repairs.

219

THE UNITED STATES AS THE WORLD'S PEACE KEEPER

The 1990s saw America drawn into regional wars, including the Iraqi invasion of Kuwait in 1990. That conflict was resolved with conventional weapons and a lightning ground campaign, but civil wars in Somalia, in the former Yugoslavia, and in Haiti could not always be resolved by military hammer-blows.

The Battle of Mogadishu

Somalia, an impoverished nation in East Africa, suffered from drought and famine in 1992 and was torn apart by civil war. Various Somali warlords and factions fought for power while its suffering population was in dire need of humanitarian aid.

United Nations relief workers, their convoys and aid stations, were often in danger and were attacked by armed gangs. In the last half of the year, the United States worked with the UN to launch "Operation Provide Relief," bringing in thousands of tons of supplies. Through the first half of 1993, approximately 30,000 American and 10,000 troops from other UN member nations moved in to stop the civil strife in "Operation Restore Hope."

The leading Somali warlord, Mohammed Farah Aidid, opposed the UN, attacking and killing 23 Pakistani troops who attempted to take control of his radio station. Aidid now became a target of Task Force Ranger—Army Rangers and the Special Forces unit, Delta Force. On October 3, Task Force Ranger raided a compound in the center of the city of Mogadishu, where Aidid was believed to be living. They failed to snare Aidid, and instead ran into heavy ground fire that brought down two Black Hawk helicopters. Surrounded, the Americans had to fight their way out of the city in a 17-hour battle against thousands of Somali gunmen. They broke out the following day, after losing 18 dead and 84 wounded. Somali casualties were estimated at 500-1,000 dead and 1,000 wounded.

American public opinion now turned against helping Somalia build itself into a modern nation, and President Bill Clinton withdrew the troops by March 1994.

SECURITY CHECKPOINT A Marine shows a Haitian family through security on their way to a humanitarian assistance center at St. Terese in December 1998.

Haiti, Bosnia, and Kosovo

Nation-building was more successful in Haiti, which was taken over in 1990 by a military junta that threw out elected president Jean-Bertrand Aristide. The UN called for Aristide's reinstatement but was ignored. In September 1994, an American naval task force and paratroopers prepared an assault, but at the last moment the junta agreed to permit Aristide's return. To enforce the agreement, 20,000 American and 2,000 UN troops entered Haiti, which was placed under temporary UN management.

American air power was used in strife-wracked Bosnia, a former republic of Yugoslavia, which dissolved in 1991. Centuries-old hostility among the former Yugoslavia's Greek Orthodox Serbs, Catholic Croats, and Muslims sparked fierce fighting, massacres, and the ejection of minority populations—so-called "ethnic cleansing." By 1993, the Bosnian city of Sarajevo, mainly Muslim, was under ruthless siege and bombardment by Bosnian Serbs, who opposed Bosnian independence. Led by President Slobodan Milosevic, Serbia supplied Bosnian Serb forces and encouraged the killing.

In September 1995 NATO finally began "Operation Deliberate Force," an air campaign against the Bosnian Serb

"Every bomb is a political bomb."

—U.S. AIR FORCE GENERAL MICHAEL RYAN, NATO AIR COMMANDER, "OPERATION DELIBERATE FORCE," INSISTING ON LIMITING CASUALTIES

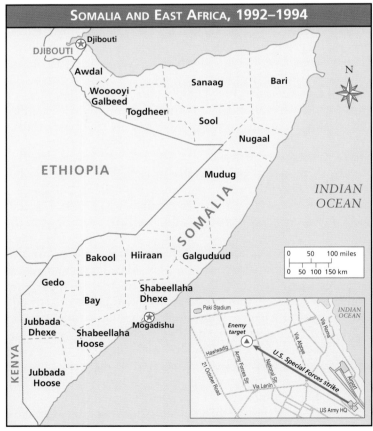

WARRING SOMALIS Led by an American task force, UN troops attempted to keep the peace among feuding Somali warlords and clans. Efforts to capture the warlord Mohammed Farah Aidid in Mogadishu brought on a bloody battle in October 1994.

THE END OF YUGOSLAVIA By 1991, this nation of six republics was falling apart. As Slovenia, Croatia, and Bosnia-Herzegovina left the federation, civil war raged until NATO air attacks against Bosnian Serbs and a peacekeeping force—with Russians as well as 20,000 Americans—intervened in 1995.

positions besieging Sarajevo. American warplanes flew 65 per cent of the more than 3,500 NATO sorties. Three-weeks of air attacks compelled the Serbs to negotiate a settlement, known as the Dayton Peace Accords, brokered by President Clinton at Dayton, Ohio. That December, 20,000 American soldiers deployed in Bosnia as part of a peacekeeping mission that included NATO and former Warsaw Pact troops.

NATO air power was even more devastating in 1999, when Serbia's Milosevic orchestrated ethnic cleansing against Muslims living in the province of Kosovo. Military, transportation, and industrial targets in Serbia and Kosovo were struck in "Operation Allied Force," with 38,000 sorties flown from March to June. Milosevic withdrew his army from Kosovo, which saw the immediate arrival of peacekeeping troops in "Operation Joint Guardian." Led by NATO commanders, the 42,500 peace keepers of Kosovo Force, or KFOR, came from 28 countries and included 7,000 American soldiers and Marines.

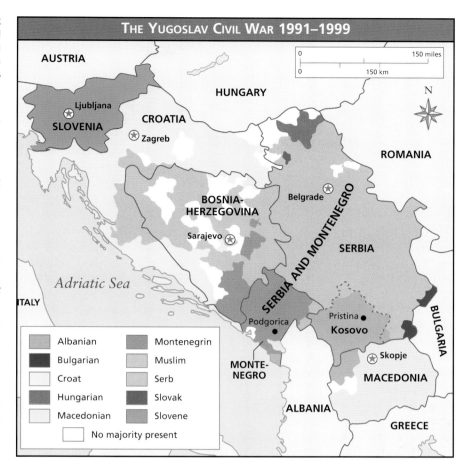

THE YUGOSLAV CIVIL WAR 1991–1999

- Albanian
- Bulgarian
- Croat
- Hungarian
- Macedonian
- Montenegrin
- Muslim
- Serb
- Slovak
- Slovene
- No majority present

INSPECTION TOUR A Bosnian Serb leads American combat engineers of the NATO Implementation Force (IFOR) looking for prohibited weapons in Serb bunkers.

THE ACCORDS PARTITION After more than four years of civil war, a "Zone of Separation" divided the Bosnia/Muslim/Croat Federation from the Bosnian Serb Republic.

26: MIDEAST TREMBLES AS IRAQ INVADES KUWAIT

SADDAM HUSSEIN Exhorting his people, Saddam governed Iraq with an iron hand, exploiting his country's oil wealth to win financial and military support from Western powers that overlooked his oppressive rule.

"There will be a lasting role for the United States in assisting the nations of the Persian Gulf . . . to deter future aggression."

—PRESIDENT GEORGE H.W. BUSH, TO JOINT SESSION OF CONGRESS, SEPTEMBER 11, 1990

The Iraqi dictator, President Saddam Hussein, commanded one of the world's most powerful armies, which by 1990 had been battle-hardened in the brutal Iran-Iraq War (1980–1988), also called the First Persian Gulf War, which cost each side half a million dead. There seemed to be no one standing in Saddam's way when he asserted Iraq's historical right to annex the tiny, oil-rich emirate of Kuwait, to his south. Also, Saddam accused Kuwait of drilling for oil under Iraqi soil by means of "slant drilling."

Kuwait not only had eight per cent of the world's oil reserves—Iraq had 20 percent—but its capital, Kuwait City, is an excellent port on the Persian Gulf.

Plan for domination

Saddam in Kuwait would threaten Saudi Arabia, which controlled another 25 percent of the world's oil, thus making his international influence enormous. In late July, he queried April Glaspie, the American ambassador to Iraq, about the possible United States response to his annexation of Kuwait. Glaspie said, "We have no opinions on the Arab-Arab conflicts, like your border disagreement with Kuwait." Saddam took this to mean he would not be prevented from invading Kuwait.

A week later, on August 2, six Iraqi divisions rumbled across the Kuwait border, brushing aside the few border guards, and sweeping into Kuwait City. On the day of the invasion, the United Nations Security Council voted unanimously to demand immediate withdrawal. Within a few more days, President George H.W. Bush began the deployment of American forces to the region under General H. Norman Schwarzkopf, head of the United States Central Command, which covered the Middle East.

"Operation Desert Shield"

Saudi King Fahd was reluctant to permit American troops on his soil, but when Saddam refused to withdraw from Kuwait, and at the same time massed forces on the Saudi border, the king relented.

Bush organized a massive Coalition force from Western and Muslim countries, which began to build up in Saudi Arabia. Other Middle East nations feared Iraqi aggression, and they provided troops and aircraft, and offered ports of entry for Coalition forces. This defense of Saudi Arabia was "Operation Desert Shield" and included the arrival of six aircraft carrier groups in the Persian Gulf and Red Sea.

The massing of Coalition troops, armor, and air and naval power proceeded into winter. All the while, Saddam was defiant, refusing to withdraw his army, estimated at more than 350,000 troops and 4,280 tanks, arrayed along the Iraqi frontier and in Kuwait. The Coalition assembled a land force of 540,000 troops in seven American army divisions—armored, armored cavalry, airborne, and mechanized infantry—two Marine Corps divisions, a British armored division, a French light armored division, and Arab units that equaled four more divisions, including armor. A Marine task force was on board ship in the Persian Gulf.

In September, Iraq's Revolutionary Command Council issued the statement—usually attributed to Saddam Hussein—that "This battle is going to become the mother of all battles."

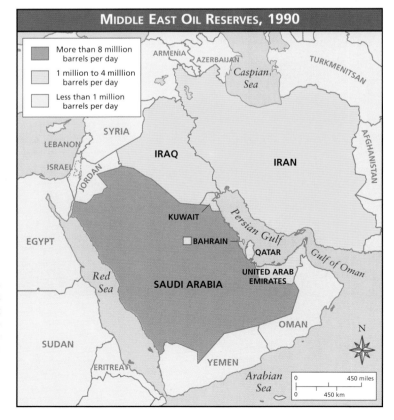

MIDDLE EAST OIL RESERVES, 1990

More than 8 milllion barrels per day

1 million to 4 milllion barrels per day

Less than 1 million barrels per day

OIL-RICH STATES Petroleum fields beneath the desert sands of the Middle East had brought 80 years of wealth and warfare to Saudi Arabia, Iraq, Kuwait, and principalities on the Persian Gulf.

THE IRAQI OCCUPATION OF KUWAIT, 1990

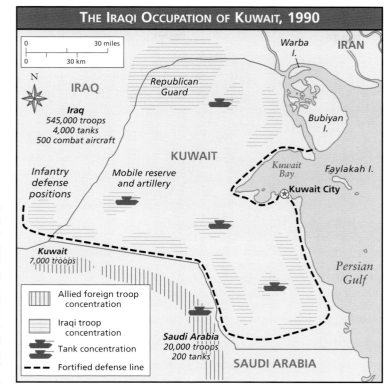

IRAQI FORCES IN KUWAIT Saddam's massive army was arrayed defensively around Kuwait to meet the anticipated UN offensive. His best force, the Republican Guard, was held in reserve and largely escaped the subsequent destruction that wiped out much of Iraq's army.

Saddam had a formidable air defense, with 8,000 anti-aircraft pieces, surface-to-air missile batteries, and a sophisticated radar air-warning system that communicated with the weaponry and with Iraq's 800 aircraft, 300 of which were classified as "interceptor" planes for fighting enemy intruders. As 1991 began, and it became apparent that Saddam intended to fight, Schwarzkopf and General A. Charles Horner prepared an air campaign to destroy the Iraqi air defenses, air force, and also its mobile Scud missile system. These Scuds were capable of reaching as far as Israel. (In order to persuade Muslim nations to join the coalition, Israel was not asked to participate in the campaign.)

Saddam let a UN January 15 deadline pass, and two days later, on January 17, Schwarzkopf put into action his air-assault plan, "Instant Thunder," to prepare for the ground attack.

THE DESERT STORM ALLIES

The 540,000-strong United Nations Coalition force, led by 430,000 Americans, was made up of troops from 36 nations: Afghanistan, Argentina, Australia, Bahrain, Bangladesh, Belgium, Canada, Czechoslovakia, Denmark, Egypt, France, Germany, Greece, Hungary, Honduras, Italy, Kuwait, Morocco, The Netherlands, New Zealand, Niger, Norway, Oman, Pakistan, Poland, Portugal, Qatar, Saudi Arabia, Senegal, South Korea, Spain, Syria, Turkey, the United Arab Emirates, and the United Kingdom

ALLIED TROOPS A British Scorpion combat reconnaissance vehicle speeds through the desert. The black inverted "V" identified all Allied vehicles.

THE U.S.-LED COALITION AGAINST IRAQ, 1990–1991

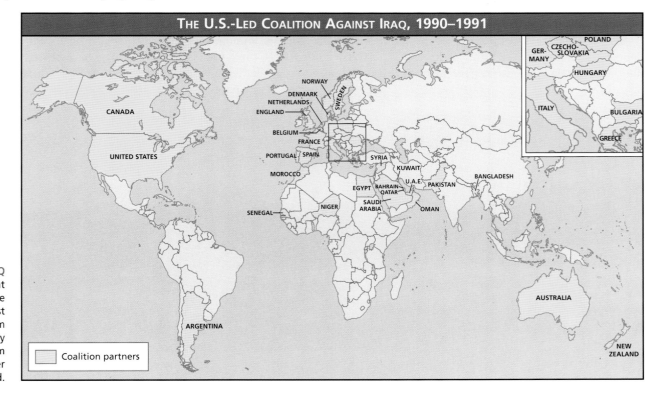

COALITION VS. IRAQ The 36 nations that formally joined the UN's coalition to oust Saddam Hussein from Kuwait in January 1991 came from almost every corner of the world.

THE MOST EFFECTIVE AIR BOMBARDMENT IN HISTORY

"The day we executed the air campaign, I said, 'We gotcha!'"

—GENERAL H. NORMAN SCHWARZKOPF, DESERT STORM COMMANDER

IN-FLIGHT REFUELING The B-2 Spirit Bomber is termed the "flying wing" because of its shape; a "stealth" bomber, its design and technology make it almost invisible to radar. B-2 bombers based in Missouri took part in the 1991 war to push Iraq out of Kuwait.

Within days of Iraq's invading Kuwait, the Coalition had begun building up its tactical air force, starting with F-15 fighters that immediately flew from the United States to Saudi Arabia. By January 1991, the Coalition had 1,736 fixed-wing aircraft from 12 countries ready for action, including fighters, bombers, refueling tankers, and transports.

This force operated from a number of bases: 10 in the United Arab Emirates and in Saudi Arabia, two in Turkey, and one in Cyprus. Aircraft flew from the decks of eight carriers, and heavy bombers were available from bases in Germany, Great Britain, Spain, and the Indian Ocean island of Diego Garcia, with B-52s from as far away as Barksdale air base in Louisiana.

"Operation Instant Thunder"

Two days after the air campaign began on January 17, Iraq's electrical system was shut down, its air defense network almost wiped out, and its anti-aircraft weaponry badly damaged. The bombardment continued for five weeks, raining down 88,500 tons of ordnance on Iraq and on its troops occupying Kuwait. Of this ordnance, 6,500 tons were precision-guided weapons that homed in on targets with a devastating accuracy never before known in wartime. In addition, hundreds of naval cruise missiles were fired at Iraqi targets.

Saddam could do little in response, soon losing 200 of his interceptor warplanes while failing to win a single air battle. The Coalition flew some 109,000 sorties, losing only 38 aircraft. By mid-February, much of Iraq's ground force was reduced to 50 percent effectiveness by the bombing campaign, considered the most devastating ever launched.

Iraq immediately fired Scuds against Israel, hoping to draw her into the war and thus shatter the Coalition's unity.

Israel refused to be provoked, although 40 Scuds were fired against her cities, causing deaths and injuries and much uncertainty. Another 46 Scuds were fired against Saudi Arabia, and one killed 28 Americans when it hit a barracks in Dhahran. Almost 60 percent of Iraq's total Scud firings took place within the first 10 days of the war. Batteries of Patriot missiles shot down some Scuds, which were largely ineffective.

Saddam's offensive thrust

Almost 600 "hardened" Iraqi bunkers were destroyed by laser-guided bombs, which blew up many shelters protecting Iraqi combat aircraft. Saddam was compelled to send more than 120 of his planes to Iran in hopes of saving them from destruction. There, they were confiscated as repayment for damage done in the Iran-Iraq War.

On January 29, the Iraqis launched a desperate offensive, a three-pronged advance across a 30-mile front into Saudi Arabia toward the Persian Gulf coastal town of Khafji, which had been abandoned. Coalition aerial surveillance had already observed the buildup, and defensive works had been strengthened, especially Iraqi field artillery emplacements. Collaboration between high-flying air force observers and forward Marine spotters in foxholes brought down a crushing air attack that stopped the advance in its tracks. The Iraqi offensive was soon defeated in the Battle of Khafji. The Americans suffered 11 deaths, all Marines, accidentally killed by "friendly

PREPARING FOR ACTION An F-18 fighter-bomber is refueled and rearmed at an American air base in Saudi Arabia; the air war supporting the American-led coalition in the "Desert Storm" lightning campaign devastated Iraq's forces occupying Kuwait.

fire." Under constant air bombardment Saddam could mount only this limited offensive.

Air power supreme

After Iraq's communications were shattered, its anti-aircraft and transportation targets reduced, Coalition pilots concentrated on pounding ground troops, their support units, and infrastructure.

Thousands of Iraqi soldiers found themselves in desert trenches without food or water, supply columns unable to reach them. Moreover, their contact with headquarters often was cut off by the bombing. In the face of the massive air bombardment, so many Iraqis began deserting from the front-line divisions that by mid-February, only 183,000 still held in those positions.

Now came the second phase of Desert Storm, the ground attack.

CHEMICALS AND SCUDS Iraq's chemical-warfare and Scud missile facilities were attacked by Coalition air and missile strikes. A number of Scuds were fired at Israel, but they caused few casualties.

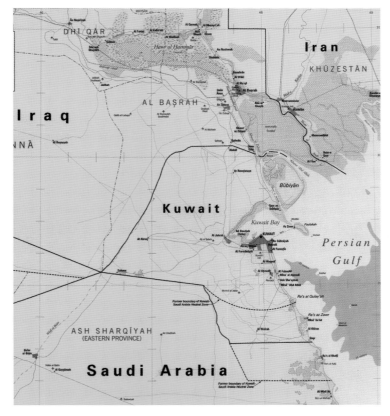

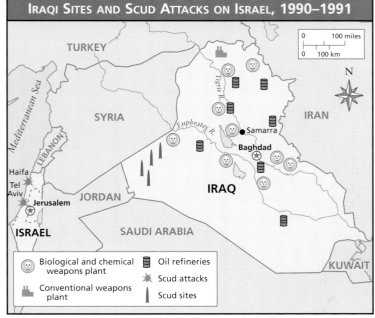

IRAQI SITES AND SCUD ATTACKS ON ISRAEL, 1990–1991

Biological and chemical weapons plant

Conventional weapons plant

Oil refineries

Scud attacks

Scud sites

STRATEGIC KUWAIT The Arab emirate of Kuwait not only possesses vast oil reserves, but its capital, Kuwait City, is one of the best ports on the Persian Gulf, which has few comparable harbors.

THE BATTLE OF KHAFJI

On the night of January 29, 1991, elements of three Iraqi mechanized and armored divisions moved across the Saudi border toward Khafji. The daily destruction of Iraqi armor and artillery from the air prompted Saddam to bring on a land battle while his ground forces were still intact. If they inflicted heavy casualties, that might dull the Coalition's taste for a full-scale war.

High-flying Air Force E-8 aircraft monitoring southern Kuwait with sensors detected the Iraqi columns moving. At this time, a massive Coalition deployment was underway 200 miles to the west. That maneuver could not be stopped to counter the Khafji attack, or the entire Desert Storm offensive would be thrown off schedule. The crisis had to be met by air power in cooperation with Marines and Saudi troops near Khafji. Sorties scheduled that night for A-10 and A-6 ground-support aircraft were diverted to the Khafji front, and AC-130 Gunships were scrambled. The Iraqi armor came under ferocious attack, and their offensive was brought to a halt. Marines supported by artillery and air power (including Marine Corps FA-18s) drove back the offensive, and Saudi forces retook Khafji on January 31.

The Battle of Khafji demonstrated something new in warfare: air power could stop enemy armored forces moving at night without needing a simultaneous counterattack on the ground.

IRAQI ARMOR A Soviet-built Iraqi tank lies in ruins, destroyed by attacks from Coalition aircraft. Tank-busting A-10 Warthog aircraft were especially effective.

DESERT STORM'S LETHAL "LEFT HOOK" LIBERATES KUWAIT

The military doctrine underlying the ground war to be waged by the UN Coalition against Iraq had been developed by NATO for possible operations against the Soviet Union in Europe. This "Air-Land" battle plan combined air power with speed of movement and mobility on the ground. The attack struck hard, with deception and surprise, aiming deep—in this case at least 100 miles—behind the enemy's front. Iraqi troop dispositions, the open desert terrain, and the training, technology, and equipment of Coalition troops were ideal for this tactical doctrine. It was called, appropriately, "Operation Desert Storm."

Desert Storm offensive

In mid-February, Saddam ignored yet another UN ultimatum to withdraw from Kuwait. Before dawn on February 24, Schwarzkopf began the offensive, first moving against Kuwait City. The 1st Marine Division attacked along the coastal road, and Arab units in "Joint Forces Command North" advanced at the Marine left. Offshore, elements of the 4th and 5th Marine divisions threatened an amphibious landing, thus keeping thousands of Iraqi defenders guessing and waiting in position.

American paratroopers 250 miles to the west flew far into Iraq to establish a forward stronghold known as "Cobra Base," which became an objective of XVIII Corp's wide-swinging force of paratroopers and French armor. The next objective was to capture Highway 8 and cut the escape route northward along the Euphrates River. This assault covered 155 miles in 31 hours. The paratroopers were supported by the swift advance of the 24th Mechanized Infantry.

In the center of the American troop dispositions was VII Corps, the most powerful force, which delayed 12 hours to allow other developments to unfold and draw in the enemy.

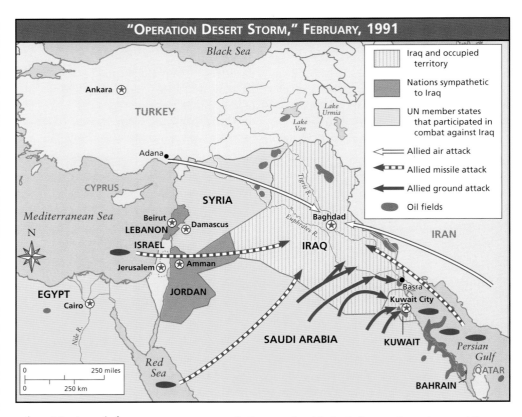

"OPERATION DESERT STORM," FEBRUARY, 1991

- Iraq and occupied territory
- Nations sympathetic to Iraq
- UN member states that participated in combat against Iraq
- ⟵ Allied air attack
- ◄◄◄ Allied missile attack
- ◄━ Allied ground attack
- ⬤ Oil fields

BOMBARDMENT Air Force and guided missile attacks on Iraq and its invasion force in Kuwait came from all sides, including carrier task forces in the waters of the region, and from bases as close as Turkey and as distant as the Indian Ocean and United States.

SURRENDERING TO THE COALITION Iraqi troops give up in the face of nearly invulnerable American M1-A1 tanks.

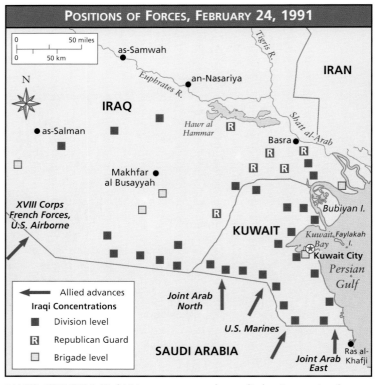

POSITIONS OF FORCES, FEBRUARY 24, 1991

- ◄━ Allied advances
- **Iraqi Concentrations**
- ■ Division level
- R Republican Guard
- ☐ Brigade level

ALLIED ATTACKS Initial UN maneuvers and assaults kept many Iraqi forces in the front lines pinned down, while the allied offensives in the West outflanked them.

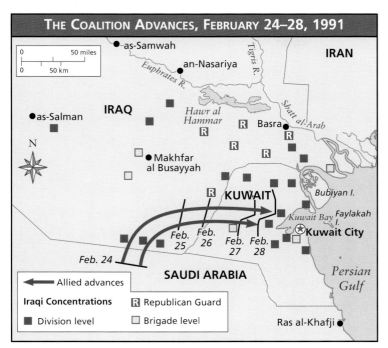

THE COALITION ADVANCES, FEBRUARY 24–28, 1991

THE LEFT HOOK With classic boxing tactics, UN forces jab straight ahead and then follow with an unexpected and savage left hook. Iraqi forces in Kuwait were overwhelmed by the assault.

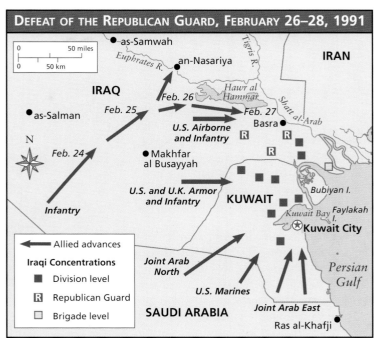

DEFEAT OF THE REPUBLICAN GUARD, FEBRUARY 26–28, 1991

DESERT STORM The tactics of deep penetration brought airborne and helicopter-borne troops to the Euphrates River, while the main UN forces attacked Kuwait. The penetration cut the main route of escape for Iraqi troops reeling from the main assault.

Then VII Corps struck, with a "left hook," and drove through Iraqi lines, where thousands of Saddam's dazed soldiers surrendered without a fight. Thousands more tried to flee northward from Kuwait City in a crowd of military vehicles, private trucks, and cars. They were massacred by relentless air attacks that gave the road the name, "Highway of Death."

Wheeling eastward to drive at Republican Guard armor and infantry divisions in northern Kuwait, VII Corps brought on massive tank battles that raged along an 80-mile front. The outgunned, outmaneuvered Iraqis were defeated at every turn, hammered by tank cannon, artillery, and air attacks. Unable to destroy more than four Coalition tanks, the Iraqis lost nearly 4,000 tanks, destroyed or captured, almost 1,500 other armored vehicles, and 3,000 artillery pieces. Only a handful of Saddam's original 43 combat divisions were still battle-ready, but the elite Republican Guard divisions mostly escaped the battle intact.

The Marine force held back and let their Kuwaiti allies enter Kuwait City first, as liberators, on February 27. President Bush called a cease fire on the morning of February 28. He believed that pushing on to Baghdad to pursue Saddam would lead to destabilization of Iraq. Civil strife would spill over into neighboring Turkey and Iran, whose own ethnic and religious groups would support one faction or another.

Second Persian Gulf War: casualties and results

In this ground war of 100 hours, more than 100,000 Iraqi soldiers died, and another 300,000 were wounded—a large proportion on the "Highway of Death." At least 150,000 Iraqis deserted, and more than 80,000 were taken prisoner. Coalition losses were light for such a massive conflict. The United States lost 148 killed in action, with 458 wounded; another 121 died from "friendly fire." Eleven American women were killed in combat.

Saddam Hussein remained in power in Iraq, strong enough to crush rebellions that rose up against him in northern Kurdish territory and in the southern Shia lands. Bush and the Coalition did not aid these uprisings, preferring that Iraq remain stable for the time being, though still under a cruel dictator. Saddam's military might, however, was broken forever, and he no longer posed a threat to the Middle East.

The campaigns of operations "Desert Shield" and "Desert Storm" made up the Second Persian Gulf War, with the earlier Iran-Iraq War known as the First Persian Gulf War.

> *"[He] led his country in . . . the Battle of Battles, where Iraq stood fast against the invasion, maintaining its sovereignty and political system."*
>
> —SADDAM HUSSEIN BIOGRAPHY, ON THE SECOND PERSIAN GULF WAR, ALSO KNOWN AS "DESERT STORM"

OIL FIRES ROAR An Iraqi tank crew watches as Kuwaiti oil wells burst into flame—sabotage carried out by Saddam's retreating army. Such damage severely polluted the region's air and the waters of the Persian Gulf.

27: TERROR IN NEW YORK, WAR IN AFGHANISTAN

On the morning of September 11, 2001, two hijacked domestic airliners crashed into the Twin Towers of the World Trade Center in New York and exploded. Soon after, a third hijacked airliner slammed into the Pentagon in Washington, and a fourth crashed in a field in Pennsylvania. These terrorist attacks killed more than 3,000 persons.

For the first time in its 52-year history, the North Atlantic Treaty Organization invoked Article 5 of its charter, declaring the attacks on America to be aggression on all 19 member states.

The United States government accused the radical terrorist Muslim organization, al-Qaida, as the perpetrators. Headed by Osama bin Laden—a Saudi Mujahedin leader who fought in the Afghan-Soviet War—al-Qaida had several terrorist training camps in Afghanistan. President George W. Bush demanded Afghanistan's ruling Muslim fundamentalist Taliban regime turn over bin Laden, but they insisted on seeing hard evidence of bin Laden's culpability before they would give him up.

AFGHAN'S PEOPLES Divided by mountain ranges, Afghanistan's 26 million population is made up of traditionally antagonistic ethnic groups: 38 percent are Pashtuns, rivals of the Tajiks, at 25 percent. About 85 percent of Afghanis are Sunni Muslims, the rest mainly Shia.

Bombarding the Taliban

On October 7, the Americans and British began "Operation Enduring Freedom," launching air strikes against Taliban military targets and al-Qaida training camps.

MOMENT OF IMPACT The Twin Towers of the World Trade Center were destroyed on September 11, 2001, when terrorists deliberately crashed two hijacked airliners into them, killing more than 2,600 persons.

Coalition airpower struck the Afghan capital, Kabul, the Taliban command base at Kandahar airport, and the cities of Herat, Kunduz, and Mazar-e-Sharif. Attacks were carried out by B-2 Spirit bombers from bases in the United States, B-1 Lancers, B-52 Stratofortresses, and F-16 Fighting Falcons. There were also carrier-based strike aircraft, and approximately 50 Tomahawk cruise missiles were fired from American and British submarines in the Arabian Sea. Pentagon officials said 85 percent of the targets were destroyed, including radar, anti-aircraft batteries and a few dozen war planes. The operation also used bases in Pakistan, Uzbekistan, and Tajikistan.

Northern Alliance attacks

The Taliban had been engaged in a civil war against warlords and anti-Taliban forces known as the Northern Alliance. This opposition was pinned in pockets of resistance in the central mountains and the northeast corner of the country. Now, American Special Forces teams were dropped to cooperate with Northern Alliance fighters, who were supplied with armaments, including some purchased from former Soviet republics. Taliban troop strength was about 40,000, including al-Qaida's force of 10,000 Arabs, Pakistanis, Chechens, and Uzbeks. The Northern Alliance had between 15-20,000 soldiers, mainly from the Tajik and Uzbek ethnic minorities, who were adversaries of the majority Pashtuns, the main backers of the Taliban.

Supported by Special Forces and a powerful air attack, the Northern Alliance began a counteroffensive that quickly picked up steam as the poorly armed Taliban government soldiers and

"The manner in which we react . . . [will] highlight our readiness and adaptability to meet the nation's needs. . . ."

—Marine Commandant, General James L. Jones, September 12, 2001

volunteer fighters were overrun or retreated. On November 13, the Taliban began a massive retreat from Kabul, and thousands were taken prisoner. War lords slaughtered many in cold blood, taking revenge for past defeats. By the onset of winter, the Northern Alliance and American troops were victorious everywhere, although most leaders of the Taliban and al-Qaida had escaped across the border with Pakistan or vanished in Afghanistan's rugged mountains.

The campaign winds down

Taliban stronghold Kandahar fell on December 7, and by mid-December, several thousand American and coalition forces were in Afghanistan, commanded by General Tommy Franks. On December 22, an interim government headed by Hamid Karzai was inaugurated in Kabul.

"OPERATION ANACONDA"

On January 4, an American Special Forces member was killed in a fire fight, the first United States soldier to die in action in the Afghanistan campaign. A number of other Special Forces troops were wounded in the battle, which occurred near the Tora Bora cave complex where Osama bin Laden was suspected to be in hiding. Major fighting was renewed in this area in March 2002, as coalition forces made a massive push to root out 1,000 al-Qaida and Taliban forces in the Shahi-Kot Valley and Arma Mountains southeast of Zormat. By March 6, eight Americans and seven Afghan government soldiers had been killed in this campaign, known as "Operation Anaconda," but bin Laden escaped. About 400 Taliban and al-Qaida forces were killed in the fighting.

IN SEARCH OF ENEMY FIGHTERS Troopers of the 101st Airborne Division scan a ridge line, scouting for Taliban and Al-Qaida bases in the rugged mountains of eastern Afghanistan.

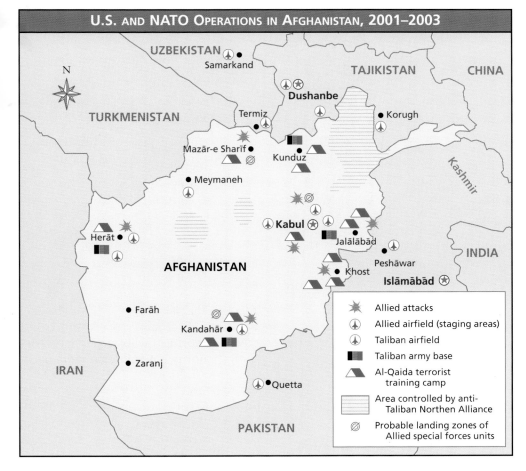

U.S. AND NATO OPERATIONS IN AFGHANISTAN, 2001–2003

Legend:
- Allied attacks
- Allied airfield (staging areas)
- Taliban airfield
- Taliban army base
- Al-Qaida terrorist training camp
- Area controlled by anti-Taliban Northen Alliance
- Probable landing zones of Allied special forces units

Karzai, a Pashtun and an American resident, had fled Afghanistan years before.

Major fighting occurred in March 2002, as Franks launched "Operation Anaconda" into the eastern mountains. Intermittent raids by Special Forces and attacks and bombings by guerrilla fighters marked the next two years of conflict in Afghanistan, where NATO troops were stationed to protect the new government. The nascent central government in Kabul had little authority beyond the city, where warlords resumed their autocratic and corrupt rule, and Islamist guerrillas waged a low-level insurgency against NATO troops, foreigners, and Kabul authorities.

ATTACK ON AFGHANISTAN Special Forces joined the anti-Taliban Northern Alliance for "Operation Enduring Freedom" in October 2001. Air and missile strikes from carrier fleets and long-range bombers reduced the Taliban's weak military infrastructure, and their major cities had fallen by December.

28: AMERICA LAUNCHES THE THIRD GULF WAR

Immediately after the terrorist attacks on the United States on September 11, 2001, President George W. Bush and his administration determined to attack Iraq. Bush and British prime minister Tony Blair accused Saddam Hussein of having links to terrorists, specifically to al-Qaida and Osama bin Laden. They also accused Iraq of possessing Weapons of Mass Destruction (WMD)—nuclear, chemical, or biological—some of which could be unleashed within hours.

The peace terms of the Second Gulf War (1991) had compelled the Iraqis to surrender or destroy any WMDs and stop their development. Recent United Nations inspections had not found WMDs in Iraq, but Bush and Blair declared those inspections to be ineffective and said Saddam was concealing ongoing WMD development. Congress and Parliament authorized their respective administrations to take whatever steps necessary, including waging war, to force Iraq to divest itself of WMDs.

Preparing to attack Iraq

Bush and Blair tried to bring other nations into a new coalition against Iraq, but unlike 1991, few militarily strong countries were willing to join. Among those nations objecting to military action against Iraq without solid proof of WMDs were France, Germany, Russia, and China. The UN refused to back military action without evidence that Saddam Hussein harbored WMDs or had ties to terrorists.

American and British forces were mobilized, and by early 2003 almost 250,000 military personnel from every branch of the service were in the Persian Gulf region. General Tommy Franks, head of Central Command (CENTCOM), was in charge of the campaign. Not counting forces involved in Afghanistan, CENTCOM had the American 3rd Infantry Division, 101st Airmobile Division, 1st Marine Division, 82nd Airborne Division, the 173rd Airborne Brigade, a Marine expeditionary unit, and several thousand Special Forces. British ground troops included the 7th Armored Brigade, the Royal Marine Commando Brigade, and air assault troops. There were also 2,000 Australians, including special forces. The offensive could count on at least five carrier groups and 1,000 warplanes. The American 4th Infantry Division and 1st Armored Division were in transit to the theater.

The Iraqi army had 25 divisions and several independent brigades, with a

WEAPONS DEMOLITION Hundreds of mortar rounds captured from Iraqi resistance fighters in April 2003 are destroyed by American ordnance disposal units near the village of Khariat.

KEY BAGHDAD SITES Weapons inspection teams from the UN identified important places around the Iraqi capital that were related to their investigations—including research centers and missile design facilities.

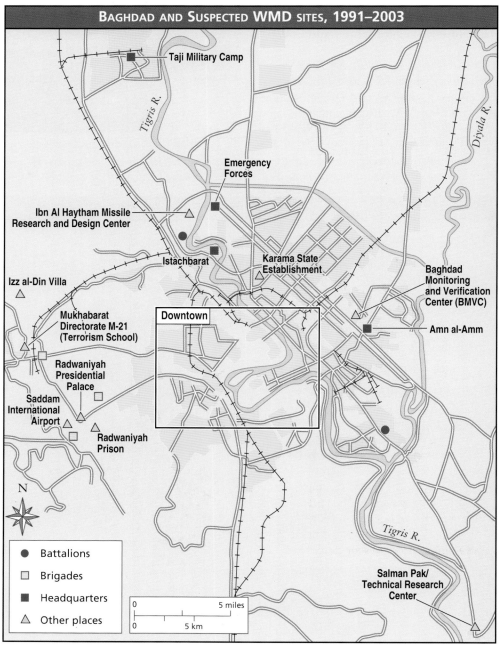

BAGHDAD AND SUSPECTED WMD SITES, 1991–2003

Taji Military Camp

Tigris R.

Diyala R.

Emergency Forces

Ibn Al Haytham Missile Research and Design Center

Istachbarat

Izz al-Din Villa

Karama State Establishment

Baghdad Monitoring and Verification Center (BMVC)

Downtown

Amn al-Amm

Mukhabarat Directorate M-21 (Terrorism School)

Radwaniyah Presidential Palace

Saddam International Airport

Radwaniyah Prison

N

Tigris R.

Salman Pak/ Technical Research Center

● Battalions
□ Brigades
■ Headquarters
△ Other places

0   5 miles
0   5 km

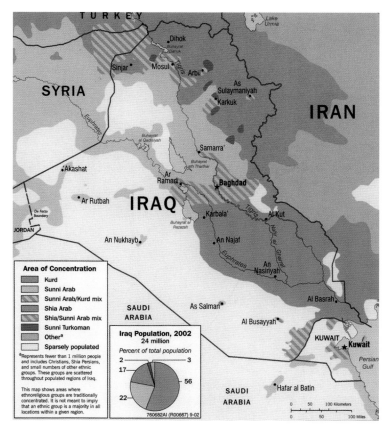

IRAQ'S POPULATION Iraq is most populous in the Southeast and center, with a few large cities in the North. Its 24 million people are 97 percent Muslim—60 per cent Shia and 36 percent Sunni. Political dominance belonged to the minority Sunni, Saddam's own persuasion.

nominal strength of 350,000, many being conscripts. There were 100,000 reservists, and also 30-40,000 volunteers in the *Fedayeen Saddam*, a paramilitary force trained in guerrilla warfare. The best Iraqi troops were the Special Republican Guards, numbering about 26,000 men and equipped with armor. Iraq had 1,800 aging tanks that were no match for modern armor and anti-tank weapons. Its air force numbered 350 planes, including 180 MiG-23s and MiG-25s, many in need of spare parts.

"Operation Iraqi Freedom"

On March 17, 2003, President Bush issued an ultimatum for Saddam Hussein and his sons, Uday and Qusay, who ruled with him, to depart from Iraq within 48 hours or face attack. Saddam and his sons refused, and the Third Gulf War, also called "Operation Iraqi Freedom," began on March 19.

The war started with a "decapitation" attack by Tomahawk Cruise missiles and strikes from F-117 Nighthawk stealth aircraft in an attempt to kill Iraq's leaders. Saddam and his sons escaped this attack, which was followed up the next morning by the 3rd ID crossing from Kuwait into southern Iraq, meeting little resistance. Special operations forces were airlifted into western and southern Iraq as American and British troops moved to seize air bases and oil fields. One object was to keep the oil fields from being set ablaze or the oil being spilled, as in the previous war. American and British forces entered the strategic port of Umm Qasr, near the major Iraqi city of Basra. Waves of air and missile attacks hit Baghdad and destroyed military targets around the country.

Coalition casualties were light. The worst loss was the crash of a Marine Sea Knight helicopter in northern Kuwait, killing the four American and eight British Marines on board.

ANTAGONISM WITH IRAQ

Throughout the 1990s, American relations with Saddam Hussein's Iraq remained raw and tense. Immediately after the Gulf War, Iraqi opposition forces had risen up against Saddam, but the United States and Britain had failed to help the insurgents other than to belatedly declare "no-fly zones," where Saddam's air force was not permitted to operate. One such zone was over northern Iraq, where anti-Saddam Kurds established an autonomous region. The other was over southern Iraq, where Saddam had massacred thousands of Shia Muslims who rebelled. Although too late to aid the Shia, there were periodic cruise missile attacks and airstrikes against Iraqi anti-aircraft installations and warplanes. A fierce three-day air campaign, "Operation Desert Fox," was waged in 1998, when President Bill Clinton objected to Saddam's placing new restrictions on WMD inspectors and failing to turn over requested documents for examination. "Desert Fox" hit dozens of Iraqi military emplacements, further weakening Saddam's air defenses.

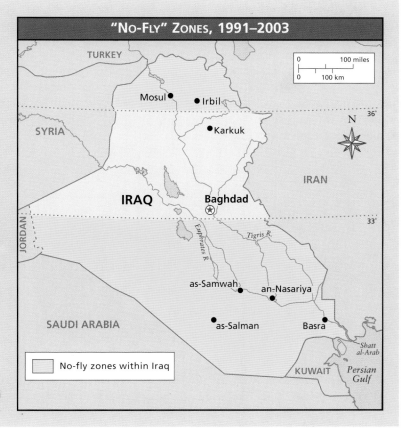

PROTECTED AREA American and British aircraft stopped Iraqi military flights over the Kurds in the North and Shia in the South.

IRAQI DEFENSES CRUMBLE, BUT A SANDSTORM HITS HARD

"This is not a war against a people, a country or a religion, and the Iraqi people . . . know this to be true."

—VICTORIA CLARKE, PUBLIC AFFAIRS
OFFICER, DEPARTMENT OF DEFENSE, IN A
MARCH 22, 2003, PRESS BRIEFING

IRAQI CAPTIVES Marines escort a column of prisoners of war to a holding area on March 21. Many Iraqi generals failed to communicate with their troops, so thousands of soldiers simply threw away their gear and went home without formally surrendering.

By March 21, most of Saddam's anti-aircraft units and warning systems had been battered into uselessness, and no enemy air force had appeared in the skies. Iraqi positions in the Hijarah Desert were captured by United States Special Forces, in large part to prevent Scud missiles from being fired at Israel from there.

The 3rd Infantry Division's drive north toward Baghdad had already covered almost 100 miles. British Royal Marines now took the strategic Faw Peninsula near Basra, while United States Navy SEALs and Coalition Special Forces seized gas and oil terminals along the Persian Gulf, finding little sabotage by retreating Iraqis. Elements of the 101st Airborne crossed into Iraq.

The following day, March 22, with Coalition forces moving rapidly northward or consolidating their positions, the 3rd ID fought with Iraqi troops, killing 45 while suffering no casualties. The division bypassed urban areas and pockets of resistance, following the doctrine of deep penetration, reaching 150 miles into Iraq—halfway to Baghdad. American Marines and British forces moved to encircle Basra, where thousands of Iraqis with artillery and armor took up defensive positions. As many as 2,000 Iraqi soldiers had been captured.

ROUNDING THEM UP 3ID soldiers secure Iraqi fighters near Karbala Gap on April 6. For a few days, Iraqi fedayeen—"Men of Sacrifice"—harassed Coalition convoys coming from the south.

Iraqis fight back

Resistance increased along the main northward routes, including Highway 8, the main line of supply for advancing Coalition troops. The Saddam Fedayeen militia and regular army troops fought fiercely at times, inflicting casualties, but suffering heavily from the guns of Coalition armor and from air strikes. Iraqi opposition was especially strong at the town of Nasiriyah, where key bridges crossed the Euphrates River. March 23 saw the first unmanned aerial vehicle (UAV) kill in Iraq, which took place near the town of Al Amarah, where a Predator drone destroyed an anti-aircraft artillery piece with a Hellfire II missile.

On March 23, the 101st Airborne conducted an air assault into southern Iraq. In northern Iraq, up to 50 cruise missiles were fired at villages occupied by the Islamist groups Ansar al-Islam (Supporters of Islam) and Komala Islami Kurdistan (Islamic Society of Kurdistan). Now, United States troops began to be airlifted into Kurdish-controlled northern Iraq to open a second battlefront. The Kurds bitterly opposed both Saddam's government and the Islamists hit by the cruise missile attack.

Also on this day, a column of the 507th Maintenance Company became lost near Nasiriyah and was ambushed by Iraqi irregulars. Five Americans were later shown as prisoners on Iraqi television and seven were missing.

On March 24, elements of the 3rd ID reached Karbala, within 50 miles of Baghdad. Attack helicopters struck at Iraqi Republican Guard positions, meeting unexpectedly intense counter fire that shot down one helicopter. Its two-man crew was captured and shown on Iraqi television.

Blinded by sand

A massive sandstorm engulfed Iraq on March 25, slowing the Coalition advance to a crawl in some places. Conflict continued amid the swirling sandstorm, which reduced visibility to a few

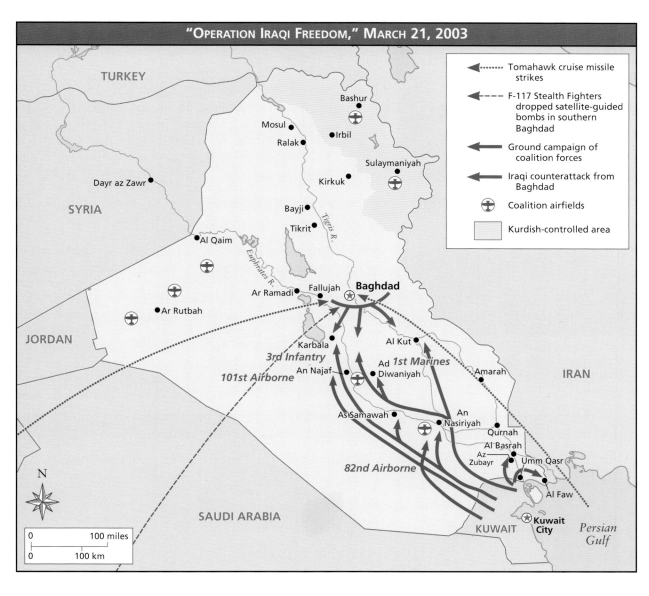

"OPERATION IRAQI FREEDOM," MARCH 21, 2003

Legend:
- ◄······· Tomahawk cruise missile strikes
- ◄----- F-117 Stealth Fighters dropped satellite-guided bombs in southern Baghdad
- ◄━━━ Ground campaign of coalition forces
- ◄━━━ Iraqi counterattack from Baghdad
- ⊕ Coalition airfields
- ☐ Kurdish-controlled area

TURKEY

Bashur

Mosul • Irbil
Ralak •
Dayr az Zawr •
SYRIA
Sulaymaniyah
Kirkuk •
Bayji •
Tikrit •
Al Qaim •
Euphrates R. Tigris R.

Fallujah • **Baghdad** ⊕
Ar Ramadi •
JORDAN
• Ar Rutbah

Karbala • Al Kut •
3rd Infantry
101st Airborne An Najaf • Ad Diwaniyah **1st Marines**
• Amarah IRAN

As Samawah • An Nasiriyah •
Qurnah •
Al Basrah •
Az Zubayr • Umm Qasr
82nd Airborne
• Al Faw

N

SAUDI ARABIA
KUWAIT Kuwait City ⊕ Persian Gulf

0   100 miles
0   100 km

ROUTES OF ATTACK
Preceded by heavy air and missile strikes on presidential palaces and military installations, Coalition troops jumping off from Kuwait sped toward their goals. British and Americans headed for Basra, while American forces aimed for Al-Najaf and Al-Kut.

feet and put fine sand in everything from tank engines to food. Marines fought to clear Nasiriyah of resistance, and the 3rd ID battled elements of Republican Guards outside Karbala. Special operations forces, Army Rangers, and paratroopers from the 82nd Airborne parachuted onto an airfield in northern Iraq and captured it. Soldiers of the 7th Cavalry Regiment fought off an attack near Najaf. Much of the resistance was loosely organized, with some of the most effective Iraqi fighting being carried out by Fedayeen militia, who struck at supply columns on the road and then slipped away.

British troops broke up an Iraqi column outside Basra, destroying 20 T-55 tanks and other armored vehicles. On this day, American planes heavily bombed Republican Guard encampments south of Baghdad, attempting to destroy defenses in that area. There was speculation that Saddam, in desperation, might use chemical weapons when Coalition troops came close to the city—crossing an imaginary "red line." Soldiers had special suits and respirators for such circumstances, but hot, dusty weather made them almost unbearable to wear.

SHELTER FROM THE STORM Stung by a seasonal sandstorm that barreled in from the western desert on March 25, these American troops carry out their normal duties while fellow soldiers huddle in nearby tents.

SADDAM'S FORCES OPPOSED ON THREE FRONTS

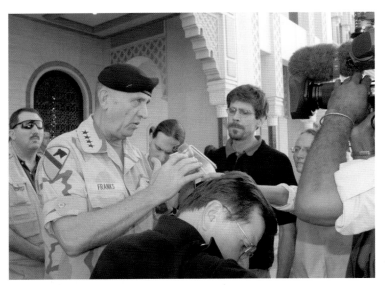

MEETING WITH REPORTERS While touring the Persian Gulf region in April, 2003, General Tommy Franks, commander and chief strategist of United States Central Command, speaks to reporters in Abu Dhabi, United Arab Emirates.

On March 26, two columns of Republican Guard vehicles heading south from Baghdad were destroyed by Coalition air attacks. To the southwest, the 3rd ID encircled Najaf, engaging in a three-day battle that killed approximately 1,000 enemy troops with few American casualties. Paratroopers of the 173rd Airborne Brigade made a night drop onto an airstrip in Kurdish-controlled northern Iraq to keep Iraq's forces in that part of the country from moving south to defend Baghdad.

Refitting for the next push

With equipment suffering wear and tear from the fine sand and heat of Iraq, many American units paused on March 27 to refit and repair. At the town of Samawah, elements of the 3rd ID fought off a determined attack by 1,500 Iraqi irregulars. On this day, soldiers from the 1st Infantry Division were airlifted northward to Bashur airstrip, while Kurdish troops and American Special Forces attacked Ansar al-Islam positions along the Iranian border.

On March 28, Apache helicopters of the 101st Airborne destroyed Iraqi tanks, trucks, and other equipment near

RESISTANCE STIFFENS Attempts by irregular and regular Iraqi forces to fight the Coalition kept Basra from immediately falling, and the city was hemmed in as nearby oil fields were secured. A sand storm slowed the advance on Baghdad, but U.S. paratroopers joined with Kurd fighters in the North.

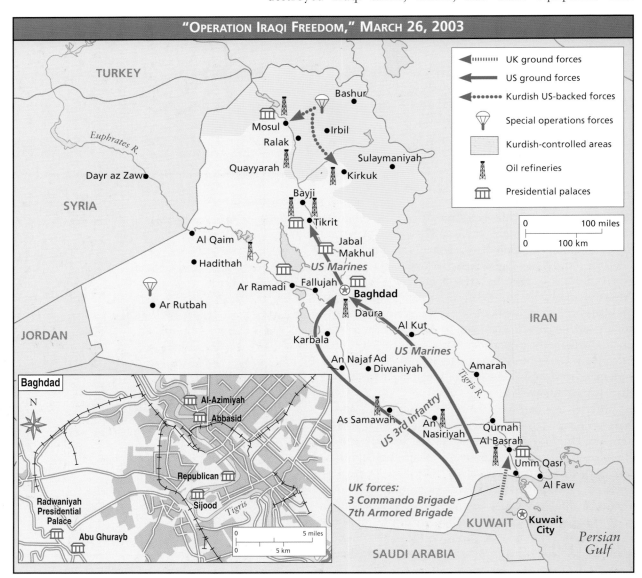

FORMING A PERIMETER American troops take defensive positions while on patrol near Samarra, Iraq, in December 2003.

Karbala. Two Apaches were damaged, but there were no American casualties. In one of the few air counterstrikes launched by Iraq, a missile hit an empty shopping center in Kuwait, with two persons suffering minor injuries.

Suicide bomb counterattacks

Four soldiers of the 3rd ID were killed at a Najaf checkpoint on March 29 when a suicide bomber blew up his taxi cab. Elsewhere on the same day, 82nd Airborne troops captured an airfield in southern Iraq and also repulsed an attack by irregulars along Highway 8. British Marines continued to fight for the port of Umm Qasr, which had not yet fallen. Widespread bombing raids continued, and Apache helicopters of the 101st Airborne joined in airstrikes on Baghdad.

On March 30, 600 British commandos attacked enemy positions near Basra, destroying tanks and capturing nearly 300 prisoners. This was the largest British assault of the war. Meanwhile, paratroopers of the 101st Airborne besieged Najaf, and units of the 3rd ID pushed northward to Hillah, while the rest of the division moved to within a few miles of Karbala. Its soldiers fought house-to-house in Hindiyah on March 31, where they destroyed the local headquarters of Iraq's ruling Ba'ath party.

Iraqi resistance was mostly ineffective, although often courageous. Whenever the enemy appeared solidly entrenched, Coalition aircraft laid down a carpet of destruction that wiped out strongpoints and blew up dug-in armor and artillery. Thousands of Iraqi soldiers were now appearing on the roadsides, out of uniform, apparently walking homeward or trying to get away from the fighting.

On April 1, Pfc. Jessica Lynch, reported missing in action since the 507th Maintenance Company was ambushed on March 23, was recovered by special operations troops from an Iraqi hospital in Nasiriyah, where she had been a patient. American women were participating in combat more extensively than ever before in history. Women were flying fighter jets and attack helicopters, patrolling streets and leading units of mostly male soldiers. By the end of 2003, nine women would die, including Lynch's friend, Pfc. Lori Piestewa, ambushed with the 507th, and the first American woman killed.

At Baghdad's door

On April 1 the 3rd ID engaged Republican Guards outside Karbala, while the 101st Airborne entered southern Najaf, and American Marines advanced on Kut. On April 2, the 3rd ID crossed the Euphrates River at Musayyib, coming within 30 miles of Baghdad. Marines crossed a canal and the Tigris River at Numaniyah to approach Baghdad from the southeast. The 3rd ID battled into Baghdad's Saddam Hussein International Airport on April 3, while Marines to the southeast came within 15 miles of the city.

No chemical or biological weapons were used against Coalition forces, which had crossed the imaginary "red line" close to Baghdad.

"Our sensors show that the preponderance of the Republican Guard divisions that were outside of Baghdad are now dead."

—GENERAL MICHAEL MOSELEY, COALITION FORCES AIR COMPONENT COMMANDER, IN AN APRIL 5, 2003, PRESS BRIEFING

MP GUNNER This military police soldier, on security duty, was one of many women in combat zones during "Operation Enduring Freedom."

AMERICAN TROOPS ENTER BAGHDAD, SADDAM FALLS

On April 4, the 3rd ID took control of Baghdad's airport while Marines were engaged in a fierce fight near southeastern Baghdad. The 101st Airborne began moving northward to secure Karbala, where strongpoints had been bypassed during the advance to Baghdad. In Basra, British troops still fought irregular forces.

Also on April 4, three United States special operations soldiers were killed by a car bomb near the strategic Haditha Dam in northwest Iraq.

Infantry and Marines take Baghdad
The 3rd ID made a show of force on April 5, sending a fast-moving armored column through southwestern Baghdad. The column ran into pockets of resistance but had no casualties. Marines were taking control of the southeastern suburbs. Now, Iraqi civilians began widespread looting of government buildings, shops, office complexes, and even schools, hospitals, and museums.

On April 5, the first Coalition aircraft landed at Baghdad airport as the 3rd ID made a second raid into the city, this time coming from the west. The 101st Airborne took full control of Karbala, and British troops finally entered the center of Basra, soon to declare that city under control. The 3rd ID again entered

ON THE ALERT After a rocket-propelled grenade attack, American soldiers take cover while cordoning off Baghdad's Abu Ghurayb Market and searching for insurgents.

Baghdad on April 7 and took over abandoned presidential palaces, while Marines pushed through the eastern sector of the city. American warplanes massively bombed a Baghdad building suspected of housing Saddam Hussein and his sons, but without success. The next day, April 8, Marines captured the Rasheed military air base in eastern Baghdad, while the 101st Airborne battled stubborn Iraqi defenders in Hillah. An A-10 Thunderbolt II was downed by an Iraqi surface-to-air missile, but the pilot was rescued.

On April 9, resistance in Baghdad collapsed. On this day, American troops hauled down a large statue of Saddam Hussein, while a number of Iraqis looked on, cheering. Coalition forces had military control of Baghdad, but unfettered looting and rampaging criminality plagued the city.

The war wound down as Kurdish fighters captured the northern city of Kirkuk on April 10, joining United States troops the next day to enter, uncontested, the city of Mosul. On April 13, Americans entered Saddam's hometown of Tikrit, where his own Sunni Muslim denomination was strongest. For decades, the Sunni had been favored by Saddam at the expense of the more numerous Shia Muslims, who resented Sunni domination.

Tikrit's limited resistance was overcome by April 15, but violence continued in Iraq in the form of guerrilla warfare.

Casualties and guerrilla war
On May 1, the Coalition declared an end to major fighting.

The United States had suffered 115 killed in action, the British 12. Iraqi military deaths were between 5–6,000, and 8–10,000 civilians died. At least 20,000 Iraqis were wounded in the war. Guerrilla resistance continued throughout 2003, with roadside bombings taking a steady toll of Coalition troops patrolling in lightly armored Humvees. By the close of the year, Americans killed in action numbered 327, British 20. An additional 32 soldiers from several Coalition countries had also died. More than 2,250 Americans had been wounded.

In July 2003, Saddam's sons Uday and Qusay were killed in a firefight with American troops. In mid-December, Saddam himself was captured. No Weapons of Mass Destruction were found in Iraq, nor were links between Saddam and international terrorists.

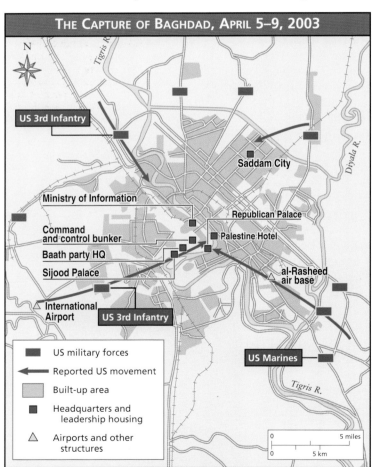

THE CAPTURE OF BAGHDAD, APRIL 5–9, 2003

N

Tigris R.

US 3rd Infantry

Saddam City

Diyala R.

Ministry of Information

Republican Palace

Command and control bunker

Palestine Hotel

Baath party HQ

Sijood Palace

al-Rasheed air base

International Airport

US 3rd Infantry

US Marines

■ US military forces

← Reported US movement

Built-up area

■ Headquarters and leadership housing

△ Airports and other structures

Tigris R.

0   5 miles
0   5 km

INTO BAGHDAD Heavily armored American troops probed from the southwest, through the international airport, and from the al-Rasheed air base to the southeast. Other than sporadic resistance, the anticipated last-ditch Iraqi defense of Baghdad never developed, and Americans moved into the city almost at will.

"IRAQI FREEDOM" COALITION

In 2003, 31 countries, in addition to the United States, offered troops for operations in Iraq. These were: Albania, Azerbaijan, Bulgaria, Czech Republic, Denmark, the Dominican Republic, El Salvador, Estonia, Georgia, Honduras, Hungary, Italy, Kazakhstan, Latvia, Lithuania, Macedonia, Moldova, Mongolia, The Netherlands, Nicaragua, Norway, Philippines, Poland, Portugal, Romania, Slovakia, South Korea, Spain, Ukraine, Thailand, and the United Kingdom. By early 2004, Japanese soldiers began to arrive in Iraq to help with reconstruction projects. This was the first time since World War II that Japanese troops had operated outside their country. Also contributing support by then were Canada and New Zealand.

By late-2004, Americans killed in Iraq numbered more than 900, and 100 other Coalition soldiers had died.

The Americans worked to build an international occupation force, but only 23,000 military personnel were contributed by 35 other nations. In July 2004, limited autonomy was handed over to a U.S.-picked government, which faced many difficulties. For one thing, the Kurds wanted more power, and like the Shia and Sunni were determined to shape their future in a country under an Iraqi-chosen government. Until then, the United States, with 140,000 troops, would remain in charge of Iraq.

"The former regime elements we have been combating have been brought to their knees."

—GENERAL RAYMOND T. ODIERNO, COMMANDER, 4TH ID, ON THE IRAQI INSURGENCY; JANUARY 22, 2004

THE DICTATOR FALLS An equestrian statue of Saddam Hussein is engulfed in a ball of flame as American explosives blow it from its perch above the Tikrit presidential palace in July 2003.

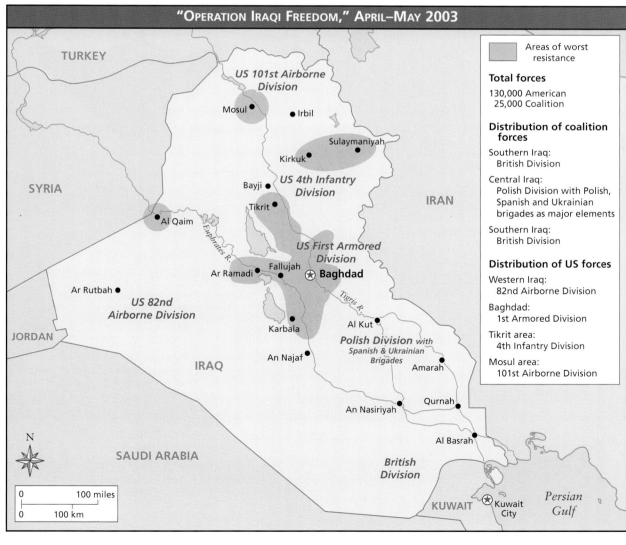

"OPERATION IRAQI FREEDOM," APRIL–MAY 2003

Areas of worst resistance

Total forces
130,000 American
25,000 Coalition

Distribution of coalition forces

Southern Iraq:
British Division

Central Iraq:
Polish Division with Polish, Spanish and Ukrainian brigades as major elements

Southern Iraq:
British Division

Distribution of US forces

Western Iraq:
82nd Airborne Division

Baghdad:
1st Armored Division

Tikrit area:
4th Infantry Division

Mosul area:
101st Airborne Division

TURKEY
SYRIA
IRAN
JORDAN
SAUDI ARABIA
IRAQ
KUWAIT

US 101st Airborne Division
Mosul • • Irbil
Sulaymaniyah •
Kirkuk •
Bayji • US 4th Infantry Division
Tikrit •
Al Qaim •
Euphrates R.
US First Armored Division
Fallujah •
Ar Ramadi • ⊛ Baghdad
Ar Rutbah •
Tigris R.
US 82nd Airborne Division
Karbala • Al Kut •
An Najaf • Polish Division with Spanish & Ukrainian Brigades
Amarah •
Qurnah •
An Nasiriyah •
Al Basrah •
British Division
KUWAIT ⊛ Kuwait City
Persian Gulf

N

0   100 miles
0   100 km

FROM INVADER TO POLICEMAN Coalition patrols found quieter towns in the mainly Kurdish north and the Shia south. They met hostility in some neighborhoods of Baghdad and in the towns of the Sunni-dominated central region. By mid-2004, U.S. Central Command had 200–225,000 military personnel in the region.

Stealth, UAVs, and Cell Phones

No military branch made better use of modern technology than the various air arms. Learning from the Vietnam War, designers developed aircraft to penetrate air defenses and precisely hit their targets. In the 1980s, software-based systems became prevalent, not only in cockpits, but in training facilities, where young pilots learned their craft in breathtakingly realistic flight-simulation equipment. Cutting-edge technology gave American pilots the great advantage of hours of simulated flying, which few militaries could match.

While speed and power were the hallmarks of supersonic aircraft like the F-15 Eagle or the radar-elusive B2 Stealth long-range bomber, designers produced one that was not so speedy, but was uncannily maneuverable: The British-designed Harrier, with its "vectored thrust," could take off and land vertically, and had the advantage of superior mobility in a close-quarters dogfight.

Many innovative technologies were tested in the Second Persian Gulf War, "Desert Storm," in 1991: computerized communications and weapons systems, composite body-armor, light machine guns, night-vision goggles, rocketry, electronics, Precision Guided Munitions, and even cell phones. From 20,000 feet, Unmanned Aerial Vehicles (UAVs) beamed down real-time camera imagery for targeting, battle-damage assessment, reconnaissance, and surveillance—and from lower altitudes they fired rockets. During the lightning invasions of Afghanistan in 2001 and Iraq in 2003, sophisticated electronics and computers, including global positioning devices, were used to great effect by both the infantryman in the desert and by command-and-control officers at distant headquarters.

A/OA-10 THUNDERBOLT II Nicknamed "Warthog," this twin-engine jet fighter was the first aircraft designed for close air support of ground forces. Maneuverable at low air speeds and altitude, A-10s are armed with Gatling Guns that fire thousands of rounds a minute and are devastatingly effective against armor.

PREDATOR This surveillance and reconnaissance Unmanned Aerial Vehicle employs radar and video cameras, and has forward-looking infrared. The images can be distributed in real time to the front-line soldier or to command headquarters.

NIGHTHAWKS United States Air Force F117-A Nighthawk stealth aircraft, with advanced navigation and attack systems, were deployed to the Persian Gulf area in 1996.

MOBILE LAUNCHER A Multiple Launch Rocket System can fire artillery rockets or missiles with explosive warheads. This launcher is mounted on a tracked vehicle, enhancing mobility.

CRUISE MISSILE The vertical launcher of the USS *Shiloh* fires a cruise missile as part of the 1996 "Operation Desert Strike" against Iraq. The cruiser is in the Persian Gulf.

ATTACK HELICOPTER The army's versatile AH-64A Apache is capable of operating against armor and of flying at night or in poor weather conditions. The Apache is armed with tank-busting Hellfire missiles, Hydra 70 rockets, and 30mm cannon.

COMMUNICATING WITH AIRCRAFT Using a satellite communications radio, this Marine in the Republic of Congo in 1997 communicates with a KC-130 Hercules aircraft of an aerial refueler transport squadron.

AMERICAN INFANTRYMAN Equipped for campaigning in desert conditions, this soldier has goggles, light machine gun, body armor, and a full backpack with bedroll. The combined weight can exceed 80 pounds.

NIGHT VISION American soldiers in Al Fallujah, Iraq, put on their night vision goggles in preparation for a raid on insurgent forces, in February 2004. Night vision goggles amplify ambient light, allowing the troops that wear them to operate at night, while enemy fighters without goggles are at a disadvantage.

MOUNTED INFANTRY The lightly armored and fast-moving Bradley Armored Fighting Vehicle can carry up to eight soldiers. The turret mounts a 25mm "chain gun" that is powerful enough to take on anything other than main battle tanks.

ABRAMS TANK The M1A1 Abrams, with its 120mm cannon and heavy composite laminate armor, is the most powerful armored vehicle of its time. In action, the Abrams is often supported by the Bradley Armored Fighting Vehicle, pictured in Iraq, above right, with soldiers of the 3rd Armored Cavalry Regiment.

BIBLIOGRAPHY & SELECTED SOURCES

Archer, Christin I., et al. *World History of Warfare*. Lincoln, Nebraska: University of Nebraska Press, 2002.

Boatner, Mark Mayo III. *The Civil War Dictionary*. New York: David McKay Co. 1959

Boatner, Mark Mayo. *Encyclopedia of the American Revolution*. Mechanicsburg, Pennsylvania: Stackpole Books, 1994

Brownstone, David, and Irene Franck. *Timelines of War: Chronology of Warfare from 100,000 BC to the Present*. Boston: Little, Brown and Company, 1994.

Chartrand, René. *American War of Independence Commanders*. Oxford: Osprey Publishing, 2003

Churchill, Winston S. *The Second World War*, 6 Vols. Boston: Houghton Mifflin Company, 1948–1953.

Commager, Henry S., and Richard Morris, eds. *The Spirit of Seventy-six*. New York: Harper & Row, 1974.

Editors. *Modern Warfare* (Series). Alexandria, Virginia: Time-Life Books, 1990.

Editors. *Picture History of the Civil War*. New York: American Heritage Publishing Co., 1960.

Editors, et. al. *Battles and Leaders of the Civil War*, 4 Vols. New York: Castle Books, 1956

Eggenberger, David. *An Encyclopedia of Battles*. New York: Dover Publications, 1985.

Frankland, Noble, ed. *The Encyclopedia of Twentieth Century Warfare*. New York: Crown Publishers, 1989

Heller, Jonathan, ed. *War & Conflict: Selected Images from the National Archives, 1765–1970*. National Archives and Records Administration, Washington, D.C. 1990.

Horne, Charles F., ed. *Source Records of the Great War*, Vol. V. National Alumni 1923

Ketchum, Richard M., ed. *The Revolution*. New York: American Heritage Publishing Company, 1958.

Kuehne, Richard E., and Michael J. McAfee. *The West Point Museum—A Guide to the Collections*. West Point, New York: U.S. Military Academy, Association of Graduates, the Class of 1932, 1987.

Long, E.B. *The Civil War Day by Day*. Garden City, New York: Doubleday & Co., 1971.

Morison, Samuel Eliot. *History of United States Naval Operations in World War II*. Boston: Little, Brown and Company, 1956.

Page, Tim, and John Pimlott, eds. *Nam: The Vietnam Experience 1965–1975*. New York: Barnes & Noble, 1995

Parker, Geoffrey, ed. *Warfare: Cambridge Illustrated History*. Cambridge: Cambridge University Press, 1995.

Rutledge, Joseph L., and Thomas B. Costain, eds. *Century of Conflict*. New York: Doubleday & Company, 1956.

Tarassuk, Leonid, and Claude Blair, eds. *The Complete Encyclopedia of Arms and Weapons*. New York: Bonanza Books, 1986.

Tucker, Spencer C. *Encyclopedia of American Military History*, 3 Vols. New York: Facts on File, 2003

SELECTED WEBSITES FOR MILITARY HISTORY RESEARCH:

The Airforce Historical Research Agency
http://www.au.af.mil/au/afhra/

American History Archive Project: Columbia University
http://www.ilt.columbia.edu/k12/history/aha.html

American Memory: Historical Collections for the National Digital Library
http://memory.loc.gov/ammem/amhome.html

The Anne S. K. Brown Military Collection, Brown University
http://www.brown.edu/Facilities/University_Library/collections/askb/

The California Military Museum
http://militarymuseum.org/

DefenseLink (U.S. Department of Defense)
http://www.defenselink.mil/

Frontier Army Museum at Fort Leavenworth, Kansas
http://leav-www.army.mil/museum/

George Washington Papers at the Library of Congress
http://lcweb2.loc.gov/ammem/gwhtml/gwhome.html

GlobalSecurity.org
http://www.globalsecurity.org/

History Net, The
http://history.about.com/

Imperial War Museum
http://www.iwm.org.uk/

Jane's Information Group (private publication which tracks military technology)
http://www.janes.com/

The Library of Congress
http://www.loc.gov/

Military History Encyclopedia on the Web
http://www.rickard.karoo.net/peopleframe.html

National Aeronautics and Space Administration History Office
http://www.hq.nasa.gov/office/pao/History/index.html

The National Archives and Records Administration
http://www.nara.gov/

National Army Museum
http://www.national-army-museum.ac.uk/

The National Parks Service
http://www.nps.gov/

Naval Historical Center
http://www.history.navy.mil/

Patton Museum of Cavalry and Armor, Fort Knox
http://knox-www.army.mil/museum/

Redstone Arsenal Historical Information
http://www.redstone.army.mil/history/

University of Kansas
http://www.ukans.edu/history/VL/topical/military.html

U.S. Army Center of Military History
http://www.army.mil/cmh-pg/

U.S. Army Engineer Museum
http://www.wood.army.mil/MUSEUM/mus_info.htm

U.S. Army information and archives
U.S. Army Military History Institute
http://carlisle-www.army.mil/usamhi/

U.S. Army Signal Corps Museum
http://www.gordon.army.mil/museum/

U.S. Civil War Center: Louisiana State University
http://www.cwc.lsu.edu/

U.S. Military Academy at West Point
http://www.usma.edu/

Virginia Historical Society
http://www.vahistorical.org/

World War I
The Great War: University of Pittsburgh
http://www.pitt.edu/~pugachev/greatwar/ww1.html

The World War I Document Archive
http://www.lib.byu.edu/~rdh/wwi/

World War II resources
http://www.ibiblio.org/pha/

ACKNOWLEDGMENTS & PICTURE SOURCES

ACKNOWLEDGMENTS: Steve R. Waddell, Associate Professor of History, United States Military Academy; Clifford J. Rogers, Associate Professor of History, United States Military Academy; Michael Moss, director of the West Point Museum; Anthony Galante; Isabelle Sigal; Damon Yasevich; Erika Rubel; Joseph Fernandez; and David Rumsey, of the David Rumsey Map Collection, www.davidrumsey.com.

PICTURE CREDITS: The source of each picture used in this book is listed below, by page. When a number of pictures appear on a page, the sources are separated by semi-colons and listed as they appear on the page from left to right and from top to bottom. A number of sources are in shortened form; for the full name, see the list below.

CMH—United States Army Center of Military History; DoF—Department of Defense; DP—Dover Publications LC—Library of Congress; DRMC—David Rumsey Map Collection; LCGMD—Library of Congress, Geography and Map Division; NA—National Archives; NPS—National Park Service; RT—image courtesy of Ron Toelke

TITLE PAGE: ii LCGMD.
TABLE OF CONTENTS: vi-vii LCGMD.
INTRODUCTION: viii-1 LCGMD.
TIMELINE: 2 LCGMD 3 LCGMD 4 LCGMD 5 LCGMD 6 LCGMD 7 LCGMD 8 LCGMD.
PART 1 CHAPTER 1
10 LCGMD 11 LC 12 LC 13 LC; LC 14 LCGMD 15 LC; Schenectady Historical Society 16 LC 17 LC; LC; LC.
CHAPTER 2
18 LC 19 LCGMD; State Historical Society of Wisconsin 20 National Archives of Canada 21 LC.
CHAPTER 3
22 LC; LC 23 Independence National Historical Park 24 LC; LCGMD; CMH 25 Don Troiani 26 LC 27 CMH 28 CMH 30 LC 31 CMH 33 Courtesy of the National Museum of the U.S. Army (Charles McBarron) 34 LCGMD 35 Independence National Historic Park 36 LCGMD; Naval Historical Center; U.S. Navy 37 Don Troiani 38 Courtesy of the National Museum of the U.S. Army (Charles McBarron) 39 Independence National Historic Park 40 LC; NPS, Museum Management Program and Valley Forge National Historical Park, photos by Carol Highsmith and Khaled Bassim; DP; DP; NPS, Museum Management Program and Valley Forge National Historical Park, photos by Carol Highsmith and Khaled Bassim; DP 41 NPS; NPS, Museum Management Program and Valley Forge National Historical Park, photos by Carol Highsmith and Khaled Bassim; NPS, Museum

Management Program and Guilford Courthouse National Military Park, photos by Khaled Bassim; NPS, Museum Management Program and Guilford Courthouse National Military Park, photos by Khaled Bassim; Kentucky Historical Society; Anne S. K. Brown Military Collection, Brown University Library.
PART 2 CHAPTER 4
42 LC; LCGMD 43 LC 44 LC 45 LC; LC 46 Naval Historical Foundation 47 LC.
CHAPTER 5
48 LCGMD 49 LC; LCGMD; CMH 50 LC; LCGMD 51 LC.
CHAPTER 6
52 LC; LC 53 LC 54 Don Troiani 55 Courtesy of the New York Historical Society; LC.
CHAPTER 7
56 LC; LC; LC 57 LC; LC 58 LCGMD; CMH 59 LC; LC.
CHAPTER 8
60 CMH 61 LC.
CHAPTER 9
63 LCGMD; Private Collection 64 LC; LCGMD 65 Private Collection; CMH 66 Courtesy of the National Museum of the U.S. Army 67 LC.
CHAPTER 10
68 LC; LCGMD 69 LC 70 DRMC; DRMC 71 LC; LC 72 RT; RT; DP; DP; DP 73 RT; DP; The West Point Museum (photographed by James Burmester); DP; LC.
PART 3 CHAPTER 11
74 LCGMD 75 NA 76 LC 77 NA 78 LC 79 LC; LC; LC 80 LCGMD 82 LC 84 LCGMD; NA 85 LC.
CHAPTER 12
86 RT 87 NA 88 LC 89 NA 90 LC 91 LCGMD; LCGMD 92 LCGMD 93 LC.
CHAPTER 13
94 LC 95 LCGMD 96 LC; LCGMD 97 LCGMD 98 LCGMD 99 LC 100 LCGMD 101 LC; LCGMD 102 LC 103 LC; LCGMD 104 Don Troiani; LC; LC; LC 105 LC; MPI Archives; NA; NA; Springfield Armory National Historic Site.
PART 4 CHAPTER 14
106 LC; LCGMD 107 LC 108 RT 109 LC 110 LC 111 LCGMD 112 LC; NPS 113 West Point Museum 114 LC; NA.
CHAPTER 15
116 LC; LCGMD 117 LC 118 NA 119 NA CMH 120 NA 121 NA 122 LCGMD; CMH 123 © Bettmann/CORBIS.
CHAPTER 16
124 LC; LCGMD 125 CMH 127 NA; NA 128 MPI Archives 129 LC; CMH 130 RT; RT; RT; RT; LC; The West Point Museum (photographed by James Burmester)131 RT; RT; RT; Old Salem Restoration, Winston-Salem, N.C.; The West Point Museum (photographed by

James Burmester).
PART 5 CHAPTER 17
132 LC; LCGMD 133 LC 134 NA 135 NA 136 LC; U.S. Navy 137 NA; NA 139 NA 140 CMH 141 NA 142 NA 143 NA; NA 144 NA; CMH 145 NA; US Air Force 146 NA 147 NA; NA.
CHAPTER 18
149 LCGMD; NA 150 RT; LC; NA; NA 151 RT; MPI Archives; NA; NA; NA; NA; The West Point Museum (photographed by James Burmester).
PART 6 CHAPTER 19
152 LCGMD; NA 153 NA 154 NA; NA 155 LC 157 NA; NA 158 U.S. Air Force 159 NA 160 NA 161 NA 163 MPI Archives; NA; NA.
CHAPTER 20
164 NA; NA 165 NA; CMH 166 U.S. Air Force Art Collection 167 RT; NA 168 NA 169 NA 170 NA 171 NA 172 LC 173 NA.
CHAPTER 21
174 NA 175 NA 176 NA 177 NA 178 NA 179 NA 181 NA; U.S.S Intrepid Museum 182 NA 183 NA; NA 184 Courtesy of Ron Toelke; Courtesy of Ron Toelke; LC; NA; NA 185 Art Explosion, Nova Development Corp.; Art Explosion, Nova Development Corp.; LC; LC; LC; NA.
PART 7 CHAPTER 22
186 LCGMD; NA 187 NA 188 NA 189 NA 190 LC 191 CMH 192 CMH 193 NA 194 NA; NA 195 NA.
CHAPTER 23
197 NA; NA 198 NA; U.S. Navy 199 NA 200 NA 201 NA; NA 202 NA; NA 203 CMH 204 A.P. Wide World 205 NA.
CHAPTER 24
206 MPI Archives 208 NA 209 U.S. Air Force; U.S. Navy 211 Courtesy of the National Museum of the U.S. Army 213 NA; © Reza; Webistan/CORBIS 214 DoF; NA; Navy Historical Center; U.S. Navy 215 DoF; DoF; DoF; NA; NA.
PART 8 CHAPTER 25
216 DoF; LCGMD 217 DoF 218 RT 219 DoF 220 DoF 221 DoF; LCGMD.
CHAPTER 26
222 Hulton Deutsch 223 © Robin Adshead; The Military Picture Library/CORBIS 224 DoF; U.S. Air Force 225 LCGMD; U.S. Air Force 226 CMH 227 U.S. Army.
CHAPTER 27
228 LCGMD; © Reuters/CORBIS 229 U.S. Army.
CHAPTER 28
230 U.S. Army 231 LCGMD 232 DoF; U.S. Army 233 DoF 234 DoF 235 U.S. Army; U.S. Army 236 U.S. Army 237 DoF 238 DoF; DoF; DoF; DoF; DoF; DoF 239 DoF; DoF; DoF; DoF; U.S. Army.

INDEX